AF759587

Making a Difference Through Marketing

Carolin Plewa · Jodie Conduit
Editors

Making a Difference Through Marketing

A Quest for Diverse Perspectives

Springer

Editors
Carolin Plewa
Adelaide Business School
The University of Adelaide
Adelaide
Australia

Jodie Conduit
Adelaide Business School
The University of Adelaide
Adelaide
Australia

ISBN 978-981-10-0462-9 ISBN 978-981-10-0464-3 (eBook)
DOI 10.1007/978-981-10-0464-3

Library of Congress Control Number: 2016930824

© Springer Science+Business Media Singapore 2016
This work is subject to copyright. All rights are reserved by the Publisher, whether the whole or part of the material is concerned, specifically the rights of translation, reprinting, reuse of illustrations, recitation, broadcasting, reproduction on microfilms or in any other physical way, and transmission or information storage and retrieval, electronic adaptation, computer software, or by similar or dissimilar methodology now known or hereafter developed.
The use of general descriptive names, registered names, trademarks, service marks, etc. in this publication does not imply, even in the absence of a specific statement, that such names are exempt from the relevant protective laws and regulations and therefore free for general use.
The publisher, the authors and the editors are safe to assume that the advice and information in this book are believed to be true and accurate at the date of publication. Neither the publisher nor the authors or the editors give a warranty, express or implied, with respect to the material contained herein or for any errors or omissions that may have been made.

Printed on acid-free paper

This Springer imprint is published by SpringerNature
The registered company is Springer Science+Business Media Singapore Pte Ltd.

Foreword

Over the past 25 years, Pascale Quester has made a unique contribution to the University of Adelaide, to the discipline of marketing internationally, and to the Australian and French higher education sectors.

Upon arriving in South Australia, she established the marketing discipline at the university while producing important research on sponsorship and consumer behaviour. But her contribution extended well beyond her individual research and teaching: she was appointed Executive Dean of the Faculty of the Professions in 2007 and then Deputy Vice-Chancellor and Vice President (Academic) in 2011. A strong advocate of global education, Pascale has developed links with institutions in Asia and Europe while holding several appointments as a visiting professor at La Sorbonne, ESSEC and the University of Nancy.

She was recognised as a distinguished Fellow of the Australia and New Zealand Marketing Academy in 2009; an honour bestowed on only a selected few academics in the marketing discipline. She was also the director of the Franco-Australian Centre for International Research in Marketing, and in 2007, she received the highest academic recognition by the French National Academic Committee to become Professor des Universities et Habilitée à Diriger la Recherche, before receiving one of France's highest honours, the Ordre national du Mérite, in 2012.

One of her most enduring legacies has been the adoption of a co-creation approach, particularly with the student body, to a range of University of Adelaide initiatives: from the development of the student learning hub to the introduction of the Small-Group Discovery Experience. Her capacity to drive results, and her boundless energy and passion sets her apart, not only as an academic but as a leader.

This Festschrift captures the achievements of a remarkable individual, a scholar with a passion for quality education and research, who has earned the long-standing respect of both colleagues and students alike. It has been a pleasure to work with her.

Prof. Warren Bebbington
Vice-Chancellor and President
University of Adelaide

Preface

With this book we would like to honour Prof. Pascale Quester and the contribution she has made to the discipline of marketing at The University of Adelaide and beyond over the past 25 years. Prof. Quester's professional impact has been outstanding, and is reflected in the many achievements, awards and honours so richly deserved. Her stellar career as a researcher with an international reputation for her work on sponsorship and customer behaviour continues to inspire generations of scholars worldwide. Indeed, her commitment to the academic excellence of students, colleagues and the university, together with her strong strategic vision and charismatic leadership, has seen her lead the marketing discipline, become Executive Dean of the Faculty, and now Deputy Vice-Chancellor and Vice-President (Academic) at The University of Adelaide.

While we could continue listing Prof. Quester's achievements, it would not highlight what she is known for. Whenever anyone speaks of Pascale they speak of her personal attributes; as well as the care and passion she has shown over the years for her countless colleagues and students. Without hesitation they acknowledge her generosity with her knowledge and her time, and reflect on how she has guided them while allowing them to learn and grow independently. Her charisma and passion encouraged students to come to her lectures, not because they were enrolled in the course but just because they loved her way of telling a story and enriching their lives. The simple fact is that she makes a difference; a difference to her students, her colleagues and collaborators, but also to the university and the broader community.

It is her ability to make a difference that has inspired this book, which offers a collection of chapters written by Prof. Quester's former and current students and collaborators. This collection of work furthers our knowledge in those areas that Prof. Quester has shaped the most.

In part one "Marketing a difference—sponsorship and sport", the chapters draw heavily on Prof. Quester's extensive contribution to the field of sponsorship. In the chapter 'The Question of Sponsorship Effectiveness', Mazodier explores the effectiveness of sponsorship, offering insight into the difference sponsorship can make to organisations. In particular, the chapter not only reviews common effects of sponsorship on consumer-based outcome variables but elaborates on how to select an event to sponsor, relevant individual consumer characteristics and sponsorship activation. Sponsorship activation is the key focus of the chapter 'Leveraging Research on Activation: Quester and Thompson's (2001) Impact on the Field of Sponsorship'. Written by Carrillat and D'Astous, this chapter outlines the difference Prof. Quester and her colleague Beverley Thompson made to the sponsorship literature with their article published in 2001, which marked the beginning of sponsorship as a major scholarly field in its own right. Khan and Burton's chapter 'Sponsorship-Linked Attitudes of Employees of Sponsoring Firms: SMEs Versus Large Organisations', further explores the ability of sponsorship to make a difference to various stakeholder groups. In particular, the authors demonstrate empirically that sponsorship can result in positive employee attitudes, with results suggesting strong implications for small and medium sized organisations. The chapter 'Connected Stadium: A Pillar for Football Clubs' Marketing Development?' written by Bal and

Fleck, is dedicated to the connected stadium, a major paradigm shift in sports marketing with a significant influence on the sporting economy and community. A comprehensive overview offers important insights into the scope, marketing challenges, technologies and implications for relevant stakeholder groups, drawing extensively on practical examples.

Part two "Making a Difference—Social Marketing and Ethics" reflects current social issues that Prof. Quester is passionate about and has made a significant contribution to understanding, including areas such as public health, young consumers, and gambling. In the chapter 'Promoting Public Health: Understanding the Limitations of Marketing Principles and the Need for Alternative Approaches', Pettigrew and Jongelenis offer insight into the ways in which marketing and social marketing knowledge should be applied to achieve well-being at the population level, utilising the health challenges of ageing and obesity as examples. Tabarashkina and Crouch shed additional light on the food consumption of young consumers, in the chapter 'Contemporary Young Consumers and Food Consumption—Implications for Social Marketing Research', identifying a range of critical gaps in the literature that should be addressed to ensure relevant policy development and social marketing campaigns can make a positive difference in the community. In the chapter 'The Ethicality of Immersive Sponsorship within a Children's Edutainment Centre', Arthur focuses on young consumers, specifically examining the ethicality of immersive sponsorship in a children's edutainment centre in Abu Dhabi. The chapter discusses the deontological, relativist and utilitarian views, offering insight that can be used by policy makers, parents and marketers to inform their actions. In the last chapter of this part, 'Emotional Advertising to Attenuate Compulsive Consumption: Qualitative Insights from Gamblers', De Vos, Crouch and Ilicic advance our understanding of emotional advertising appeals in the context of problem gambling, with compulsive consumption behaviour of particular concern. Specifically, the authors discuss the emotional appeals that can make a difference when communicating with gamblers.

Part three "Making a Difference—Customers and Brands" encompasses a collection of contributions to areas Prof. Quester advanced during her research and teaching career, including customer behaviour and experience, marketing communications, and country of origin effects. The chapter 'Revisiting the Long and Winding (Less Travelled) Road: The Road to Chaos in Marketing' by Steyer revisits and develops the eminent paper Profs. Quester and Steyer published in the Journal of Consumer Research in 2010, reminding managers of the law of imitation and the importance of social interactions. In the chapter 'The Case for Altruism in eWoM Motivations', Killian, Fahy and O'Loughlin recognise that many people in an online context offer advice, knowledge and expertise with the intention of helping others while expecting nothing in return. The ensuing discussion offers novel insight into altruism as a motivator to engage in electronic word-of-mouth and considers the role of communication channels and platform choice, valence, and the nature of the brand in this dynamic. The chapter 'Customer Experience of Value in the Service Encounter', written by Chen, explores customer experience of value and the difference it can make in transforming customer satisfaction into customer loyalty in a service setting. Yu and Pappu introduce portfolio-brand fit into the celebrity endorsement literature, with their chapter 'Multiple Celebrity Endorsement' presenting both conceptual development and empirical evidence in the context of multiple celebrity endorsement. These findings should make a difference to how marketing practitioners design and evaluate their celebrity endorsements, giving consideration to the multidimensional nature of fit in the context of multiple celebrity endorsement. The remaining chapters offer an international and cross-sectoral perspective with the key focus on country of origin effects. The chapter 'Can Country of Origin Branding be a Competitive Advantage for Agri-Products from Emerging Countries?', written by Karunaratna and Crouch, examines the concept of country of origin and its implications for agri-products, with a particular focus on emerging countries. Finally, in the chapter 'Decomposition of Country of Origin Effects in Education Services: A Conjoint Analysis Approach', Aruan and Crouch examine country of origin in a services context, offering critical insights to service providers by considering not only where the service is delivered but also the country of origin of the person providing the service.

Part four "Making a Difference—University Education and Innovation" explores topics that are critical to the higher education system today and relate both to Prof. Quester's academic and professional work. The chapter 'Knowing Me, Knowing You: Mentorship, Friendship, and Dancing Queens', written by Lu and Scholz, outlines a reflection of the supervision relationship between the authors and their Ph.D. supervisors, one of them Prof. Quester. Inspired by ABBA and informed by relationship marketing theory, the authors develop a conceptual model noting the relevance of trust, commitment and congruence to make a difference in the context of Ph.D. supervision. The chapter 'Beyond the Obvious: Facets of Diversity in Marketing Student Groups', by Sherman and Plewa, examines the difference various types of diversity in groups can make on the students' satisfaction with the process and outcome of group work. This study was undertaken in one of the core courses developed by Prof. Quester. Conduit, Karpen and Farrelly seek to better understand the nature of student engagement with the university institution, an area Prof. Quester has made a difference at The University of Adelaide. This chapter 'Student Engagement: A Multiple Layer Phenomenon', demonstrates the embedded nature of engagement with the lecturer, the course, and with the tertiary institution at a holistic level and introduces the importance of social engagement within universities. The chapter 'Marketing—Making a Difference for Entrepreneurial Universities', written by Baaken, Davey and Rossano goes beyond a student focus, discussing the difference marketing, and in particular science-to-business marketing, can make to universities in today's competitive higher education environment. Chapter 'Improving Innovation Process Performance and Service Quality in Innovation Networks', written by Plewa, Rampersad, Troshani and Kesting, further elaborates on the research and innovation of higher education, showing the difference an innovation management application can make not only to furthering innovation process performance within the network but also to the perceptions of the technology transfer office's service quality.

In much the same way that Prof. Quester has throughout her career, the chapters in this book cover a multitude of marketing perspectives, theories and contexts. While jointly advancing research in Prof. Quester's areas of passion, interest and academic contribution, this book and its individual contributions create a unique platform for cross-disciplinary and cross-sectoral dialogue. Together these contributions demonstrate the legacy of Prof. Quester, as so many of her former and current colleagues and students strive to continue to make a difference in these areas.

At this time, when we celebrate 25 years since you came to The University of Adelaide, we would like to thank you, Pascale, for the difference you have made; on behalf of your friends, colleagues, collaborators, former students and many others who have been part of your journey. This is for you.

Carolin Plewa
Jodie Conduit

Contents

Part I
Making a Difference—Sponsorship and Sport

The Question of Sponsorship Effectiveness

Marc Mazodier

Abstract This chapter summarises the effects of sponsorship on consumer behaviour. Sponsorship is a marketing communications strategy that pairs a brand with an event to enable the brand to benefit from the audience of the event and from the target audience's positive associations with the event. The effects of sponsorship have been widely researched. Pascale Quester has contributed significantly to research in this area, having published more than 20 papers on event sponsorship, substantially improving knowledge to enable managers and event organisers to maximise sponsorship benefits. This chapter reviews prior research relating to the effects of sponsorship and its moderating variables. Specifically, this chapter recaps the findings about the main effects of sponsorship and identifies some avenues for further research. Then, it reviews the role of perceived brand-event fit, consumers' event involvement and self-congruity with the event, consumer nationalism, consumers' gender, education and age, as well as sponsorship activation in sponsorship effectiveness.

Keywords Sponsorship · Ambush marketing · Congruence · Activation · Articulation · Consumer behaviour

Introduction

Pascale Quester has extensively researched the effects of sponsorship on consumer behavior and the variables that moderate these effects. Sponsorship is a (cash or kind) investment made by one organisation in an event, person, or idea for the purpose of exploiting the commercial potential of the association of the sponsoring organisation and the event, person or idea (Meenaghan 1983). In the past 40 years, sponsorship has evolved from simple, short-term corporate donations that boosted

M. Mazodier (✉)
Hong Kong Baptist University, Kowloon Tong, Hong Kong
e-mail: mmazodier@hkbu.edu.hk

M. Mazodier
University of South Australia, Adelaide, Australia

© Springer Science+Business Media Singapore 2016
C. Plewa and J. Conduit (eds.), *Making a Difference Through Marketing*,
DOI 10.1007/978-981-10-0464-3_1

management egos into long-term, economic-based relationships between the sponsor and sponsees or properties, typically grounded in complex legal agreements (Quester and Thompson 2001). Sponsorship spending has increased significantly in the past 30 years, from just $2 billion worldwide in 1984 (Sponsorship Research International 1996) to $55.3 billion in 2014 (International Events Group 2015). The increase in sponsorship activities reflects the growing belief that developing a brand through association with an event may be effective in building brand equity. Indeed, many studies demonstrate that sponsorship can increase brand equity and revenues by building brand awareness, brand attitude, brand image, brand trust and brand loyalty (Chien et al. 2011; Mazodier and Merunka 2012; Quester 1997). However, Mazodier and Rezaee (2013) report substantial negative abnormal returns following sponsorship announcements. Such a finding suggests that investors perceive sponsorship as a less efficient marketing communication strategy for improving firm performance. This chapter reviews the most common sponsorship effects on consumer-based outcome variables and their antecedents, identifying the limitations of prior studies that explain the negative reactions of shareholders to sponsorship announcements.

Summary of Main Effects and Avenues for Further Research

As noted, the effect of sponsorship activities on brand knowledge is quite well established. Specifically, sponsorship can increase brand awareness (Grohs et al. 2004; Javalgi et al. 1994; Mazodier and Chandon 2005; Quester 1997) and improve brand attitude (Grohs et al. 2004; Lardinoit and Quester 2001; Mazodier and Merunka 2012; Quester and Thompson 2001). Many studies suggest that sponsorship can improve brand image thanks to the transfer model (e.g. Grohs and Reisinger 2014; Gwinner and Eaton 1999; Woisetschläger and Michaelis 2012). In addition, research demonstrates that sponsorship can promote consumers' perceptions of corporate social responsibility (CSR) (e.g., in the context of non-profit organisations (Cornwell and Coote 2005), charitable activities (Menon and Kahn 2003), and community-based sports sponsorship (Quester et al. 2013)). Sponsorship can also positively affect brand trust (Lee and Mazodier 2015; Mazodier and Merunka 2012), brand loyalty (Mazodier and Merunka 2012; Sirgy et al. 2008) and increase purchase intent (Daneshvary and Schwer 2000; Madrigal 2000; Mazodier and Chandon 2005).

If this is the case, why do investors remain sceptical about sponsorship? First, a common criticism is "the lack of attention paid to measuring sponsorship effects relative to the investment made" (Olson and Thjømøe 2009, p. 504). The substantial negative abnormal returns reported by Mazodier and Rezaee (2013) suggest that sponsorship fees and related costs have become excessive over the last decade. Therefore, managers might be expected to direct their marketing spending on communication strategies that are more justifiable. Further research is needed to quantify financial returns on sponsorship activities and to convince financial analysts of the effectiveness of investment in sponsorship. Such research should compare sponsorship investment with other event communication strategies (e.g. advertising, ambush marketing) (Mazodier and Quester 2014a). Ambush marketing refers to any form of communication around an event that uses its characteristic signs and symbols to mislead spectators by implying that the brand is an official sponsor (Mazodier et al. 2012). The intention of such strategies is to improve brand equity through the massive audience that certain events attract. Two studies show that sponsorship improves more effectively brand loyalty and purchase intent than advertising (Olson and Thjømøe 2009; Mazodier and Merunka 2012). However, given that sponsorship incurs additional expenses (i.e. the sponsorship fees), it is conceivable that it could reduce profits even while improving brand equity. As such, marketers and investors need more guidance to identify the most effective marketing activities to improve their brand equity. Sponsorship research is also limited in that it has not uncovered a great deal of knowledge about the long-term effects of sponsorship. Most research investigates the immediate consequences of sponsorship; however, the cumulative nature of sponsorship effectiveness suggests the need to gain a perspective of the longer term effects and as such, the use of longitudinal research methodologies (Pham 1991). Recent studies have collected relevant data periodically to record the effects of sponsorship over time (Mazodier and Quester 2014b; Woisetschläger and Michaelis 2012). However, academics and professionals have called for more research on the long-term effect of sponsorship, including its effects beyond the end of sponsorship (McAlister et al. 2012).

Moderators of Sponsorship Effectiveness

Like other marketing communication strategies, sponsorship effectiveness depends on many factors that can substantially influence the return-on-investment of the sponsorship activities. Therefore, managers should know the constructs that influence consumer reactions to sponsorship and its profitability. The following sections review these constructs and discuss them from the perspective of the following considerations relating to maximising the benefits of sponsorship:

- managers select one event to sponsor based on the perceived fit between the brand and the event
- individual characteristics moderate the effects of sponsorship and managers should use sponsorship to target the consumers that react most positively to sponsorship
- sponsorship activation influences the effects of sponsorship.

How to Select One Event to Sponsor

The Role of Perceived Fit

Sponsorship research often includes the idea of perceived fit (also referred to as congruence, relatedness or match) between the sponsor and the sponsored event or activity. In the sponsorship literature, fit usually refers to consumers' perception of the similarity or consistency between the brand and the sponsored property. The extent to which the sponsor and the event are similar can depend on the functionality, attributes, image or other key associations of the sponsor and the sponsored property (Gwinner and Eaton 1999; Simmons and Becker-Olsen 2006; Speed and Thompson 2000). Several studies on sponsorship have found a positive effect of perceived overall fit on the effects of sponsorship (e.g. Deitz et al. 2012; Gwinner and Eaton 1999; Mazodier and Merunka 2012; Olson 2010; Simmons and Becker-Olsen 2006; Speed and Thompson 2000; Zdravkovic et al. 2010). Quester et al. (2013) also confirm the substantial role of perceived fit for community-based sponsorship effectiveness. For example, property CSR image only influences perceived sponsor CSR image when consumers perceive the association between the brand and the club as congruent. Perceived fit also has a direct positive effect on sponsor CSR image (Quester et al. 2013).

However, using realistic sponsorship stimuli, Olson and Thjømøe (2009) demonstrate that sponsors with a low level of fit may enjoy stronger identification than sponsors with a high level of fit primarily because people find some degree of incongruence interesting. Olson and Thjømøe (2012) find a negative effect of an initial high-level of fit between a sponsor and an event on sponsor recognition when sponsorship activation occurs. Indeed, the articulation of the sponsorship, which is the ancillary marketing communication actions purported to explain the relationship between the sponsor and the sponsored property (Cornwell et al. 2005), is likely to remove the initial advantage of a congruent sponsorship, that is, the presence of pre-existing links in the consumer memory between the event and the brand (Cornwell et al. 2006). This is because congruent associations can be overlooked or regarded as not stimulating because they conform to consumers' expectations (Jagre et al. 2001).

Thus, there appears to be a flaw in the conventional wisdom suggesting that there should be a fit between the brand and the sponsored property. This flaw can be explained by the congruence theory (Mandler 1982) and the concept of 'created fit' (Becker-Olsen and Simmons 2002). According to Mandler (1982), incongruent information can lead to superior recall and positive evaluations because incongruent messages can stimulate consumer interest. As such, the process of resolution leads to greater positive evaluations. Further, Becker-Olsen and Simmons (2002) argue that the link between a sponsor and an event can be apparent from the mere juxtaposition of their names ('native fit'), or the association may require some explanation in dedicated communication ('created fit'). Zdravkovic et al. (2010) highlight that managers should not rely on natural fit but should proactively attempt to communicate their brand's fit with the event to consumers. If sponsorship articulation leads to incongruence resolution, the brand generates arousal, is interesting, and is valued positively (Jagre et al. 2001). It is for this reason that sponsorship research, which investigates both native and created fit, demonstrates that low-fit sponsorships can generate more positive effects. Simmons and Becker-Olsen (2006) demonstrate that created fit, which they achieved by explaining how the sponsor and incongruent sponsor recipient relate, can improve evaluations of incongruent sponsorships. Mazodier and Quester (2014b) empirically validate congruence theory (Mandler 1982) and demonstrate that initial incongruence leads to a greater sponsorship-induced change in brand affect. Over time, as consumers are exposed to and become aware of sponsorship activation, the initial sponsorship incongruence is resolved, generating positive attitudes. Given that sponsorship-linked marketing improves brand affect for consumers who initially perceive the association as incongruent, managers can sponsor events that do not share a natural fit with the brand without jeopardising their marketing performance. However, Mazodier and Quester (2014b) recommend that they reserve a substantial budget to explicate their fit with the sponsored event and that they should do so early in the campaign. Indeed, incongruent sponsors that fail to explain convincingly their association with the sponsored event can face negative reactions from consumers who have not resolved the incongruence.

Individual Consumer Characteristics

Extant research indicates that sponsorship effectiveness depends on several individual consumer characteristics. Managers should run sponsorship when they target consumers who are likely to react positively.

Event Involvement

The level of consumer involvement in the sponsored property is an important predictor of sponsorship effectiveness (Mazodier and Chandon 2005; Walraven et al. 2014). Indeed, individual exposure to corporate sponsors is a function of the number of events attended or watched (Wakefield et al. 2007). Therefore, the more the consumer is involved with a particular sponsored object, the more likely they will be exposed to sponsor messages, and thus there will be a higher probability of sponsorship awareness. Event involvement not only leads to a higher probability of sponsorship exposure but also to a higher probability of sponsorship processing. As Pham (1992) posits, involvement with a sponsored event leads to higher overall attention devoted to the event, including the attention for embedded sponsorship stimuli. Likewise, Wakefield et al. (2007) argue that highly involved consumers are more willing to engage in active information processing and thus are more likely to pay attention to sponsorship exposure. Moreover, image transfer is positively influenced by a spectator's strong involvement, and attitudes towards the sponsor are more favourable when the spectator is involved in the event (Levin et al. 2001). The more the spectator is a 'fan' of the event, the more they will perceive that sponsorship helps the event. In turn, the spectator will hold more goodwill towards the sponsor (Meenaghan 2001).

Consumers' Self-Congruity with the Sponsored Event

Mazodier and Merunka (2012) and Sirgy et al. (2008) indicate that managers should select events with symbolic attributes that match their targeted consumers' self-concept. This matching process is referred to as 'self-congruity' (Sirgy 1985). Self-congruity plays an important role in both pre-purchase and post-purchase behaviours (Johar and Sirgy 1991), and according to self-congruity theory, a fit between the brand and the consumer's self-image arises when a value-expressive brand triggers the consumer's self-schema, which contains self-knowledge related to the product's perceived image (Sirgy 1985). Sirgy et al. (2008) and Mazodier and Merunka (2012) extend research on self-image congruence to a sponsorship context by demonstrating that self-congruity with a sponsored event strengthens the effects of sponsorship on brand trust, brand affect and brand loyalty.

Demographic Variables

Further, various demographics may influence sponsorship effectiveness. Prior research provides contradictory results. Some research finds no significant difference in the effectiveness of sponsorship, regardless of age or gender (Daneshvary and Schwer 2000; Quester 1997), whereas other research suggests that young people remember brand sponsors better than do older people (Walliser 1994). These results coincide with research on memory, which has demonstrated that memory of the source of a message decreases with age (Spencer and Raz 1995). Given that younger people are more able to associate a sponsor with an event, sponsorship should have a more significant effect on this group. Moreover, older people are less comfortable with sports sponsorship, and have greater negative attitudes towards the sponsor (Dalakas and Kropp 2002). Mazodier and Chandon (2005) and Walraven et al. (2014) confirm that older age (of the consumer) has a negative effect on sponsorship awareness and purchase intent.

Discussing the gender effect, Pham (1992) observes higher awareness scores among men exposed to sponsorships, and Kinney et al. (2008) and Walraven et al. (2014) indicate that men are more likely than women to recall and recognise sponsors correctly. In contrast, according to McDaniel and Kinney (1998), women respond more positively to sponsorship in the areas of awareness, attitudes, and purchase intentions. These results are confirmed by McDaniel (1999) and Mazodier and Chandon (2005). It is likely that the effect of gender depends on the event and further research should investigate the interaction effect between gender and event involvement.

Kinney et al. (2008) and Walraven et al. (2014) indicate that education level has positive effects on sponsorship recall.

The Role of Consumer Nationalism

As market globalisation exposes foreign firms to potential backlash from consumer nationalistic orientation towards their products, sponsorship strategies must consider the interplay between nationalistic sentiment and sponsorship effects. While foreign sponsors are typically preoccupied with determining the fit between their brand and a local event, they must also consider individual-level nationalistic sentiment. The success of companies in foreign markets depends on creating favourable country-directed consumer attitudes. Sponsorship research indicates that an event with a foreign sponsor tends to be evaluated less favourably than an event with a domestic sponsor (Ruth and Simonin 2003; Yue et al. 2014). Lee and Mazodier (2015) demonstrate that consumer ethnocentrism and animosity negatively moderate sponsorship effectiveness, while cosmopolitanism has a positive effect on sponsorship effectiveness. Therefore, the presence of foreign brands in a sponsored event invokes ethnocentric feelings among local consumers, which dampens sponsorship goodwill and other positive sponsorship outcomes. Hence, the strategic uses and outcomes of international sponsorship must be considered in conjunction with consumers' perceptions of foreign brands from a nationalistic perspective.

Sponsorship Activation

The terms 'leverage' and 'activation' are often used to define marketing communication campaigns that intend to remind consumers of the sponsorship (Carrillat et al. 2015). Sponsorship-linked marketing activities often span many days, weeks or years and imply repeated exposure to sponsor messages. It is ultimately the marketer's responsibility to make consumers aware of the link between the event and the brand, using advertising, public relations, promotion, and merchandising. For example, at the 2013 Hong Kong Rugby Sevens tournament, co-sponsor Cathay Pacific created a popup store in Causeway Bay that used equipment to allow consumers to momentarily 'become' rugby players - conveying the excitement of the game to them on an individual level. It is well established that sponsorship activation is key to maximising sponsorship effectiveness (Carrillat et al. 2015; Chadwick and Thwaites 2005; Quester and Thompson 2001; Weeks et al. 2008). As noted, one objective of sponsorship activation is to communicate the meaning of the association between the sponsor and the event to leverage the benefits of sponsorship (Quester and Thompson 2001). Therefore, 78 per cent of sponsorship managers invest as much in sponsorship activation as they do in fees to acquire the official rights to the sponsorship (International Events Group 2013). Nevertheless, Olson and Thjømøe (2009) report that the ratio of activation spending to sponsorship spending has an inverted U-shape relationship with sponsorship effectiveness, with the optimum being approximately the two or three threshold.

Conclusion

Over more than 15 years and 20 articles, Pascale Quester has considerably improved our knowledge about sponsorship. Quester has established sponsorship as an effective marketing communication strategy and identified several variables that drive sponsorship effectiveness. Nevertheless, more research is needed to establish the financial return on investment of sponsorship (particularly its long-term effects) and to compare the return on investment of sponsorship with other event communication strategies such as traditional advertising or ambush marketing.

References

Becker-Olsen K, Simmons CJ (2002) When do social sponsorships enhance or dilute equity? Fit, message source, and the persistence of effects. Adv Consum Res 29(1):287–289

Carrillat F, d'Astous A, Couture MP (2015) How corporate sponsors can optimize the impact of their message content mastering the message: Improving the processability and effectiveness of sponsorship activation. J Advertising Res 55

Chadwick S, Thwaites D (2005) Managing sport sponsorship programs: Lessons from a critical assessment of english soccer. J Advertising Res 45(3):328–338

Chien PM, Cornwell BT, Pappu R (2011) Sponsorship portfolio as brand image creation strategy. J Bus Res 64:142–149

Cornwell BT, Coote LV (2005) Corporate sponsorship of a cause: The role of identification in purchase intent. J Bus Res 58:268–276

Cornwell BT, Weeks CS, Roy DP (2005) Sponsorship-linked marketing: Opening the black box. J Advertising 34(Summer):21–42

Cornwell BT, Humphrey MS, Maguire AM, Weeks CS, Tellegen CL (2006) Sponsorship-linked marketing: The role of articulation in memory. J Consum Res 33(3):312–321

Dalakas V, Kropp F (2002) Attitudes of youth toward purchasing from sponsors: A cross-cultural perspective. J Euromarketing 12(1):19–39

Daneshvary R, Schwer RK (2000) The association endorsement and consumers' intention to purchase. J Consum Mark 17(3):203–213

Deitz GD, Myers SW, Stafford MR (2012) Understanding consumer response to sponsorship information: A resource-matching approach. Psychol Mark 29:226–239

Grohs R, Reisinger H (2014) Sponsorship effects on brand image: The role of exposure and activity involvement. J Bus Res 67:1018–1025

Grohs R, Wagner U, Vsetecka S (2004) Assessing the effectiveness of sport sponsorship–An empirical examination. Schmalenbach Bus Rev 56(April):119–138

Gwinner KP, Eaton J (1999) Building brand image through event sponsorship: The role of image transfer. J Advertising 28:47–57

International Events Group (2013) Survey: Sponsors require more agency support, spend less on activation. http://www.sponsorship.com/About-IEG/Press-Room/Survey:Sponsors-Require-More-Agency-Support.aspx. Accessed 18 June 2013
International Events Group (2015) Sponsorship spending report: Where the dollars are going and trends for 2015. http://www.sponsorship.com/Resources/Sponsorship-Spending-Report–Where-The-Dollars-Are.aspx. Accessed 18 May 2015
Jagre E, Watson JJ, Watson JG (2001) Sponsorship and congruity theory: A theoretical framework for explaining consumer attitude and recall of event sponsorship. Adv Consum Res 28:439–445
Javalgi RG, Taylor MB, Gross AC, Lampman E (1994) Awareness of sponsorship and corporate image: An empirical investigation. J Advertising 23:47–58
Johar GV, Sirgy MJ, (1991) Value expressive versus utilitarian appeals: When and why to use which appeal. J Advertising 20:23−34
Kinney L, McDaniel SR, DeGaris L (2008) Demographic and psychographic variables predicting NASCAR sponsor brand recall. Int J Sports Mark Sponsorship 9(3):169–179
Lardinoit T, Quester PG (2001) Attitudinal effects of combined sponsorship and sponsor's prominence on basketball in Europe. J Advertising Res 30:48–57
Lee R, Mazodier M (2015) The roles of ethnocentrism, animosity, and cosmopolitanism in sponsorship effects: A latent growth modeling approach. Eur J Mark 49(5/6):919–942
Levin AM, Joiner C, Cameron G (2001) The impact of sports sponsorship on consumers' brand attitudes and recall: The case of NASCAR's fans. J Curr Issues Res Advertising 23(Fall):23–31
Madrigal R (2000) The influence of social alliances with sports teams on intentions to purchase corporate sponsor's products. J Advertising 29:13–24
Mandler G (1982) The structure of value: Accounting for taste. Affect Cogn 17:3–36
Mazodier M, Chandon JL (2005) Gender, age and group norms moderate the impact of sport sponsorship on awareness, attitudes and intentions to buy. Revue Sciences de Gestion 48:65−87
Mazodier M, Merunka D (2012) Achieving brand loyalty through sponsorship: The role of fit and self-congruity. J Acad Mark Sci 40(6):807–820
Mazodier M, Quester P (2014a) Leveraging sport events over time: A comparison of sponsorship and sport event advertising [Research Commentary]. Int J Res Mark 31(1):33–34
Mazodier M, Quester P (2014b) The role of sponsorship fit for changing brand affect: A latent growth modeling approach. Int J Res Mark 31(1):16–29
Mazodier M, Rezaee A (2013) Are sponsorship announcements good news for the shareholders? Evidence from international stock exchanges. J Acad Mark Sci 41(5):586–600
Mazodier M, Quester P, Chandon J-L (2012) Unmasking the ambushers: Conceptual framework and empirical evidence. Eur J Mark 46(1/2):192–214
McAlister AR, Kelly SJ, Humphreys MS, Cornwell BT (2012) Change in a sponsorship alliance and the communication implications of spontaneous recovery. J Advertising 41(1):5–16
McDaniel SR (1999) An investigation of match-up effects in sport sponsorship advertising: The implications of consumer advertising schemas. Psychol Mark 16(2):163–184
McDaniel SR, Kinney L (1998) The implications of recency and gender effects in consumer response to ambush marketing. Psychol Mark 15(4):385–403
Meenaghan JA (1983) Commercial sponsorship. Eur J Mark 17(7):5–74
Meenaghan T (2001) Understanding sponsorship effects. Psychol Mark 18:95–122
Menon S, Kahn BE (2003) Corporate sponsorships of philanthropic activities: When do they impact perception of sponsor brand? J Consum Psychol 13:316–327
Olson EL (2010) Does sponsorship work in the same way in different sponsorship contexts? Eur J Mark 44(1/2):180–199
Olson EL, Thjømøe HS (2009) Sponsorship effect metric: Assessing the financial value of sponsoring by comparisons to television advertising. J Acad Mark Sci 37:504–515
Olson EL, Thjømøe HM (2012) The relative performance of TV sponsorship versus television sport advertising. Eur J Mark 46(1):1726–1742
Pham MT (1991) The evaluation of sponsorship effectiveness: A model and some methodological considerations. Gestion 2000(7):47–66

Pham MT (1992) Effects of involvement, arousal and pleasure on the recognition of sponsorship stimuli. Adv Consum Res 19(1):85–93

Quester PG (1997) Awareness as a measure of sponsorship effectiveness: The Adelaide Formula One Grand Prix and evidence of incidental ambush effects. J Mark Commun 3(1):1–20

Quester PG, Thompson B (2001) Advertising and promotion leverage on arts sponsorship effectiveness. J Advertising Res 41:33–47

Quester P, Plewa C, Palmer K, Mazodier M (2013) Determinants of the community-based sponsorship impact on self-congruity. Psychol Mark 30(11):996–1007

Ruth JA, Simonin BL (2003) 'Brought to you by brand A and brand B': Investigating multiple sponsors' influence on consumers' attitudes toward sponsored events. J Advertising 32(3):19–30

Simmons CJ, Becker-Olsen KL (2006) Achieving marketing objectives through social sponsorships. J Mark 70(4):154–169

Sirgy MJ (1985) Self-image/product-image congruity and consumer decision making. Int J Manag 2:49–63

Sirgy MJ, Lee D-J, Johar JS, Tidwell J (2008) Effect of self-congruity with sponsorship on brand loyalty. J Bus Res 61:1091–1097

Speed R, Thompson P (2000) Determinants of sports sponsorship response. J Acad Mark Sci 28(2):226–238

Spencer WD, Raz N (1995) Differential effects of aging on memory for content and context: A meta-analysis. Psychol Aging 10:527–539

Sponsorship Research International (1996) Worldwide sponsorship values. SRI, London

Wakefield KL, Becker-Olsen KL, Cornwell BT (2007) I spy a sponsor. J Advertising 36(4):61–74

Walliser B (1994) Les déterminants de la mémorisation des sponsors. Revue Française du Marketing 150:83–95

Walraven M, Bijmolt THA, Koning RH (2014) Dynamic effects of sponsoring: How sponsorship awareness develops over time. J Advertising 43(2):142–154

Weeks CS, Cornwell BT, Drennan JC (2008) Leveraging sponsorships on the internet: Activation, congruence, and articulation. Psychol Mark 25(7):637–654

Woisetschläger DM, Michaelis M (2012) Sponsorship congruence and brand image: A pre-post event analysis. Eur J Mark 46:509–523

Yue M-L, Thwaites D, Pillai KG (2014) Effectiveness of olympic sponsorship by foreign and domestic companies: The influential role of consumer ethnocentrism. Int J Sports Mark Sponsorship 15(2):107–123

Zdravkovic S, Magnusson P, Stanley SM (2010) Dimensions of fit between a brand and a social cause and their influence on attitudes. Int J Res Mark 27(2):151–160

Leveraging Research on Activation: Quester and Thompson's (2001) Impact on the Field of Sponsorship

Francois A. Carrillat and Alain d'Astous

Abstract Sponsorship activations—that is, the ancillary marketing communication actions purported to enhance the association between sponsees and sponsors—are what make sponsorships come to life. Activations are generally considered to be critical elements of a sponsorship strategy; for some, perhaps even more so than the sponsorship itself. The work of Quester and Thompson (2001) was a landmark contribution to the study of sponsorship activation on conceptual, empirical, and methodological grounds. It led the way to a host of studies and, to this day, still strongly influences sponsorship research. This chapter highlights why at the time Quester and Thompson (2001) was a significant leap forward in the context of the existing sponsorship literature, calling attention to the fact that this article presented the results of the first study to put to the test the common belief that increasing the intensity of sponsorship activation is beneficial for sponsors. This chapter also makes the point that the rigorous methodological approach of Quester and Thompson (2001), which cleverly addressed issues of both internal and external validity, enhanced the impact of their research in the field of sponsorship. Finally, the chapter discusses the research studies that followed up on Quester and Thompson's (2001) study, the current research topics that echo its contribution today, as well as the future research directions that it suggests.

Keywords Sponsorship · Activation · Repeated exposure · Quester · Thompson

F.A. Carrillat (✉)
University of Technology Sydney, Sydney, Australia
e-mail: Francois.carrillat@uts.edu.au

A. d'Astous
HEC Montréal, Montréal, Canada
e-mail: Alain.dastous@hec.ca

© Springer Science+Business Media Singapore 2016

C. Plewa and J. Conduit (eds.), *Making a Difference Through Marketing*,
DOI 10.1007/978-981-10-0464-3_2

Key Contributions

Quester and Thompson's (2001) article (hereafter Q&T) improved upon the sponsorship research literature of its time in many different ways. Sponsorship research was then at a critical point, at a juncture between perpetuating a tradition of context-specific findings, where practical considerations often took precedence over scientific standards, and establishing itself as a full-blown academic field. The publication of Q&T, with its significant conceptual, empirical, and methodological contributions, clearly marked the beginning of the scholarly and empirically driven phase of sponsorship research, which by all accounts continues to this day. Fittingly, the same year as the publication of Q&T, Cornwell et al. (2001), in a survey of key US sponsorship managers across many different industries, showed that managers considered activations as the most important weapon in the sponsor's arsenal; and yet, at that time, academic research on the topic was very limited.

Conceptual Innovation

The concept of sponsorship activation is rooted in the sponsorship-linked marketing framework that was put forward by Cornwell (1995), an influential scholar in the field of sponsorship. Sponsorship-linked marketing consists in coordinating all marketing activities across stakeholders in order to enhance the sponsee-sponsor association. One important contribution of Q&T was to provide a rigorous empirical investigation of this framework's activation component; explicitly testing its added value as a sponsorship strategy. As sponsorship researchers and practitioners know, the up-front investments made by sponsors in the form of property right fees only buy the visibility that the sponsee provides directly. This visibility is usually limited and generic for all sponsors in a given tier (signages in and around the location of the event, logos in brochures, etc.). This is why sponsors generally engage in supplementary communication activities aimed at enhancing their association with the sponsored entity. The purpose of these activations—that not only take the form of advertising, but also of sweepstakes, packaging, samples, special product editions, etc. (Cornwell et al. 2005)—is "to exploit the commercial potential of the association between a sponsee and a sponsor" (Weeks et al. 2008, p. 639). For instance, *Procter & Gamble*'s widely recognised "Proud sponsor of moms" advertising campaign that ran during the 2012 and 2014 Olympic Games, was aimed at promoting the link between the corporation, as well as its brands, and this event. Through the use of media vehicles apart from the event itself, *P&G* wanted to communicate to a larger audience the very fact that it was sponsoring the Olympics. Hence, above all, the fees paid to sponsees give a sponsor the right to activate this link and to use exclusive trademarks such as an event's logo, mascot, or taglines. Sponsorship researchers and practitioners alike consider that the bulk of a firm's sponsorship budget ought not to be devoted to the fees required to become a sponsor, but rather to investments in various sponsorship activations (e.g. Crimmins and Horn 1996; Olson and Thjómóe 2009). Thanks to its empirical investigation, Q&T contributed to shed light on the specific role of sponsorship activations. In doing so, it solidified the conceptual stance initiated by Cornwell (1995) according to which in order to maximise their benefits, sponsorship programs should be supported by various marketing communication activities.

Empirical Breakthrough

The research question tackled by Q&T was innovative and the results obtained painted a very clear, yet contrasted picture. These findings consolidated a series of results from isolated studies, in which experimental and statistical controls were not as stringent, that had explored the potential benefits of sponsorship activations. In her own previous research, Pascale Quester had already shown a keen interest in the study of activations through two papers based on the Adelaide Formula One Grand Prix. In the first one (Quester 1997), sponsor awareness of residents of the city of Adelaide was higher for those sponsors that engaged in activations than for those that did not. Interestingly, the findings included a breakdown of the different activations that sponsors engaged in. For instance, then General Motors/Holden, enjoyed the highest awareness level of any sponsor performing activations by supporting the 'celebrity race'; a peripheral event to the main race. These findings were confirmed in the article published the following year (Quester and Farrelly 1998) where the least visible sponsors in terms of activation reaped the smallest benefits from their investment.

Relevant research on activation was conducted by other researchers. Among these precursors, Crimmins and Horns (1996), through their analysis of NBC's exclusive "Olympic Watch" data, showed that sponsors of the Olympics having invested in activations were generally able to create stronger associations with this event. For instance, 64 % of sponsors that used activations succeeded in creating a link with the Olympic Games in comparison with only 4 % of sponsors that did not. In addition, their results revealed that establishing this link was a necessary, but not sufficient, condition for achieving perceptual changes of the sponsor's brand image. In the same vein, Cornwell et al. (1997) found that sponsors of a basketball team that did not advertise during the game were not recalled by attendees and Otker and Hayes (1987), for their part, observed that sponsors gaining the most from their sponsorship during the 1986 World Cup were those with the greatest advertising presence during the event. However, although relevant, these studies did not allow a systematic investigation of the impact of activations on sponsorship effectiveness as no data were available regarding the type and amount of activation spending.

Building on these important prior findings, Q&T was a landmark empirical contribution to the research domain of sponsorship activation. Above all, the methodology employed was rigorous as well as relevant. For the first time, a study on sponsorship activation was conducted with a tight control on extraneous factors while taking place in the field, aiming for both internal and external validity. Within the context of a real event, the *Adelaide Festival of the Arts*, a sample of city inhabitants was selected to participate in a two-stage treatment with control design where pre- and post-event measures were obtained from a first group that attended one of the events of the festival (treatment) and a second group that did not attend any of the festival's event (control). Participants in the treatment conditions had bought tickets for an event sponsored by one of three firms who dedicated various budget amounts to the activation of their sponsorship: 75 cents of activation spending for every dollar of sponsorship fee, 25 cents for every dollar, and no activation at all, respectively. The results showed the strongest awareness and attitude gains (pre- *vs.* post-event measures) among people who had attended an event sponsored by the firm with the strongest investment intensity, followed by the firm with an intermediary level of intensity; whereas the firm that did not activate did not reap much from its sponsorship. This yielded great insights, not only from the point of view of research validity because it was a well-crafted field experiment (i.e. use of a control group, inclusion of a no activation condition, before and after measures, sample of adult consumers, real event and real sponsors), but also because it investigated the effects of sponsorship activation at different levels of intensity (0.75 ratio *vs.* 0.25). It would be another 8 years before Olson and Thjómóe (2009) would address again the issue of activation budget-sponsorship fee ratio. Critically, using experiments with strong external validity, they found that this ratio can reach decreasing marginal returns in terms of sponsorship effectiveness beyond a certain level. In sum, Q&T's empirical impact on the field of sponsorship was seminal because it offered the first rigorous test of activation's benefits by relying on a stringent experimental design with longitudinal data gathered into the field.

Methodological Advances

Although Q&T's method did not allow investigating the effectiveness of different type of activation strategies, it nonetheless provided for the first time empirical evidence for the relationship between sponsorship activation intensity and favourable consumer responses. Indeed, before the publication of Q&T's article, the sponsorship research literature had not seen a rigorously controlled field experiment. The majority of empirical papers were either descriptive in nature (e.g. Gardner and Shuman 1987), based on case studies, best practice reports, or post-event surveys that left much insight to guesswork (e.g. Amis et al. 1999; Bennet 1999). Although Pham (1992) as well as d'Astous and Bitz (1995) used an experimental design approach, their stimuli and data collection procedures were modelled on the laboratory experiment. While the work of Meenaghan (1983; 2001) and his collaborators (e.g. Meenaghan and Shipley 1999) had laid the conceptual foundations for what was to come empirically, it was not until Q&T that this became a full-fledged reality. Building on these important previous works, Q&T brought experimental designs to the field.

Lasting Influence on the Field of Sponsorship

In addition to being a significant contribution in the area of sponsorship activation, many subfields of sponsorship are indebted to Q&T regarding their progress in the advancement of knowledge, either empirically or theoretically.

Conceptual Refinements of the Activation Concept

First and foremost, Q&T led the way to a series of rigorous empirical studies on activation itself. These papers cover a broad array of activation tools such as advertising (e.g. Grohs et al. 2004; Olson and Thjómóe 2009), product packaging (Woodside and Summers 2012), product trials during the event (Sneath et al. 2005), and websites (Weeks et al. 2008). The results of these studies have confirmed the benefits of sponsorship activation across a variety of applications. In addition to spurring researchers to further investigate sponsorship activation and its benefits, Q&T also fostered further conceptual developments of the activation construct. This is particularly evident in the research program of Bettina Cornwell and her collaborators where important refinements to the notion of activation were made. Cornwell et al. (2005) popularised the concept of articulation, a special case of activation, where the activation message is purported not only to strengthen the sponsee-sponsor link, but also to explain the relationship between the sponsee and the sponsor. Message articulation is usually relied upon by sponsors that are incongruent, or lacking natural fit with the sponsee. *McDonald*'s campaign articulating its sponsorship of the 2014 Sochi Olympic Games offers a good illustration of message articulation. Titled "being together", the campaign featured a family sharing a meal at a *McDonald*'s restaurant while watching the games on TV. A subsequent study by Cornwell et al. (2006) showed the beneficial effects of articulation message on sponsor recall, whether the sponsors are congruent or not with the sponsee. Interestingly, their findings also revealed that the detrimental impact of the presence of competitors of the focal sponsor in the communication landscape can be alleviated by well-conceived articulation messages. The positive impact of articulation messages on sponsor evaluation was confirmed by Simmons and Becker-Olsen (2006) and Coppetti et al. (2009) who showed that articulation can foster image transfer—that is, whereby the image characteristics of the sponsee rub off the image of its sponsor. More recently, Olson and Thjómóe (2011) showed that articulation can improve the perceived congruence of the sponsee-sponsor pair, confirming that the benefits of articulation are explained in good part by this enhanced congruence.

The concept of activation was further refined by Weeks et al. (2008) who made the distinction between leveraging and activating. While leveraging represents a somewhat passive way to communicate the association between the sponsee and the sponsor, activation reflects a more proactive strategy, a strategy that requires inputs from consumers. This distinction is particularly relevant in an online context because of the many possibilities for consumers to interact with sponsors through their website (e.g., proactive actions, such as clicking through, can be requested), as compared with merely being on the receiving end of activation messages. Their findings revealed that leveraging is not as good as activation from the point of view of sponsorship effectiveness. In an effort to further examine the impact of the interactivity that online contexts afford, Carrillat et al. (2014b) took the study of activation into the realm of social media by showing that event-related Facebook postings that require more engagement from Facebook users (solving riddles, thinking metaphorically about the objectives of the event, etc.) are more effective at promoting favorable responses.

Repeated Exposures to Sponsorship Activations

Although in most real-world situations, target consumers are exposed several times to a sponsor's activation initiatives over time (e.g. the multiple exposures to *P&G* 'Moms' campaign), only a few studies have examined the impact of message repetition in the context of sponsorship activation. Even if it is fair to assume that consumers in Q&T were exposed more than once to activations regarding the sponsored artistic events, their data did not relate systematically message frequency with consumer responses. Several recent papers have however investigated the effect of message repetitions. Mazodier and Merunka (2012) examined the effects of exposing consumers to three activation messages at intervals of 3 or 4 days. Their results showed that repetition leads to significantly more positive consumer responses toward the sponsor than no sponsorship activation at all. Another approach to studying activation message repetition is to rely on activation expenditures as a proxy for message exposure frequency to the target market, such as in Walraven et al. (2014). Their longitudinal data showed that the benefits reaped by *Heineken*, the UEFA Champions' League main sponsor since 2005, in terms of brand name recall and recognition over a 4-year period, were significantly and positively related to the size of the activation budget.

Sponsorship Clutter

If activation is meant to make the sponsee-sponsor link more vivid among stakeholders, it can also be a way to inoculate against sponsorship clutter, that is, when there are competitors in the perceptual space occupied by a focal sponsor, whether they themselves are sponsors of the same, or another, sponsee (e.g. sponsoring athletes taking part in a sponsored event), or are not sponsors at all. Although Q&T reported a high level of clutter in the sponsorship environment of their study, mentioning for instance 33 different logos of various sponsors in the Festival Booking Guide, they did not systematically investigate whether activation messages can reduce in some way the possible negative effects of sponsorship clutter. This question was examined in the aforementioned study by Cornwell et al. (2006) who showed that the presence of a competitor in the sponsorship environment creates some clutter that is detrimental to sponsor recall and that articulation can circumvent this problem to some extent. Ruth and Simonin (2006) on the other hand showed that clutter can be detrimental to consumer appreciation of the sponsee when the sponsor's commercial objectives are apparent, but that these evaluations improve when the motivations behind the sponsorship are perceived as benevolent. While the work of Cornwell et al. (2006) and that of Ruth and Simonin (2006) have revealed a negative impact of sponsorship clutter on memory of sponsors and evaluation of the sponsee, its effects on sponsor evaluation were not addressed. Carrillat et al. (2005) did not observe a negative impact of sponsorship clutter on attitudinal responses toward sponsors. However, they found that when clutter results from concurrent sponsorship (i.e. the presence of other brands sponsoring the same event), the image of all the sponsors may transfer between each other; which can be detrimental or beneficial, depending on the sponsor's held images.

Broadening the Scope of Sponsorship Research

One would be hard pressed to find an empirical study prior to Q&T that investigated something else than sports properties. Although Q&T did not specifically frame their findings within the realm of arts sponsorship, this was noticeably one of the first studies to bring sponsorship research outside of the sports domain. In doing so, Q&T paved the way for subsequent studies to be conducted in the context of the arts and culture. In addition, this prompted questions about the generalisation of sponsorship findings outside of sports, an issue brought up by Meenaghan (2001) who highlighted the importance of accounting for effects associated with different levels of sponsorship, such as the type of activity sponsored (sports, arts, cause, etc.). In this sense, Q&T represents a significant research episode in the debate concerning the generalisability of findings across different sponsored entities. In an article devoted to this issue, Olson (2010) concluded that for the most part, research findings appear to hold across different sponsored activities. However, this is an isolated study that does not account for all possible variations across contexts. A rigorous meta-analysis of the effectiveness of sponsorship using the sponsee's domain of activity as a moderator would allow to address this question systematically.

As shown above, up to the publication of Q&T, many sponsorship studies were plagued with methodological and conceptual fragility. Hence, Q&T not only represented a sharp turn in this regard, but it did so in a domain very sparingly examined previously. One consequence is that more papers on sponsorship began to appear in the arts management research literature. For instance, the *International Journal of Arts Management*, which rarely discussed sponsorship issues before the 2000s, witnessed a growing number of contributions in this area (e.g. d'Astous et al. 2005; Ropo and Sauer 2003) in the wake of the publication of Q&T.

Ambush Marketing

Q&T also revived important questions related to ambush marketing, that is, when non-sponsor firms attempt to be perceived as actual sponsors by means of diverse strategies, such as sponsoring the broadcast of the event, using non restricted event-themed elements in their communication materials, sponsoring a competing event, etc. (Carrillat et al. 2014a). The issue of ambush marketing was investigated by scholars early on (i.e. Sandler and Shani 1989), but for more than a decade this research topic remained quite dormant. One contribution of Q&T was to present empirical evidence related to involuntary ambushing, that is, when non-sponsor brands become associated with an event although no intended attempt was made at posing as real sponsors. Always in the vanguard of new developments, years later, Pascale Quester and collaborators looked at the so-called 'name and shame' strategy used by sponsors to retaliate against ambushers by unmasking them to the general public (Mazodier et al. 2012).

Activation and Event-Sponsor Congruence

One of the most often studied concepts in sponsorship is sponsor-sponsee congruence, or the extent to which the sponsee and the sponsor fit well together (e.g. Speed and Thompson 2000). Sponsorship researchers generally distinguish between sponsorships that seem to fit naturally (e.g. *Nike* and sport properties such as events, athletes or teams) and others where fit is not as obvious (e.g. *Visa* and the Olympics or *Nike* and an art exhibit) or downright inexistent (e.g. *Camel* cigarettes and off-road car racing). Pascale Quester made significant contributions in the specific area of sponsor-sponsee congruence as well, specifically regarding the underlying dimensions of congruence (Fleck and Quester 2007). Researchers working in this area are interested in establishing on what bases (image, concrete features, brand concept, geographical match, etc.) is congruence formed (e.g. Carrillat et al. 2013; Olson and Thjómóe 2011). Later, Quester tackled the issue of activation and congruence by examining how they combine to influence sponsorship effectiveness over time (i.e. Mazodier and Quester 2014). This article's contribution resides in its findings that affective reactions toward the brand improves more sharply over time for sponsors that invest heavily in activations. Set during the 2010 FIFA World Cup and the 2012 London Olympics, respectively, the two studies bring important insights to the debate concerning whether congruent or incongruent sponsorships produce the best results. This question essentially opposes human memory associative theorists who argue that congruent sponsorships facilitate the spreading activation of associations in consumers' minds, which is a source of positive affect (Carrillat et al. 2005), and cognitive elaboration theorists who believe that incongruence leads to deeper information processing, which produces greater attitude change and better memory for sponsors (Jagre et al. 2001).

According to Mazodier and Quester (2014), such an opposition might be misguided. What sponsorship researchers and managers should rather look at is whether activating a sponsorship is more or less effective over time as a function of the initial level of sponsee-sponsor congruence. Their results show that the apparent superior effectiveness of congruent sponsorships may be in fact punctual, due to sponsorship research having generally focused on immediate, or short-term effects. Thanks to the longitudinal design adopted in this study, the results show that, over time, the potential for improvement of mildly incongruent sponsee-sponsor associations, through diverse sponsorship activations and articulations, is greater than that of congruent sponsee-sponsor pairs. In addition, the rate of improvement of the effectiveness of mildly incongruent sponsorship is faster than that of congruent sponsorships. The incongruence resolution process that is at the source of the superiority of mild incongruence apparently requires some time to significantly impact consumer's evaluative reactions, a phenomenon that Mazodier and Quester's (2014) design could unearth. With this article, Pascale quester's work came full circle; starting in 2001 with research on the effectiveness of activations that triggered many contributions, this 2014 paper nicely mixes together, in a longitudinal perspective, activations and sponsee-sponsor congruence, two of the cornerstone concepts of sponsorship.

Conclusion

Sponsorship research has improved drastically within the last 15 years; there is now greater attention paid to theoretical developments, more rigorous and relevant research designs, better sampling methods, more sophisticated measuring instruments and analyses, and greater consideration of internal and external validity issues. This evolution can be traced to the hard work of many scholars devoted to making sponsorship research a truly scientific enterprise. Among them, Pascale Quester stands as a prominent figure. Her research approach, oftentimes based on longitudinal measurements taken in the field, with a tight experimental control, maximises both relevance and rigor; characteristics that have become more widespread in sponsorship studies. Q&T significantly contributed to bring sponsorship research into its modern phase. At a time when the sponsorship literature was almost exclusively focused on sports events, and when descriptive and non-causal research designs were all too common, this article marked a clear divide between two eras.

Research by Q&T and their followers has brought many important advances in our understanding of sponsorship activation and articulation, but there is still a great deal to accomplish. We would like to conclude this homage to Pascale Quester by suggesting some directions for future research.

To this day research on sponsorship activation and articulation has essentially focused on the reinforcement of the sponsor-sponsee link. While this emphasis is understandable, it must recognised that activation messages can be articulated around various dimensions. As a first example, recently we have been interested in our laboratory in looking at a quite common although, strangely enough, understudied phenomenon: sponsor change, that is, the situation where, for some reasons, a current sponsor exits from a sponsorship and is replaced by another. We discovered that when presented with this fact, consumers naturally engage in developing various causal explanations of the behaviors of the former as well as the new sponsors. For instance, they might think that the former sponsor had attained its objectives or, in contrast, that it considered the sponsorship as unprofitable. Inferences are also made in relation with the new sponsor, for example that it was an opportunistic move. In addition we found that, depending on various characteristics of the sponsor change situation, notably, the duration of the former partnership, these inferences vary and are likely to impact consumer responses (e.g. purchase intentions). Managing consumer inferences in this type of situation is therefore critical, and this must be done by communicating adequately with consumers. Hence, new sponsors in this situation should consider the possibility of activating their sponsorship not only to reinforce their link with the sponsee but also, and perhaps, more importantly, with the objective of creating among consumers, through proper articulation, durable impressions of support and continuity.

A second example, issued also from research in our laboratory, concerns the importance of attenuating the inferences that consumers often make about the apparent commercial motivations of sponsors. As discussed elsewhere (Carrillat and d'Astous 2012), the advertising-sponsorship interface is something that sponsorship researchers and practitioners should always consider carefully, and manage, since consumers may sometimes develop impressions that a sponsor is more interested in exploiting an entity (e.g. an event) than supporting it. The goodwill that is often associated with sponsorship is in jeopardy whenever consumers make such inferences and concrete actions should be taken to harness them. Activating the sponsorship with adequate articulation can serve this purpose and could be done with the objective of convincing consumers of the altruistic nature of the sponsor's intentions. Research is needed on this important aspect of sponsorship management. It would be relevant in particular to verify if inferences of commercial exploitation made by consumers depend on the type of property that is sponsored (e.g. arts, sports or cause-related actions) and compare the effectiveness of articulation in attenuating these inferences across these different types. In their research, Q&T found that their participants had positive perceptions of the sponsors of the Adelaide Festival of the Arts, but did not have the data to test or even speculate about possible differences with other sponsorship contexts.

Another relevant direction for future research concerns the important issue of sponsorship portfolio, that is, the situation where a firm sponsors several entities (Chien et al. 2011). To this day, research on sponsorship activation and articulation has mostly centered on single-entity sponsoring. Yet, it is quite common that firms sponsor several entities which may, or may not, be consistent with respect to their domain of activity and their reputation. As recent research in our laboratory has demonstrated, any given sponsor-sponsee link in a sponsorship portfolio might suffer from these multiple connections, because consumers may not only have some difficulty in establishing several sponsor-sponsee links, but also in giving meaning to these numerous associations, especially when there is high variance among the sponsees. Activating a given sponsorship in the context of a sponsorship portfolio should therefore be made with a consideration of consumers' knowledge of the sponsor's involvement with other properties and the objective of facilitating the establishment of distinctive and coherent sponsor-sponsee associations.

References

Amis J, Slack T, Berret T (1999) Sport sponsorship as distinctive competence. Eur J Mark 33(3−4):250−272

Bennett R (1999) Sport sponsorship, spectators recall and false consensus. Eur J Mark 34 (3/4):291–313

Carrillat FA, Colbert F, Feigné M (2014a) Weapons of mass intrusion: The leveraging of ambush marketing strategies. Eur J Mark 48(1/2):314–335

Carrillat FA, d'Astous A (2012) The sponsorship-advertising interface: Is less better for sponsors? Eur J Mark 46(3/4):562−574

Carrillat FA, d'Astous A, Davoine V (2013) The sponsor-event geographical match as a dimension of event-sponsor fit: An investigation in Europe and North America. Australas Mark J 21 (4):264−270

Carrillat FA, d'Astous A, Morisette Grégoire E (2014b) Event sponsorship activation in the social media: A facebook experiment. Internet Res 24(4):474−495

Carrillat FA, Lafferty BA, Harris EG (2005) Investigating sponsorships effectiveness: Do less familiar brands have an advantage over more familiar brands in single and multiple sponsorship arrangements? J Brand Manag 13(1):50–64

Chien PM, Cornwell TB, Pappu R (2011) Sponsorship portfolio as a brand-image creation strategy. J Bus Res 64(2):142–149

Coppetti C, Wentzel D, Tomczak T, Henkel S (2009) Improving incongruent sponsorships through articulation of the sponsorship and audience participation. J Mark Commun 15(1):17–34

Cornwell TB (1995) Sponsorship-linked marketing development. Sport Mark Q 4:13−24

Cornwell TB, Humphreys MS, Maguire AM, Weeks CS, Tellegen CL (2006) Sponsorship-linked marketing: The role of articulation in memory. J Consum Res 33(3):312–321

Cornwell TB, Maignan I, Irwin R (1997) Long-term recall of sponsorship sources: An empirical investigation of stadium and sport café audiences. Asia-Australia Mark J 5(1):45–57

Cornwell TB, Roy DP, EAS II (2001) Exploring managers' perceptions of the impact of sponsorship on brand equity. J Advertising 30(2):41−51

Cornwell TB, Weeks CS, Roy DP (2005) Sponsorship-linked marketing: Opening the black box. J Advertising 34(2):21–42

Crimmins J, Horn M (1996) Sponsorship: From management ego trip to marketing success. J Advertising Res 36:11−21

d'Astous A, Bitz P (1995) Consumer evaluations of sponsorship programmes. Eur J Mark 29 (12):6–22

d'Astous A, Colbert F, Parmentier MA (2005) Consumer perception of private versus public sponsorship of the arts. Int J Arts Manag 8(1):48−60

Fleck N, Quester P (2007) Birds of a feather flock together… definition, role and measure of congruence: An application to sponsorship. Psychol Mark 24(11):975−1000

Gardner MP, Shuman PJ (1987) Sponsorship: An important component of the promotions mix. J Advertising 16(1):11–17

Grohs R, Wagner U, Vsetecka S (2004) Assessing the effectiveness of sport sponsorships—An empirical examination. Schmalenbach Bus Rev. 56:119–138

Jagre E, Wilson JJ, Watson JG (2001) Sponsorship and congruity theory: A theoretical framework for explaining consumer attitude and recall of event sponsorship. In: Advances in Consumer Research, vol 28. Valdosta, GA

Mazodier M, Merunka D (2012) Achieving brand loyalty through sponsorship: The role of fit and self-congruity. J Acad Mark Sci 40(6):807–820

Mazodier M, Quester P (2014) The role of sponsorship fit for changing brand affect: A latent growth modeling approach. Int J Res Mark 31(1):16–29

Mazodier M, Quester PG, Chandon J-L (2012) Unmasking the ambusher: Conceptual framework and empirical evidence. Eur J Mark 46(1/2):192–214

Meenaghan T (1983) Commercial sponsorship. Eur J Mark 25(11):5–10

Meenaghan T (2001) Understanding sponsorship effects. Psychol Mark 18(2):95–121

Meenaghan T, Shipley D (1999) Media effect in commercial sponsorship. Eur J Mark 33 (3/4):328–347

Olson EL (2010) Does sponsorship work in the same way in different sponsorship contexts? Eur J Mark 44(1/2):180–199

Olson EL, Thjømøe HM (2009) Sponsorship effect metric: Assessing the financial value of sponsoring by comparisons to television advertising. J Acad Mark Sci 37(4):504–515

Olson EL, Thjømøe HM (2011) Explaining and articulating the fit construct in sponsorship. J of Advertising 40(1):57–70

Otker T, Hayes P (1987) Judging the efficiency of sponsorship: Experience from the 1986 soccer world cup. Eur Res 15(4):3–8

Pham MT (1992) Effects of involvement, arousal, and pleasure on the recognition of sponsorship stimuli. Adv Consum Res 19:85–93

Quester P (1997) Awareness as a measure of sponsorship effectiveness—The Adelaide formula one grand prix. J Mark Commun 3(2):1–20

Quester P, Farrelly F (1998) Brand association and memory decay effects of sponsorship: The case of the australian formula one grand prix. J Prod Brand Manage 7(6):539–556

Quester PG, Thompson B (2001) Advertising and promotion leverage on arts sponsorship effectiveness. J Advertising Res 41:33−47

Ropo A, Sauer E (2003) Partnerships of orchestras: Towards shared leadership. Int J Arts Manag 44−55

Ruth JA, Simonin BL (2006) The power of numbers. J Advertising 35(4):7–20

Sandler DM, Shani D (1989) Olympic sponsorship versus "Ambush" marketing: Who gets the gold? J Advertising Res 29(9/14):38–43

Simmons CJ, Becker-Olsen KL (2006) Achieving marketing objectives through social sponsorships. J Mark 70:154–169

Sneath JZ, Finney RZ, Close AG (2005) An IMC approach to event marketing: The effect of sponsorship and experience on event attitude. J Advertising Res 45(4):373–381

Speed R, Thompson P (2000) Determinants of sports sponsorship response. J Acad Mark Sci 28 (2):226–238

Walraven M, Bijmolt THA, Koning RH (2014) Dynamic effects of sponsoring: How sponsorship awareness develops over time. J Advertising 43(2):142−154

Weeks CS, Cornwell TB, Drennan JC (2008) Leveraging sponsorships on the internet: activation, congruence, and articulation. Psychol Mark 25(7):637–654

Woodside FM, Summers J (2012) The impact of sponsorship awareness in low involvement setting. Contemp Manag Res 8(3):205–228

Sponsorship-Linked Attitudes of Employees of Sponsoring Firms: SMEs Versus Large Organisations

Aila Khan and Suzan Burton

Abstract Corporate sponsorship is often used to develop positive attitudes towards a brand or a firm, among its customers and/or potential customers. Depending on the size of the organisation, corporate sponsorship may involve high-profile entities (such as the Olympics), or smaller local groups or individuals, but the prominence of large entities means that sponsorships by large organisations attract most media and research attention. A less commonly studied effect of sponsorship is the effect on the attitudes of the sponsoring organisations' own employees. In this area, as with consumer-focused sponsorship, large organisations are likely to have substantial advantages. Large firms have the resources to leverage their sponsorship both internally and externally. Large organisations also have the expertise to effectively communicate their sponsorship-relationship to internal audiences. Yet smaller organisations may also be successful in engaging employees by sponsoring local entities at far lower cost, and providing opportunities for employee participation in the sponsorship. This research compares sponsorship-linked attitudes of 405 employees at small and medium-sized enterprises (SMEs) and large organisations. Despite large organisations' bigger budgets, sponsorship-linked attitudes were not significantly lower among SME employees. For one measure, sponsorship-linked organisational identification, SME employees rated significantly higher than employees of large organisations. The findings suggest that sponsorship can result in positive employee attitudes, even in SMEs—and may in fact be even more cost-effective for SMEs. These results may be due to increased communication within SMEs, or because SME employees may have stronger affiliations with sponsored entities. Implications for research and practice are discussed.

Keywords Sponsorship · Employees · Organisational size · Perceived external prestige · Organisational identification

A. Khan (✉) · S. Burton
Western Sydney University, Parramatta, NSW, Australia
e-mail: a.khan@westernsydney.edu.au

S. Burton
e-mail: s.burton@westernsydney.edu.au

© Springer Science+Business Media Singapore 2016

C. Plewa and J. Conduit (eds.), *Making a Difference Through Marketing*,
DOI 10.1007/978-981-10-0464-3_3

Introduction

Corporate sponsorship may have its roots in patronage, but today, it is regarded as being similar to advertising, as an investment made to progress corporate objectives (Meenaghan and Shipley 1999). This view of corporate sponsorship as an investment is reflected in a definition of corporate sponsorship by Quester and Thompson (2001, p. 34) as "*an investment, in cash or in kind, in an activity, person or event (sponsee), in return for access to the exploitable commercial potential associated with that activity, person or event by the investor (sponsor)*".

Although, like advertising, sponsorship is generally seen as an investment, a key differentiating factor between sponsorship and advertising is the former's ability to deliver a benefit to society while assisting in meeting marketing objectives. As a result of this societal benefit, consumers generally receive sponsorship communications in a 'halo of goodwill', so sponsorship communications are viewed less critically than advertising messages (Meenaghan 2001). Sponsors can also benefit from the gratitude that arises among audiences who have a strong liking for the 'sponsee', that is, for the sponsored event or property (Crimmins and Horn 1996).

In addition to providing benefits by creating positive associations among consumers, a sponsor's own employees are an important second, internal, audience for sponsorship-related objectives. Just as an external communication tool—advertising—has effects on internal audiences (Gilly and Wolfinbarger 1998), corporate sponsorship—though primarily aimed at customers—may also have an impact on employees. A company's sponsorship of a popular event or "worthy cause" can be viewed by different stakeholders, including employees, as making a valuable contribution in strengthening the relationship between the sponsor and the community (Lacey et al. 2010). The benefit of sponsorship can be enhanced by leveraging the sponsorship with employees. For example, Nike-sponsored athletes '…give motivational talks, host sales meetings,…play golf with clients and employees and help in product development' (Amis et al. 1999, p. 6). Thus, a sponsored athlete becomes an integral part of the company, with employees viewing the athlete as more of a 'colleague' than a star (Amis et al. 1999).

A key aspect of sponsorship implementation is the sponsor's investment in the activation or leveraging of the sponsorship-relationship. Activation includes all marketing activities that a company conducts to promote its involvement in sponsorship. Such a marketing expenditure is over and above the rights fee paid to the sponsored property (IEG 2010). According to some estimates, the activation-sponsorship fee ratio can be as high as 8:1 in order to fully reap the rewards from the sponsorship deal (O'Reilly and Horning 2013).

Large organisations, besides bigger budgets, are often able to benefit from the media coverage that comes with high-profile sponsorships. As a result, most public and research attention has focused on sponsorship by large organisations. For example, Nike could afford to sign up Michael Jordan for US$2.5 million a year when he was in his senior year at university and still had to prove himself as a professional player (Amis et al. 1999). The sponsorship resulted in Air Jordan shoes and Jordan-related apparel contributing over US$200 million a year in sales for Nike (Katz 1994).

Although the majority of research has focused on sponsorship by large organisations such as Nike, small and medium-sized enterprises (SMEs) may also be able to benefit from sponsorship by supporting activities at a community-level, or by supporting smaller, more affordable entities (Mack 1999). When an organisation is seen as being caring and supportive towards an entity that employees are passionate about (such as a local football team), employees may feel obliged to reciprocate the generosity (Eisenberger et al. 2001). One way of reciprocating is through more favourable employee attitudes and behaviours towards the employer (Jones 2010).

While large organisations may also support neighbourhood entities, their support of local community events is often overshadowed by their support of other more high-profile events. In contrast, over 50 % of SMEs regularly sponsor local events and charities (Webb and Carter 2001), but would rarely, if ever, sponsor major events. Perhaps in part due to their association with community based sponsorships, SMEs have been found to have a more direct connection with the local community (Russo and Perrini 2010). People in the community often know the local small business owners—and their family members—by name. Customers can put a face to the business (Koch 2013). Such deep connections cannot be realised by bigger corporations.

But sponsorships are expensive, and the outcomes often uncertain. For smaller organisations, the benefits of sponsorship are even less certain. Smaller organisations will have lower sponsorship budgets, and so be less able to capitalise on the media attention given to high-profile sponsees. Similarly, a smaller organisation will not be able to offer its employees the chance to get the privileged access to high-profile sportspeople offered by large sponsors such as Nike. Under these conditions, it is not clear whether small organisations can hope to obtain the positive effects on employee attitudes that large organisations can achieve through their more expensive and higher profile sponsorships.

Despite this important challenge for understanding the effects of sponsorship in different size organisations, there has been only limited research attention to sponsorships by small to medium organisations (SMEs), and even less into the effects (if any) of those sponsorships on the employees of SME sponsors. As a result, this research compared the response of employees from large organisations and SME sponsors, to explore whether sponsoring SMEs can achieve equivalent positive responses from their employees, despite considerably lower budgets and lower profile sponsees. In the next section, we discuss examples of sponsorship by large and small organisations, and then describe the study, the results, and the implications for businesses and for research.

Leveraging Corporate Sponsorship

Worldwide, expenditure on sponsorship has been increasing faster than other forms of promotion such as advertising (Meenaghan 2001). According to one estimate, the expenditure on sports sponsorship in Australia and New Zealand alone is approximately A$927 million per year (IMR Sports Marketing 2013). The 2006 Commonwealth Games in Melbourne were estimated to have involved around $AUD130 million in associated sponsorship from 50 sponsors (Webb 2006). One of the eight principal corporate sponsors of the Games was the National Australia Bank (NAB), and a spokesperson at the time said that NAB would have recouped the cost of the sponsorship in new business even before the Games started.

However, corporate sponsorship is not limited to large organisations. While SMEs cannot usually afford to sponsor large events or other well-known sponsees, they can be involved in supporting small-scale, local and regional properties at much lower cost. One study found that smaller businesses paid up to $20,000 to sponsor regional sporting events (Lamont 2005). For example, a real estate agency in Western Australia, Abel McGrath, sponsored an event organised by a primary school's P&C. The event encouraged locals to immerse themselves in culture in a relaxed picnic setting. The firm's owner played auctioneer on the night, auctioning off items donated by the locals. Money raised from the evening went towards an art program at the primary school. Such sponsorship arrangements can be a cost-effective way for SMEs to achieve their communication goals (Gardner and Shuman 1988). Even with a relatively small communication budget, SMEs can therefore reach their publics in a significantly cheaper way than media-based advertising (Lamont 2005).

While the majority of public and research attention has been directed to the effects of high-profile sponsorship on customer attitudes, sport sponsorship can also result in significant positive effects on the staff of the sponsoring organisation. For example, as mentioned above NAB was one of the major sponsors of the 2006 Commonwealth Games. As well as providing what the bank believed was an effective commercial return on its sponsorship, an NAB spokesperson said that the Games proved to be 'a huge staff motivational tool', with 30–40 % of staff involved, and resulting in more than 6500 positive emails from staff (Webb 2006). So while the impact of sponsorship is recognised in large corporate sponsorships, the sponsorship literature has largely neglected any effect of sponsorship on employees in SMEs. This could be partly because a mere 5 % of SME managers report any substantial benefits in terms of improved employee relations resulting from the firm's involvement in corporate sponsorship (Webb and Carter 2001). Another study found that none of the surveyed SMEs listed any employee-related goals in their sponsorship objectives (Lamont and Dowell 2008). However SME employees may still be positively impacted by sponsorship by their employer, particularly if the employer supports an entity that an employee is passionate about.

The effects of sponsorship on external and internal audiences are summarised in Fig. 1. Sponsorship can have a direct effect on the sponsor's external publics (including its existing and potential customers), creating, and/or reinforcing a

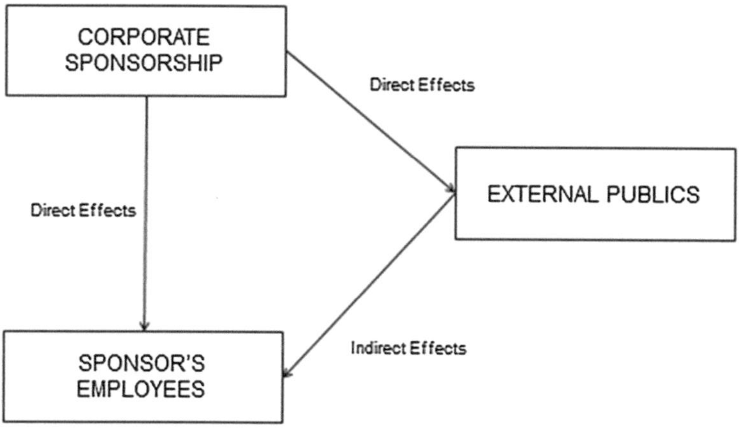

Fig. 1 The effects of sponsorship on employees—adapted from Acito and Ford (1980)

favourable corporate image. At the same time, the sponsorship is likely to have a direct effect on the sponsor's employees. A direct effect on employees could occur when they are exposed to their employers' sponsorship messages, by hearing about the sponsorship themselves, or by experiencing the sponsorship firsthand. Employees may experience the sponsorship by getting involved in their organisations' sponsorship related internal marketing activities—such as Nike's programs to bring sponsored athletes and staff together, or NAB's employee volunteering opportunities in its Commonwealth Games sponsorship.

Employees may also be indirectly affected by their employers' sponsorship activity, as shown in Fig. 1. Indirect effects occur when external stakeholders—such as customers, suppliers, and/or government officials—see or hear about the organisation's sponsorship activities. When these stakeholders interact with the employees, they may talk about their impressions of the firm's sponsorship. In this way, employees form an image of how outsiders view their organisation—a 'construed external image' (Dutton et al. 1994). Research has shown that individuals can 'bask in reflected glory' when associated with successful others, and increase their attachment to that other (Cialdini et al. 1976). Consistent with that effect, if outsiders view a sponsor's contribution as valuable, the sponsor's employees may feel more positively about their employer, and thus experience increased motivation at work.

Do Employee Attitudes to Sponsorship Vary Between Large and Small Organisations?

Both direct and indirect effects are likely to be greater for sponsorships by large organisations, since such sponsorships will involve larger sums of money and higher levels of organisational competence in leveraging sponsorship activities.

In addition, sponsees—either individuals, such as sporting stars, or major events—that receive large amounts of sponsorship are likely to receive much more media attention than the lower-profile sponsees typically sponsored by SMEs. The ever-increasing attention by large organisations to leveraging their sponsorship investment is thus likely to result in significant direct effects on employees. Such sponsorships would also have increased indirect effects as more people are likely to notice, and possibly talk about, prominent sponsors (Wakefield et al. 2007).

As a result of the greater ability of large organisations to leverage sponsorship efforts, employees of large organisations might be expected to have more positive attitudes to their employer's sponsorship arrangements, see that sponsorship as more prestigious in the community, and as a result, have greater identification with the organisation, due to the 'reflected glory' effect of the organisation's sponsorship(s) (Cialdini et al. 1976). Alternatively, it is possible that an SME sponsorship that is focused on a local community within which employees live and socialise may be viewed as more effective by the employee because they might see the results of the sponsorship themselves, and possibly accrue personal prestige. For example, the Abel McGrath sponsorship of the primary school discussed above would be very visible to employees whose children go to the school. Such employees, would be likely to see the direct benefit of the sponsorship for a school which otherwise would have limited sponsorship options. Even if an employee does not have any children attending the specific school, he or she may hear about the sponsorship through other community members or friends.

The preceding discussion suggests that an employee's response to their employer's sponsorship arrangement can be assessed with three measures:

(1) *Specific Attitudes toward Employer's Sponsorship*

The first measure assesses employees' specific attitudes toward their employers' sponsorship activity, because measures of specific attitudes offer the greatest explanatory power in understanding behaviour (Zielke and Dobbelstein 2007). The construct reflects previous discussion of specific attitudes by Eagly and Chaiken (1993), and in this context, thus reflects employees' predisposition to respond in a favourable or unfavourable way to their employers' sponsorship activity.

(2) *Sponsorship-Linked Perceived External Prestige*

Sponsorship-linked Perceived External Prestige reflects the extent to which an employee feels proud of their organisation's sponsorship program due to recognition and endorsement by important external publics (e.g. customers, friends, family members, media and business associates). The construct is derived from the work of Bergami and Bagozzi (2000).

(3) *Sponsorship-Linked Organisational Identification*

The third measure assesses the extent to which employees see themselves as possessing the same attributes as their employer, reflecting previous research on Organisational Identification (Dutton et al. 1994).

In the following section, we describe the study used to compare the responses of employees from sponsoring SMEs and large organisations to their employers' sponsorships.

Methodology

Data was collected using an online survey. Inclusion criteria were (1) that the employee was working at an organisation employing more than five employees, and (2) that the employee was aware of some activity being currently sponsored by the employer (see definition below).

Screening questions were used to categorise respondents as employed by large or SME organisations, consistent with definitions used by the Australian Bureau of Statistics (2001)—a large organisation being one employing 200 or more workers, a medium-sized organisation having twenty to 199 employees, and a small organisation five to nineteen employees. (Organisations with fewer than five employees are termed micro-enterprises, and micro-enterprise employees were not included in the study). As corporate sponsorship may easily be confused with other marketing and promotional activities, a definition of sponsorship was provided to respondents during the screening process and at the start of the study:

> Corporate sponsorship is "the provision of assistance, either financial or in-kind, to an activity by a commercial organisation for the purpose of achieving commercial objectives". Thus, giving donations purely for philanthropic reasons does not form part of corporate sponsorship. The sponsor must be interested in leveraging the sponsorship-relationship to achieve certain business-related objectives. This could be done by sponsoring a charity or a public service (e.g. the Fire Brigade) as well.

A quota sampling method was used to ensure a sufficient sample from both small and large organisations, resulting in a final sample of 405, with 205 (51 %) from large organisations, and 200 (49 %) from SMEs. The incidence rate for the survey was 19 %. Sample characteristics are given in Table 1.

Table 1 Respondent profile

Variable	Frequency	%	Variable	Frequency	%
Gender			Firm size		
Males	228	56.30	Large	205	50.62
Females	177	43.70	SMEs	200	49.38
Age			Status		
18–35	185	45.68	Full-time	340	83.95
36–50	137	33.83	Part-time	65	16.05
51+	83	20.49			

Measures

Specific Attitudes Toward Employers' Sponsorship

The employees' attitude to their employer's sponsorship was measured with four items, drawn from four different sponsorship studies (Dees et al. 2008; Irwin et al. 2003; Madrigal 2001; Rifon et al. 2004).

1. My employer's sponsorship improves my impression of my company
2. My employer's sponsorship effort makes me feel more favourable toward my employer
3. My employer's sponsorship activity improves my perception of my employer
4. My employer's sponsorship activity makes me like my employer more.

The first item was modified from a previous study that used a single item to measure spectator attitudes to sports sponsorship (Irwin et al. 2003). In view of the recommendation to use multiple items to generate valid estimates of reliability, additional items were included from three studies measuring consumers' specific attitudes (Dees et al. 2008; Madrigal 2001; Rifon et al. 2004).

Sponsorship-Linked Perceived External Prestige

Sponsorship-linked Perceived External Prestige was measured with five items modified from a consumer-focused sponsorship study by Cornwell and Coote (2005), who adapted the scale from Mael and Ashforth (1992). Following these authors, two items were reverse coded, as shown below. However, those items were subsequently dropped from analysis due to poor correlations with other items—presumably due to response errors during the survey completion caused by the reverse coding.

1. People in my community think highly of my employer's sponsorship activity
2. In my community, it is considered positive for my employer to have sponsored an activity
3. My employer is considered to be generous because it sponsors an activity in order to help out
4. As far as support through sponsorship is concerned, my employer does not have a good reputation in my community (Reverse coded)
5. People in other similar businesses look down at my employer's sponsorship activities (Reverse coded).

Sponsorship-Linked Organisational Identification

Sponsorship-linked Organisational Identification was measured with six items modified from the consumer-focused measures used by Cornwell and Coote (2005).

1. If someone criticises my employer's sponsorship efforts, it feels like a personal insult
2. I am very interested in what others think about my employer's sponsorship activities
3. When I talk about my employer's sponsorship, I usually say "we" rather than "they"
4. The successes of such sponsorship activities are my successes
5. If a story in the media criticised my employer's sponsorship activities, I would feel embarrassed
6. When someone praises my employer's sponsorship efforts, it feels like a personal compliment.

General Beliefs and Attitude Toward Sponsorship

Since employees of large organisations may have different general attitudes to sponsorship, which might, in turn, influence their attitude to their employer's sponsorship, a fourth measure, 'General Beliefs and Attitude to Sponsorship' was assessed to ensure there was no systematic difference in attitude to sponsorship between the employees from SMEs and large organisations. This variable was assessed with five items, adapted from Lachowetz et al. (2002).

1. Sponsorship creates a positive image for the sponsoring organisation
2. Sponsorship is a positive thing in organisations today
3. Sponsorship should be a regular part of a company's activities
4. I am positively impressed with an organisation that sponsors anything or anyone
5. I like to see companies supporting worthy causes or events.

All items were measured on a five point Likert scale, ranging from 1 (Strongly disagree) to 5 (Strongly agree). Validity and reliability scores were found to be satisfactory (see Tables 3 and 4 in Appendix). A single, summated scale was computed for each construct by averaging responses to items of each construct (Hair et al. 2010). Thus, the possible range of scores for each measure is from 1.0 to 5.0, with higher scores reflecting stronger attitudes. Independent-samples *t*-tests were used to compare mean differences between the two groups of employees, after testing of appropriate assumptions (i.e. approximately normal distributions and variance for the groups being compared).

Results

General Beliefs and Attitude Toward Sponsorship

General beliefs and attitudes to sponsorship did not vary between employees from SMEs and large organisations, with both groups having the same beliefs and attitude, in general, when rounded to one decimal place (see Table 2). This lack of difference was expected, and is not surprising, since people's general attitudes are likely to have been formed from their experiences outside the workplace, rather than being primarily driven by any experience of their employer's sponsorship programs. The lack of difference in general attitude thus allowed a comparison of employees' attitudes toward their employers' sponsorship under the assumption that the groups had the same general attitude to sponsorship.

Specific Attitudes Toward Employers' Sponsorship

There was no difference in the mean attitude of employees to their employer's sponsorship across large organisations and SMEs ($p > 0.1$). In fact, SME employees had a slightly—but not significantly—more positive attitude to their employee's sponsorship efforts (see Table 2). Thus despite what would be presumed to be much higher sponsorship expenditure by large organisations, the attitude of employees in SMEs to their employer's sponsorship was no less positive—and, as discussed above, was, on average, more positive, though not significantly so. Lower expenditure on sponsorship by SMEs does not therefore appear to be a barrier to achieving any positive effects on employee attitude to sponsorship.

Sponsorship-Linked Perceived External Prestige (PEP)

There was no significant difference in Sponsorship-linked PEP across the respondents from SMEs and large organisations ($p > 0.1$) (see Table 2). Indeed, as with attitudes to their employer's sponsorship, employees from SMEs rated the Sponsorship-linked PEP of their employer higher than those from large organisations (though not significantly higher). As shown in Table 2, SME employees rated

Table 2 Sponsorship-linked employee attitudes—large organisations versus SMEs

Variables	Large		SMEs		Difference	
	Mean	SD	Mean	SD	t-value	p-value
General beliefs and attitude	3.41	0.66	3.37	0.60	−0.55	0.58
Specific attitudes	3.43	0.89	3.46	0.86	0.36	0.71
Sponsorship-linked PEP	3.35	0.78	3.46	0.74	1.50	0.13
Sponsorship-linked OI	2.82	0.81	2.99	0.85	−1.98	0.04[a]

[a]Significant difference between means

the external prestige of their employer's sponsorship 3.46 on the five-point scale, compared to an average rating 3.35 for employees from large organisations. The result is somewhat surprising, since the large corporate events sponsored by large organisations would be expected to have higher visibility in the broad community.

One possible explanation for the higher rating by SME employees may be the repeated reference to 'in my community', and an evaluation of an employer as 'generous' in its sponsorship in the measurement items. These features of the measure may have focused SME respondents' attention on the benefits of local, and less clearly commercial, sponsorship often used by SME sponsors, with a commensurate higher evaluation of the local community's evaluation of that sponsorship. Whatever the reason for the lack of significant difference (and the higher rating by SME employees), the result does suggest that SME sponsorship arrangements are viewed by their employees as resulting in community prestige (at least for the local community) that is at least equivalent to, and possibly even higher than, the prestige associated with much larger and high-profile sponsorships.

Sponsorship-Linked Organisational Identification (OI)

Employees of large organisations had significantly lower average levels of Sponsorship-linked OI than SME employees, as shown in Table 2. Employees of large organisations, on average, rated their identification as 2.82 on the five-point scale, compared to an average of 2.99 for employees of SMEs.

The result is somewhat surprising, since Sponsorship-linked OI would be expected to be higher due to the higher profile of sponsorships by large organisations, and the associated opportunities for promoting those sponsorships, either through advertising, public relations, or employee-directed activities. The result may reflect lower levels of organisational identification among employees of large organisations, but suggest that creating sponsorship-linked identification with an employer is not solely dependent on the firm being a big player in the market or sponsoring more prominent, high profile events. Based on these results, SMEs with smaller budgets and more low-key sponsees can still generate higher levels of OI amongst their employees than large organisations. One possible explanation is the opportunity for SME employees to establish face-to-face interaction with the owner-manager of the firm, possibly resulting in a transfer of values and principles. Such an environment of open interaction and communication is an important factor in building identification toward the firm (Smidts et al. 2001). Given the size and structure of a typical SME, it is also possible that employees participate in deciding which property to sponsor, resulting in higher levels of Sponsorship-linked OI.

Sponsorship-linked OI would be expected to be higher when Sponsorship-linked perceived external prestige is high, consistent with evidence that individuals can 'bask in reflected glory' due to their association with a prestigious entity (Smidts et al. 2001). Consistent with that view, there was a positive linear association between Sponsorship-linked organisational identification and Sponsorship-linked perceived external prestige ($r = 0.665$; $p < 0.01$).

Discussion

The results suggest that organisation size (and by extrapolation, organisational budget) is not a barrier to sponsors achieving positive effects on employee attitudes from their sponsorship. These results showed no significant difference between employees from large and small organisations in Specific attitudes towards their employers' sponsorship, or in Sponsorship-linked perceived external prestige—indeed, ratings of Sponsorship-linked perceived external prestige were higher for SME employees. While the difference was not statistically significant for all but one outcome measure, it shows that sponsorship-related feelings of prestige amongst employees are not just triggered by sponsorship publicity and high-profile events. While smaller firms may not obtain the widespread media coverage of a sponsored event that would be common for larger sponsors, any form of employee-directed communication—such as an organisational newsletter, a brief email, or an informal chat which positively portrays the organisation's position in society—may assist in creating favourable employee perceptions about the sponsorship. As summarised by Collett and Fenton (2011, p. 89), "a small budget should not be perceived as a barrier to sponsorship, (it is) merely a catalyst for greater creativity in activation".

The results are even more striking in regards to Sponsorship-linked organisational identification. Employees of SMEs had significantly higher levels of Sponsorship-linked organisational identification than those from large organisations, suggesting that even with much lower sponsorship budgets, SMEs can obtain more positive results than large organisations in this area. The result is particularly surprising, since SMEs are likely to be able to only modestly leverage their sponsorship program with their employees compared to large organisations. However, based on these results, scarce resources do not appear to limit the potential effect of sponsorship on employee attitudes. SMEs, in spite of their size and resource limitations, appear to still be able to generate favourable sponsorship-related attitudes amongst their employees. As these results demonstrate, these attitudes can be as strong—or even stronger—than those of individuals employed by large organisations. A possible explanation is that due to the structure and operations of SMEs, employees are in a position to come close to the owner/manager (Longenecker et al. 1989), and thus gain first-hand information regarding the organisation's operations. This more informal environment and flatter hierarchy may result in the higher levels of identification with the employer and/or the firm shown by the SME employees in this study.

Implications

The results have implications for sponsoring organisations and for sponsorship researchers. For sponsors, the results show that sponsorship, which is usually targeted towards customers can result in favourable employee attitudes, even for

SMEs with low sponsorship budgets. The effectiveness of sponsorship has been shown to be related to the degree to which sponsors are willing to leverage their investment with additional promotional activities (Quester and Thompson 2001). These results extend that work, by showing that SMEs can achieve equivalent, or in some cases more favourable, employee attitudes than large organisations. The positive effects of sponsorship on the SME employees in this study also suggest that leveraging sponsorship with employees may be particularly important when employees belong to the community benefitting from the corporate sponsorship.

A direct or indirect focus on employees' communities is increasingly common by sponsoring organisations.. For example Telstra, the largest Australian telecommunications company, states that it is "… dedicated to supporting the communities in which our …employees live and work" (Telstra 2015). The Bank of Melbourne (a regional subsidiary of one of Australia's largest banks) explicitly states that any requests for sponsorship will be evaluated against opportunities for involving bank's employees with the sponsored activity (Bank of Melbourne 2015). Another large Australian B2B agribusiness, Graincorp, states its belief in supporting '… employees and their communities by investing in the things that matter to them' (GrainCorp 2015). However the higher levels of Sponsorship linked OI found in employees of SMEs in this study suggests that community based sponsorships—whether by large or small organisations—may have a more positive effect on employee attitudes if the sponsor can effectively leverage its sponsorship program by ensuring that its employees get involved with the campaign. An example of successful leverage of sponsorship is Vodafone Ireland, which has an integrated internal communications program that informs and engages 1100 employees with the company's external sponsorship activities (Lombardi 2013). The internally-directed program includes sponsorship updates for employees through the firm's intranet, weekly newsletter, and broadcasts to plasma screens located around the office premises. Other methods of increasing employee engagement with the campaign include invitations for employees to 'mini-launches' of sponsored events, internal competitions for event tickets, opportunities for employees to volunteer, and sponsored-artist performances for Vodafone staff.

Campaigns such as Vodafone's, which engage staff with a sponsorship program, have two particular advantages in leveraging the sponsorship internally. Employees are able to get an insight into how the sponsorship investment pays off for the company internally and externally. In addition, employees can be a powerful channel for conveying messages to external stakeholders (Dawkins and Stewart 2003). When employees mention their workplaces positively and with pride, external stakeholders are likely to be influenced to align their perceptions of the organisation with the reported experiences of employees.

Effective leverage of sponsorship can also have the effect of making the sponsor a more attractive employer to both current and potential employees. For example financial firm UBS has sponsored Alinghi, twice winner of the prestigious America's Cup yacht. UBS used sponsorship to highlight values common to both UBS and the Alinghi team—responsibility, informed and rapid decision making, drive to succeed, teamwork and the Swiss identity (Farrelly and Greyser 2007).

When an organisation supports and identifies with a popular sponsored-property such as Alinghi, employees can merge the identity and the success of the property with that of their employer (Hickman et al. 2005). While we did not measure employees' identification with the sponsored property, previous research (Hickman et al. 2005) has shown that employees who have an interest in the company sponsored activity are more likely to have a strong sense of firm identification. Promoting the sponsorship relationship to potential employees can also be beneficial as individuals are more likely to apply for and work for organisations that are likely to possess similar values as them (Maignan et al. 1999).

There has been much debate about adequate measurement of the effects of corporate sponsorship, but with little consensus (e.g. Crompton 2004). Moreover, most of the work on sponsorship measurement has been undertaken with reference to consumer audiences (Cornwell and Maignan 1998). In view of the findings from this research, marketers should ensure that the measurement of sponsorship effectiveness is not limited to consumer audiences. Corporate sponsorship's value to a sponsor can be assessed more broadly—and more accurately—by also taking into account its impact on internal audiences.

This study examined employee attitudes towards corporate sponsorship in general. Future research could investigate the response towards different categories of sponsorship, such as sport, art and social causes. Previous research has shown that different categories of sponsorship carry different levels of goodwill and image with consumer audiences (Meenaghan and Shipley 1999), so it would be useful to see if a similar pattern is seen with employee-audiences. Researchers should also use experiments, as well as pre-sponsorship and post-sponsorship measurements, to explore the different factors influencing the impact of sponsorship.

Conclusion

The growing expenditure on sponsorship, coupled with increasing pressure on marketers to demonstrate the cost-effectiveness of their expenditure, will together increase the pressure on sponsors to demonstrate that any sponsorship programs are cost-effective. These results are a reminder that sponsors should ensure their sponsorship program is able to target multiple audiences, including employees, and that the results of sponsorship should be measured for multiple audience groups. For employers, that may mean that before and after measures of employee attitudes are used to assess the effect of any sponsorship program.

For SMEs, however, the results are encouraging: although this study did not assess the effect of sponsorship on external publics, the results show that SME sponsorships can be evaluated by measuring employees' sponsorship-related attitudes. Findings from this study show that sponsorship-related attitudes for SME employees are equivalent to, or in some cases more positive than those of employees of large organisations.

Appendix

See Tables 3 and 4.

Table 3 Reliability of variables

Variables	Number of items	Cronbach's alpha
Specific attitudes	4	0.95
Sponsorship-linked PEP[a]	4	0.68
Sponsorship-linked OI	6	0.87
General beliefs and attitude	5	0.89

[a]Initially, a 5-item scale. However, two items deleted at EFA and CFA stage

Table 4 Confirmatory factor analysis of variables

Variables	Items	CMIN/df	p	RMSEA	GFI	AGFI	CFI
Specific attitudes	4	1.87	0.15	0.05	0.99	0.99	0.99
Sponsorship-linked PEP[a]	3	0.82	0.44	0.00	0.99	0.99	1.00
Sponsorship-linked OI	6	1.49	0.17	0.03	0.99	0.97	0.99
General beliefs and attitude	5	1.18	0.04	0.02	0.99	0.99	1.00

[a]Initially, a 5-item scale. However, two items deleted at EFA and CFA stage

References

Acito F, Ford JD (1980) How advertising affects employees. Bus Horizons 23(1):53–59

Amis J, Slack T, Berrett T (1999) Sport sponsorship as distinctive competence. Eur J Mark 33 (3/4):250–272

Australian Bureau of Statistics (2001) Small business in Australia. Retrieved http://www.abs.gov.au/ausstats/abs@.nsf/mf/1321.0. Accessed on 24 April 2015

Bank of Melbourne (2015) Corporate sponsorship. Retrieved from https://www.bankofmelbourne.com.au/about/sponsorship. Accessed on June 13, 2015

Bergami M, Bagozzi RP (2000) Self-categorization affective commitment and group self esteem as distinct aspects of social identity in the organization. Br J Soc Psychol 39(4):555–577

Cialdini RB, Borden RJ, Walker MR, Freeman S, Sloan LR (1976) Basking in reflected glory: three football field studies. J Pers Soc Psychol 34(3):366–375

Collett P, Fenton W (2011) The sponsorship handbook: essential tools, tips and techniques for sponsors and sponsorship seekers. Wiley, San Francisco, CA

Cornwell TB, Coote LV (2005) Corporate sponsorship of a cause: the role of identification in purchase intent. J Bus Res 58(3):268–276

Cornwell TB, Maignan I (1998) An international review of sponsorship research. J Advertising 27(1):1–21

Crimmins J, Horn M (1996) Sponsorship: from management ego trip to marketing success. J Advertising Res 36(4):11–21

Crompton JL (2004) Conceptualization and alternate operationalizations of the measurement of sponsorship effectiveness in sport. Leisure Stud 23(3):267–281

Dawkins J, Stewart L (2003) CSR in stakeholder expectations, and their implication for company strategy. J Bus Ethics 44(2/3):185–193

Dees W, Bennett G, Villegas J (2008) Measuring the effectiveness of sponsorship of an elite intercollegiate football program. Sport Mark Q 17:79–89

Dutton JE, Dukerich JM, Harquail CV (1994) Organizational images and member identification. Adm Sci Q 39(2):239–263

Eagly AH, Chaiken S (1993) The psychology of attitudes. Harcourt Brace Jovanovich, Fort Worth, TX

Eisenberger R, Armeli S, Rexwinkel B, Lynch PD, Rhoades L (2001) Reciprocation of perceived organizational support. J Appl Psychol 86(1):42–51

Farrelly FJ, Greyser SA (2007) Sports sponsorship to rally the home team. Harvard Bus Rev 85:22–24

Gardner MP, Shuman P (1988) Sponsorships and small businesses. J Small Bus Manage 26 (4):44–52

Gilly MC, Wolfinbarger M (1998) Advertising's internal audience. J Mark 69–88

GrainCorp (2015) Sponsorship. Retrieved from http://www.graincorp.com.au/about-graincorp/community-and-sponsorship/sponsorship. Accessed on 5 June 2015

Hair JF, Black WC, Babin BJ, Anderson RE (2010) Multivariate data analysis—a global perspective. Pearson, New York

Hickman TM, Lawrence KE, Ward JC (2005) A social identities perspective on the effects of corporate sport sponsorship on employees. Sports Mark Q 14(3):148–157

IEG (2010) Sponsorship spending receded for first time; better days ahead: IEG sponsorship report

IMR Sports Marketing (2013) Australia/New Zealand sponsorship worth $880 million. Retrieved from http://www.imrpublications.com/newsdetails.aspx?nid=44. Accessed on 1 June 2015

Irwin RL, Lachowetz T, Cornwell TB, Clark JS (2003) Cause-related sport sponsorship: an assessment of spectator beliefs, attitudes, and behavioral intentions. Sport Mark Q 12(3): 131–139

Jones DA (2010) Does serving the community also serve the company? Using organizational identification and social exchange theories to understand employee responses to a volunteerism programme. J Occup Organ Psychol 83(4):857–878

Katz D (1994) Just do it: the nike spirit in the corporate world. Random House, New York

Koch, D (2013) Setting up solid communications. Retrieved from http://blog.slicemedia.com/setting-solid-communications-david-koch/. Accessed on 18 Aug 2015

Lacey R, Close AG, Finney ZR (2010) The pivotal roles of product knowledge and corporate social responsibility in event sponsorship effectiveness. J Bus Res 63(11):1222–1228

Lachowetz T, Clark J, Irwin R, Cornwell TB (2002) Cause-related sponsorship: a survey of consumer/spectator beliefs, attitudes, behavioral intentions and corporate image impressions. Paper presented at the American Marketing Association

Lamont MJ (2005) Small and medium business sponsorship of regional sport tourism events (PhD), Southern Cross University, Lismore NSW

Lamont MJ, Dowell R (2008) A process model of small and medium enterprise sponsorship of regional sport tourism events. J Vac Mark 14(3):253–266

Lombardi G (2013) Vodafone Ireland leverages the brand internally. Retrieved from http://www.simply-communicate.com/news/internal-communication/vodafone-ireland-leverages-brand-internally. Accessed on 1 June 2015

Longenecker JG, McKinney JA, Moore CW (1989) Do smaller firms have higher ethics? Bus Soc Rev 71(Fall):19–21

Mack RW (1999) Event sponsorship: an exploratory study of small business objectives, practices and perceptions. J Small Bus Manage 37(3):25–30

Madrigal R (2001) Social identity effects in a belief-attitude-intentions hierarchy: implications for corporate sponsorship. Psychol Mark 18(2):145–165

Mael F, Ashforth BE (1992) Alumni and their alma mater: a partial test of the reformulated model of organizational identification. J Organ Behav 13(2):103–123
Maignan I, Ferrell OC, Hult GTM (1999) Corporate citizenship: cultural antecedents and business benefits. Acad Mark Sci 27(4):455–469
Meenaghan T (2001) Understanding sponsorship effects. Psychol Mark 18(2):95–122
Meenaghan T, Shipley D (1999) Media effect in commercial sponsorship. Eur J Mark 33(3/4): 328–348
O'Reilly N, Horning DL (2013) Leveraging sponsorship: the activation ratio. Sport Manag Rev 16 (4):424–437
Quester P, Thompson B (2001) Advertising and promotion leverage on arts sponsorship effectiveness. J Advertising Res 41(1):33–47
Rifon NJ, Choi SM, Trimble CS, Li H (2004) Congruence effects in sponsorship. J Advertising 33(1):29–42
Russo A, Perrini F (2010) Investigating stakeholder theory and social capital: CSR in large firms and SMEs. J Bus Ethics 91(2):207–221
Smidts A, Pruyn ATH, Riel CBMV (2001) The impact of employee communication and perceived external prestige on organizational identification. Acad Manag J 44(5):1051–1062
Telstra (2015) Community and environment. Retrieved from http://www.telstra.com.au/aboutus/community-environment/awards-grants-sponsorship/. Accessed on 5 June 2015
Wakefield KL, Becker-Olsen K, Cornwell TB (2007) I spy a sponsor: the effects of sponsorship level, prominence, relatedness, and cueing on recall accuracy. J Advertising 36(4):61–74
Webb R (2006) Everyone's a winner here, the Age. Retrieved from http://www.theage.com.au/news/business/everyones-a-winner-here/2006/03/04/1141191884457.html. Accessed on 25 May 2015
Webb J, Carter S (2001) Sponsorship activities and the small firms sector. Managing Leisure 6(3): 168–179
Zielke S, Dobbelstein T (2007) Customers' willingness to purchase new store brands. J Prod Brand Manag 16(2):112–121

Connected Stadium: A Pillar for Football Clubs' Marketing Development?

Charles Bal and Nathalie Fleck

Abstract In this chapter, we explore the notion of *connected stadium* and its affiliate concepts of *stadium 2.0* and *m-stadium*. The connected stadium is indeed a game-changer in the sport industry as it brings within the premises of a stadium a new range of consumption behaviours, based on technology, connectivity and instantaneity. By doing so, the connected stadium comes with new stakes and ambitions for brands, spectators and the clubs operating their stadium. More importantly, the connected stadium stands at the crossroad of two major societal and consumption trends: second screen and the *Internet of Things*. Yet, this major technological shift does not come without deep cultural questioning, especially in France, where stadiums are still seen as a theatre for performances rather than a place to spend time... and and money! Following an introduction into the notion of the connected stadium and its use across multiple stakeholder groups, the chapter concludes with a discussion of what the future holds.

Keywords Connected stadium · Sport consumption · Technology · Football clubs · France

Introduction

With over 300,000 spectators in one single day of Ligue 1—a symbolic record set in October 2014—several stadiums revamped for Euro 2016 and a potential of 100,000 additional seats in the aftermath of the competition, all seemed to be a

C. Bal (✉)
Université Panthéon Sorbonne, Paris, France
e-mail: Bal_charles@yahoo.fr

C. Bal
University of Adelaide, Adelaide, Australia

N. Fleck
University of Maine, Le Mans, France
e-mail: Nathalie.fleck@univ-lemans.fr

© Springer Science+Business Media Singapore 2016

C. Plewa and J. Conduit (eds.), *Making a Difference Through Marketing*,
DOI 10.1007/978-981-10-0464-3_4

green light for French football and its economy. Yet despite this positive momentum, two key data tarnish the most optimistic projections: firstly, the average occupancy rate of Ligue 1 stadiums has been stagnating around 70 % since the 2011–2012 season; and secondly, growing disinterest for stadiums among younger fans, while their interest for sport has not faded (Hammond 2014).

This raises the question of why younger fans tend to abandon football stadiums, while there are still many seats available for them. Why do youngsters prefer the comfort of their couch, or the friendliness of a bar, to the fervour of a stadium? Why do they prefer qualitative TV broadcasts (HD, slow motion, expert analysis, statistics, etc.) to the proximity of a game and emotions that happen a few metres away from them? Why can they no longer stand to be cut off from their online community for 90 min, or prefer a screen over the spectacle of a stadium? In other words, why are younger fans—who are also the most connected—going to the stadium less and less?

Sporting event consumption is a complex phenomenon. All fans are not "ultras"; they do not all see their team as a way to express their own identity, and they do not all remain faithful to one team for a lifetime (Jäger 2013). This results in very diverse sport consumption behaviours, to which recent technological developments (global mobile data traffic increased by 81 % between 2013 and 2014, over 66 % of mobile data will be videos in 2017, 27.7 million mobile users in France and over 50 % of French equipped in smartphone) and new communication habits (7.5 M French access social networks via their mobile) have contributed.

However, instead of bringing the fan to the very source of his emotions—the stadium—his increasing connectivity has brought him closer to his community and the greatest common denominator he shares with it: television. Indeed, television's new digital and social functions promote a collective use of it: richer, more engaging and more participatory; a new function that now positions television as the fiercest competitor of the stadium in France. This evolving competitive landscape pushed Samuel Guillardeau, Stadium Manager of Nice's Allianz Riviera stadium, to affirm that "*before competing against other stadiums, a stadium is competing against television*". Therefore, it is no more surprising to find among sporting event spectators similar expectations to those of TV viewers: access to more content (replays, analysis, slides, etc.), immediate consumption (no queue, no order deadlines, etc.) and continuous connection with their communities (Jäger 2013).

Hence, there is a struggle against lowering occupancy rates and falling ticketing revenues, in which both professional clubs and stadium operators have sought answers to their audiences' new expectations, and to provide them with a real consumer experience on top of the sporting spectacle. This has led to sporting events being enriched with new offers going beyond sports performance, to venture into stands, control rooms and the never-ending relationship that the fans maintain with their communities. This evolution has literally transformed the physical and symbolic boundaries of the stadium, and thus its role among the various stakeholders of a sporting event: teams, fans, sponsors and media. From an isolated place, cut off from the rest of the world and centred on the sport spectacle, the stadium has become open, turned towards the spectators and, through them, to countless (social) communities outside the stadium. And the stadium has become *connected*.

The connected stadium is revolutionising economic and marketing development models of many clubs, challenges fans' consumption habits—especially in France, where stadiums are more readily considered spectacle venues than social and collective life venues (Söderman and Dolles 2013)—and contests the existing power balance between stadium and television when it comes to sport consumption. For all these reasons, the connected stadium is a major paradigm shift in sports marketing.

The purpose of this chapter, dedicated to the connected stadium and its influence in football economy, is to understand its scope, issues and usages, and to question further the upcoming evolutions.

Definition, Challenges and Technological Developments of the Connected Stadium

In 2012, Facebook revealed the 25 biggest social landmarks in the world, that is to say the 25 most privileged places for fans to geo-locate themselves on the social network. Among them, eight sports stadiums and arenas, including the famous Staples Center of Los Angeles, San Francisco's Wrigley Fields, Barcelona's Nou Camp or Auckland's Eden Park. And when it comes to focusing on the 8 most active cities on Facebook (New York, London, Paris, Berlin, Melbourne, Seoul, Tokyo and Sao Paulo), one to two sports venues are consistently found among the top 5 social landmarks. Two years later, chances are great that the combination of a galloping mobile consumption and the Brazilian World Cup had propelled the mythical Maracana and Arena Corinthians stadiums to being among the most popular venues on Facebook, in 2014!

What should we think about geo-location, as an example of digital interaction happening in a stadium? Is it more related to the concept of connected stadium, stadium 2.0 or m-stadium? What differences should we make among these three stadiums? How do we articulate them? At this stadium, a semantic clarification is important to distinguish these three concepts, and lay the basis for a reflection about the stakes of the connected stadium as we understand it today.

Connected Stadium, Stadium 2.0, M-Stadium: Definition

In its most common usage, the connected stadium is a generic concept denoting a sporting venue which provides its users—clubs, media, brands, spectators—with a number of technologies facilitating the flow of information during an event.

The massive concentration of simultaneous mobile connections resulting in the saturation of 3G and 4G networks, the connected stadium defines by extension a stadium that offers alternative modes of connection for the thousands of people gathered at that time.

However, one may substitute this rather generic definition with the following hierarchy of definitions:

- The **connected stadium** consists of facilitating the operation of a stadium by means of computer and network assistance before, during and after a sporting event. A connected stadium will utilise any technologies enabling the arena to optimise its filling rate, to maximise it match-day revenue (dynamic management of access points, automated restocking of outlets, targeted promotions on the different LCD screens of the arena) and to interact with its environment in order to facilitate the organisation of the event (such as the Amsterdam Arena which automatically sends an SMS to fans advising them about the different commuting options and informing them about the weather forecast for the event).
- **Stadium 2.0** consists of the implementation of technologies that promote the digitalisation of the viewer's experience. This is about enriching the fan's match-day experience by allowing him to operate the lever of the statutory geo-location ("*I was there!*"), to realise his need for tribal experiences (uninterrupted discussion with his community) and to satisfy his expectations for qualitative content (videos, etc.). According to Helleu, the stadium 2.0 refers to "*the idea of a stadium that exists outside of the event, which speaks on social networks and interacts with fans*"; in other words, a stadium meeting spectators' needs for interactivity, before, during and after the sporting event (Chanavat et al. 2014).
- In turn, the **m-stadium** suggests the use of contactless, seamless mobile technology throughout the audience journey in the stadium. The smartphone has thus become a preferred interface, allowing the user to interact with the stadium: to get there, to enter the premises, to find his seat, etc.

As shown by the three definitions above, the connected stadium is a broader and more complex concept than it seems. Indeed, in its broadest approach, the connected stadium encompasses both stadium 2.0 and the m-stadium, in a set of measures that ultimately enrich the spectator experience: easing the access to the stadium, enriching the content offered, encouraging sharing behaviours with the out-stadia and multiplying consumption opportunities.

This "augmented" stadium experience answers several marketing issues, that we propose to detail in the following section.

The Marketing Stakes of the Connected Stadium

To question the marketing challenges of the connected stadium is to put into perspective the interests of the various stakeholders of a stadium—brands, media, supporters and clubs—in enriching match-day experience.

For **brands**, the connected stadium is the opportunity to evolve from a branding logic to a brand experience logic. Thanks to a boosted connectivity and an improved network of screens, the connected stadium makes it possible to enrich brand visibility, to multiply interaction touch points—hence data collection—with the viewer, and immerse him in an "augmented" consumption experience. By engaging the fan in the context of a shared commitment to a team or an event, brands lay the basis for a favourable persuasion context (Crimmins and Horn 1996; Bal et al. 2009) and may identify and characterise more finely their communications to spectators.

For **spectators**, the challenge of the connected stadium is to satisfy their growing needs for enhanced consumer experiences. In 2015, a stadium can no longer be a disconnected enclave! For the modern fan, living the live experience "for real" must no longer mean agreeing to disconnect from his community. Now, the modern supporter requires more than the sporting event that takes place on the field. He wants to access the event without wasting his time on commuting, he wants to comment live on the game with his community, access exclusive content, play games to win tickets or jerseys, benefit from targeted promotions from the official store or bar, and order items without even moving from his seat. Therefore, the connected stadium appears to be a logical evolution of sports marketing, towards more experience, more interactivity and more exclusivity.

For **clubs**, the connected stadium is an ideal tool to bring the fans back in the stands and to generate additional revenue. Indeed, given the economic constraints imposed by the financial fair play, the connected stadium is a way for many clubs to monetise their audience and thus achieve the necessary economic equilibrium. The stakes are high since an attractive stadium—like the new Juventus stadium, 18,000 places smaller than the aging Stadio Delle Alpi, but more comfortable and better equipped, principally in terms of commercial offerings (Palvarini and Tosi 2013)—is a lever to grow customer loyalty by means of match day experience (Shilbury et al. 2009) and to develop new revenue: dematerialised ticketing, in-stadia consumption, access to premium content, etc. For professional football clubs such as PSV Eindhoven or Olympique Lyonnais, for example, the ambition is to generate 30 and 70 M€ respectively of yearly additional revenue through the equipment of their stadiums with connected technologies. These additional revenues will help to reinforce their squad in order to have a chance to take part to the Champions League and its lucrative TV rights.

However, the economic and organisational model of most major stadiums in France (owned by local authorities, built and operated by large private companies and rented by professional clubs) greatly complicates the funding—often considerable—of a connected stadium. Investments that rise to tens of millions of euros, and sometimes to more than a hundred million euros, as was the case in San Francisco, to equip the Levi's 49ers Stadium with 680 hotspots, 12,000 Ethernet ports and 1700 beacons. Then, who must bear the burden of transforming the stadium into a profit centre? And most importantly, who can benefit from it?

Because in terms of profits, the outlook is booming. Indeed, only 13 % of the French Ligue 1 clubs' annual revenues come from match day profits (essentially, ticketing and in-stadia consumption), while the figure has risen to 25 and 44 % for the British and German counterparts respectively (LFP Report/DNCG 2013)!

For all these reasons, it is now clear that the economic success of French professional football clubs is now closely linked to the place occupied by their stadium in their business model, and to the efforts they will make in order to develop stadium-related income sources (Monna 2013). Indeed, a connected stadium promotes the diversification of match day incomes, maintains these revenue opportunities when the stadium is occupied by another event, and helps control—at least commercially—sports hazards (Chanavat et al. 2014).

However, none of the above-mentioned marketing challenges would be possible without the application of some recent, major technological developments to the sports marketing world in general, and to stadiums and arenas in particular. We intend to present these technological evolutions in the next paragraph.

Overview of the Technologies Implemented in Connected Stadiums

Wi-Fi, RFID, NFC… The technologies employed in connected stadiums are of course many and varied, as shown in Tables 1 and 2, but they all have in common a series of communication goals: they allow us to access information, to store it, analyse it and broadcast it. Among the technologies present in the stadiums, we distinguish *identification* technologies, *capture* technologies, *connectivity* technologies and *analysis* technologies.

Identification technologies are designed to recognise objects and download their data; they usually take the form of bar codes, RFID (Radio Frequency Identification) or NFC (Near Field Communication). Appearing more recently, RFID solutions have gradually replaced barcodes, which are considered too limited in the information and interaction opportunities they offer. RFID chips indeed have the advantage to be read remotely (up to one metre) by the simple means of a radio wave, where bar codes require an optical laser and therefore the installation of

Table 1 Application examples

• The 680 hotspots of San Francisco 49ers Levi's Stadium allow 25,000 spectators to watch—simultaneously—slow motion sequences on their smartphone
• The Tampa Bay Lightning season-ticket holders receive during the pre-season a team jersey equipped with a RFID chip that allows them to enter the stadium without tickets, to receive special offers and to make all their purchases seamlessly in the arena
• In Pretoria's Loftus Versveld Stadium, fans can download their tickets directly into their smartphones and flash their devices before the NFC entrance portals to access the stadium

Table 2 Comparing 32 NFL stadiums connectivity in 2014

NFL teams	Stadium	Capacity	Wi-Fi	DAS	Beacon
Baltimore Ravens	M&T Bank Stadium	71,008	No	856 antennas	No
Cincinnati Bengals	Paul Brown Stadium	65,515	Yes	Yes	No
Cleveland Browns	FirstEnergy Stadium	73,200	In 2015	Yes	No
Pittsburgh Steelers	Heinz Field	65,500	193 terminals	339 antennas	No
Buffalo Bills	Ralph Wilson Stadium	71,757	No	200 antennas	No
New England Patriots	Gillette Stadium	68,756	Yes	Yes	No
Miami Dolphins	Sun Life Stadium	75,540	1100 terminals	Yes	Yes
New York Jets	MetLife Stadium	82,500	850 terminals	600 antennas	No
Houston Texans	NRG Stadium	71,054	No	No	No
Indianapolis Colts	Lucas Oil Stadium	63,000	Yes	Yes	No
Jacksonville Jaguars	EverBank Field	67,297	Yes	No	No
Tennessee Titans	LP Field	69,149	Yes	Yes	No
Denver Broncos	Sports Authority Field	76,125	Yes	Yes	No
Kansas City Chiefs	Arrowhead Stadium	76,416	600 terminals	Yes	No
Oakland Raiders	O.Co Coliseum	56,057	No	Yes	No
San Diego Charger	Qualcomm Stadium	70,561	No	Yes	No
Detroit Lions	Ford Field	65,000	Yes	Yes	No
Green Bay Packers	Lambeau Field	80,735	No	Yes	No
Minnesota Vikings	TCF Bank Stadium	52,000	Limited	Yes	No
Atlanta Falcons	Georgia Dome	71,280	500 terminals	Yes	No
Carolina Panthers	Bank of America Stadium	74,455	645 terminals	Yes	No
New Orleans Saints	Mercedes-Benz Superdome	76,468	600 terminals	Yes	No
Tampa Bay Buccaneers	Raymond James Stadium	65,890	Yes	Yes	No

(continued)

Table 2 (continued)

NFL teams	Stadium	Capacity	Wi-Fi	DAS	Beacon
Dallas Cowboys	AT&T Stadium	105,121	1525 terminals	1374 antennas	No
New York Giants	MetLife Stadium	82,500	850 terminals	600 antennas	No
Philadelphia Eagles	Lincoln Financial Field	69,176	600 terminals	Yes	No
Washington Redskins	FedExField	85,000	Limited	Yes	No
Arizona Cardinals	Univ. of Phoenix Stadium	65,000	100 terminals	Yes	No
San Francisco 49ers	Levi's Stadium	68,500	1200 terminals	700 antennas	1700 terminals
Seattle Seahawks	CenturyLink Field	72,000	Yes	Yes	No
St. Louis Rams	Edward Jones Dome	66,000	No	Yes	No

Mobile Sports Report (2014)

specific applications on mobile receivers (such as smartphones). NFC solutions, for their part, are not limited to only reading information. They allow the exchange of encrypted data between two devices over a short distance (about 10 cm), thus emulating complex objects such as payment cards.

Capture technologies allow gathering of information related to events happening on the pitch or in the stadium. Miniaturised sensors enrich the sporting spectacle by adding a new set of data to existing data, aiming at capturing and analysing players' movements, physical parameters and environmental factors. For example, this takes the form of the Goal Line technology adopted during the 2014 FIFA World Cup or the Hawk Eye technology which is now in use in most major professional tennis tournaments, whose use largely feeds the event's broadcast.

Connectivity technologies are related to the synchronisation of different systems. From EDGE to Wi-Fi to 4G, it is all about connecting smartphones or tablets to the Internet or a local network. EDGE, 3G+ or 4G are technologies that provide access to wireless internet within almost all of the territory. While the download capacity offered by mobile operators is increasingly high, sometimes the system cannot bear the burden of a stadium's thousands of simultaneous connections. Local connection technologies, such as Wi-Fi, are then used to decongest the network by offering a multicast content distribution. In other words, the information is not broadcast as many times as there are receivers, but only once to a group of receivers, allowing a substantial saving of bandwidth.

Lastly, **analytical technologies** analyse and transfer data to physically and virtually optimise the stadium life. This is the case for example of the Command Center software developed by American company Roundarch, allowing the MetLife Stadium in New York to monitor, analyse and manage in real time the fans' behaviour in the stadium and to find and implement the appropriate answers:

management of the stadium entry and exit streams, real-time replenishment of stadium outlets, personalisation of the promotions run on the hundreds of screens installed throughout the arena based on the consumer profiles located in each stand, deployment of a "flying" sales force to take in-advance orders when the queues exceed a certain size, etc.

Alex LOTH, *Director of Information Systems*
French Tennis Federation

What is the current position in France, when it comes to Connected Stadium?

The question of the adoption of connected stadiums in France is subject to strong disagreements. Two different schools are arguing: on one hand, those who see in new technologies a way to adapt themselves to new consumption patterns; and, in the other hand, those who reject this idea advocating the very essence of the sport spectacle and the necessary proximity between the fans and the players. Personally, I am a strong supporter of the connected stadium and I believe new technologies really help to enrich the viewer's experience.

What is the "most connected" stadium you went to?

In my opinion, the Kansas City stadium offers, since 2011, the models the more in line with current practices. The audience takes part to the show, from the moment they enter the stadium to the moment they leave it. For example, when the fans flash their ticket at the entry gates, they automatically download on their smartphone a video customized depending on the location of their seat. And few minutes before the game, the fans are invited to turn their phone toward the pitch to take part a giant video tiffo! Fans can also access the coach's explanations about different game strategies, via a dedicated mobile application and a micropayment.

These are all experiences that have helped multiply by 5 in-stadia sales in only few years and raise the average spectators' basket to US$112.

How can a connected stadium contribute to the economic development of a federation?

The multiplication of connected objects and the diversification of mobile device uses make of everyone an actor of the connectivity. But before addressing the ROI question, we must adapt our offers to these evolutions while preserving the sporting spectacle. By allowing the spectator to become a "spect'actor" and accepting his new interaction needs, new business opportunities will logically appear for stadiums operators and advertisers.

For an event like Roland Garros, which lasts three weeks and has no existence the rest of the year, the objectives are primarily to enrich the fans experience at the event and to improve our understanding of our clients in order to provide them with a personalized experience. In this logic, Roland Garros connectivity aims at offering a qualitative services and differentiating experiences, in order to be, in a near future, eligible for an increase in internal and external revenues.

What are the basics of a connected stadium?

Before even thinking about networks and connection technologies, one must wonder about the nature of the services to offer: What do we want to offer to our customers? Then you must think about how to integrate the necessary technologies in the stadium: these are mainly reflections and thoughts of an architectural order. Indeed, it is essential to integrate the objective of connectivity from the earliest stages of the design of the stadium, since it will influence the choice of the construction materials, the architectural principles underpinning the project and the programming of the building.

What do you think will be tomorrow's technology in connected stadiums?

Today, 4G—and the upcoming 5G—carries a lot of rich experiences, especially around video content. In this context, we must expect a transformation of carriers' networks and the emergence of connected services that enhance the multicast consumption of videos. The Internet of Things will also drastically increase the number of interactions stadium networks will have to be able to absorb, and generate new data that will need to be capture, sorted, analyse and actioned. This obviously appeals to the concept of "predictive technologies" which are utterly important to any marketer.

When it comes to information diffusion and relationships with our customers, the Beacon is a technology that we want to experience. Without necessarily being intrusive, the Beacon provides a push of practical information related to transportation, signage, catering or even ticketing that we would like to offer to Roland Garros visitors.

The "MASS Wi-Fi" is also an evolving technology allowing to create a dense and "private" communications belt, permitting the implementation of new service lines able to maintain the best in-stadia relations with our customers…

Finally, in front of regulatory constraints and the necessary debate about Wi-Fi and mobile waves emission fields power, the Li-Fi (i.e. LIght-FIdelity), a wireless communication technology based on the use of visible light, could offer an alternative to existing technologies without generating electromagnetic "pollution"…!

On the Uses of the Connected Stadium

Technologies with previous exposure allow stadium operators and brands to innovate in order to meet consumers' expectations. But of course, implementing these innovations is not an end in itself. To be able to bear fruit, this approach has to satisfy expectations or enable further development of uses meant for enriching the experience in the stadium.

Between sporting and marketing problematics, the uses of the newly connected stadiums have multiplied though this process.

For Spectators and TV-Viewers

The combination of a place (the stadium), a moment (the match) and means (new technologies) has moved some sporting events into a real crowd-centric communication platform, oriented towards fans. To meet the expectations of a hyper-connected generation, willing to consume more information and to share it, innovations have been implemented to enrich spectators' experiences in the stadium, but also outside the stadium. Three main trends have then emerged: in-stadia interactions, interactions towards the outside and the second screen applied to the stadium.

In-stadia interactions enable spectators to interact more easily with the stadium, teams or athletes, and other spectators. They are supported by innovations, ranging from the dematerialisation of the ticket to applications developed by the stadium itself (e.g. at the Amsterdam Arena or at the Barclays Center of New York), which give information to spectators in real time about the ease of access to the facilities, help them to find their way around the stadium thanks to an interactive map, to participate in promotional games and competitions, to reach exclusive content (composition of the teams in preview, live in the changing-room, access to the microphones of the referees and coaches, etc.) or enable them to order food or other products from their seats.

Interactions towards the outside are based on at least three levers identified by academic research: the need for emotions (Raman and Chattopadhyay 1995), the need to share them (Rimé 2009) and the need for statutory self-assertion, close to the need for belonging by Maslow (1943). Satisfying this latest need requires sharing the event with one's community. In this regard, social networks such as Twitter, Facebook, Foursquare or Instagram are all tools that enable spectators to declare the now 'sacrosanct' "I was here!"

Finally, regarding the practice of supplementing a first source of content, **the second screen** is also a tool in the connected stadium arsenal of services. As the stadiums consider television as their main competitor, they have to propose at least the same services to compete (statistics, solutions of live broadcast, replay, etc.). Thus the second screen enables the spectator to reach, in real time, enriched content linked to the match. To this end, more and more stadiums create their own applications and make use of specialised technological solutions, such as the StadiumVision Mobile solution created by the American giant Cisco. For example, this is the case for the Barclays Center of New York or for the stadium Santiago Bernabéu of Real Madrid. This technology makes it possible, amongst other things, to broadcast information in multicast via Wi-Fi, thus allowing live-watching of a video stream without any saturation of the network. Integrated with proprietary applications, this solution enables people to re-examine all the actions of the match from the different viewing angles of the video production, and to access, in real time, the diverse statistics of the match. In France, the Olympique Lyonnais's Grand Stade will use this solution to be able to give content simultaneously to 25,000 mobiles.[1]

For Brands and Organisers

The emergence of the second screen and the *Internet of Things* establishes new stakes concerning logistics and business for all the stakeholders: organisation, sponsors and sport teams.

In terms of logistics, connected stadiums provide numerous opportunities to optimise the footsteps of spectators and facilitate the success of events. Two hours before each match, Bayern Munich's Allianz Arena takes control of the traffic lights surrounding the stadium within a radius of 20 km to ensure vehicle flow and fluidity of the access to the stadium!

For organisers, these services represent a boon to optimising the arrival of spectators and the time they spend in the premises. Controls at entry and analysis of spectators' flows enable them to efficiently manage the stock replenishment of stadium outlets.

Regarding business, the stakes of the connected stadium are colossal! For organisers, these services are interesting in that they are extending the time spent by spectators in the stadium. The better the event is organised, the earlier spectators will arrive and/or the later they will leave, thus spending more time… to consume.

Multiplying contact points with people then becomes an essential stake for organisers. First to increase buying opportunities, but also to optimise the visibility of the different partners of the event. For example, the AT&T Stadium, residency of the Dallas Cowboys, organises, with its partners, prediction contests on Twitter, inviting internet users to guess who will score the next goal. Winners are then showcased on the giant screens, offering in the process a little bit more qualified visibility to the partners of the stadium.

For the Sport

Summing up the connected stadium as an enriched offer addressed to spectators would mean forgetting the reason why they are going to the stadium: to enjoy a

[1]Source: http://www.lesechos.fr/thema/entreprise-digitale-2/0203545110326-un-stade-connecte-pour-vivre-autrement-les-matchs-de-lolympique-lyonnais-1011044.php?qMv5Jp6CpIicUP32.99.

sporting spectacle. Some technologies implemented in the stadium also serve the interests of the sport and its athletes, before those of the media and spectators.

Since sport has become professional, the perpetual quest for performance helped push ever further the limits of effort. The continuous improvement of equipment, training methods or nutritional plans is part of a desire to advance the human body ever further. In this context, trajectories, heart rates, respiratory rates, acceleration rates, body temperatures, etc. have become data to measure, analyse and (potentially) communicate in a stadium.

Many tools now enable the measurement of these parameters and some are able to emerge. In 2011, American sporting goods provider Under Armour announced the creation of a smart jersey—called "E39"—making it possible to know these physical indicators in real-time. If the tool is only used for training by the Tottenham Football Club for the moment, for the purposes of the medical staff particularly, it would not be surprising that it is used one day during a match to enrich with data a communication addressed to fans.

Sports accessories are also subject to many connected changes. In tennis, the Babolat rackets launched a "Play and Connect" model that enables us to monitor real-time data such as the speed of the ball or the effect upon it by the player, so that it could significantly enrich the viewing of the match for spectators. In football, Adidas also embraced the topic in 2014 by unveiling its connected ball, the "mi-Coach Smart Ball", which can instantly measure information on the shooting power, trajectory, spin and accuracy. All these objects are used to further push the science of sport and to give more entertainment to fans.

What Is the Future for the Connected Stadium?

With ten stadiums built or upgraded for the purpose of hosting EURO 2016 matches, French Ligue 1 clubs will benefit from 100,000 new seats for the 2016–2017 season and onwards.[2] To make this heritage a blessing rather than a problem, leaders of French football have no other choice but to start to learn *stadium seat marketing*. Indeed, in a championship where the stadiums' occupancy rates hardly exceed 70 %—when the occupancy rates are above 90 % every weekend in English and German stadiums[3]—there is no certainty that these 100,000 new seats will be occupied if nothing is done to attract populations to stadiums that do not usually go there or have given up going.

But is making connected stadiums enough to fill them? Obviously not, because the connected stadium is not only a technological evolution, it is an evolution of clubs' economic and marketing models, which deeply affect the role and place of

[2]Source: http://www.lepoint.fr/sport/euro-2016-un-heritage-de-100-000-places-qui-pose-probleme-17-10-2014-1873449_26.php.

[3]Same source.

the stadium in the lives of clubs and spectators. When connected, a stadium fosters the implementation of effective loyalty programs, personalised CRM programs according to the stand and the type of ticket of the spectator, algorithms in order to track and optimise the waiting time at the stadium's outlets (snack bars, shops) and real-time restocking. All these services will allow France to catch up a huge lag in terms of filling a stadium and generating match day revenues.

From a sporting theatre, the connected stadium has evolved into an immersive experience; from an entertainment venue, it has become a consumption and communication platform connected with the world. In terms of user experience, the key words become convenience, real time, (enriched) content, interactivity, and of course, monetisation.

As such, and the ambition of Olympique Lyonnais or OGC Nice demonstrates it well, the connected stadium is expected to play a central role in the economic and marketing development of clubs that will invest in it. By concentrating all attention and focusing on fans, and by multiplying opportunities and reasons to consume, football clubs can expect to attract and retain customers, develop new uses and especially attract new revenue.

But to achieve this, the actors of French football will have to align the quality and connectivity of their stadiums with these new ambitions. In effect, the many debates that surround the uses and challenges of connected stadiums—as rich and passionate as they are—will be in vain until the issue of the connections are solved, or at least considered. It is instructive to note that the specifications to be met by stadiums designated to host EURO 2016 matches do not contain a single word about connectivity. Apart from the new stadiums of Lyon or Nice, nothing today indicates that the work conducted in all other French stadiums will actually lead to better connected places.

However, a note of optimism remains in the landscape of French stadiums, considering that the development of clubs' incomes, made possible by connected stadiums, could ultimately partly benefit local authorities. Indeed, some of them—particularly Marseille (with Olympique de Marseille) and Saint-Etienne (with AS Saint-Etienne)—have succeeded in indexing club revenue as a part of the rent these clubs have to pay to use their stadium[4]!

Technologically, the solution to the problem of networks in stadiums could come from the works of the Internet Engineering Task Force on mobile ad hoc networks (MANET for Mobile ad hoc networks), through which devices connect to each other, becoming in turn receiver and router, to form a larger network without requiring a central infrastructure.

But even if the question of technology could be resolved one day, the cultural question will, however, remain. If the connected stadiums have great successes in the United States, in England or in Germany, can we expect a similar success in France, where fans still see the stadium as a theatre for performances rather than a

[4]Source: http://sport24.lefigaro.fr/football/euro-2016/actualites/euro-2016-ou-en-est-le-chantier-des-stades-718234.

place to spend time… and money? Could there be, in the French stands, protest movements similar to those of PSV Eindhoven[5] fans who accused the club management—who decided to equip the stadium with Wi-Fi—of diverting them from their primary function: singing and cheering for a team? Or will we see new examples of schizophrenic clubs like Manchester United who, after having decided to offer a Wi-Fi connection to fans, seeks to prohibit them to share pictures and videos on social networks, in order to protect their broadcasters' exclusive rights?

As the top-level sport, the future of the connected stadium is full of uncertainties. This is probably why studying it still fascinates us so much!

Samuel GUILLARDEAU, *Stadium Manager*
OGC Nice

How could a connected stadium contribute to the economic development of a club?

Simply because it enables a club to generate additional revenue through new offerings and new partners. Today, our partners are no longer looking for only panel advertising or VIP seats; they have to tell a story and express their proximity to the club and to the fans. And this is precisely what the connected stadium makes possible. This will be done through connected applications and video content that will be accessible only in the stadium.

Today, the biggest competitors of a club and its stadium are mainly TV broadcasters. We must find and propose in the stadium additional and exclusive contents that are able to counter the contents now surrounding the TV broadcasts of the matches. And we have imperatively to manage to offer that directly in the sport places.

Today, we are no longer mere ticket sellers for football games. We design and sell genuine experiences to increasingly demanding customers.

Who has the responsibility for these connected projects in a stadium like the Allianz Riviera?

The various stakeholders of a stadium do not always have the same interests, except perhaps on the question of the connected stadium. The connected stadium is indeed an added value for the operator of the stadium in its desire to develop a multifunctional use, and for a club like OGC Nice which will use it to attract new fans, develop new revenue, etc.

In Nice, we share a lot about this topic to find solutions, organize investments and the sharing of revenues they generate.

How did it materialize at the Allianz Arena?

We have launched with the stadium operator and the naming partner Allianz many experiments involving Google Glasses, *social walls* for fans, *social rooms* for bloggers and influencers, etc.

[5]Source: http://rue89.nouvelobs.com/rue89-sport/2014/08/19/pourquoi-supporters-foot-plaignent-wifi-gratuit-254272.

Today, if we found ways to make those who did not go to the stadium want to come here, we still have to make progress on the activities offered to the spectators in the stadium. This will require equipment and a still more efficient network, contents to offer and share between fans, etc.

References

Bal C, Quester P, Plewa C (2009) Event-related emotions: a key metric to assess sponsorship effectiveness. J Sponsorship 2(4):367–378

Chanavat N, Renaud M, Desbordes M (2014) Naming et modularité: les clés de la réussite? Jurisport 142:41–45

CISCO (2014) Cisco visual networking index: global mobile data traffic forecast update, 2013–2018. Retrieved from: http://www.cisco.com/c/en/us/solutions/collateral/service-provider/visual-networking-index-vni/white_paper_c11-520862.pdf

Crimmins J, Horn M (1996) Sponsorship: from management ego trip to marketing success. J Advertising Res 36(4):11–21

Hammond T (2014) Stadiums race to digitize: how sports teams are scrambling to keep Millennials coming to games. Retrieved from http://www.techrepublic.com/article/how-sports-teams-are-scrambling-to-keep-millennials-coming-to-games

Havas Sports and Entertainment (2014) FANS.PASSIONS.BRAND. The eight logics of engagement, étude réalisée en partenariat avec le University of Southern California's Annenberg Innovation Lab. Retrieved from: http://www.havas-se.com/news/global-fans-decoded-through-the-logics-of-engagement-in-fans-passions-brands-study

Jäger M (2013) The connected stadium—the advent of the fan experience 2.0 through Wi-Fi? Research report, Institute for Sport Economics and Sport Management, German Sport University Cologne

Maslow AH (1943) A theory of human motivation. Psychol Rev 50:370–396

Mobile Sports Report (2014) Stadium tech report. The football issue: Levi's stadium leads the way for NFL technology deployments. Retrieved from http://stadiumtechreport.com/documents;id=DOC04/

Monna O (2013) Club, collectivité, investisseur privé: organiser au mieux le ménage à trois. Jurisport 128:15–19

Palvarini P, Tosi S (2013) Globalisation, stadiums and the consumerist city: the case of the new Juventus stadium in Turin. Eur J Sport Soc 10(2):161–180

Raman NV, Chattopadhyay P (1995) Do consumers seek emotional situations: the need for emotion scale. Adv Consum Res 22(1):537–542

Rapport LPF/DCNG (2013) Situation du football Professionnel – Saison 2013–2013, Ligue de Football Professionnel – Direction Nationale du Contrôle de Gestion. Retrieved from: http://www.lfp.fr/corporate/dncg

Rimé B (2009) Emotion elicits the social sharing of emotion: theory and empirical review. Emot Rev 1(1):60–85

Shilbury D, Westerbeek H, Quick S, Funk DC (2009) Strategic sport marketing, 3rd edn. Allen & Unwin, Crows Nest, NSW

Söderman S, Dolles H (2013) Handbook of research on sport and business. Edward Elgar Publishing, Cheltenham, UK

Part II
Making a Difference—Social Marketing and Ethics

Promoting Public Health: Understanding the Limitations of Marketing Principles and the Need for Alternative Approaches

Simone Pettigrew and Michelle I. Jongenelis

Abstract This chapter comments on marketing and social marketing principles and how they may or may not apply to major public health challenges. Marketing insights make it clear that the primary focus of public health efforts needs to be on upstream rather than downstream approaches. In the typical absence of adequate funding to undertake the basic principles of marketing at the downstream level (e.g. segmentation and competitor analysis) and the inappropriateness of delivering to consumers what they say they want (a fundamental assumption of the marketing concept that doesn't usually work in public health), marketing knowledge needs to be applied in different ways to improve well-being at the population level. The two health issues of ageing and obesity are presented as examples of cases in which (social) marketing strategies will not be effective unless implemented as recommended in the literature—they need to be thoroughly researched, strategically implemented, well-resourced, and persistent in nature.

Keywords Public health · Marketing · Social marketing · Ageing · Obesity

Introduction

Numerous factors are coinciding to focus governments' attention on stemming the tide of rapidly escalating health costs in both developed and developing nations. Despite impressive advances in immunisation and treatment, infectious diseases remain a constant threat (WHO 2015). However, the focus of this chapter is on non-communicable diseases, which are consuming a large and growing proportion of public health budgets worldwide (WHO 2013). In particular, the two trends of population ageing and obesity pose enormous challenges in terms of health

S. Pettigrew (✉) · M.I. Jongenelis
School of Psychology and Speech Pathology, Curtin University, Perth, Australia
e-mail: Simone.pettigrew@curtin.edu.au

M.I. Jongenelis
e-mail: Michelle.jongenelis@curtin.edu.au

© Springer Science+Business Media Singapore 2016

C. Plewa and J. Conduit (eds.), *Making a Difference Through Marketing*,
DOI 10.1007/978-981-10-0464-3_5

promotion, along with associated effects on national productivity levels and the costs of delivering a wide range of related community services (Productivity Commission 2013).

Ageing and obesity are conditions that are greatly affected by both the actions of individuals and the environments in which they live. Worldwide there has been a trend to consider the actions of individuals to be the most important focus for public health interventions (Hastings 2015; Pykett et al. 2014; Roberto et al. 2015). This is likely to be due to a reluctance or inability to make the huge infrastructure investments necessary to fundamentally alter physical and social environments to make them more conducive to good health, along with the 'nanny state' rhetoric that is encouraged by certain industries that profit from the current state of affairs (Moodie et al. 2013; Moore et al. 2015). The resulting focus on the responsibilities of individuals to look after their own health has led to a reliance on the market to present solutions (e.g. weight loss products, fitness centres, retirement housing, and hearing devices). To a lesser extent, governments have also selectively embraced the principles of social marketing in their attempts to encourage individuals to act in their own best interests (Pykett et al. 2014). In these two ways, marketing has permeated the health sector by constituting an apparent solution to the perceived need for individuals to make appropriate health-related decisions. This situation calls for a close examination of the nature of marketing and whether (in either its commercial or social forms) it represents an adequate solution to current major public health problems.

This chapter provides descriptions of marketing and social marketing with a view to assessing the efficacy of these approaches in addressing major public health objectives. The specific health problems of ageing and obesity are presented as mini case studies to demonstrate that the application of social marketing approaches to date has been inadequate to achieve public health goals, and in fact has been detrimental in terms of the opportunity costs associated with selecting these approaches over other potentially more effective alternatives. Suggestions are made for ways in which these approaches could and should be combined with other strategies to more comprehensively address the antecedents of unhealthy ageing and obesity. The analysis has implications for other health problems that are also proving resistant to improvement through current approaches (e.g. alcohol consumption, mental health, oral health, and injury prevention).

Marketing Principles

The discipline of marketing is based on the fundamental principle of 'the marketing concept'. This concept relates to the adoption of a customer focus that involves designing organisations' operations around the profitable satisfaction of consumers' needs (Quester et al. 2001). An underlying assumption is that consumers' choices are malleable, and will change in favour of marketers who can provide the most attractive goods and services at affordable prices. Directly applying this notion to the public health sphere is clearly problematic because of the tendency for people's stated preferences (e.g. for energy-dense foods, alcohol and tobacco products, and a sedentary lifestyle) to be in fundamental conflict with health optimisation.

As an example of this lack of translation, market segmentation suggests that since different consumers have different needs, it is usually necessary to focus on a particular segment of consumers to effectively satisfy these needs. This ensures that the marketed good or service comes as close as possible to meeting the specific needs of the selected market segment. A related concept is that of competition. The assumption is that competitors will enter profitable markets, resulting in the need to address the preferences and requirements of specific segments to enhance competitiveness. The idea of exchange is also relevant due to the recognition that (i) the choice of one product represents an opportunity cost in terms of a competitor's product and (ii) the customer must 'give' something (usually money, but also time and effort) to 'get' the product. These notions are again problematic in the health domain because of the need to provide health-related goods and services to broad sections of the population rather than specific market segments. The provision of these goods and services is often a loss-making situation rather than a profit-generating opportunity, with demand often exceeding supply. Further confounding the problem is competition in the form of industries that heavily promote goods and services that create the problems in the first place (Hastings 2015; Moodie et al. 2013; Moore et al. 2015). The public health sector cannot compete for the 'share of mind' obtained by these industries through their intensive use of promotion and distribution strategies to ensure that their products are well known and widely available.

Marketing theory and practice are heavily oriented around what are known as the '4 Ps'—product, price, promotion, and place. Once specific consumer needs have been identified, the market segmented, and the competition analysed and accounted for, the 4 Ps are used to maximise sales within the target market. For example, a commercial food company that produces functional foods may choose to target middle class retirees with health concerns because of their spending power, growing segment size, and willingness to make changes to their food choices to enhance their health as they age. With the population segmented to identify this specific target market, the company will then develop the functional food to meet the taste preferences of this group ('Product'), ensure the product meets cost expectations ('Price'), advertise the product in media used by older people ('Promotion'), and distribute the product in supermarkets and other food stores located within residential areas that are heavily populated by older people ('Place'). Compare this to the public health practitioner's goal of encouraging the majority of the population to consume fewer unhealthy foods, eat more fruits and vegetables, and engage in much greater levels of physical activity. While consideration of the marketing approaches of segmentation, competition, and the 4 Ps may be of some assistance in developing social marketing programs (as outlined below), the behaviour change task is substantially different from a commercial marketing task, which limits the extent to which marketing principles that primarily focus on individual decision-making can be usefully translated to the public health context.

Social Marketing Principles

The Journal of Marketing was established in 1963, signifying the official birth of the discipline. The sub-discipline of consumer behaviour subsequently evolved to specifically address the complexities associated with understanding and influencing individuals' consumption decisions (Quester et al. 2013). Similarly, the sub-discipline of social marketing emerged in response to the needs of policy makers and practitioners to encourage consumers to engage in behavioural change in non-commercial contexts (Kotler and Zaltman 1971). At the time of its inception, social marketing was defined as "The design, implementation, and control of programs calculated to influence the acceptability of social ideas and involving considerations of product planning, pricing, communication, distribution, and marketing research" (Kotler and Zaltman 1971, p. 5).

Social marketing borrows the primary elements of commercial marketing (and their associated assumptions) by focusing on individuals' preferences and needs, market segmentation, the notions of competition and exchange, and operational strategy in the form of the 4 Ps (Andreasen 2002; Donovan and Henley 2010). It is therefore a complex, multi-component process (Carins and Rundle-Thiele 2014). Despite recognition of this at a conceptual level, real-world interventions classified as social marketing are often merely advertising campaigns and/or education programs (Aschemann-Witzel et al. 2012; Herrick 2007; Rothschild 1999), and as such have limited success beyond increased awareness of the particular issue being raised (Croker et al. 2012). To be truly effective, social marketing efforts need to address not only individuals' behaviours (i.e. those occurring in the 'micro' environment), but also those occurring in the 'meso' and 'macro' environments that constitute social groups (e.g., families) and broader environments respectively (Carrete and Arroyo 2014; Langford and Panter-Brick 2013; Stead et al. 2007). In theory, this is achieved by engaging in the full social marketing process rather than selectively applying individual components of the social marketing repertoire. For example, reviews of social marketing programs targeting nutrition and obesity have found that program effectiveness is associated with the extent of adherence to the full social marketing process (Carins and Rundle-Thiele 2014; Gracia-Marco et al. 2010).

Social marketing is inherently more difficult than commercial marketing due to (i) the need to focus on broad issues rather than specific product purchases and (ii) the difficulties associated with measuring success in the absence of accessible metrics in the form of sales revenues, market share, and profitability (Aschemann-Witzel et al. 2012). In addition, there is the need to consider not just those in the specified target market, but also important other stakeholders such as policy makers, health practitioners, and affected family members (Hoek and Jones 2011). To increase the likelihood of achieving behavioural change in this complex environment, social marketing relies heavily on empirical evidence from previous campaigns and theories of social behaviour (Grier and Bryant 2005; Hastings 2003). The following sections focus on specific health issues that have proven largely resistant to efforts to date, including the use of social marketing approaches.

Public Health Case Studies

Ageing

The world's population is ageing rapidly. In Australia, the proportion of the population aged 65 years and older will increase from around one in seven people currently to one in five in 2061 (ABS 2013, 2014). This will have enormous implications for the national health budget because of the much higher health costs per capita among members of this age group (AIHW 2005; Productivity Commission 2013). To reduce these costs, as well as optimise quality of life among members of this substantial population segment, it is critical that older people stay fit and functional for as long as possible (Pettigrew 2014). This objective is confounded by social norms relating to 'slowing down' in later life and corresponding reductions in physical activity levels with age (ABS 2012). An important but difficult public health objective is therefore to markedly increase the amount of physical activity undertaken by the large majority of seniors.

The private sector can assist to some extent through the development, provision, and promotion of a range of goods and services that facilitate physical activity among older people (e.g. modified exercise clothing, equipment, and facilities) (Moschis and Pettigrew 2011; Pettigrew and Moschis 2012). However, companies selling these products must overcome ageing stereotypes to build a market for their products, and a further obstacle for at least some companies will be the potential to alienate their younger target markets by associating their products and organisations with older people (Long 1998). Therefore, commercial marketing may not be the most suitable and effective approach to address this health issue.

Environmental-level approaches have much greater potential to favourably alter seniors' activity levels. Examples include designing neighbourhoods to encourage and facilitate walking as a method of transport, incorporating healthy ageing content into medical training for general practitioners, further raising the retirement age, and encouraging older people to become volunteers (King et al. 2011; Pettigrew and Moschis 2012; Pettigrew et al. 2015a). Such approaches require a longer time horizon and ongoing investment, but have considerable potential to make population-level improvements to seniors' health and a corresponding reduction in the costs of ageing to the community as a whole (Productivity Commission 2013).

Obesity

Not only is the world's population becoming older, it is also becoming fatter (OECD 2014; WHO 2014). The World Health Organization (2014) reports a doubling of global obesity rates since 1980, which has had disastrous consequences for national health budgets (OECD 2014). Many individuals exist within obesogenic environments that promote the excessive consumption of unhealthy foods, discourage physical activity, and encourage sedentary behaviours (Osei-Assibey et al. 2012; Swinburn and Egger 2002). Much food-related decision-making occurs at a subconscious level (Wansink and Chandon 2014) and is subject to humans' poor ability to understand the impact of time discounting on their food intake decisions (i.e. they tend to automatically favour consumption now over improved health later: Richards and Hamilton 2012). Regardless, most attempts to curtail the obesity epidemic have focused on attempting to convince individuals to consciously change their eating patterns—an approach that has been deemed a failure in the face of continuing increases in obesity rates (Rekhy and McConchie 2014; Tuorila 2014; Witham and Avenell 2010). In addition, the marketplace has been largely left to address the problems associated with the quality of the food supply, but the minor modifications that have been made in the form of marginal improvements in the nutrition profiles of some foods are not sufficient to make a meaningful difference to population obesity levels (Moodie et al. 2013).

Once again, well-resourced, macro-level initiatives are better suited to address this serious public health problem. The scale of the required effort is evident in the global child obesity program EPODE (Ensemble Prévenons l'Obésité des Enfants'—translated as "Together Let's Prevent Childhood Obesity": Borys et al. 2012). This comprehensive program that is based on social marketing principles adopts a community-based approach to social norms relating to nutrition and physical activity. It involves a large number of stakeholders within each country cooperating to embed healthy lifestyle messages and activities into children's physical and social environments (Borys et al. 2012; Pettigrew et al. 2014, 2015c). Although evaluation studies are in progress, early results indicate that this approach has been able to achieve significant improvements in child obesity rates in intervention areas relative to control areas (Vinck et al. 2015). Tackling child obesity is critical because of the strong association between child and adult obesity (Magarey et al. 2003), however comprehensive programs targeting child obesity alone will not be adequate to address population levels of obesity because of the increased prevalence of the condition with age (Weksler 1999). As such, similar programs need to be developed and implemented to prevent and treat adult obesity. As demonstrated by the EPODE example, such programs need to include a large number of stakeholders, incorporate the many physical and social contexts in which adults live, and receive sustained attention and funding to achieve favourable outcomes.

For both children and adults, substantial improvement in obesity levels requires systems-level planning and implementation (Roberto et al. 2015; Swinburn et al. 2013). This includes (i) food supply factors, such as the foods made available to children in school canteens (Pettigrew et al. 2012) and the way in which nutrition information is supplied on food packages in supermarkets (Blewett et al. 2011) and (ii) food promotion factors, such as the extent to which unhealthy products can dominate food-related messages in the media, thereby creating social norms that favour these kinds of products (Pettigrew et al. 2015b; Roberts et al. 2013). Such changes are beyond the scope of traditional social marketing campaigns.

An Alternative Approach: Environment First, Individual Decision-Making Second

As shown in these two mini case studies, relying on social marketing processes to encourage individual behaviour change will not be adequate to address the enormous social problems represented by population ageing and high levels of obesity. This is due to the inability to (i) undertake some of the basic principles of marketing at the downstream level (e.g., segmentation to select the most profitable target group from within the larger market), (ii) compete with massively resourced competitors, and (iii) deliver to consumers what they say they want (a fundamental assumption of the marketing concept that does not always apply in public health). As such, social marketing efforts that seek to encourage individuals to change their behaviours in favour of their long-term health need to be substantially augmented with structural changes that support healthy decisions. Insights into how this may be achieved may be obtained from other research domains as outlined below.

Two disciplines that are related to social marketing are psychology and behavioural economics. Both provide conceptual inputs into many marketing theories and practices, but they also provide insights into why governments should not rely solely or primarily on social marketing to advance public health. The discipline of psychology is based on theories that demonstrate the complexity of achieving lasting behavioural change in individuals. For example, Ryan and Deci's (2000) self-determination theory proposes that while human beings are active agents who have evolved to make positive developmental changes over time, social and cultural factors can facilitate or undermine self-motivation to make these changes. Individuals' motivations thus operate as a function of the environment in which they exist, and this environment can either support or undermine intrinsic motivation, self-regulation, and, ultimately, healthy development and well-being. Creating an environment that fosters self-determined motivation sustains health-promoting behaviour (Owen et al. 2014), making change at the environmental level critical for promoting the adoption and maintenance of healthy behaviours among individuals.

Behavioural economics incorporates knowledge from psychology, economics, and other disciplines to provide insight into ways of modifying physical, social, and financial contexts to encourage behavioural change (King et al. 2013; Lui et al. 2014). This burgeoning area of work explicitly recognises the benefits of altering environments to make them more conducive to particular behaviours. Across various behavioural domains (e.g. food choices, gym usage), interventions based on the principles of behavioural economics demonstrate the ability to improve outcomes for individuals (Gittelsohn and Lee 2013; Lui et al. 2014; Milkman et al. 2013). This evidence highlights the need for public health initiatives to move beyond encouraging individuals to make 'rational' behavioural changes for the sake of their future well-being, and instead combine any such attempts with comprehensive environmental modifications that make the healthy choice the easy choice.

Conclusion

Fundamental differences exist between the use of marketing principles in the commercial sector and the problems faced by policy makers and practitioners working in public health. While marketers seek to change a specific behaviour, public health problems are highly complex, with multiple behavioural changes typically required to address multifactorial health issues. For example, addressing obesity requires dietary and physical activity changes at the population level, both of which can take many forms and as a consequence defy simple behavioural prescriptions. A case in point is nutrition—a healthy diet involves the adequate inclusion of certain types of foods and the limiting of other types of foods. This is a much more difficult communication and persuasion task compared to "Try/buy brand X of breakfast cereal". This fundamental difference in the behaviour change task needs to be fully appreciated by the public health sector before decisions are made to prioritise social marketing approaches over more structural approaches that seek to create environments that are conducive to healthy decisions and behaviours. While social marketing conceptually includes such macro approaches (Andreasen 2002), rarely in practice does it take this form. Instead, the 'Promotion P' in the form of advertising and/or education is often implemented in isolation, which is unlikely to achieve the desired outcomes (Aschemann-Witzel et al. 2012; Croker et al. 2012; Rothschild 1999). The potential of social marketing is thus not being realised.

There are, however, opportunities presented by social marketing that can be taken forward for public health purposes. Both marketing and social marketing highlight the importance of a comprehensive and sustained approach to changing behaviour. The substantial theoretical and practical advancements of these disciplines should assist in providing cogent arguments to policy makers about the characteristics of effective public health behaviour change initiatives. The complex behaviours that are the focus of public health efforts are much more difficult to address than the marketer's task of encouraging new product trial or brand switching, illustrating the even greater need in public health for behaviour change programs to be thoroughly researched, strategically implemented, well-resourced, and long-term in nature (Rekhy and McConchie 2014).

Perhaps most importantly, the theoretical and applied aspects of social marketing should make it clear to policy makers that attempting to change individuals' behaviours is not, as is often assumed, the easy path relative to introducing structural changes. Adopting a social marketing approach entails employment of the full range of strategic marketing processes, not just the development of an advertising campaign. Learnings from the discipline of psychology also show how difficult it is to stimulate and support meaningful behavioural change in individuals. This is especially the case where environments continue to encourage the opposite behaviours to those being recommended. Large and sustained investments in marketing efforts are needed to (i) make individuals aware of the need for change, (ii) advise them of the various behavioural options available to them and how they can be enacted, (iii) convince individuals of the superiority of the recommended behaviours over their current behaviours, and (iv) support them to maintain any new behaviours until they become habitual and preferred.

Ultimately, as indicated by behavioural economics, in many cases it is likely to be easier, faster, and more cost-effective to invest in the environmental and infrastructure changes that can subtly and often subconsciously encourage individuals to change their behaviour. Developing, implementing, and sustaining complex strategies to prompt behavioural change in contexts that remain conducive to existing unhealthy behaviours is an expensive, time-consuming, and potentially futile task. However, taking the upstream approach requires political will, strong leadership, and a prioritising of public health over the vociferous interests of industries that will be adversely affected by the sought changes in consumer behaviour. Let's hope our leaders are up to the task.

References

Andreasen AR (2002) Marketing social marketing in the social change marketplace. J Public Policy Mark 21(1):3–13

Aschemann-Witzel J, Perez-Cueto FJ, Niedzwiedzka B, Verbeke W, Bech-Larsen T (2012) Lessons for public health campaigns from analysing commercial food marketing success factors: a case study. BMC Public Health 12(1):139–149

Australian Bureau of Statistics (2012) Australian health survey: first results, 2011–12. Catalog No. 4364.0.55.001. ABS, Canberra

Australian Bureau of Statistics (2013) Population projections, Australia, 2012 (base) to 2101. Catalog no. 3222.0. ABS, Canberra

Australian Bureau of Statistics (2014) Population by age and sex, Regions of Australia, 2013. Catalog no. 3235.0. ABS, Canberra

Australian Institute of Health and Welfare (2005) Health system expenditure on disease and injury in Australia, 2000–01. Catalog no. HWE 28. AIHW, Canberra

Blewett N, Goddard N, Pettigrew S, Reynolds C, Yeatman H (2011) Labelling logic. Commonwealth of Australia, Canberra

Borys JM, Le Bodo Y, Jebb SA, Seidell JC, Summerbell C, Richard D, De Henauw S, Moreno LA, Romon M, Visscher TLS, Raffin S, Swinburn B (2012) The EEN study group: EPODE approach for childhood obesity prevention: methods, progress and international development. Obes Rev 13:299–315

Carins JE, Rundle-Thiele SR (2014) Eating for the better: a social marketing review (2000–2012). Public Health Nutr 17(07):1628–1639

Carrete L, Arroyo P (2014) Social marketing to improve healthy dietary decisions: insights from a qualitative study in Mexico. Qual Mark Res Int J 17(3):239–263

Croker H, Lucas R, Wardle J (2012) Cluster-randomised trial to evaluate the 'change for life' mass media/social marketing campaign in the UK. BMC Public Health 12(1):404

Donovan R, Henley N (2010) Principles and practice of social marketing, 2nd edn. IP Communications, Victoria

Gittelsohn J, Lee K (2013) Integrating educational, environmental, and behavioral economic strategies may improve the effectiveness of obesity interventions. Appl Econ Perspect Policy 35(1):52–68

Gracia-Marco L, Vicente-Rodriguez G, Borys JM, Le Bodo Y, Pettigrew S, Moreno LA (2010) Contribution of social marketing strategies to community-based obesity prevention programmes in children. Int J Obes 35(4):472–479

Grier SA, Bryant C (2005) Social marketing in public health. Annu Rev Public Health 26:319–339
Hastings G (2003) Relational paradigms in social marketing. J Macromarketing 23(1):6–15
Hastings G (2015) Public health and the value of disobedience. Public Health. doi:10.1016/j.puhe.2015.03.010 showArticle Info
Herrick C (2007) Risky bodies: public health, social marketing and the governance of obesity. Geoforum 38(1):90–102
Hoek J, Jones SC (2011) Regulation, public health and social marketing: a behaviour change trinity. J Soc Mark 1(1):32–44
King AC, Sallis JF, Frank LD, Saelens BE, Cain K, Conway TL, Kerr J (2011) Aging in neighborhoods differing in walkability and income: associations with physical activity and obesity in older adults. Soc Sci Med 73(10):1525–1533
King D, Greaves F, Vlaev I, Darzi A (2013) Approaches based on behavioral economics could help nudge patients and providers toward lower health spending growth. Health Aff 32(4):661–668
Kotler P, Zaltman G (1971) Social marketing: an approach to planned social change. J Mark 35:3–12
Langford R, Panter-Brick C (2013) A health equity critique of social marketing: where interventions have impact but insufficient reach. Soc Sci Med 83:133–141
Liu PJ, Wisdom J, Roberto CA, Liu LJ, Ubel PA (2014) Using behavioral economics to design more effective food policies to address obesity. Appl Econ Perspect Policy 36(1):6–24
Long N (1998) Broken down by age and sex—exploring the ways we approach the elderly consumer. J Mark Res Soc 40(2):73–91
Magarey AM, Daniels LA, Boulton TJ (2003) Predicting obesity in early adulthood from childhood and parental obesity. Int J Obes 27:505–513
Milkman KL, Minson JA, Volpp KG (2013) Holding the hunger games hostage at the gym: an evaluation of temptation bundling. Manage Sci 60(2):283–299
Moodie R, Stuckler D, Monteiro C, Sheron N, Neal B, Thamarangsi T, Lincoln P, Casswell S (2013) Profits and pandemics: prevention of harmful effects of tobacco, alcohol, and ultra-processed food and drink industries. The Lancet 381(9867):670–679
Moore M, Yeatman H, Davey R (2015) Which nanny–the state or industry? Wowsers, teetotallers and the fun police in public health advocacy. Public Health. doi:10.1016/j.puhe.2015.01.031
Moschis G, Pettigrew S (2011) Understanding consumer well-being in later life: business strategies for enhancing quality of life. In: Kohlbacher F, Herstatt C (eds) Marketing and innovation in the aging society. Springer, Berlin, pp 229–238
OECD (2014) Obesity update 2014. Organisation for economic co-operation and development; 2014. Available http://www.oecd.org/els/health-systems/Obesity-Update-2014.pdf
Osei-Assibey G, Dick S, Macdiarmid J, Semple S, Reilly JJ, Ellaway A, Cowie H, McNeill G (2012) The influence of the food environment on overweight and obesity in young children: a systematic review. BMJ Open 2:e001538. doi:10.1136/bmjopen-2012-001538
Owen KB, Smith J, Lubans DR, Ng JY, Lonsdale C (2014) Self-determined motivation and physical activity in children and adolescents: a systematic review and meta-analysis. Prev Med 67:270–279
Pettigrew S (2014) Energetic ageing: it's the only way. Medicus 54(5):34–35
Pettigrew S, Moschis G (2012) Consumer well-being in later life. In: Mick D, Pettigrew S, Ozanne J, Pechmann C (eds) Transformative consumer research for personal and collective wellbeing. Taylor and Frances, New York, pp 565–581
Pettigrew S, Pescud M, Donovan R (2012) Stakeholder support for expansion of an Australian school food policy. Health Educ Res 27(6):996–1004
Pettigrew S, Borys JM, Ruault du Plessis H, Walter L, Huang T, Levi J, Vinck J (2014) Process evaluation outcomes from a global child obesity prevention intervention. BMC Public Health 14:757–766

Pettigrew S, Jongenelis M, Newton RU, Warburton J, Jackson B (2015a) A research protocol for a random controlled trial of the health effects of volunteering for seniors. Health Qual Life Outcomes 13:74. doi:10.1186/s12955-015-0263-z

Pettigrew S, Jongenelis M, Quester P, Chapman C, Miller C (2015b) Dimensions of parents' attitudes to unhealthy foods and beverages. Food Qual Prefer 44:179–182

Pettigrew S, Weir L, Williams M, Rundle-Thiele S (2015c) Using publicity to enhance the effectiveness of a child obesity prevention program. In: Wymer W (ed) Innovations in social marketing and public health communication: improving the quality of life for individuals and communities. Springer Wellbeing and Quality-of-Life Series, Heidelberg

Productivity Commission (2013) An ageing Australia: preparing for the future. Commission Research Paper Overview, Canberra

Pykett J, Jones R, Welsh M, Whitehead M (2014) The art of choosing and the politics of social marketing. Policy Stud 35(2):97–114

Quester P, McGuiggan RL, McCarthy EJ, Perrault WD (2001) Basic marketing, 3rd edn. McGraw-Hill, New York

Quester P, Pettigrew S, Sally Rao Hill SR, Kopanidis F (2013) Consumer behaviour, 7th edn. McGraw-Hill, Hawthorn

Rekhy R, McConchie R (2014) Promoting consumption of fruit and vegetables for better health: have campaigns delivered on the goals? Appetite 79:113–123

Richards TJ, Hamilton SF (2012) Obesity and hyperbolic discounting: an experimental analysis. J Agri Resour Econ 37:181–198

Roberto CA, Swinburn B, Hawkes C, Huang TT, Costa SA, Ashe M, Brownell KD (2015) Patchy progress on obesity prevention: emerging examples, entrenched barriers, and new thinking. The Lancet 385:2400–2409

Roberts M, Pettigrew S, Chapman K, Quester P, Miller C (2013) The advertised diet: an examination of the extent and nature of food advertising on Australian television. Heath Promot J Austral. doi:10.1071/HE12926

Rothschild ML (1999) Carrots, sticks, and promises: a conceptual framework for the management of public health and social issue behaviors. J Mark 63(4):24–37

Ryan RM, Deci EL (2000) Self-determination theory and the facilitation of intrinsic motivation, social development, and well-being. Am Psychol 55(1):68

Stead M, McDermott L, Hastings G (2007) Towards evidence-based marketing: the case of childhood obesity. Mark Theor 7(4):379–406

Swinburn B, Egger G (2002) Preventive strategies against weight gain and obesity. Obes Rev 3:289–301

Swinburn B, Sacks G, Vandevijvere S, Kumanyika S, Lobstein T, Neal B, Barquera S, Friel S, Hawkes C, Kelly B, L'Abbé M, Lee A, Ma J, Macmullan J, Mohan S, Monteiro C, Rayner M, Sanders D, Snowdon W, Walker C (2013) For INFORMAS: INFORMAS (International network for food and obesity/non-communicable diseases research, monitoring and action support): overview and key principles. Obes Rev 14(S1):1–12

Tuorila H (2014) From sensory evaluation to sensory and consumer research of food: an autobiographical perspective. Food Qual Prefer. doi:10.1016/j.foodqual.2014.05.006

Vinck J, Brohet C, Roillet M, Dramaix M, Borys JM, Beysens J, Jebb S, De Laet C, Nève J (2015) Downward trends in the prevalence of childhood overweight in two pilot towns taking part in the VIASANO community-based programme in Belgium: data from a national school health monitoring system. Pediatr Obes. doi:10.1111/ijpo.12022

Wansink B, Chandon P (2014) Slim by design: redirecting the accidental drivers of mindless overeating. J Consum Psychol 24(3):413–431

Weksler ME (1999) Obesity: age-related weight gain and the development of disease. Geriatrics 54(11):57

Witham MD, Avenell A (2010) Interventions to achieve long-term weight loss in obese older people: a systematic review and meta-analysis. Age Ageing 39:176–184

World Health Organization (2013) Global action plan for the prevention and control of noncommunicable diseases 2013–2020. WHO, Geneva. Available http://www.who.int/nmh/publications/ncd-action-plan/en

World Health Organization (2014) Obesity and overweight, fact sheet no. 311. Available http://www.who.int/mediacentre/factsheets/fs311/en

World Health Organization (2015) Millennium development goals (MDGs), fact sheet no. 290. Available http://www.who.int/mediacentre/factsheets/fs290/en/

Contemporary Young Consumers and Food Consumption—Implications for Social Marketing Research

Liudmila Tarabashkina and Roberta Crouch

Abstract Marketing has undergone profound changes during the past 30 years with a shift from television advertising to digital marketing and development of more engaging campaigns between brands and individuals. This change has also affected young consumers (i.e. children aged less than 13 years), who attracted marketers' attention in the mid-1980s, who have ever since been marketing aggressively to this group across multiple media channels, engaging in the so-called "cradle-to-grave" marketing. Research shows that exposure to food advertising is associated with biased product evaluations extending into adulthood and the last two decades have also noted a substantial increase in the rates of childhood obesity and overweight levels worldwide. Although research about young consumers and their food consumption started more than 40 years ago, current discussion centres predominantly around the impact of food advertising on children and extant knowledge remains fragmented and inconclusive in relation to a number of *external,* as well as *internal influences.* In particular, it is still unclear how children choose healthy and less healthy foods under the influence of different socialisation agents and their own consumer knowledge about advertising or nutrition. Extant gaps impede effective policy development and successful social marketing campaigns since the full extent of children's susceptibility to food advertising remains unclear. This paper was inspired by work conducted under PhD candidature supervision by Prof. Pascale Quester and provides a review of social marketing literature to highlight the gaps in our knowledge and delineate important directions for future social marketing research in relation to young consumers' food consumption.

Keywords Young consumers · Food consumption · Gaps · Review

L. Tarabashkina (✉)
The University of Adelaide, Adelaide, Australia
e-mail: liudmila.tarabashkina@adelaide.edu.au

R. Crouch
School of Marketing & Management, The University of Adelaide, Adelaide, Australia
e-mail: Roberta.crouch@adelaide.edu.au

R. Crouch
Groupe ESC Dijon Bourgogne, School of Wine and Spirits, Dijon, France

© Springer Science+Business Media Singapore 2016

C. Plewa and J. Conduit (eds.), *Making a Difference Through Marketing*,
DOI 10.1007/978-981-10-0464-3_6

Introduction

Transformation of Food Industry

In contrast to other products, food not only represents a vital source of sustenance, but also has symbolic value (i.e. being a vegetarian) as well as being the occasional indulgence (Rappoport 2003). Over the past 40 years, economic development and advances in agricultural practices have lead to an increase in the variety of available foods (Drewnowski 1997), resulting in an improved capacity to produce crops irrespective of seasonality (Kearney 2010). In fact, the number of grocery items available for consumption nowadays has increased threefold, and contemporary children consume foods which did not exist when their parents were young (Rappoport 2003). The nature of meals has changed—that is, where and with whom they are shared (Benton 2004; Livingstone 2005). Lifestyles have become more hectic—individuals are more mobile; they look for foods which are easy to eat on a move (Grocer 2008), resulting in steady annual growth rates for the snacking product category globally ("Snack Attack" 2014). Frozen, canned or packaged convenience foods nowadays are easily accessible through supermarkets, replacing to some extent, traditional food preparation and cooking (Osman et al. 2014). Parents who are especially busy during weekdays can dine out or buy take away foods for their families (Osman et al. 2014). Additionally, diets have changed towards more energy dense foods which contain higher amount of fats, added sugars and saturated fats from animal sources (Drewnowski and Popkin 1997) and average daily calories available for consumers have increased by approximately 600 calories (Dietary Guidelines for Americans 2010). This trend has been accompanied by a reduced intake of complex carbohydrates, fibre, fruit and vegetables (Drewnowski and Popkin 1997) and an increase in portion sizes (Dietary Guidelines for Americans 2010).

Changes in the food industry have coincided with a worldwide increase in the rates of adult overweight and obesity (Benton 2004). Overall, it is projected that by 2030 around 60 % of the worldwide adult population will be overweight or obese (Kelly et al. 2008c). From the public health perspective, the cost of obesity is high and likely to double by 2025 (Aitken et al. 2009). Alarmingly, the younger generation is gaining weight faster than their parents (Hebden et al. 2012) and there are significant health implications relating to the development of overweight and obesity amongst children which have been widely documented (WHO 2015). Obesity has both genetic and environmental origins, where the latter represents an outcome of prolonged poor lifestyle habits (Caroli et al. 2004). Although having obese parents certainly represents a risk factor for young children who have not yet developed obesity (Wardle et al. 2001), scholars seem to agree that the worldwide increase in rates of childhood obesity support an environmental rather than genetic explanation for current obesity trends in the younger population (Hill et al. 2003).

Young Consumers and Food Industry: A Segment Worth Conquering

The changes in the nature of the food industry have coincided with significant shifts in the role of children in the market space. Before the 1950s, much of the advertisers' attention while promoting products designed for children was aimed at adult consumers, in other words their parents (McNeal 1994). However, the advent of television and children's programs have dramatically changed the nature and the scope of advertising to children (Schor 2004). Over time, marketers' perceptions of children have changed—in the 1930s, they were perceived as growing machines, which needed education; in the 1950s, they were novelty seekers (Cook 2000). In the 1960s, children's market potential was still not considered seriously (McNeal 1999), but from the 1990s onwards, children have been treated as autonomous and savvy individuals (Cook 2000).

Children are important to marketers for a number of reasons—they influence their parents' consumer behaviour; they will be future consumers (Martin and Bush 2000); and they already exercise considerable spending power in the market space and influence their parents (McNeal 1999). Although young consumers are targeted by the manufacturers of multiple products, *foods* are more accessible to children through their own pocket money and purchase requests addressed to their parents (Harris et al. 2009). Worldwide, children aged 8–14 years spend and influence a market worth $1.88 trillion (Lindstrom and Seybold 2003). Hence, from the commercial point of view, childhood represents an important stage to build brand loyalty, where "cradle-to-grave marketing" is considered to represent a key to a long and sustainable relationship between food manufacturers and children (Hastings et al. 2003).

Because children represent a fast-growing and attractive market segment for the food industry (Livingstone and Helsper 2006), food advertising to children has substantially increased in the last decades (Byrd-Bredbenner 2002) outnumbering other product categories especially on television (Hastings et al. 2006). Food and beverage companies currently heavily invest in a promotion of their brands through interactive social media and mobile marketing (Montgomery et al. 2012), capitalising on capabilities of these technologies. Food advertising landscape has significantly changed over time showing an increase in non-core food categories (Roberts et al. 2013). From the public health perspective, childhood represents an important period not only for the development of obesity (Venn et al. 2007), but also food and consumer preferences (Birch 1999; Nestle 2002). Hence, it is not surprising why research, as well as obesity prevention policies, have recently focused on children (Reisch and Gwozdz 2011). Despite long research efforts in this area, our knowledge about factors that influence children's food consumption leading to weight gain still remains fragmented (Hastings et al. 2003), impeding policy development. Twelve major gaps still exist in our knowledge, which have been identified through a literature review of studies conducted between 1970 and 2014. These gaps are discussed in detail below, delineating important directions for future social marketing research, contributing to the current discussion about children's food consumer socialisation.

Gaps in Knowledge About Young Consumers' Food Consumption

Of all factors suggested as in the literature as possible causes of childhood obesity, which relate to reduced physical activity, snacking, and food advertising—the latter represents the most widely debated factor (OfCom 2004). Numerous studies have exposed the intensity of food advertising targeting children (Cairns et al. 2009; Desrochers and Holt 2007), highlighting their poor reflection of dietary recommendations (Byrd-Bredbenner 2002). Typically, if a child watches two and a half hours of commercial television every day, he or she would be exposed to 11 "junk" food advertisements per day, and to around 77 of them per week (Neville et al. 2005). Past research has shown that exposure to advertisements in childhood can be associated with biased product evaluations in adulthood (Connell et al. 2014) and the current discussion of childhood obesity frequently evolves around the issue of food promotion, where children are typically depicted as being susceptible to advertising (Buijzen et al. 2010). As a result, restrictions on food advertising have been nominated as one of the most effective interventions to fight the obesity pandemic (Haby et al. 2006). Although several ecological studies tend to support such an approach (Dhar and Baylis 2011; Lobstein and Dibb 2005), stricter regulations of food advertising are challenging due to a number of reasons.

First, any policy restrictions on food marketing targeting children need to have a precise definition of the types of foods that are considered inappropriate, which can be provided by the government or industry self-regulation policies (Hawkes 2007), where the latter is still missing in many countries (Hebden et al. 2010). National policies regarding the control of food advertising aired on television also vary substantially (IASO 2010), and even more work is required to regulate promotion on the Internet and other channels used by marketers (mobile phone apps, etc.). Second, advertising represents only one of the many *external (social level) factors* that influence children in addition to *individual level factors* (Livingstone and Helsper 2004), highlighting the complexity of the obesity problem. In particular, children start learning about foods first from their parents (Benton 2004) and as they grow up, food marketing (Brand 2007) and peers become influential(Birch and Fisher 1998). While the presence of influencers operating both on *individual and social levels* was highlighted a decade ago (Livingstone and Helsper 2004), the determinants of children's food choices have not yet been studied while controlling for both *social* and *individual level influences* (*gap 1*, Fig. 1). Recently, empirical studies looking at the magnitude of influence of different *external influences* have been assessed, and the impact of food advertising on children's food consumption has been evaluated as a modest, but not as a significant independent determinant (Cairns et al. 2013). So far, only five studies have looked into the influence of several factors on children's dietary behaviour (Baker et al. 2003; Bolton 1983; Buijzen et al. 2008; Norton et al. 2000; Stoneman and Brody 1981). They vary substantially in terms of methodology used (experiment vs. survey) and have not assessed the influence of all relevant *social level* factors simultaneously, leaving a gap in our knowledge about the *overall magnitude of the influence* of food advertising compared to *parents*, *peers*, and *school* (*gap 2*, Fig. 1).

Furthermore, past research has predominantly concentrated on behavioural outcomes in children (food preferences or food consumption) (Halford et al. 2007) and more insights are required about *children's nutritional* and *persuasion knowledge* in food consumption decision making—the *individual level factors*. Both nutritional and persuasion knowledge increase with age (Tallarini et al. 2013; Wiman and Newman 1989) and designate more *rational* and *logical approach to* food selection. Nutritional knowledge is related to better understanding of nutritional information (Grunert et al. 2013), but empirical results about its influence on children are still mixed, providing inconclusive support for its potentially positive effect on children's diets (Gibson et al. 1998). Furthermore, It is generally assumed that persuasion knowledge would act as a filter, protecting children from advertising

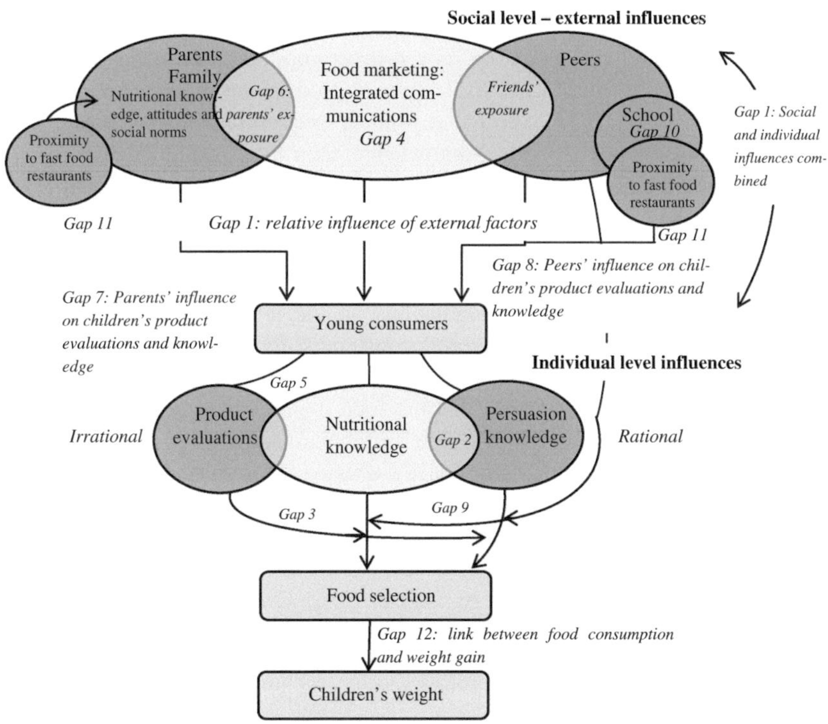

Fig. 1 Extant gaps in knowledge relating to young consumers' food consumption

(Rozendaal et al. 2009). Older children are generally expected to be less susceptible to persuasive tactics due to more advanced cognitive and social development skills that help them grasp bias in advertising (Seiders and Petty 2007). Although children's persuasion knowledge has always been central to the debate about the influence of food advertising on young consumers (Martin 1997), currently more is known about the age at which understanding of advertising intent emerges, rather than its application by children (Mallinckrodt and Mizerski 2007; Rossiter and Robertson 1974). Currently, experimental literature suggests that advertising influences children's post-experimental food preferences (Borzekowski and Robinson 2001), however, whether children's nutritional knowledge combined with persuasion knowledge can mitigate the effects of promotion on dietary behaviour is still missing (*gap 3*, Fig. 1). Future studies in this area need to be carefully designed because extant research suggests that adult consumers do not always utilize their nutritional knowledge when they select foods (Saarela et al. 2013). Consumers may still choose to purchase a brand even when they are fully aware of marketers' persuasive intent due to positive brand or product evaluations (i.e. *emotional influences*). *Product evaluations* that are likely to influence children's food consumption relate to *taste, social appeal,* and *fun*, which represent the themes that are consistently deployed by the food marketers (Cairns et al. 2013) and may impact on children's liking of unhealthy food advertisements (Tarabashkina et al. 2011). Emotional mood enhancement and food craving are typically used for the promotion of less healthy product categories (Pettigrew et al. 2012) and it has been suggested that emotional advertising may distract children from other aspects of advertisements, such as nutritional disclaimers or product information (Wicks et al. 2009). While it is logical to expect that *product evaluations* have a potential to undermine persuasion and nutritional knowledge, their *moderating effects* have not yet been examined calling for a more holistic understanding of factors that influence young consumers where assessing both rational and irrational components of food consumption represents an important direction for social marketing. Hence, future research needs to broaden the scope of enquiry by examining the potential moderating influences of product evaluations on the relationship between nutritional and persuasion knowledge on young consumers' food choices (*gap 4*, Fig. 1).

Literature review has also revealed a number of gaps in relation to *external factors*. Scholars consistently report that the food media environment has become more diversified (Cairns et al. 2009) where children are exposed to food promotion across multiple channels, including not only television (Morton et al. 2005), but also magazines (Kelly et al. 2008b), supermarkets (Chapman et al. 2006), websites (Kelly et al. 2008a), and more recently, smartphones. Contemporary young consumers have access to digital technology not experienced by previous generations (Schor 2004). Yet, the assessment of the influence of *integrated marketing communication* is still missing (*gap 5*, Fig. 1). More research is required about children's susceptibility to new, non-traditional marketing techniques, such as advergames and social media on children (Montgomery et al. 2012). Whether advertising is capable of altering children's nutritional knowledge, impacting positively on product evaluations represents another unexplored area (*gap 6*, Fig. 1).

Next, *parents' role* in the childhood obesity problem represents another area for exploration because both children and parents are exposed to food advertising (Grier et al. 2007). Research about parents' susceptibility to food promotion suggests that advertising can influence parents' product perceptions (nutritional benefits, taste, fun, and social appeal) (Jones and Fabrianesi 2007), likelihood of consumption of the commonly advertised energy-dense foods (Pettigrew et al. 2013), and selection of energy dense products over healthy alternatives when products are advertised using sport celebrities or nutritional messages (Dixon et al. 2011). Advertising of energy dense and low in nutrient foods aimed at children has recently shifted towards parents (Dixon et al. 2011) and their inability to withstand food advertising may be harmful for young consumers. In particular, research has shown that parents' *attitudes* (favourable or unfavourable evaluation of an object or behaviour (Fishbein and Ajzen 1975, p. 6)) and *social norms* about less healthy foods (beliefs about what constitutes an appropriate behaviour amongst people (Fishbein and Ajzen 1975)) are associated with more frequent consumption of fast foods by children, where a positive association was also observed between parents' exposure to fast food advertising and social norms (Grier et al. 2007). Because younger children depend on their parents for food provision, it is logical to assume that exposure to unhealthy role models may predispose them to unhealthy lifestyles, which is supported by the Social Cognitive Theory (Bandura 2002). Although favourable attitudes and social norms can reinforce misconceptions about specific behavioural patterns (Hawkins and Pingree 1982), the literature does not explain how parents' attitudes and social norms may influence *children's product evaluations, persuasion and nutritional knowledge* (*gap 7*, Fig. 1).

Another external factor, which requires further research is *peers*. Extant literature suggest that pre-schoolers' vegetable choice can change within four days after children start having lunch with peers who have different vegetable preferences (Birch 1980) and there is also support for perceived food consumption resemblance between friends for soft drinks (Perkins et al. 2010) and less healthy foods (Feunekes et al. 1998). The above-mentioned influences, however, have been examined in relation to behavioural outcomes. As a result, peers' influence on young consumers' *product evaluations, nutritional* and *persuasion knowledge* remains under-researched, limiting our understanding of potential pathways of peer influence on the formation of favourable attitudes amongst young consumers (*gap 8*, Fig. 1). Futhermore, although peer influence may undermine children's use of their persuasion and nutritional knowledge as a result of conformity when foods are consumed with friends, this potential moderating effect has not yet been tested (*gap 9*, Fig. 1).

In the context of food consumption, *school* represents another location where learning about foods and nutrition may take place, not only as a result of educational programs, but also due to *foods' availability* in canteens. Although consumption of snacks and soft drinks is higher when they are available at schools (Wouters et al. 2010), more research is encouraged to investigate how schools contribute to the development of unhealthy lifestyles and *favourable product evaluations* amongst young consumers (*gap 10*, Fig. 1). Likewise, *proximity to fast food restaurants* represents another area for investigation—there is some evidence suggesting an association between proximity and consumption of fast foods in disadvantaged areas (Forsyth et al. 2012). Children belonging to low socio-economic background also tend to have higher weight (O'Dea et al. 2014) and consume less healthy foods more often (Ambrosini et al. 2009; Larson et al. 2008). Yet, it is still not clear how availability of fast foods impacts on *wider social norms* and *perceptions of less healthy foods' acceptability* both amongst *parents* and *their children* (*gap 11*, Fig. 1).

Finally, the influences of food advertising have been previously studied in relation to two separate variables—food preferences or food consumption (behavioural outcomes) (Utter et al. 2006) and weight (health diet-related outcome) (Proctor et al. 2003). At the moment, the extant literature suggests only an association between children's weight and TV watching and the link between the consumption of less healthy foods and children's weight is still tenuous (Jolly 2011) (*gap 12*, Fig. 1). The absence of such conclusive evidence has been frequently used as an argument against a ban of "junk" food advertising aimed at young consumers (Jolly 2011). Should the influence of food advertising as a precursor to children's weight be proven, this relationship needs to occur through food consumption (food advertising → consumption → weight) (IOM 2006) and should be assessed controlling for the influence of *external* and *internal factors*.

Conclusion

This review has identified a number of important gaps in our knowledge about young consumers' food consumption, delineating several directions for future research. As shown above, food choices represent a complex consumer and social phenomenon, where factors that are likely to influence food consumption may not only operate on *individual* and *social levels* (Livingstone and Helsper 2004), but may also be *moderated* by individual (product evaluations) or external factors (peers). In agreement with the childhood obesity and social marketing literature (Livingstone 2004), there is an urgent need to examine a wider range of factors influencing children's food choices—such an approach would be able to examine the strength of each external agent affecting children's dietary behaviour and finally provide evidence as to whether food advertising exerts a small influence on children, as previously claimed by marketing professionals (WFA 2010). Since food advertising continues to use integrated marketing techniques reaching out to children, their parents, and peers (Cairns et al. 2013), more research is encouraged to assess the influence of new non-traditional methods of advertising, as well as *integrated marketing communications*. Based on the gaps outlined in this review, scholars are encouraged to develop a comprehensive, yet parsimonious conceptual framework of the factors that influence children's dietary behaviour leading to obesity. The absence of a conceptual framework impedes research in social marketing, as well as the development of effective obesity prevention strategies. The role of research remains crucial in advising public policy-makers, parents, and health practitioners about the strategies to improve young consumers' diets. Yet, the translation of research into policy, unfortunately, lags behind and remains substantially outpaced by the innovation and development in the food industry. This review has provided a detailed assessment of extant gaps about the factors that have not yet been examined, but may be related to children's food consumption, providing a clear guidance for future research to make original contributions to the field of social marketing.

References

Aitken RJ, Allman-Farinelli MA, King LA, Bauman AE (2009) Current and future costs of cancer, heart disease and stroke attributable to obesity in australia—A Comparison of Two Birth Cohorts. Asia Pac J Clin Nutr 18:63–70

Ambrosini GL, Oddy WH, Robinson M, O'Sullivan TA, Hands BP, de Klerk NH, Beilin LJ (2009) Adolescent dietary patterns are associated with lifestyle and family psycho-social factors. Public Health Nutr 12(10):1807–1815

Baker WC, Little T, Brownell K (2003) Predicting adolescent eating and activity behaviors: the role of social norms and personal agency. Health Psychol 22(2):189–198

Bandura A (2002) Social cognitive theory of mass communication. In: Bryant J, Zillman D (eds) Media effects: advances in theory and research. Lawrence Erlbaum Associates, Hillsdale, NJ, pp 121–155

Benton D (2004) Role of parents in the determination of the food preferences of children and the development of obesity. Int J Obes 28:858–869

Birch LL (1980) Effects of peer models' food choices and eating behaviors on preschoolers' food preferences. Child Dev 51(2):489–496

Birch LL (1999) Development of food preferences. Annu Rev Nutr 19:41–62

Birch LL, Fisher JO (1998) Development of eating behaviours among children and adolescents. Pediatrics 101(3):539–549

Bolton RN (1983) Modeling the impact of television food advertising on children's diet. In: Leigh JH, Martin CR (eds) Current issues and research in advertising. Division of Research, Graduate School of Business Administration, University of Michigan, Ann Arbor, pp 173–199

Borzekowski DL, Robinson TN (2001) The 30-second effect: an experiment revealing the impact of television commercials on food preferences of preschoolers. J Am Diet Assoc 101:42–46

Brand JE (2007) Television advertising to children: a review of contemporary research on the influence of television advertising directed to children: Australian Communications and Media Authority

Buijzen M, Schuurman J, Bomhof E (2008) Association between children's television advertising exposure and their food consumption patterns: a household diary-survey study. Appetite 50:231–239

Buijzen M, van Reijmersdal EA, Owen LH (2010) Introducing the PCMC model: an investigative framework for young people's processing of commercialized media content. Commun Theory 20:427–450

Byrd-Bredbenner C (2002) Saturday morning children's television advertising: a longitudinal content analysis. Fam Consum Sci Res J 30(3):382–403

Cairns G, Angus K, Hastings G (2009) The extent, nature and effects of food promotion to children: a review of the evidence to december 2008: Institute for Social Marketing. University of Stirling and the Open University, United Kingdom

Cairns G, Angus K, Hastings G, Caraher M (2013) Systematic reviews of the evidence on the nature, extent and effects of food marketing to children. A retrospective summary. Appetite 62 (March):209–215
Caroli M, Argentieri L, Cardone M, Masi A (2004) Role of television in childhood obesity prevention. Int J Obes 28:S104–S108
Chapman K, Nicholas P, Banovic D, Supramaniam R (2006) The extent and nature of food promotion directed to children in Australian supermarkets. Health Promot Int 21(4):331–339
Connell PM, Brucks ME, Nielsen JH (2014) How childhood advertising exposure can create biased product evaluations that persist into adulthood. J Consum Res 41(1):119–134
Cook DT (2000) The rise of "the toddler" as subject and as merchandising category in the 1930s. In: Gottdiener M (ed) New forms of consumption: consumers, culture, and commodification Rowman & Littlefield Publishers, Inc
Desrochers DM, Holt DJ (2007) Children's exposure to television advertising: implications for childhood obesity. J Publ Policy Mark 26(2):182–201
Dhar T, Baylis K (2011) Fast-food consumption and the ban on advertising targeting children: the Quebec experience. J Mark Res XLVIII:799–813
Dietary Guidelines for Americans (2010) U.S. Department of Agriculture and U.S. Department of Health and Human Services, 7th, Printing Office. Washington, DC
Dixon H, Maree S, Wakefield M, Kelly B, Chapman K, Donovan R (2011) Parent's response to nutrient claims and sports celebrity endorsement on energy-dense and nutrient-poor foods: an experimental study. Public Health Nutr 10:1–9
Drewnowski A (1997) Taste preferences and food intake. Annu Rev Nutr 17:237–253
Drewnowski A, Popkin BM (1997) The nutrition transition: new trends in the global diet. Nutr Rev 55(2):31–43
Feunekes GIJ, de Graaf C, Meyboom S, van Staveren WA (1998) Food choice and fat intake of adolescents and adults: associations of intakes within social networks. Prev Med 27 (5):645–656
Fishbein M, Ajzen I (1975) Belief, attitude, intention, and behavior: an introduction to theory and research reading. Addison-Wesley, MA
Forsyth A, Wall M, Larson N, Story M, Neumark-Sztainer D (2012) Do adolescents who live or go to school near fast-food restaurants eat more frequently from fast-food restaurants? Health Place 18(6):1261–1269
Gibson EL, Wardle J, Watts CJ (1998) Fruit and vegetable consumption, nutritional knowledge and beliefs in mothers and children. Appetite 31(2):205–228
Grier SA, Mensinger J, Huang SH, Kumanyika SK, Nicolas N (2007) Fast-food marketing and children's fast-food consumption: exploring parents' influences in an ethnically diverse sample. J Publ Policy Mark 26(2):221–235
Grunert KG, Wills JM, Fernandez-Celemín L (2013) Nutrition knowledge, and use and understanding of nutrition information on food labels among consumers in the UK. Appetite 55:177–189
Guide to snacking (2008) The Grocer: 2–50
Haby MM, Vos T, Carter R, Moodie M, Markwick A, Magnus A, Swinburn B (2006) New approach to assessing the health benefit from obesity interventions in children and adolescents: the assessing cost-effectiveness in obesity project. Int J Obes 30:1463–1475
Halford JC, Boyland EJ, Hughes G, Oliveira LP, Dovey TM (2007) Beyond-brand effect of television food advertisements/commercials on caloric intake and food choice of 5-7-year-old children. Appetite 49:263–267
Harris JL, Brownell KD, Bargh JA (2009) The food marketing defense model: integrating psychological research to protect youth and inform public policy. Soc Issues Policy Rev 3 (1):211–271
Hastings G, Stead M, McDermott L, Forsyth A, MacKintosh AM, Rayner M, Angus K (2003) Review of research on the effects of food promotion to children. Centre Soc Mark, Glasgow
Hastings G, McDermott L, Angus K, Stead M, Thomson S (2006) The extent, nature and effects of food promotion to children: a review of the evidence. World Heath Organization

Hawkes C (2007) Regulating and litigating in the public interest. Am J Public Health 97 (11):1962–1973. doi:10.2105/AJPH.2006.101162
Hawkins RP, Pingree S (1982) Television's influence on social reality. In: Pearl D, Bouthilet L, Lazar J (eds) Television and behavior: ten years of scientific progress and implications for the eighties, vol 2. National Institute of Mental Health, Rockville, MD, pp 224–247
Hebden L, King L, Kelly B, Chapman K, Innes-Hughes C, Gunatillaka N (2010) Regulating the types of foods and beverages marketed to Australian children: how useful are food industry comments? Nutr Diet 67:258–266
Hebden L, Chey T, Allman-Farinelli M (2012) Lifestyle intervention for preventing weight gain in young adults: a systematic review and meta-analysis of RCT. Obes Rev 13:692–710
Hill J, Wyatt H, Reed G, Peters J (2003) Obesity and the environment: where do we go from here? Science 203:853–856
IASO (2010) The PolMark Project. Policies on marketing food and beverages to children. International Association for the Study of Obesity
IOM (2006) Food marketing to children and youth: threat or opportunity?. The National Academies Science, Institute of Medicine, Washington, DC
Jolly R (2011) Marketing obesity? Junk food, advertising and kids. Parliament of Australia Department of Parliamentary Services, Canberra
Jones SC, Fabrianesi B (2007) Gross for kids but good for parents: differing messages in advertisements for the same products. Publ Health Nutr 11(6):588–595
Kearney J (2010) Food consumption trends and drivers. Philos Trans Biol Sci 365 (1554):2793–2807
Kelly B, Bochynska K, Kornman K, Chapman K (2008a) Internet food marketing on popular children's websites and food product websites in Australia. Public Health Nutr 11 (11):1180–1187
Kelly B, Cretikos M, Rogers K, King L (2008b) The commercial food landscape: outdoor food advertising around primary schools in Australia. Aust N Z J Public Health 32(6):522–528
Kelly T, Yang W, Chen CS, Reynolds K, He J (2008c) Global burden of obesity in 2005 and projections to 2030. Int J Obes 32:1431–1437
Larson NI, Neumark-Sztainer D, Story MT, Wall MM, Harnack LJ, Eisenberg ME (2008) Fast food intake: longitudinal trends during the transition to young adulthood and correlates of intake. J Adolesc Health 43:79–86
Lindstrom M, Seybold P (2003) Brandchild: Remarkable insights into the minds of today's global kids and their relationship with brands. Kogan Page Publishers, London
Livingstone S, (2004) A Commentary on the Research Evidence Regarding the Effects of Food Promotion on Children: Research Department of the Office of Communications
Livingstone S (2005) Assessing the research base for the policy debate over the effects of food advertising to children. Int J Advertising 24(3):273–296
Livingstone S, Helsper E (2004) Advertising foods to children: understanding promotion in the context of children's daily lives: Research Department of the Office of Communications
Livingstone S, Helsper E (2006) Does advertising literacy mediate the effects of advertising on children? A critical examination of two linked research literatures in relation to obesity and food choice. J Commun 56:560–584
Lobstein T, Dibb S (2005) Evidence of a possible link between obesogenic food advertising and child overweight. Obes Rev 6:203–208
Mallinckrodt V, Mizerski D (2007) The effects of playing an advergame on young children's perceptions, preferences, and requests. J Advertising 36(2):87–100
Martin MC (1997) Children's understanding of the intent of advertising: a meta-analysis. J Publ Policy Mark 16(2):205–216
Martin C, Bush A (2000) Do role models influence teenagers' purchase intentions and behavior? J Consum Res 17(5):441–453
McNeal J (1994) Kids as customers: a handbook of marketing to children. Lexington Books, New York

McNeal JU (1999) The kids market: Myths and realities. Paramount Market Publishing Inc, Ithaca, NY
Montgomery KC, Grier SA, Chester J, Dorfman L (2012) The digital food marketing landscape: challenges for researchers. In: Williams JD, Pasch KE, Collins CA (eds) Advances in Communication Research to Reduce Childhood Obesity, pp 221–242
Morton H, Stanton R, Zuppa J, Mehta K (2005) Food advertising and broadcasting legislation—A case of system failure? Nutr Diet 62:26–32
Nestle M (2002) Food politics: how the food industry influences nutrition and health. University of California Press, Berkeley, Los Angeles
Neville L, Thomas M, Bauman A (2005) Food advertising on Australian television: the extent of children's exposure. Health Promot Int 20(2):105–112
Norton PA, Falciglia GA, Ricketts C (2000) Motivational determinants of food preferences in adolescents and preadolescents. Ecol Food Nutr 39(3):169–182
O'Dea JA, Chiang H, Peralta LR (2014) Socioeconomic patterns of overweight, obesity but not thinness persist from childhood to adolescence in a 6 -year longitudinal cohort of Australian schoolchildren from 2007 to 2012. BMC Public Health 14(1):1–9
OfCom (2004) Childhood obesity—food advertising in context: Office of Communications
Osman I, Osman S, Mokhtar I, Setapa F, Shukor S, Azreen M, Temyati Z (2014) Family food consumption: desire towards convenient food products. Procedia—Soc Behav Sci 121:223–231
Perkins JM, Perkins W, Graig DW (2010) Misperceptions of peer norms as a risk factor for sugar-sweetened beverage consumption among secondary school students. J Am Diet Assoc 110:1916–1921
Pettigrew S, Roberts ME, Chapman K, Quester P, Miller C (2012) The use of negative themes in television food advertising. Appetite 58(2):496–503
Pettigrew S, Tarabashkina L, Roberts M, Quester P, Chapman K, Miller C (2013) The effects of television and internet food advertising on parents and children. Public Health Nutrition, pp 1–8
Proctor MH, Moore LL, Gao D, Cupples LA, Bradlee ML, Hood MY, Ellison RC (2003) Television viewing and change in body fat from preschool to early adolescence: the Framingham Children's Study. Int J Obes 27(7):827–833
Rappoport L (2003) How we eat: appetite, culture, and the psychology of food. ECW Press, Toronto
Reisch LA, Gwozdz W (2011) Chubby cheeks and climate change: childhood obesity as a sustainable development issue. Int J Consum Stud 35:3–9
Roberts M, Pettigrew S, Chapman K, Quester P, Miller C (2013) The advertised diet: an examination of the extent and nature of food advertising on Australian television. Health Promot J Austral 24(2):137–142
Rossiter JR, Robertson TS (1974) Children's TV commercials: testing the defenses. J Commun, 137–145
Rozendaal E, Buijzen M, Valkenburg P (2009) Do children's cognitive defenses reduce their desire for advertised products? Communications 34(3):287–303
Saarela A-M, Lapveteläinen AT, Mykkänen HM, Kantanen TT, Rissanen RL (2013) Real-life setting in data collection. The role of nutrition knowledge whilst selecting food products for weight management purposes in a supermarket environment. Appetite 73:196–208
Schor JB (2004) Born to buy: the commercialized child and the new consumer culture. Scribner, New York
Seiders K, Petty RD (2007) Taming the obesity beast: children, marketing, and public policy considerations. J Publ Policy Mark 26(2):236–242
Snack Attack (2014) Prepared Foods 183(11): 21–24
Stoneman Z, Brody GH (1981) Peers as mediators of television food advertisements aimed at children. Dev Psychol 17(6):853–858
Tallarini A, Zabeo A, Ferraretto A (2013) Nutritional knowledge in an Italian population of children, pre-adolescents and adolescents. Publ Health Nutr 17(3):708–714

Tarabashkina L, Quester P, Habel C (2011) Advertising literacy, peer–child communication, popular foods and children's food related behavior: mediating or non-existent effects? Obes Res Clin Pract 5(Sup 1):38

Utter J, Scragg R, Schaaf D (2006) Associations between television viewing and consumption of commonly advertised foods among New Zealand children and young adolescents. Publ Health Nutr 9(5):606–612

Venn AJ, Thomson RJ, Schmidt MD, Cleland VJ, Curry BA, Gennat HC, Dwyer T (2007) Overweight and obesity from childhood to adulthood: a follow-up of participants in the 1985 Australian Schools Health and Fitness Survey. Med J Aust 186(9):458–460

Wardle J, Guthrie C, Sanderson S, Birch L, Plomin R (2001) Food and activity preferences in children of lean and obese parents. Int J Obes 25(7):971–977

WFA (2010) WFA analysis: what next for food marketing? World Federation of Advertisers. http://www.wfanet.org/en/global-news/wfa-analysis-what-next-for-food-marketing. Accessed 13 Dec 2012

WHO (2015) Obesity and overweight. http://www.who.int/mediacentre/factsheets/fs311/en/. Accessed 8 Mar 2010

Wicks JL, Warren R, Fosu I, Wicks RH (2009) Dual-modality disclaimers, emotional appeals, and production techniques in food advertising airing during programs rated for children. J Advertising 38(4):93–105

Wiman AR, Newman LM (1989) Television advertising exposure and children's nutritional awareness. J Acad Mark Sci 17(2):179–188

Wouters EJ, Larsen JK, Kremers SP, Dagnelie PC, Geenen R (2010) Peer influence on snacking behavior in adolescence. Appetite 55:11–17

The Ethicality of Immersive Sponsorship Within a Children's Edutainment Centre

Damien Arthur

Abstract In a shift away from traditional advertising, brands are increasingly embedding themselves into children's lived experiences. Immersive brand placements within educational vehicles such schools, textbooks and edutainment centres are worthy of an ethical examination as children may find it difficult to understand their persuasive intent. This study investigates the ethicality of immersive sponsorship within a children's edutainment centre. Pre, post, and follow-up interviews were undertaken with 17 children and one of their parents who visited the heavily branded edutainment venue, Kidzania. Applying a deontological perspective, the results suggest that immersive sponsorship is inherently wrong, as children aged twelve and under are generally unable to determine the persuasive intent of the sponsoring brands. Embedded within an educational and entertaining setting, the children engaged with the brands in a very positive light, unaware of persuasive intentions and unable to apply a cognitive defence. In contrast, the vast majority of parents perceived the immersive sponsorships to be ethical. Those who applied a relativist argument saw the act as ethical in the cultural context of our contemporary and commercialised world, and specifically the city of Dubai. In contrast, those who applied the utilitarian approach argued that the act was a form of corporate social responsibility, producing a net benefit for society by helping to fund and run a realistic educational experience, and increasing the confidence of the child participants. While the opposing conclusions make it difficult to provide clear policy guidance, one recommendation is to focus on advancing the marketing literacy of children.

Keywords Immersive sponsorship · Children · Ethical perspectives · Edutainment · Persuasive intent

---

D. Arthur (✉)
Zayed University, Abu Dhabi, United Arab Emirates
e-mail: damien.arthur@zu.ac.ae

© Springer Science+Business Media Singapore 2016

C. Plewa and J. Conduit (eds.), *Making a Difference Through Marketing*,
DOI 10.1007/978-981-10-0464-3_7

Introduction

The ethicality of marketing communications directed at children has been the subject of much debate. Policy has generally focused on protecting children from the potential harm that exposure to certain types of advertising may encourage (Owen et al. 2013). The typical aim is to protect children from sexualised, frightening and violent content, and those that promote an inactive or unhealthy lifestyle. Another ethical concern regards the "fairness" of targeting children when they may not be capable of understanding the purpose of marketing communications (Garde 2011). As brands move away from traditional television advertising, they are increasingly embedding themselves into children's experiences in other ways (Linn and Golin 2006). These include brand placements within educational vehicles such as schools, textbooks and edutainment centres. When brands are embedded within an educational context, children may find it even more difficult to understand the persuasive intent of the marketing communications. The ethicality of this form of promoting to children is the focus of this chapter, specifically in the context of a children's edutainment centre.

Children's Understanding of the Persuasive Intent of Marketing Communications

Academic research has attempted to uncover the age when children become aware of the persuasive intent of television advertising (Chan 2000; Moses and Baldwin 2005; Wright et al. 2005). Determining if awareness of persuasive intent exists is important to the ethicality argument, as without it, children are unable to apply a cognitive defence. If children cannot determine the persuasive purpose of advertising, then they are being deceived and can be easily manipulated. As a result children are especially vulnerable to advertising and are in need of protection. As such, governments and regulatory bodies around the world have either banned advertising to children (e.g. Sweden), or more commonly, applied some restrictions to it (e.g. Australia and Belgium) (Oates et al. 2002).

In a seminal study of persuasive intent, Robertson and Rossiter (1974) found that an understanding of the purpose of television advertising emerges at around eight years of age, and is further refined during the analytical stage of development (between the ages of seven and eleven) (John 1999). While 'around eight' is generally supported in the literature (e.g. Chan 2001; Roedder 1981), Oates et al. (2002) found only a quarter of eight year olds, and a third of 10 year olds, were capable of identifying the persuasive intent of television advertising. Similarly, Rozendaal et al. (2010) found that while an understanding of the persuasive intent of television advertising had emerged in children by eight, by twelve it was still not equivalent to an adult's understanding. From a deontological perspective, these results imply that television advertisements targeting children of less than eight fail a moral imperative, as they are inherently deceptive. As eight to 12 year olds have generally been found to have a basic understanding of the purpose of television advertising, but are still developing the cognitive skills necessary to fully comprehend persuasive intent, television advertising aimed at them is morally questionable.

While many researchers have examined children's awareness of the persuasive intent of television advertising, very few studies have investigated the more immersive forms of marketing communications. Given that television advertising is ubiquitous and contains distinct cues that allow viewers to easily distinguish between programming and advertising, it is intuitive to assume that children would find the persuasive intent of more embedded forms of marketing communications difficult to identify. The limited research that exists supports this assertion. For example, Owen et al. (2013) found children to have a significantly more sophisticated understanding of television advertising than product placement, product licensing, program sponsorship, and advergames. Similarly, Van Reijmersdal et al. (2012) found that seven to 12 year olds had difficulties in understanding the commercial nature and intent of advergames. In a study examining the sponsorship of a theme park, Grohs et al. (2012) found a rudimentary understanding of persuasive intent emerged in the 10 year olds, which appeared to be fully developed in those aged twelve. Applying the deontological perspective once again, these more immersive forms of marketing communications are also unethical when targeting children who are not yet capable of determining persuasive intent. The research supports the notion that this occurs at a later age than for television advertising, most likely at around twelve.

While researchers have begun to investigate the age at which children can identify the persuasive intent of the more immersive forms of marketing communications, no study to date has provided an in-depth examination of the ethicality of brands immersed within an educational vehicle. In a broad 'ethics in advertising' study, Triese et al. (1994) measured perceptions of ethicality from the general public's perspective. They found their sample to be particularly concerned about advertising in public schools, far more so then toward unhealthy food commercials targeting children. Given the public concern, the positive perceptions and trust we place in educational environments, combined with children's lack of cognitive defence and the immersive nature of the brand placements, makes the practice of integrating brands within an educational vehicle worthy of ethical examination. Thus, this study investigates the ethicality of immersive sponsorship within a children's edutainment centre.

The Edutainment Centre as a Sponsorship Vehicle

The portmanteau 'edutainment' refers to the interactive pedagogy that converges learning with a fun and entertaining experience (Okan 2003). While interest in the convergence of education with entertainment has increased significantly with the explosion of new and interactive technologies (Addis 2005), over the past two decades it has become an increasingly common marketing practice, and the subject of retail studies. For example, Feenstra et al. (2015) examined how child-oriented educational workshops and events conducted in-store by retailers create active, multi-sensory, social experiences. Whereas Creighton (1994) examined how theme-park style, heavily commercialised edutainment centres provided educational experiences designed to help children become 'good consumers' through play. It is a contemporary version of the latter, Kidzania, that provides the context of the current study.

Kidzania is positioned as an informal learning environment where children learn about adult occupations and responsibilities through playing 'grown-ups' and undertaking occupational and consumer tasks in a replica city (Baker 2014). A leader in the field, the firm currently operates 16 centres in 13 countries, with 24 expected to be operating in 21 countries later this year (Marsh and Bloom 2014; Kidzania 2015a). Within the Kidzania in Dubai, the extent of the sponsorship, and the immersion and engagement of the sponsoring brands is noteworthy. To enter the fantasy metropolis children are issued Emirates tickets and then board a replica Emirates airplane. Once inside the children can learn to be a kitchen hand at McDonalds, a factory worker in the Coca-Cola bottling plant, a courier for FedEx, a chocolatier in the Kinder Chocolate factory, a dentist with the assistance of Colgate, or a Doctor with the help of Dettol. For working in their chosen professions the children receive 'KidZos', the Kidzania currency, which they can deposit in their Al Hilal bank accounts, or spend at a number of real retail outlets within Kidzania. In fact, within the Dubai Kidzania children can take on any of 70 occupational roles including television presenter, police officer, and hairdresser, and experience interactions with over 35 real world brands including Sony, Kellogg's, and Dunkin' Donuts.

Research Questions

In examining the ethicality of immersive sponsorship within a children's edutainment centre we focused on two research questions:

1. Is immersive sponsorship within a children's edutainment centre inherently unethical?
2. Do parents perceive immersive sponsorship within a children's edutainment centre as unethical?

In addressing the first research question we have primarily adopted a deontological approach, attempting to ascertain whether this form of marketing communication is inherently right or wrong based on whether the children are deceived by the brand's persuasive intent. As parents are the primary guardians of children and have a responsibility to protect them from harm, the second question aims to better understand their varying perspectives. As ethical determinations can vary depending on which ethical theory of moral philosophy is applied, deontological, relativist and utilitarian perspectives are discussed.

Methodology

As part of a larger study investigating consumer socialisation within a marketer-sponsored children's edutainment centre, pre, post, and follow-up interviews were undertaken with 17 children and one of their parents, who had never previously been to Kidzania. Pre and post interviews were conducted immediately prior to entering, and after exiting the venue, whereas the follow-up interviews took place approximately one week after the experience. While all 87 interviews were considered as data and analysed in NVIVO for the purpose of this study, the post and follow up interviews with the children were the most useful in determining an understanding of persuasive intent, whereas the pre and post interviews with the parents were most useful in determining their perceptions of ethicality.

As persuasive intent has been found to emerge at around eight for television advertising, and around twelve for more immersive forms of marketing communications, children aged between seven and twelve were recruited for this study. A demographic profile of the participants, including pseudonyms, is provided in Table 1. The author conducted pre, post and follow-up interviews with the ten children who were native English speakers and their respective parent. Student researchers who were native in Arabic conducted pre, post and follow-up interviews with the remaining children and their respective parent. To ensure the children's interviews were suitable for their cognitive capacity, Peracchio and Mita's (1991) guidelines were followed.

Table 1 Demographic profile of participants

Child	Gender	Age	Native Language	Parent
Andrew	Male	7	English	Mother of Andrew
Danielle	Female	7	English	Mother of Danielle, Amy and Lizzie
Mohammed	Male	7	Arabic	Mother of Mohammed, Layla and Saif
Moza	Female	7	Arabic	Mother of Moza and Afra
Yoosuf	Male	7	English	Father of Yoosuf
Afra	Female	8	Arabic	Mother of Moza and Afra
Declan	Male	8	English	Mother of Declan
Jen	Female	8	English	Mother of Jen
Layla	Female	8	Arabic	Mother of Mohammed, Layla and Saif
Mel	Female	8	English	Mother of Mel
Miles	Male	8	English	Mother of Miles
Noura	Female	9	Arabic	Mother of Noura
Amy	Female	10	English	Mother of Danielle, Amy and Lizzie
Brain	Male	10	English	Mother of Brian
Lizzie	Female	11	English	Mother of Danielle, Amy and Lizzie
Saif	Male	11	Arabic	Mother of Mohammed, Layla and Saif
Shaima	Female	12	Arabic	Mother of Shaima

Results and Discussion

Is Immersive Sponsorship Within a Children's Edutainment Centre Inherently Unethical?

Persuasive intent is central to the argument that immersive sponsorship within a children's edutainment centre is inherently unethical. Academics have argued that if children are unable to understand the persuasive intent of the sponsors, then the practice is unethical, as children cannot enact a cognitive defence. While it could be argued that the marketers behind the sponsoring brands within Kidzania were not intending to persuade, but performing an act of social responsibility, this is certainly not in line with Kidzania's partner seeking web page which promises 'increased sales', 'long-term ROI', 'exposure', 'brand recognition' and 'loyalty' all in the first two sentences (Kidzania 2015b). Regardless of the intent, evidence suggests that implicitly acquired affective associations through engaging with brands in a fun and exciting environment do influence behaviour (Nairn and Fine 2008). The results of the larger consumer socialisation study support this, with a 34 % shift in brand preferences toward the sponsoring brands (see Arthur and Sherman (2015) for a full analysis). Therefore, even if the intent of the sponsorship was entirely well meaning, from a deontological perspective, it is not necessarily the understanding of persuasive intent that is important, but perhaps more accurately an understanding of persuasive capability.

Putting these semantic differences aside, the analysis revealed that while the children were very aware of the many brands that were present within Kidzania, their understanding of the sponsor's intentions and the communication's ability to persuade was weak. When probed, the children overwhelmingly attributed an assistive intent to the sponsoring brands, expressing that they were there to educate and entertain them. In this way the children viewed the brand placements in a very positive light: as fun, famous and there to inform them about potential occupations. Take the following quotes for example.

> Lizzie: They were there because if you want to work in one of those brands, it's a learning experience.
>
> Danielle: To tell you what you can do when you grow up.

Only two of the 17 children identified the persuasive intent of the brand sponsors, and neither of these was phrased in a manner to suggest that the children were executing a cognitive defence. Specifically Noura stated "[The brands help us] to learn how to work, order things, and when we grow up, we can go there and be customers", and Jen said "Because they want to make the company better, so more people come, so they can get more money". Given their relatively young age (nine and eight respectively), it was interesting that these two children were the only ones who identified the persuasive intent of the sponsors. None of the older children aged between ten and twelve exhibited any understanding of persuasive intent. Upon interviewing Jen's mother it become apparent that Jen's parents had deliberately spoken to their daughter on a number of occasions about the purpose of marketing communications and the 'tricks' marketers apply. While Noura's mother didn't offer up any such explanation, the results do suggest an ability to identify the persuasive intent of sponsors within an immersive and educational setting may have more to do with education and discussions about the topic than age. It is also worth noting that the Kidzania experience did instigate a number of parent-child conversations about brands, which provided an avenue for parents to approach the topic if they felt it was appropriate.

In summary, in the children's edutainment centre investigated, 15 of the 17 children could not identify the sponsoring brands' intentions to persuade, but the vast majority could identify and understand the parallel educational and entertainment objectives. While all of the children were aware of the existence of sponsoring brands, their deep immersion into the educational and entertaining setting likely masked their persuasive capability and intent. As such, immersive sponsorship within a children's edutainment centre is inherently unethical in that children are unaware of the persuasive intent of the sponsors and are being easily manipulated, as they are incapable of enabling a cognitive defence. While the harm caused by the sponsoring brands is by no means life threatening, the act itself should be considered as morally wrong.

Do Parents Perceive Immersive Sponsorship Within a Children's Edutainment Centre as Unethical?

The parents' initial perceptions of Kidzania were generally in line with the firm's positioning. They perceived it as an interactive learning centre where their children would socialise while learning about and playing professions. Attitudes toward the sponsorship within the centre were rarely mentioned in the pre-interviews, and after probing were for the most part generic 'wait and see' statements. Upon leaving the centre, having been exposed to the brand sponsorships, their attitudes became increasingly specific and elaborate.

In contrast to our conclusion above where we found immersive sponsorship within a children's edutainment centre to be inherently unethical, only one of the twelve parents adopted this particular deontological view. This parent, Mel's mother, felt it was deceptive of the brands to promote the educational nature of the centre, when a persuasive intent was their primary purpose.

> Mel's Mother: I don't like it in general… I don't like this pushing of big brands and trying to make it look like it is educational… [They're] just trying to brand it as educational, but actually what you have is just big brands pushing their own products.

Upon leaving the centre another parent was 'slightly cynical' of the sponsorship, and a third reported being shocked by the 'in your face' nature of the branded environment. However, neither of these attitudes led to a negative ethical evaluation. There was however one parent who provided an unethical evaluation of a single component of the Kidzania experience. For Lizzie's mother, the exclusive inclusion of 'junk food' sponsors with no healthy alternatives was perceived as intrinsically unethical. Indeed, having children interact with brands that promote an unhealthy lifestyle, and providing no other food alternatives is morally wrong from a number of perspectives.

Interestingly, none of the parents identified the removal of the children from them as they undertook their various occupational roles and interacted with the brands as an ethical cause for concern. Depending on the activity, parents could generally look in on the children through a window to see what they were doing, but without being up close they couldn't hear or see the brand sponsored information that was being communicated.

It is perhaps less surprising, but still worth noting, that none of the parents identified the extremely structured play environment as a cause for concern. This line of moral reasoning has been argued by Linn (2013) and suggests the constant commercial pressures that children are exposed to inhibit them from creative play, an act essential to the development of creativity. Directed play in the form of electronic media, instructions, kits and in this case, occupational and consumer roles where children are shown only a single way to complete the task, hinders experimentation, inventiveness and creative problem solving. While no parents identified the issue, whether edutainment centres that focus on introducing and developing consumer and occupational roles in children are in effect taking away some of their childhood innocence, is worthy of consideration.

The vast majority of parents perceived the immersive sponsorship within the edutainment centre to be either entirely, or for the most part, ethical. Those who adopted the latter perspective generally applied a relativist lens. According to theory of relativism, no universal rules exist, and our normative beliefs are a function of our culture. Four of the parents applied this reasoning as to why they were ok with the brands immersing themselves in an educational environment and engaging with their children. Take the following quotes for example.

> Yoosuf's father: I am in Dubai now. I kind of expect that kind of thing. It doesn't bother me. It's just there. It's there in the background. It doesn't bother me.

> Brian's mother: You see them everywhere anyway, so they're just getting their marketing inside there… It's not a concern at all.

The remaining parents generally adopted a utilitarian perspective as to why the sponsorships were ethical. With utilitarian ethics, the 'end justifies the means', and in this case, the positive value the sponsors created by helping to fund an engaging educational facility was perceived to outweigh the negative act and potential negative consequences. The parents identified positive value as created in many different ways, the obvious being the education provided by the centre to their children. Specifically, they discussed how their children learnt about the world of work, the diversity of occupations, different occupational roles, local organisations, and financial literacy. A less obvious but even more frequently mentioned benefit to the children was the increase in confidence gained from speaking to a variety of strangers and performing a number of tasks they had never previously conducted.

Regardless of where they perceived the value to be gained, the majority of parents felt the brands were providing an act of corporate social responsibility. The parents rarely identified the persuasive intent of the brands; rather they perceived their purpose to not only help fund and provide an educational experience, but to do so in a more realistic manner than would otherwise be possible. Gratitude was often expressed in that the experience and venue would not be of the same standard without the realism and financial support that the sponsoring brands provided. Take the following quotes for example.

> Miles' Mother: I actually quite like it, because I'm really big into social responsibility, I really think that it's a good thing. Now, whether it's subliminal marketing of their brand, which inevitably it would be, the fact that they're socially responsible enough to have a facility that people rave about in a more shopping sort of way, that kids can interact with and learn about, and do. For me, it's just fantastic! I think that, because it takes a lot of money and effort to set something like this up… whoever is behind it, they're companies that I'm more likely to shop with because of the fact that they care about education.

> Declan's Mother: Having been to a similar place in Leeds, and obviously nothing was branded there, it's interesting, because I think the setup wasn't as good. I mean, here, I thought the setup was very good, everything worked. Whereas when we went to the one in Leeds, things didn't work, things had fallen off, and, again, the money wasn't obviously being put into it, whereas here everything is sort of spick and span and ready to go.

Finally, it is worth mentioning that the utilitarian argument, that such centres play an essential economic function in society by matching needs and wants in the community and socialising children as consumers to sustain retail expenditure, was never mentioned.

Conclusion

The results reveal that immersive sponsorship within a children's edutainment centre is inherently unethical. A deontological examination of the moral worth of the practice found the vast majority of seven to 12 year olds did not understand the persuasive intent of the sponsorships. Embedded within an educational and highly entertaining setting, the children engaged and interacted with the brands in a very positive light, unaware of their persuasive capabilities and unable to apply a cognitive defence. Based on this moral interpretation, policy makers should enact strict rules and regulations on immersive marketing communications targeted at children, particularly those that are embedded within educational vehicles, such as schools, textbooks and edutainment centres. Adopting a minimum age requirement of at least twelve for when immersive marketing campaigns can target children, and educating children who are approaching this age about the persuasive intent of advertisers so that they can apply a cognitive defence, seems appropriate.

In contrast, the vast majority of parents did not apply this deontological perspective and instead viewed the immersive sponsorship within a children's edutainment centre as ethical. These parents generally adopted either a relativist or utilitarian view. The relativists perceived immersive sponsorship targeting children as ethical in the cultural context of our contemporary and commercialised world, and specifically within the city of Dubai. In contrast, those who applied the utilitarian approach to their ethical reasoning argued that the edutainment centre was a form of corporate social responsibility, producing a net benefit for society by helping to fund and run an educational experience, by providing a degree of realism to that experience, and by building confidence within the children. In stark juxtaposition to the earlier deontological conclusion, the parents' application of utilitarian and relativist theory reversed the moral outcome. These opposing views make it difficult to provide clear guidance to policy makers. However, if marketing communications targeting children continue to become increasingly immersive, one recommendation to minimise the potential harm would be to launch a program with the help of teachers and parents to advance the marketing literacy of children.

While the findings presented in this chapter further our understanding of the ethicality of immersive sponsorship within a children's edutainment centre, they are subject to certain limitations. First, while parents who had never previously been to Kidzania were recruited for the study, it is likely that parents who are morally opposed to sponsored edutainment centres, and were aware of the existence of brands within Kidzania, would have chosen not to subject their children to the experience, and would have been unmoved by the incentive of free admission. Second, the standard limitations of qualitative research do apply, and therefore to better assist policy makers, future studies should attempt to determine the age at which children generally become aware of the persuasive intent of immersive sponsorship by analysing a larger sample of children inclusive of teens.

References

Addis M (2005) New technologies and cultural consumption-edutainment is born! Eur J Mark 39 (7/8):729–736

Arthur D, Sherman C (2015) Consumer socialisation in a marketer-sponsored edutainment centre. In: 2nd international colloquium on kids and retailing, Budapest, Hungary, June 2015

Baker F (2014) Reflections on an informal learning environment with invocations for classroom learning in Dubai, the United Arab Emirates. Int J Adolesc Youth 19(1):50–66

Chan K (2000) Hong Kong children's understanding of television advertising. J Mark Commun 6(1):37–52

Chan K (2001) Children's perceived truthfulness of television advertising and parental influence: A Hong Kong study. Adv Consum Res 28:207–212

Creighton MR (1994) Edutaining children: Consumer and gender socialization in japanese marketing. Ethnology 33(1):35–52

Feenstra F, Muzellec L, de Faultrier B, Boulay J (2015) Edutainment experiences for children in retail stores, from a child's perspective. J Retail Consum Serv 26:47–56

Garde A (2011) Advertising regulation and the protection of children-consumers in the european union: In the best interests of… commercial operators? Int J Child Rights 19(3):523–45

Grohs R, Wagner U, Steiner R (2012) An investigation of children's ability to identify sponsors and understand sponsorship intentions. Psychol Mark 29(11):907–917

John DR (1999) Consumer socialization of children: A retrospective look at twenty-five years of research. J Consum Res 26(3):183–213

Kidzania (2015a) Kidzania: Current locations. http://www.kidzania.com/current-parks.php. Accessed 18 Mar 2015

Kidzania (2015b) Why partner with us http://www.kidzania.ae/en/Partnership/WhyPartnerwithUs.aspx. Accessed 2 Sept 2015

Linn S (2013) The case for make believe: Saving play in a commercialized world, The New Press

Linn S, Golin J (2006) Beyond commercials: How food marketers target children Loy. LAL Rev 39:13

Marsh S, Bloom M (2014) The KidZania story: Great data, rich experience and customer loyalty. J Brand Strategy 2(4):322–327

Moses LJ, Baldwin DA (2005) What can the study of cognitive development reveal about children's ability to appreciate and cope with advertising? J Public Policy Mark 24(2):186–201

Nairn A, Fine C (2008) Who's messing with my mind? The implications of dual-process models for the ethics of advertising to children. Int J Advertising 27(3):447–470

Oates C, Blades M, Gunter B (2002) Children and television advertising: When do they understand persuasive intent? J Consum Behav 1(3):238–245

Okan Z (2003) Edutainment: is learning at risk? Br J Education Tech 34(3):255–264

Owen L, Lewis C, Auty S, Buijzen M (2013) Is children's understanding of nontraditional advertising comparable to their understanding of television advertising? J Public Policy Mark 32(2):195–206

Peracchio LA, Mita C (1991) Designing research to assess children's comprehension of marketing messages. Adv Consum Res 18:23

Robertson TS, Rossiter JR (1974) Children and commercial persuasion: An attribution theory analysis. J Consum Res 1(1):13–20

Roedder DL (1981) Age differences in children's responses to television advertising: An information-processing approach. J Consum Res 8(2):144–153

Rozendaal E, Buijzen M, Valkenburg P (2010) Comparing children's and adults' cognitive advertising competences in the Netherlands. J Child Media 4(1):77–89

Treise D, Weigold MF, Conna J, Garrison H (1994) Ethics in advertising: Ideological correlates of consumer perception. J Advertising 23(3):59–69

Van Reijmersdal EA, Rozendaal E, Buijzen M (2012) Effects of prominence, involvement, and persuasion knowledge on children's cognitive and affective responses to advergames. J Interact Mark 26(1):33–42

Wright P, Friestad M, Boush DM (2005) The development of marketplace persuasion knowledge in children, adolescents, and young adults. J Public Policy Mark 24(2):222–233

Emotional Advertising to Attenuate Compulsive Consumption: Qualitative Insights from Gamblers

Svetlana De Vos, Roberta Crouch and Jasmina Ilicic

Abstract Compulsive consumption behaviours such as smoking, drinking, and gambling are serious public health concerns that impact consumers globally. Research examining emotional advertising appeals that specifically induce help-seeking in the problem gambling context remains limited. A qualitative study through the use of focus groups was conducted to inductively explore gamblers' perceptions of effective health messages, investigating how, why, and which emotional advertising appeals would best impact on their decision to seek help. Participants proposed that positive, negative, and mixed emotional appeals can be utilised to most effectively communicate with gamblers. In addition, response efficacy (the extent people believe a recommended response effectively deters or alleviates a health threat), self-accountability (an assessment of the degree to which oneself is responsible for the situation), and perceived benefits (beliefs about the positive outcomes associated with help-seeking behaviour) are also highlighted as important message elements. This study should serve as a starting point to develop effective health messages in compulsive consumption contexts, including gambling.

Keywords Emotional appeals · Gambling · Self-accountability · Response efficacy · Perceived benefits · Help-seeking

S. De Vos (✉) · R. Crouch
School of Marketing and Management, The University of Adelaide, Adelaide, Australia
e-mail: svetlana.devos@adelaide.edu.au

R. Crouch
e-mail: Roberta.crouch@adelaide.edu.au

R. Crouch
School of Wine and Spirits, Groupe ESC Dijon Bourgogne, Dijon, France

J. Ilicic
Monash Business School, Monash University, Melbourne, Australia
e-mail: jasmina.ilicic@monash.edu

© Springer Science+Business Media Singapore 2016

C. Plewa and J. Conduit (eds.), *Making a Difference Through Marketing*,
DOI 10.1007/978-981-10-0464-3_8

Introduction

The negative impact of critical public health issues on individuals and societies challenges social marketing and public health professionals for novel communication strategies to address these concerns. Problem gambling has emerged as a serious public health issue (Adams et al. 2009). Some scholars argue that the liberalisation of the gaming industry from a welfare economic perspective (Fong et al. 2011; Livingstone and Adams 2011) together with the widespread use of the Internet for gambling, contributes to the global rise of problem gambling among young individuals and adults (King et al. 2010; Kairouz et al. 2012).

A common feature among these seemingly different public health concerns (e.g. gambling, smoking, alcohol abuse) is their compulsive nature. As such, afflicted consumers have an overriding, uncontrollable, chronic, and repetitive craving to consume the product/service (Hirschman 1992). Hodgins and El-Guebaly (2000) maintain that compulsive consumption problems (e.g. problem gambling) are best addressed through specialised services, such as psychological counseling and medical support. Therefore, it is essential for health messages to induce help-seeking attitudes and behaviours among afflicted consumers.

Relative to other compulsive consumption contexts, such as smoking or alcohol drinking, less is known about effective communication strategies to encourage help-seeking among gamblers (Calderwood and Wellington 2013). This qualitative study aims to uncover the emotional content and important associated message characteristics that problem gamblers perceive as effective emotional advertising appeals in health messages. Five focus groups were conducted in an inductive manner to reveal which emotional advertising appeal is efficient to boost help-seeking among problem gamblers. The appeal of focus groups for social marketing researchers lies in the potential for group interaction to provide researchers with data that demonstrates participants' responses and opinions about the phenomenon of interest (Stewart et al. 2007). Furthermore, focus groups may be effectively utilised to study sensitive topics in different contexts (Farquhar and Das 1999; Bagozzi et al. 2013), including problem gambling (Calderwood and Wellington 2013).

A recent study by Gainsbury et al. (2014) found few problem gamblers seek professional help, suggesting low awareness of professional help services. To address this gap, this research explored the potential benefits of various emotional appeals on help-seeking intentions among Australian at-risk gamblers and offers practical findings for social marketers and public health professionals working in the gambling context.

Literature Review and Research Questions

Emotions in Advertising

Emotion-based persuasion has been used in the social and health-related context with the aim to influence individual judgements, attitudes, and behaviours. Emotions not only energise and direct behaviour (Lazarus 1991), but are also known to enhance an individual's ability to engage in meaningful deliberation (Marcus et al. 2011).

Previous research has shown evidence to suggest that advertisements portraying negative emotions were better remembered and recalled more frequently in comparison to the ads showing warm, or other positive feelings, or no emotional content (Snipes et al. 1999). More recent studies claim that negative emotions, such as fear, act as a motivator to engage in intensive and thoughtful ad message processing (de Hoog et al. 2007). Fear facilitates attention to the message, which enables individuals to capture information helpful to evaluate the threat (Ordoñana et al. 2009). Other scholars have identified that positive emotions expand the attention scope and thought-action of an individual (Fredrickson and Branigan 2005), and enhance interaction with cognitive control, a key part of which is the ability to hold and update behaviourally relevant information with a facilitating effect on working memory maintenance and processing of information (Lindström and Bohlin 2011). Other empirical evidence also suggests that individuals experiencing positive emotions are flexible, creative, and efficient in their information processing and, therefore, positive affect generates more elaborative networks of association in memory (Lee and Sternthal 1999; Isen 2003). Negative, and to a lesser extend positive, emotions have been utilised in social marketing campaigns in various compulsive consumption contexts.

Emotional Appeals in Consumption Contexts

Negative emotions (e.g. fear, guilt, shame) are often used in preventive social marketing communications to induce the audience to pay greater attention to the problem issues at hand and prompt respondents to avoid harms (Brennan and Binney 2010). However, the persuasive effectiveness of negative emotional appeals remains inconclusive (Peters et al. 2012). For example, despite the fact that negative emotional appeals, such as fear, can be an effective communication strategy (Terblanhe-Smit and Terblanche 2010), previous research has also raised questions of fear appeal ethicality (Arthur and Quester 2003; Williams 2011; Racela and Thoumrungroje 2012), claiming that fear appeals boost chronic anxiety in vulnerable audience members such as children, the elderly, the infirm, and addicts (Hastings et al. 2004). Several authors suggest that individuals afflicted with smoking (Brown and Smith 2007; Diehr et al. 2011) or excessive drinking (Brown and Locker 2009; Lennon and Rentfro 2010) tend to inhibit processing of fear appeals. Furthermore, in line with social neurocognitive evidence (Kessels et al. 2010), threatening graphical information placed on cigarette packaging causes disengagement from message processing among smokers. Similarly, Gallopel-Morvan et al. (2011) reported that fear-eliciting health warnings on cigarette packaging provoked avoidance reactions and needed to be combined with self-efficacy (the strength of one's belief in one's own ability to reach goals) and action cues (taking action to reach the goal) for cessation support. Likewise, Puhl et al. (2013) identified that messages that imply personal responsibility and blame for excess weight (e.g. 'the more you gain, the more you have to lose', or 'chubby kids may not outlive their parents') received more negative/less positive ratings and were considered as stigmatising among individuals.

On the contrary, Fishbein et al. (2002), in a study testing 30 anti-drug ads, found that youth perceptions of ad effectiveness was significantly positively associated with negative emotion, realism, and knowledge accumulation, and was negatively associated with positive emotion. Furthermore, Morales et al. (2012) reported that fear appeals co-elicited with disgust prompted better compliance with the recommendations enclosed in the message. The authors maintained that immediate avoidance action tendencies of disgust co-activated with a fear appeal effectively altered first-time methamphetamine use among teenagers. Block (2005) reported that higher levels of guilt led to greater persuasion in a drink-driving context, based on guilt-induced self-responsibility for the risk consequences. Jäger and Eisend (2013) examined the efficacy of fear appeals in comparison to humorous social marketing advertising for individuals who differed in their prior attitude towards safe driving, finding that the advertisements with humorous elements were more effective for individuals with less favourable prior attitudes towards save driving behaviour. However, fear appeals tend to enhance safe driving behavioural intentions for recipients who have more favourable prior attitudes towards save driving.

Similar empirical findings in the gambling context reported by Munoz et al. (2010) indicate that warnings had to be threatening to increase cognitive responses which, in turn, affected attitude change towards help-seeking behaviour. The authors maintain that, in a sample of 258 Canadian gamblers, fear caused by threatening warnings was efficient in the case of attitude change and professional help-seeking. Furthermore, Muñoz et al. (2013) found that the presence of a graphic enhanced both cognitive appraisal and fear, and had positive effects on the depth of information processing in 103 gambling participants. In particular, graphic content combined with family disruptions was effective for changing attitudes and complying with the gambling warning. However, the effectiveness of appeals based on negative emotions in the gambling context is inconclusive. For example, Calderwood and Wellington (2013) reported qualitative findings on the opinions of Canadian problem gamblers ($\underline{n}$ = 17) and their family members (n = 14) in developing billboards to promote a local problem gambling service. Participants identified issues such as guilt and shame as emotions that would turn them off of the advertisement, and a fear of the advertisement leading to a scam or hoax.

Research Questions

Perceptions, beliefs, and opinions of the target population allow for the investigation of the determinants of risk behaviour and permit evaluation of the effectiveness of various communication strategies to alter these determinants (Brownson et al. 2006). Carter et al. (2011) argued that disregarding participants' perceptions, opinions, and beliefs may result in message misinterpretation and non-compliance. Identifying the right emotional themes is crucial to reach the desired target audiences in order to create attitudinal and behavioural change (Andreasen 2006), and the current exploratory research seeks to investigate gamblers perceptions of what constitutes effective emotional advertising. In particular, this qualitative study addresses the following questions: Which emotional advertising would best motivate help-seeking attitudes and intentions in an at-risk population (i.e. moderate risk or problem gamblers)? Which specific message elements should be highlighted in communications?

Method

Sampling Procedure

Five focus groups were conducted with self-reported problem gamblers (age range from 20 to 65 years old) within the metropolitan area of Adelaide, South Australia. A convenience sample, consisting of 43 participants, was drawn from the population, which is suitable for exploratory research (Malhotra and Birks 2007). An average sample size of 9 participants per focus group was drawn, totalling 43 participants (24 men, 16 women). All participants reported gambling on video lottery terminals, slot machines, or video poker machines on a weekly or daily basis. The Canadian Problem Gambling Index (CPGI) (Ferris and Wynne 2001) was used in order to determine problem gambling prevalence rates amongst the recruited participants. Participants scoring 3–27 points (i.e., moderate and problem gamblers) on the CPGI were admitted to the focus groups. Data collection was conducted until saturation was reached (Patton 2002). The digital recordings were transcribed verbatim by the researchers. A financial incentive (gift card) was offered to each participant. All participation was voluntary and each participant was assured anonymity. The names of the participants were omitted.

Prior to conducting the focus groups, a semi-structured discussion guide was developed. Issues raised in the discussion guide permitted insight into the attitudes, beliefs, and feelings towards social marketing advertising campaigns in various compulsive consumption contexts, including gambling. Several questions prompted gamblers to specifically outline the message content and message characteristics as being the most effective in communicating the risk associated with excessive gambling and encouraging help-seeking behaviour. A digital recording device was used to audiotape all focus group discussions. The focus groups consisted of two parts. Part 1 followed a semi-structured discussion arising from participants recalling their exposure to social marketing campaigns in the past or present, which impacted them emotionally. Participants were prompted to give examples of such campaigns. Next, a series of print advertising stimuli in various social marketing contexts, including gambling, were shown to participants. Participants were asked to provide their immediate feelings and reactions toward each advertisement, and were prompted to explain their reaction towards specific elements within the message that turned individuals in or out of message processing. During the second part, participants were encouraged to imagine and describe their own advertisements in the gambling context, and discuss message features that they consider important to communicate.

Research Approach: Thematic Analysis

A comprehensive analysis of focus group discussions was conducted using thematic analysis (Boyatzis 1998). Thematic analysis is the process of identifying patterns, or themes, within qualitative data, and is considered a flexible, accessible, and widely-used method of qualitative data analysis (Braun and Clarke 2006). Several steps of inductive coding were performed to identify emerging themes. First, open coding of raw text was used to find general themes evolving within the content (Thomas 2006). Next, categories were created defining the emerging themes. Finally, a selective coding system was used to narrow the themes. The researchers compared notes relevant to the themes to confirm inter-coder reliability.

Findings

Perception of Gambling Among Participants

During the focus groups participants spontaneously expressed their feelings in regards to their own gambling. Specifically, their gambling was referred to as "greed-rooted", or perceived by some participants as a "weakness" or a "costly pleasure". Several participants reported feelings of "total loss and desperation," "feeling sick, both physically and emotionally" or "lonely, deserted, and isolated" as the result of their gambling activities.

> It is an emotional thing [gambling], you know. When I am angry I feel like gambling. When I am lonely I feel like gambling. It's the habituation of it. Terrible things. I can gamble because I am happy. I am happy, so I will throw the money into this machine (Female, 53 years old).

Participants acknowledged that excessive gambling activities prevented them from "seeing and living real life, which goes beyond gambling." Two participants mentioned that they tend to personalise their relationship with the video lottery terminal; attributing some "human qualities to the machine, which kind of talks to you when you feel isolated and lonely." One participant in particular reported "feeling safe in a funny and weird way" while interacting with the video terminal. Another participant stated that problem gamblers exhibit a "different psychology", characterised by focusing on and prioritising gambling, and "being absorbed" into gambling activity.

> You become very internal; you become very focused on what you are doing with the pokies. Your family does not exist, your life does not exist, and the only thing which exists to you is the "pokies" (Female, 54 years old).

In line with previous qualitative research, participants utilise excessive gambling as means to moderate emotional discomfort (Hills et al. 2001); an attempt to regulate or alleviate their emotions (mostly negative) resulting from various life events. Life events ranged from "death in the family," "empty nest syndrome and disconnection with the children," to "accidental gambling" when participants unexpectedly won some large amounts of money in a casino and felt elated to continue gambling. Nevertheless, increased emotional and financial costs of their gambling intensified their attempts for behavioural change. These findings parallel the notion that negative emotions are among the primary motives for behaviour change among problem gamblers (Hodgins and El-Guebaly 2000).

Recalled Social Marketing Campaigns

Participants equally recalled social advertising campaigns in relation to drinking and driving, tobacco/smoking prevention, and binge eating/obesity. Some participants perceived that majority of the recalled social marketing campaigns used positive emotional messages, advocating for help-seeking behaviours in the context where people have less control over the situation (e.g. a context such as eating disorders). The top three most powerful emotions associated with these ads were fun, hope, and feeling inspired. Participants recalled that mostly negative emotional content was presented in social advertising, portraying contexts such as smoking, binge drinking, and drink-driving. The top three most powerful emotions associated with these ads were fear, guilt, and disgust. Additionally, anger, loss, sadness, rage, and shame were mentioned.

The opinions among participants were polarised as to whether negative emotional content is an appropriate strategy for social marketing advertising. Some participants strongly supported the use of negative emotions in the smoking and drink-driving contexts, whereas others were against it. Supportive participants favoured negative emotional content, claiming that negative emotions heighten individual or societal awareness of behavioural risks and their consequences.

> I still cannot get rid of a scene out of my head where the ad showed a guy coughing up blood and his wife and kids in the kitchen and he coughs that blood. It impacted me personally. I used to be a smoker and I decided to quit (Female, 34 years old).

Data from this study supports the notion proposed by LaTour and Rotfeld (1997) that responses to negative emotional content, and fear appeals in particular, cannot be generalised across health contexts, as participants react differently to health and/or social marketing campaigns based on personal relevance. For example, one participant mentioned that she was persuaded by fear appeals she recalled in a texting and driving context, however, she engaged in such behaviours infrequently. Being a smoker, she articulated some degree of fatalism in her response toward recalled anti-smoking fear and described it as "unconvincing" and "not impactful".

> These fear ads or graphic warnings on cigarette packs do not make any impact on me because if I decided to smoke and die because of it- so be it. I have seen death - no impact on me (Female, 34 years old).

Other participants expressed preferences for positive emotional content in social marketing advertisements they recalled. Participants debated on the effectiveness of a recalled anti-smoking ad, where the physical and financial benefits of quitting smoking were outlined. One participant mentioned that such information evoked "excitement" and "inspiration", and was considered "persuasive", boosting her "power to achieve". For another participant such ads defined the "reasons for change". However, some participants, who were smokers, did not perceive the benefits of quitting smoking outlined in the ad as immediately motivational, but admitted that knowing the various benefits was reassuring.

Negative Emotional Advertising in the Gambling Context

Each participant was prompted to imagine and describe his/her own health message in the gambling context. Several participants proposed to design advertising stimuli based on negative emotions. Several participants, of both genders, advocated employing negative emotional appeals, which heighten gambler responsibility for their own risky behaviour and emphasise how excessive gambling affects their lives (see Table 1).

Some participants mentioned that threats such as separation, divorce, loss of rights as a parent, threats of losing property, and significant financial debt may elicit negative emotions (i.e. fear, sadness) and prompt help-seeking action. Notably, participants strongly opposed shock tactics or the use of extreme fear appeals, as they believed that they offer "a wrong way out" or can "tip somebody over the edge". Rage and anger would be evoked in response to the shocking message prompting gamblers to dismiss help-seeking information and ultimately disengage from the message processing.

Table 1 Examples of negative emotional advertising scenarios

Age and gender of participants	Examples of proposed scenario
Female, in her 50s	You can win big but you lose more [when you gamble]. Gambling is like a trap-you cannot get out anymore. Venues are like fly traps in my advertisement. Do not get trapped!
Male, in his 20s	Money, family, house, and everything in one corner. On the opposite side the guy is having a night out in a casino and gambles. The next day he watches as the car leaves and you see his wife and kids left. Combine all the threats together by showing how much there is to lose. That night in a casino cost this guy his family life
Female, in her 60s	I would use negative emotions; isolation, loneliness, and sort of that. For me personally, gambling is a very isolating thing, it's not social, because I do the "pokie thing."
Male, in his 30s	In my ad I will be trying to get people saying that there is more at stake here than me; there is a relationship and family, whatever, so I can relate to this. Issue is bigger than just me. It's bigger than me and what I am doing. Think about the other people that you are affecting. That's how I see it. Show more of the consequences of what you are doing. If you are doing problem gambling it would lead to something negative. Think about people external to you that may be affected by your gambling. It makes you feel responsible for the situation."
Male, in his 60s	I think it [my advertisement] should be as hard as it can possibly be to get the bloke [man] to face the reality and the problems he caused. I have got to see some sort of a picture of a woman with children lining up at some charitable organisation, whether it is for food or clothing, and the person who actually caused this sort of problems feels as guilty as hell. It can be in other fields too, not only gambling. When you cause grief to your family, I do not think it can get lower than that, even though it was not necessarily meant to do when you are gambling, but at the end of the day it's is exactly what the end result is

Positive Emotional Advertising and Focus on the Gambler

Participants argued that behaviour change messages evoking negative emotions, such as guilt, fear, or shame, would not motivate gamblers to seek help. Instead, these negative emotions are perceived as stigmatizing individuals and psychologically barring them from help-seeking.

> Guilt evoked in the ad crashes you, actually. It is very strong. For a gambler, it is really, really strong. It hits you. It can also lead you down to the pokies especially for those who are tittering or have not gotten themselves under control. They just gone through that, they just lost everything and with that slap in their face, bang, they will be back to the machine. Guilt puts a really negative blame on the gambler. Gamblers have a disease, they need help, they do not need ridicule, they do not need to be put down, they do not need to be seen as an ogre in society or within a family or something like that. That negative ad stigmatises you (Female, 57 years old).

These participants proposed to use a strategically different approach in emotional advertising. They suggested that utilising positive emotions such as hope, fun, love, optimism, and focusing on the gambler themselves, is a better social marketing approach in the gambling context. One participant strongly emphasised to focus attention in advertisements on the affected person (e.g. the gambler), instead of concentrating on others (e.g. family). The same participant explained that communications should be highlighting the changes that gamblers will undergo after seeking help and rehabilitation leading to desirable consequences and the positive impact on significant others. Most importantly, the participant stated that the change has to start from the gambler himself/herself. The motivation to change risky behaviour would be encouraged by eliciting positive emotions in the message, with a strong emphasis on hope and opportunities that a gambling-free life would bring (see Table 2.).

Importantly, the participants suggested that it is crucial to design a message that boosts the gambler's self-worth, self-esteem, and offers an opportunity to search for a new identity as a result of positive change. The meaningful benefits resulting from help-seeking behaviour included "coming back to life", "family reunion", "re-connection with children and closed ones", "start of work", "changed lifestyle with the exploration of positive dimensions in life", "acquired self-worth and self-esteem", "meeting new people with positive ideas." One participant highlighted the importance of a "second chance in life to be lived with honesty and integrity".

Mixed Emotional Advertising

By constructing their own creative advertisements, other participants suggested indirectly that a combination of both negative and positive emotions might condition participants to pay attention to the stimuli. These participants argued that help-seeking would be motivated by a personal growth prospective which, in turn, evokes positive emotions. One scenario reflects a mixed emotional format, in which negative emotions are evoked by the threat appraisal and, combined with positive emotions, encourages growth and the possibility of achievement as a counterweight to gambling. The participant in that scenario used fear provoking information communicated through the loss of control and developing a gambling addiction (*tittering and slipping down the steep and slippery slope*) and the hardship of recovery (*hard to get back*) at the beginning of her message. However, she also included positive emotional content incorporated into the message statement, which may evoke hope, eagerness, and determination to resist the problem (*Build yourself from here! Life has hope! You are worthwhile!*) and focused on personal benefits arising from action. She enforced the message with meaningful dreams and achievements as a counterweight to the gambling, and implied that gamblers can achieve in themselves (*Your dreams and achievements now mean more than a press of a button!*). Another participant provided her personal life example of how a

Table 2 Examples of positive emotional advertisings scenarios

Age and gender of participants	Examples of proposed scenario
Female, in her 50s	You are trying to uplift, not to put down, not to make feel guilty, not make to think about the damage you have done, not the lies you have told, not to think about the deceit you have undergone to make the money to gamble. Instead of other people you have to have a gambler there [in the social advertisement]. The gambler is the centre: to give the gambler hope, to give the gambler the positive affect that they can find their life, their self-esteem. Because using others uses a guilt factor to make a connotation on a gambler. They have enough negative connotations to actually deal with. They have a lot of negativity in their life. Focus has to come that they are worthwhile and they are positive. In my ad I would probably say: "Life is more that the clink of a coin." When we are sitting behind these machines, our life is that clink of a coin. Alright, we are looking for a way out of that life at times because we do not see anything beyond that click of a coin. So in my ad it would be written: "Your life, your self-worth that is more important than that clink of that coin. Explore what your life could be! My self-worth has gone up and I am more than that "poker" machine!"
Female, in her 30s	Meeting someone that has things similar to you is amazing. That is going to help me. Togetherness. It feels inspiring and exciting. Somewhere, there are people like me and we have the same little habits. Advertise that getting help will be fun and you meet other people similar to you
Male, in his 50s	This is all [negative emotional content] "ohhh you have gone too far!" Can you come back from there? Maybe! When you are in the zone [excessive gambling], you can think about coming back to life. "Come back from the dark side into the light!"—that should be in the message

mixed emotional experience motivated her to reassess her gambling behaviour and to initiate behavioural change.

> One of the turning points for me in deciding to give up gambling, was that my counsellor put all the bad things that I was doing (gambling, drinking) on my route to destruction on the board and on the other side of the board we worked out what my life would look like without doing that, if I changed. You know, if I kept going the way I was - suicidal and the rest of it - that would probably be the end of it [life]. But on the other side of the white board we started to talk about things like connecting back to my children, being a worthwhile person, thinking about working again, all those sort of things. The thing that happened to me in my journey was that I lost my identity, that I lost the person I was. Now, I have come through it all, I have a new identity, and it's very, very clear to me that I lost it to my addictions. These things written on that board, made me think. Slowly seeing that sort of hope, things that I wanted to do in a positive way, because I was lost, totally lost, made the difference (Female, 64 years old).

Such qualitative findings from the current study suggest that mixing negative and positive emotions are considered to be a credible communication approach by some at-risk gamblers. This parallels the notion from positive psychology research, which suggests that positive and negative emotions co-activated simultaneously allows individuals to make sense of stressors, and gain mastery over future stressors, stimulating information processing, and helping them to transcend traumatic experiences (Larsen et al. 2003). Theory, such as the Heuristic Systematic Model, supports the notion that a feeling of ambivalence, created by the experience of conflicting emotions (i.e., mixed emotions or simultaneously evoked positive and negative emotions) may prompt more effortful information processing (Chaiken et al. 1989). Such theory stipulates that ambivalence can decrease attitude confidence to a level below the sufficiency threshold (Chaiken et al. 1989). This, in turn, generates motivation for systematic processing due to the consumer's need to preserve a desired level of attitude confidence (Chaiken et al. 1989). Recent empirical evidence confirms that participants who feel ambivalent tend to process information systematically when exposed to advertising in an obesity and junk food consumption context (Yan 2014). Similarly, ambivalence positively influenced the perceptions of message effectiveness in an anti-smoking context, through affective processing of the message (Xiaoquan and Xiaomei 2008).

Important Message Elements

Several participants highlighted the role of help-seeking action steps which they would include in their message. The message cues and action steps incorporated in their own advertising campaigns included information on readily-available specialised help executed professionally, anonymously, and non-judgementally. Participants acknowledged that in the gambling context, professional help is an essential component of recovery and provides an opportunity for treatment in a hospitable and supportive environment. Without well-pronounced action steps, the advertisement would leave participants either with anxiety, non-resolution, or both.

> Not many people could self-diagnose when they are truly in that critical moment. Try to make person on the other side feel- "Hey, no judgment! This is where you get help when you are ready. This is what you do. Did you know that is a treatable condition? These are your options." Show them-go there, it's anonymous. Hey, do not wait till it's too late-go there, and seek some help (Male, 28 years old).
>
> You cannot change this [problem gambling] without help, you cannot do it alone. You have to get yourself into an environment that is stabilising and supportive and it's not always family, because they are very hurt. You have to inform in the ads where they [target population] can go and seek help because they cannot do that [recover or stop gambling] on they own (Male, 45 years old).

Two participants mentioned that at risk gamblers may be reluctant to seek help and may feel intimidated by the social stigma attached to their problem-gambling status. In order to prompt consumers to enquire into information about specialised services, the health message should normalise help-seeking. One way of normalising help-seeking is to outline in the message that the initiative to seek-professional help comes from the gamblers themselves. Personalised decisions to "get myself out of gambling" emphasises the individual's accountability for help-seeking actions.

> "I am getting myself out of gambling. It's OK to ask HOW!"-would be a more encouraging message. Try to personalise the message, because it's ME talking. I am not being talked down. I am not being told what to do. It is my own decision! (Male, 62 years old).

Several participants advised against using visual stimuli portraying dice, video lottery terminals, or slot machines, maintaining that such gambling attributes dominate their attention and entice them into risky behaviour. Other participants suggested that problem gamblers would avoid paying attention to the social marketing materials displayed in the venue. One participant explained that the prevention material would be ignored in order to avoid the negative feelings (e.g. guilt) aroused by a message prompting them to stop gambling "as one has decided already to come and engage into gambling". Instead, these participants suggested that health messages would have a better chance to be attended to and processed outside the venue. They claimed that "the right and reflective state of mind" is compromised while engaged with the gambling activity in the venue; hence, the message is most likely to be disregarded.

> When you are in the venue, you are in the zone; you are not worried about anything else around you. You are not interested because you are gambling. When I am quiet, calm, and reflective I can be receptive to that ad and I can sit quietly and receive the information. I am not going to receive any information while I am gambling in a venue while I am trying to chase my dollar, feeling anxious (Female, 54 years old).

Discussion, Implications and Future Research

This study provides a starting point for the development of emotional advertising appeals to encourage individuals to seek help in compulsive consumption contexts, such as gambling. The majority of gamblers in the study agreed that emotional advertising has the capacity to motivate behaviours and influence help-seeking attitudes, intentions, and behaviours. However, opinions regarding whether negative versus positive emotional advertising are the most effective were polarised. Proponents of the negative emotional content highlighted the persuasiveness of guilt and fear emotional advertising in compulsive contexts. Scenarios revealed that some gamblers perceived guilt as an emotion that intensifies responsibility for the harmful gambling outcomes on significant others; particularly in the family context. Guilt would motivate at-risk gamblers to reassess their behaviour and prompt them to seek help. Some participants also propose fear emotion as an effective appeal. Fear prevailed as a loss of control over gambling, loss of identity, loss of trust, loneliness, and isolation. Monetary concerns were also incorporated into fear scenarios. Notably, extreme forms of fear appeals/shocking tactics are harmful and should not be used in the gambling context. Anxiety and depression, which often co-occur with pathological gambling, may prompt at-risk consumers to be overly distressed by shocking messages.

Gamblers support positive emotional appeals utilising hope, fun, feelings of inspiration, and excitement; with uplifting emotions prompting help-seeking action. In parallel with Calderwood and Wellington (2013), some Australian gamblers perceive guilt and fear-based health messages as stigmatising and harmful. In addition, positive expectations should be incorporated within messages targeting gamblers to seek help. Notably, perceived help-seeking benefits in the form of various intrinsically motivating positive expectations are regarded as antecedents of positive emotions such as hope, enthusiasm, or eagerness.

Furthermore, gamblers perceived other novel communication strategies, based on mixed emotional appeals, to be effective in curbing compulsive behaviour. For example, gamblers perceived effective communications as those that highlight emotions such as fear (e.g. *slipping down the steep and slippery slope* as a metaphorical expression of losing control over excessive gambling) mixed with hopefulness, determination, and resistance to the problem/issue (*Build yourself! Life has hope! You are worthwhile!*). These original findings in the gambling context parallel the notion of mixed emotional appeal effectiveness in sun screen usage contexts (Passyn and Sujan 2006). Moreover, recent findings on mediated advertising stimuli effectiveness in anti-marijuana context (Wang et al. 2012; Lang et al. 2013) point out that co-activated messages (e.g. mixed negative and positive emotional content) gain further attention from afflicted individuals based on their ability to condition individuals for information intake, better encoding, and storage of information. The findings from the current study suggest that the combination of negative emotions (e.g. fear) mixed with positive emotions (e.g. hope, eagerness, determination) are perceived as efficient to boost help-seeking in a gambling context.

Another finding from this study is that response-efficacy and self-accountability for help-seeking action are considered important elements that should be incorporated in messages to gambling-affected individuals. Personalised self-accountability (e.g. "I am getting myself out of gambling! Its OK to ask How") and clear guidance on how and were to seek help, highlights the importance of these elements in the message. Additionally, the current research indicates that advertising stimuli should exclude any explicit gambling cues, such as images of dice or slot machines screens, as these may trigger afflicted audiences to gamble. This notion parallels the findings from smoking contexts, which demonstrate that pictures of individuals smoking, or even conditioned smoking stimuli, are appetitive, pleasurable, and increase the desire of smoking a cigarette in smokers (Winkler et al. 2011).

The controversy regarding whether positive or negative emotional content is more effective in compulsive contexts calls for future research to consider the tailoring of emotional advertising to different consumers profiles (Rimer and Kreuter 2006). Future qualitative research should also explore if a mixed emotional advertising format is perceived as an effective communication strategy to prompt quitting among smokers, or healthy eating in overweight consumers. Furthermore, quantitative methods to produce more generalisable findings on emotional advertising effectiveness in compulsive contexts, with a particular focus on mixed emotions, should be utilised.

The current research provides original insights into the effectiveness of various emotional appeals from a gamblers perspective. However, the qualitative nature of this research induces a number of limitations. Given that this was a qualitative research study, the findings from this research are not generalisable. Additionally, given the convenience nature of the sample, research findings may not be representative. Although a part of every focus group was dedicated to triangulate participants answers, the audience may have been inadvertently cued by the researchers to provide socially acceptable or desirable responses.

Acknowledgement This study was a part of a Ph.D. project in which Professor Pascale Quester has been an irreplaceable member of a supervisory board and provided invaluable advice and guidance throughout all stages of the research project.

References

Adams PJ, de Raeburn J, Kawshi S (2009) A question of balance: prioritizing public health responses to harm from gambling. Addiction 104(5):688–691
Andreasen AR (2006) Social marketing in the 21st century. Thousand Oaks, CA Sage
Arthur D, Quester P (2003) The ethicality of using fear for social advertising. Australas Mark J 11 (1):12–27
Bagozzi RP, Sekerka LE, Hill V, Sguera F (2013) The role of moral values in instigating morally responsible decisions. J Appl Behav Sci 49(1):69–94
Block LG (2005) Self-referenced fear and guilt appeals: the moderating role of self-construal. J Appl Soc Psychol 35(11):2290–2309
Boyatzis RE (1998) Transforming qualitative information: thematic analysis and code development. Sage Publications, Thousand Oaks, London
Braun V, Clarke V (2006) Using thematic analysis in psychology. Qual Res Psychol 3(2):77–101
Brennan L, Binney W (2010) Fear, guilt, and shame appeals in social marketing. J Bus Res 63 (2):140–146
Brown SL, Smith EZ (2007) The inhibitory effect of a distressing anti-smoking message on risk perceptions in smokers. Psychol Health 22(3):255–268
Brown S, Locker E (2009) Defensive responses to an emotive anti-alcohol message. Psychol Health 24(5):517–528
Brownson RC, Kreuter MW, Arrington BA, True WR (2006) Translating scientific discoveries into public health action: how can schools of public health move us forward? Publ Health Rep 121(1):97–103
Calderwood KA, Wellington WJ (2013) Social marketing strategies for stigmatized target populations: a case example for problem gamblers and family members of problem gamblers. Qual Rep 18:1–19
Carter OBJ, Pollard CM, Atkins JFP, Marie-Milliner J, Pratt IS (2011) 'We're not told why-we're just told': qualitative reflections about the Western Australian Go for 2&5(R) fruit and vegetable campaign. Publ Health Nutr 14(6):982–988
Chaiken S, Liberman A, Eagly AH (1989) Heuristic and systematic processing within and beyond the persuasion context. In: Uleman J, Bargh JA (eds) Unintended thought. Guilford, New York

de Hoog N, Stroebe W, de Wit JBF (2007) The impact of vulnerability to and severity of a health risk on processing and acceptance of fear-arousing communications: a meta-analysis. Rev Gen Psychol 11(3):258–285

Diehr P, Hannon P, Pizacani B, Forehand M, Meischke H, Curry S, Martin DP, Weaver RM, Harris J (2011) Social marketing, stages of change, and public health smoking interventions. Health Educ Behav 38(2):123–131

Farquhar C, Das R (1999) Are focus groups suitable for "sensitive topics"? In: Barbour R, Kitzinger J (eds) Developing focus group research: politics, theory and practice. SAGE, London

Ferris J, Wynne H (2001) The canadian problem gambling index: final report. Canadian Center on Substance Abuse, Ottawa, ON

Fishbein M, Hall-Jamieson K, Zimmer E, von Haeften I, Nabi R (2002) Avoiding the boomerang: the need for experimental tests of the relative effectiveness of anti-drug public service announcements prior to their use in a national campaign. Am J Publ Health 92:238–245

Fong DKC, Fong HN, Li SZ (2011) The social cost of gambling in Macao: before and after the liberalisation of the gaming industry. Int Gambl Stud 11(1):43–56

Fredrickson BL, Branigan Christine (2005) Positive emotions broaden the scope of attention and thought-action repertoires. Cogn Emot 19(3):313–332

Gainsbury S, Hing N, Suhonen N (2014) Professional help-seeking for gambling problems: awareness, barriers and motivators for treatment. J Gambl Stud 30:503–519

Gallopel-Morvan K, Gabriel P, Le Gall-Ely M, Rieunier S, Urien B (2011) The use of visual warnings in social marketing: the case of tobacco. J Bus Res 64(1):7–11

Hastings G, Stead M, Webb J (2004) Fear appeals in social marketing: strategic and ethical reasons for concern. Psychol Mark 21(11):961–986

Hills AM, Hill S, Natalie M, Dickerson M (2001) Induced mood and persistence at gaming. Addiction 96(11):1629–1638

Hirschman EC (1992) The consciousness of addiction: toward a general theory of compulsive consumption. J Consum Res 19(2):155–179

Hodgins DC, El-Guebaly N (2000) Natural and treatment-assisted recovery from gambling problems: a comparison of resolved and active gamblers. Addiction 95(5):777–789

Isen AM (2003) Positive affect, systematic cognitive processing, and behaviour: toward integration of affect, cognition, and motivation. In: Dansereau F, Yammarino FJ (eds) Multi-level issues in organizational behavior and strategy. JAI/Elsevier Science, Oxford, UK

Jäger T, Eisend M (2013) Effects of fear-arousing and humorous appeals in social marketing advertising: the moderating role of prior attitude toward the advertised behavior. J Current Issues Res Advertising 34(1):125–134

Kairouz S, Paradis C, Nadeau L (2012) Are online gamblers more at risk than offline gamblers? Cyberpsychol Behav Social Networking 15(3):175–180

Kessels LTE, Ruiter RAC, Jansma BM (2010) Increased attention but more efficient disengagement: neuroscientific evidence for defensive processing of threatening health information. Health Psychol 29(4):346–354

King D, Delfabbro P, Griffiths M (2010) The convergence of gambling and digital media: implications for gambling in young people. J Gambl Stud 26(2):175–187

Lang A, Sanders-Jackson A, Wang Z, Rubenking B (2013) Motivated message processing: how motivational activation influences resource allocation, encoding, and storage of TV messages. Motivation and Emotion 37(3):508–517

Larsen JT, Hemenover SH, Norris CJ, Cacioppo JT (2003) Turning adversity to advantage: on the virtues of the coactivation of positive and negative emotions. In: Aspinwall LG, Staudinger UM (eds) A psychology of human strengths: fundamental questions and future directions for a positive psychology. The American Psychological Association, Washington, DC

LaTour MS, Rotfeld HJ (1997) There are threats and (maybe) fear-caused arousal: theory and confusions of appeals to fear and fear arousal itself. J Advertising 26(3):45–59

Lazarus RS (1991) Emotion and adaptation. Oxford University Press Inc, New York

Lee AY, Sternthal B (1999) The effects of positive mood on memory. J Consum Res 26:115–127
Lennon R, Rentfro R (2010) Are young adults fear appeal effectiveness ratings explained by fear arousal, perceived threat and perceived efficacy? Innovative Mark 6(1):58–65
Lindström BR, Bohlin G (2011) Emotion processing facilitates working memory performance. Cogn Emot 25(7):1196–1204
Livingstone C, Adams PJ (2011) Harm promotion: observations on the symbiosis between government and private industries in Australasia for the development of highly accessible gambling markets. Wiley, New York
Malhotra NK, Birks DF (2007) Marketing research. An applied approach, 3rd edn. Prentice Hall, London
Marcus G, MacKuen M, Neuman W (2011) Parsimony and complexity: developing and testing theories of affective intelligence. Polit Psychol 32(2):323–336
Morales AC, Wu EC, Fitzsimons GJ (2012) How disgust enhances the effectiveness of fear appeals. J Mark Res 49(3):383–393
Muñoz Y, Chebat J-C, Borges A (2013) Graphic gambling warnings: how they affect emotions, cognitive responses and attitude change. J Gambl Stud 29(3):507–524
Munoz Y, Chebat J-C, Suissa S (2010) Using fear appeals in warning labels to promote responsible gambling among VLT players: the key role of depth of information processing. J Gambl Stud 26(4):593–609
Ordoñana JR, González-Javier F, Espín-López L, Gómez-Amor J (2009) Self-report and psychophysiological responses to fear appeals. Human Commun Res 35(2):195–220
Passyn K, Sujan M (2006) Self-accountability emotions and fear appeals: motivating behavior. J Consum Res 32(4):583–589
Patton MQ (2002) Qualitative research and evaluation methods, 3rd edn. Sage Publications, Thousand Oaks, CA
Peters G-JY, Ruiter RAC, Kok G (2012) Threatening communication: a critical re-analysis and a revised meta-analytic test of fear appeal theory. Health Psychol Rev 1–24
Puhl R, Peterson JL, Luedicke J (2013) Fighting obesity or obese persons? Public perceptions of obesity-related health messages. Int J Obes (Lond) 37(6):774–782
Racela OC, Thoumrungroje A (2012) The perceived ethicality and efficacy of fear appeals: the use of graphic warning labels in Thailand. J Int Bus Econ 12(4):106–113
Rimer BK, Kreuter MW (2006) Advancing tailored health communication: a persuasion and message effects perspective. J Commun 56:S184–S201
Snipes RL, LaTour MS, Bliss SJ (1999) A model of the effects of self-efficacy on the perceived ethicality and performance of fear appeals in advertising. J Bus Ethics 19(3):273–285
Stewart D, Shamdasani P, Rook D (2007) Focus groups: theory and practice, vol 20. Sage, Thousand Oaks, CA
Terblanhe-Smit M, Terblanche N (2010) The effect of fear appeal HIV/AIDS social marketing on behaviour: evaluating the importance of market segmentation. Theor Appl Econ XVII 11:79–90
Wang Z, Solloway T, Tchernev JM, Barker B (2012) Dynamic motivational processing of antimarijuana messages: coactivation begets attention. Human Commun Res 38(4):485–509
Williams KC (2011) Improving fear appeal ethics. J Acad Bus Ethics 5:1–24
Winkler MH, Weyers P, Mucha RF, Stippekohl B, Stark R, Pauli P (2011) Conditioned cues for smoking elicit preparatory responses in healthy smokers. Psychopharmacology 213(4):781–789
Xiaoquan Z, Xiaomei C (2008) The role of ambivalence in college nonsmokers' information seeking and information processing. Commun Res 35(3):298–318
Yan C (2014) Persuading people to eat less junk food: a cognitive resource match between attitudinal ambivalence and health message framing. Health Commun 30(3):251–260

Part III
Making a Difference—Customers and Brands

Revisiting the Long and Winding (Less Travelled) Road: The Road to Chaos in Marketing

Recteur Alexandre Steyer

Abstract In this chapter I revisit the fruitful but also very time consuming paper Pascale Quester and I published in 2010. We consider here a group of consumers that are all the same and adopt a given product with the same probability p. This simplest case leads to nothing of interest. However we add a sociological model based on imitation and reactance. This law of social imitation was validated on both theoretical and empirical levels. It consists of a very simple equation that is non-linear (Eq. 4). This dramatically changes the richness of the consumers' behaviour. Because of their social interactions, the group can be stable, oscillating or even chaotic. More precisely, we have shown six different dynamic regimes depending on the individuals' probability of adopting the product p_0. This shows very clearly that a group is not the sum of the individuals. More than this, very elementary individual behaviour can aggregate within an interacting social group, leading to complexity and chaos.

Keywords Social imitation · Social chaos · Choice · Probability · Consumer behaviour

Introduction

In 2010 Pascale Quester and I published a very fruitful but also very time consuming paper (Quester and Steyer 2010). Pascale went to the Sorbonne for a sabbatical year and we were looking for something that would conjugate her remarkable ability to manage experimental science with my interest in social interactions which I developed in both my physics and marketing PhD theses.

In the literature, we found a great current base on imitation as a source of diffusion in the process of innovation. But in social psychology, we also found the concept of reactance that prevents people from imitating each other. I developed in my PhD thesis (Steyer 1992) a model called *avalanche theory* in which both

R.A. Steyer (✉)
University of Paris 1 Pantheon Sorbonne, Paris, France
e-mail: Alexander.steyer@univ-paris1.fr

© Springer Science+Business Media Singapore 2016
C. Plewa and J. Conduit (eds.), *Making a Difference Through Marketing*,
DOI 10.1007/978-981-10-0464-3_9

imitation and reactance were taken into account. The result is an equation with three parameters as in the classical Bass model, but with much better prevision ability on the same data. Thus, I validate the coexistence of both imitation and reactance, but only in an indirect way.

Pascale and I decided to show this in a direct experimental way and developed two experiments. The first concerns Sorbonne students after a fictional lottery. We asked them, one after the other, to choose the chocolate bar that they would like to win. We were able to control exactly what they knew about their friends' choices, and they were unconscious of the real aim of the experiment. A second study was the statistical analysis of real data in a restaurant similar to the Ariely and Levav (2000) one.

A mathematical model was built and estimations made. It showed that both imitation and reactance took place, depending of the level of unanimity within the group. As a result, the relationship between the proportion of choices in the group and the probability of choice for an individual in the group is strongly non-linear. In this paper I use this relationship to show the behavioural consequences within the group, which are highly counterintuitive.

My derivation is mathematical, but it is important to realise what is at the beginning and at the end of it. The beginning is an equation validated by Pascale and I in two totally different situations. As it is the same equation, we hope to have established some very general law of imitation that could be validated in many others fields. At the end of the demonstration we demonstrated chaos in marketing, not by either conceptual or purely empirical evidence. We demonstrated chaos by the precise mathematical and sociological mechanism, which is a very innovative approach in our field.

Toward a Law of Imitation

The two studies (Quester and Steyer 2010) are different and complementary. In the chocolate bar experiment, the control of the other's choices is total on both synchronicity and diachronicity. The second one is less controlled, but totally realistic. The first one took place in a classroom of the Sorbonne. There was no discussion between the students. They only saw the choices made by their friends before they wrote on the paper. The possible consummation of the bar was a future and individual one. On the contrary, in the restaurant there was lot of discussion. The choice of the beverage was individual, but the consummation was collective. The choice was exposed to others, indicating something of the personality and the role played in the group. In particular, they had to choose between an alcoholic beverage or not. The chocolate mark is not a social marker; on the contrary, there is no context effect.

Because of these differences, one could have expected to obtain different results in each experiment. Even if the global equation could be the same, the parameters could be very different in each case. In reality, this was not the case. Both experiments led to the same equations with the same parameters, except one. In the 2010 paper, we show the curves of the probability of choice with respect to the proportion of group choice, and it is the same curve in both experiments except for a translation. The parameter that varies and the translations of the curves are due to differences of intrinsic choice of the different products regardless of imitation.

Being more quantitative, the chocolate bar experiment gave for a logit transformation of the probability choice, the equation:

$$\text{Logit of probability} = \underset{(6.3)}{-37.3\,\pi} + \underset{(14.4)}{70.9\,\pi^2} \underset{(9.4)}{-40.2\,\pi^3} + \text{constant} \tag{1}$$

where π is the proportion of consumer's choice on paper, and the numbers in brackets are the standard deviations of the estimates.

For the restaurant experiment, the equation is:

$$\text{Logit of probability} = \underset{(3.4)}{-35.0\,\pi} + \underset{(8.6)}{82.2\,\pi^2} \underset{(5.6)}{-48.3\,\pi^3} + \text{constant} \tag{2}$$

It is remarkable that the two equations are almost the same. The coefficients are very close to one another, and the differences are lower than two times the standard deviations, so they are not statistically significant different. The constants that reflect the attractions of the brands are different, but the other coefficients that reflect the social behaviour arc the same. Of course, more studies need to confirm this result, but at this time two studies confirm equality of the three social coefficients. For students making choices in a classroom and for consumers in a restaurant, the three coefficients are the same.

Waiting for additional research, I suggest the following equation as the non-linear social law of imitation:

$$\text{Logit of probability} = -35.5\,\pi + 79.2\,\pi^2 - 46.1\,\pi^3 + \text{constant} \tag{3}$$

This equation is an average of Eqs. 1 and 2. I will now show all of the consequences of this apparently very simple equation in the following sections of this paper.

Social Chaos

Equation 3 gives the probability p of a consumer choosing a product, taking into account the fact that a proportion π of the group has made the same choice. We have to make the equation dynamic, because when one consumer has made a choice, the proportion π within the group changes automatically. According to Eq. 3, this change of π will change the probability p, and so on from time to time.

Intuitively, one could expect the process to stabilize at some level of probability but we will demonstrate that this is almost never the case…

For simplicity, we will concentrate on the simplest case, in which each consumer can only choose one product or nothing. Thus, p is the probability of choosing the product. We can think of a basic restaurant which proposes only one starter on the menu that the consumer could choose or not. We note p(0) the probability of choosing this product at the beginning before any interaction within the group, and p(t) the probability at time t during the interactions. The probability of choosing the product one time depends on the precedent proportion of consumers π in the group that would adopt the product. The expectancy of π is simply the mean of $p(t-1)$, so we can write the recursive law of imitation according to Eq. 3 with the logit transformation:

$$1/p(t+1) = 1 + (1/p_0 - 1)\exp\left(-35.5\ p(t) + 79.2\ p(t)^2 - 46.1\ p(t)^3\right) \quad (4)$$

where exp is the exponential function. P_0 is the probability of choosing the product when nobody has already done it, so without social interactions.

Intuitively, one could expect that p(t) will evolve within the group according to Eq. 4, until it reaches a stable value. Even if social interactions are complex, the group will stabilise in a mixture of two types of consumers: some will adopt and others not, and Eq. 4 would give identical values for p(t) and p(t + 1). This could effectively happen for only a few values of p_0. In most cases the dynamic behaviour of the group will be much richer than this, as we will see.

When p_0 is greater than 0.93, the group converges to a stable situation with about 8 consumers adopting the product and 2 out of 10 not adopting. Figure 1 shows such a group. Of course in the real world it is infrequent to observe groups in which such unanimity exists a priori. Let us examine cases with p_0 lower than 0.93 whose behaviour is totally new in the literature of social interactions.

Figure 1 shows the dynamics of the group beginning with $p_0 = 0.94$. Figure 2 shows the group beginning with $p_0 = 0.932$ which is very near 0.94.

One could expect the same behaviour in a group that is convergent to some stability. It is the case at the beginning. Until time 23, the group converges, but after that there is a collapse and the group becomes totally unstable. The probability of adopting the product is fluctuating every time, making it impossible to predict what proportion of people will choose the product. This is social chaos. But behind this chaos there is a non-random and simple equation which is the fourth in this paper, and for this reason, physicists call these kinds of situation *deterministic chaos*. We have shown that because of the coexistence of both imitation and reactance in the groups, they can exhibit chaotic, unpredictable, and unstable behaviour. Chaos is a well known phenomenon and has already been evocated in marketing literature, but without empirical evidence and without psycho-sociological mechanisms that would make it emerge (Diamond 1993; Doherty and Delener 2001; Gault and Jaccaci 1996; Glass 1996; Herbig 1990).

We can remark that, in this example, individual consumers have a great tendency to adopt about 90 %, but at the group level it oscillates around 25 % because of the

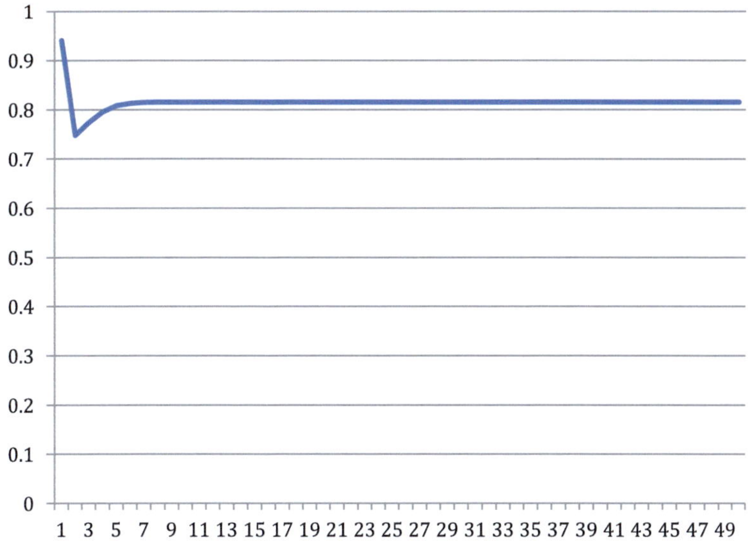

Fig. 1 Temporal evolution of the probability of choosing the product with p_0 = 0.94

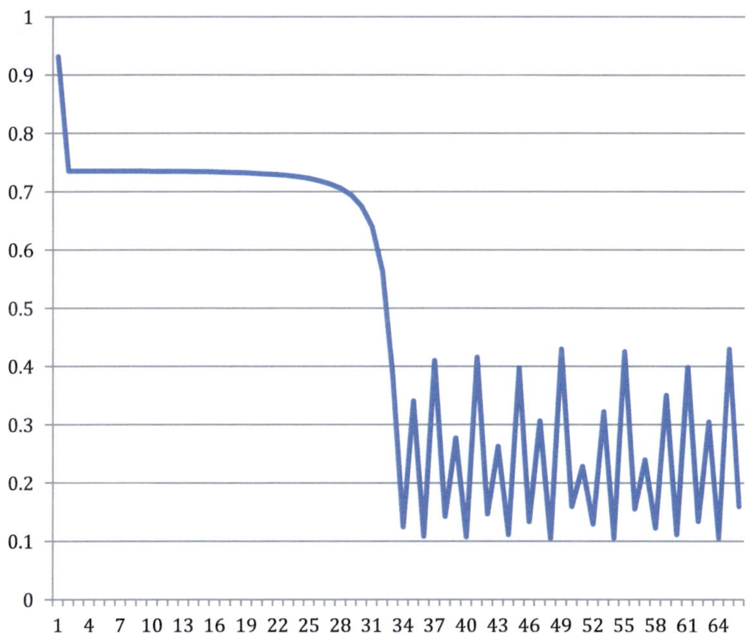

Fig. 2 Temporal evolution of the probability of choosing the product with p_0 = 0.932

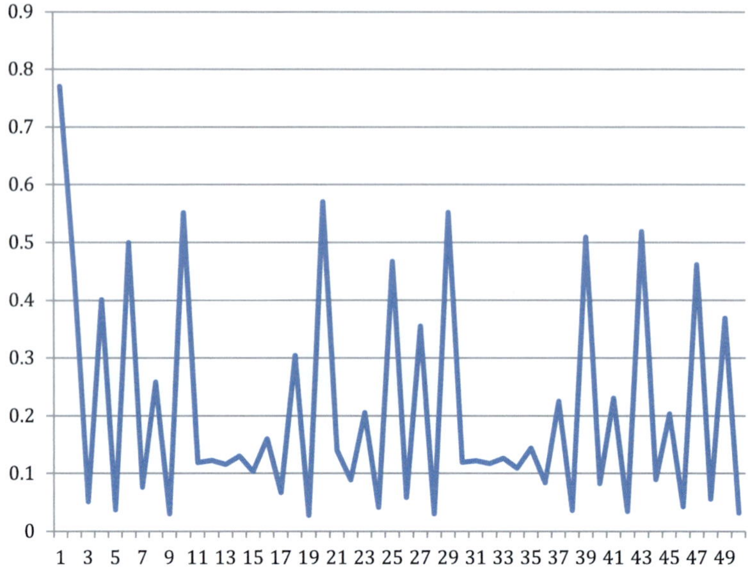

Fig. 3 Temporal evolution of the probability of choosing the product with $p_0 = 0.77$

reactance effect or variety seeking. When we lower p_0, the apparently initial stable state disappears and we observe pure chaos. Figure 3 shows such an example.

Probability of choice evolved in a totally random and apparently a totally non predictable way, even if in fact it is perfectly deterministic as in Eq. 4. In this state of chaos, what the group will ultimately choose depends mainly at the time at which the waiter asks for the choice. All the time dedicated to discussion and social interactions just enhance the randomness within the group.

When p_0 lowers, the randomness changes naturally. In chaos, all values of p can be observed. When p is lower than 0.7, the group oscillates randomly between some more or less definite values. Figure 4 shows such a case with about 3 values of attraction. The smaller p_0 is, the less chaotic the dynamic of the group is. Under $p_0 = 0.5$ there is no more chaos.

Chaos takes place in a pure oscillation between two very precise values of probability p. One is near the value of p_0 that reflects the individual tendency to adopt the product and the other is near 0, which reflects the effect of reactance. The two states are incompatible, but nevertheless they exist, and so as a consequence is that the group does a bivalent oscillation between the two indefinitely. Figures 5 and 6 show such oscillations for two different values of p_0.

When p_0 is still lower, oscillation of bivalence becomes attenuated. The amplitude becomes lower and lower, until it disappears. After that, the group is again stable, but this time with nobody adopting the product as shown in Fig. 7.

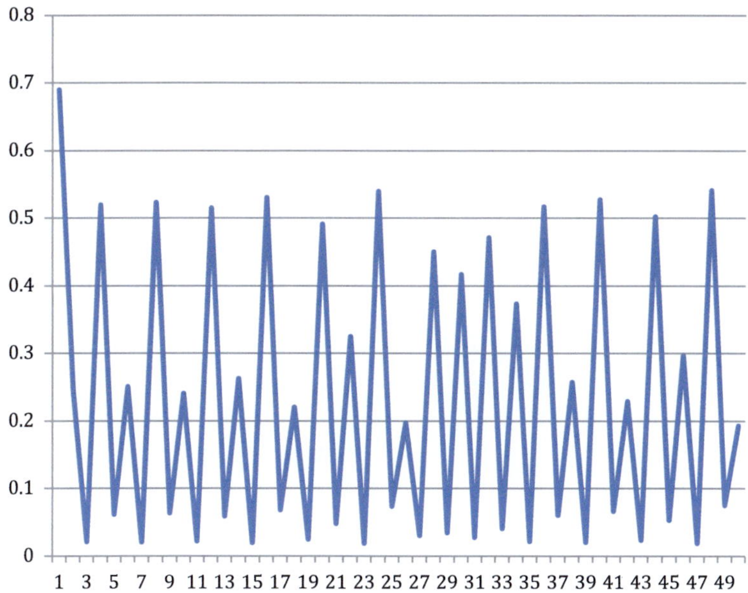

Fig. 4 Temporal evolution of the probability of choosing the product with $p_0 = 0.69$

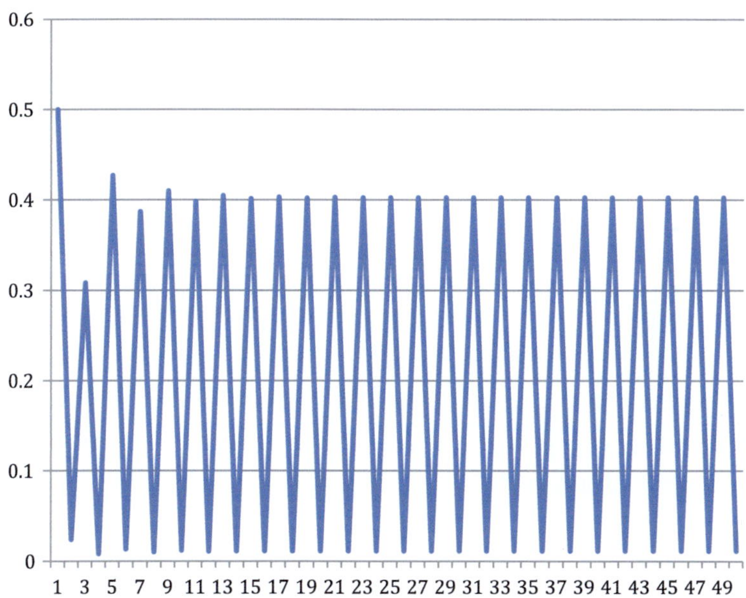

Fig. 5 Temporal evolution of the probability of choosing the product with $p_0 = 0.5$

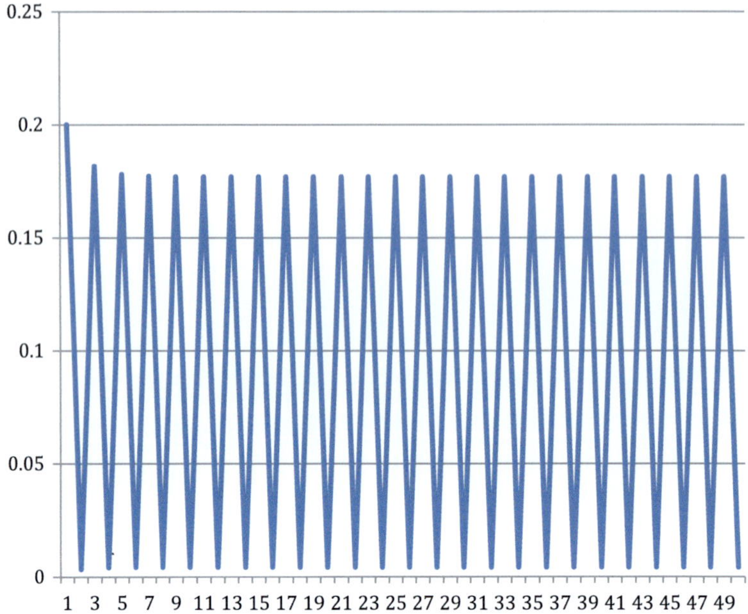

Fig. 6 Temporal evolution of the probability of choosing the product with $p_0 = 0.2$

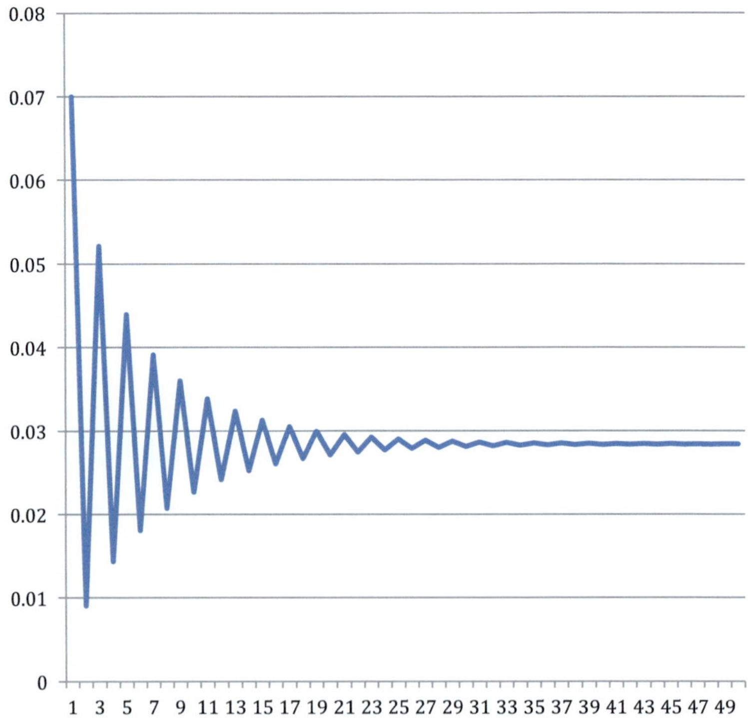

Fig. 7 Temporal evolution of the probability of choosing the product with $p_0 = 0.07$

Conclusion

In this paper we consider a group of very simple consumers. They are all the same and adopt a given product with the same probability p. This simplest case leads to nothing of interest. However we add a sociological model based on imitation and reactance. This law of social imitation was validated on both theoretical and empirical levels. It consists of a very simple equation that is non-linear (Eq. 4). This dramatically changes the richness of the consumers' behaviour. Because of their social interactions, the group can be stable, oscillating or even chaotic. More precisely, we have shown six different dynamic regimes depending on the individuals' probability of adopting the product p_0.

1. When p_0 is near 1, the group is stable. Almost everyone adopts the product
2. When p_0 is near 0.93, the group begins to adopt the product in a great majority. But after some time, the majority breaks and the probability becomes totally chaotic with respect to time
3. When $0.91 > p_0 > 0.7$ there is nothing but pure chaos
4. When $0.7 > p_0 > 0.5$ chaos become to structure around some less instable positions
5. When $0.5 > p_0 > 0.1$ the group oscillate between two opposite states. One of non-adoption and another of adoption.
6. When $p_0 < 0.1$ initial bivalence diminish until total non adoption of the product

This shows very clearly that a group is not the sum of the individuals. More than this, very elementary individual behaviour can aggregate within an interacting social group, leading to complexity and chaos.

The applications of these findings are straightforward. Whyte (1954) has shown, a long time ago, that social interactions are ubiquitous in marketing. Internet and social networks have made them increasingly accurate. So the law of imitation we found with Pascale Quester must always be in the manager's mind.

When faced with these three empirical facts:

1. A low market share, together with high purchase intention in market research
2. A very complex market share with chaotic evolution in all directions
3. Sudden change from stability to instability in the market share

the manager should ask himself if the cause is in the psychology of the consumers, or in the social interactions between them. Traditionally, more emphasis has been placed on the first reason. These simulations show that the second is as important as the first.

References

Ariely D, Levav J (2000) Sequential choice in group settings: taking the road less traveled and less enjoyed. J Consum Res 27(December):279–290
Diamond AH (1993) Chaos science. Mark Res 5(4):9–15
Doherty N, Delener N (2001) Chaos theory: marketing and management implications. J Mark Theory Pract 9(4):66–75
Gault S, Jaccaci A (1996) Complexity meets periodicity. Learn Organ 3(2):33–39
Glass N (1996) Chaos, non-linear systems and day-to-day management. Eur Manag J 14 (1):98–105
Herbig PA (1990) Marketing chaos—when randomness can be deterministic. J Int Mark Market Res 16(2):65–84
Quester P, Steyer A (2010) Revisiting individual choices in group settings: the long and winding (less traveled) road? J Consum Res 36(5):1050–1057
Steyer A (1992) la théorie des avalanches, PhD thesis, HEC, Jouy en Josas
Whyte WH (1954) The web of word of mouth. Fortune 50:140–143

The Case for Altruism in eWoM Motivations

Michelle Killian, John Fahy and Deirdre O'Loughlin

Abstract The Internet has revolutionised how consumers interact by facilitating the free exchange of information and opinions between individuals across the globe. However it is still not clearly understood why individuals help strangers by volunteering information, sharing opinions and making recommendations online. Surprisingly, much of this activity appears to involve non-reciprocal sharing, raising the question why would an individual share information or offer advice online with those they are unlikely to encounter again? Individuals who are contributing online have no guarantee of receiving anything in return for their efforts whereas freeloaders can benefit without making any contribution. The purpose of this work is to explore altruism in the context of eWoM in order to further the understanding of consumers' motivation to share information and opinions online. Altruism has been identified in the literature as a motive for eWoM although its' significance has been consistently overlooked by researchers and marketers. Whilst much online activity may be motivated by self-interest some individuals do appear to act more altruistically by offering advice, knowledge and expertise with the intention of helping others. Moreover, altruistic consumers share information and opinions without any expectation of reward. This makes them a reliable source of unbiased information for consumers seeking recommendations and an important spokesperson for marketers communicating their brands.

Keywords Altruism · eWoM · Motivations · Knowledge sharing · Online

M. Killian · J. Fahy (✉) · D. O'Loughlin
Kemmy Business School, University of Limerick, Limerick, Ireland
e-mail: John.Fahy@ul.ie

M. Killian
e-mail: Michelle.Killian@ul.ie

D. O'Loughlin
e-mail: Deirdre.OLoughlin@ul.ie

© Springer Science+Business Media Singapore 2016

C. Plewa and J. Conduit (eds.), *Making a Difference Through Marketing*,
DOI 10.1007/978-981-10-0464-3_10

Introduction

Why do consumers help strangers by volunteering information, sharing opinions and making recommendations online? Moreover why are they willing to invest time and energy helping individuals they do not know and are unlikely to ever meet in person and for no tangible reward? Indeed why are some individuals consistently more helpful than others even when it is unlikely that their efforts will be reciprocated?

Theories of kin selection (Hamilton 1963) can account for altruism towards relatives but what might be the reason for altruism towards strangers? Alexander (1987) proposed that individuals behave pro-socially in order to gain an altruistic reputation through a process of indirect reciprocity that provides them with benefits over the long term. However it is predicted that this will only occur where the likelihood of knowing someone's reputation is greater than the cost-benefit ratio of the altruistic act (Alexander 1987; Nowak and Sigmund 1998; Nowak 2006). In the case of eWoM there is likely to be much uncertainty regarding the prospect of receiving future benefits. The anonymous environment characteristic of online communications suggests that something more profound than having a personal relationship or close social tie might explain communicators' motivations for generating electronic word-of-mouth (eWoM).

Belk (2013) has drawn attention to the evolutionary and biological forces that may influence behaviour in an online environment, ultimate drivers that are often overlooked by consumer researchers who typically focus on proximate explanations for consumer motivations (Belk 2013). He argued that "non-kin relationships (e.g. close friendships) are an integral element of human sociality, which is oiled by two evolutionary processes: our evolved capacity to foster bonds of reciprocity and our innate coalitional psychology ("us vs. them")" (Belk 2013, p. 362). This suggests that motivations to share opinions online may ultimately be driven by evolutionary forces that lead to pro-social behaviours such as eWoM.

Whilst there is a burgeoning interest amongst researchers into electronic word-of-mouth, it is still not fully understood why consumers offer opinions and share information online. With increased clutter and competition online and empirical findings still relatively scarce (Breazeale 2009), it is becoming increasingly urgent to gain a deeper understanding of the underlying mechanisms of eWoM and drivers of its dissemination (Wien and Olsen 2014). Extant research investigating eWoM is extremely fragmented (Cheung and Thadani 2010), conceptualisations have tended to be simplistic and inconclusive (Chan and Ngai 2011) and despite the development of various classification frameworks and conceptual models (Chan and Ngai 2011; Cheung and Thadani 2010; Munzel and Kunz 2013), there still doesn't appear to be any over-arching theory that explains eWoM, much less the motivations why consumers engage in it. Although eWoM has been explained primarily from an individual rational perspective, a more diverse theoretical approach that focuses on motivations is also required (Cheung and Lee 2012). Consequently, it is important to address this deficit given that eWoM generation is crucial to the WoM cycle, which includes creation, transmission, receipt and adoption of information online. Indeed, without having consumers motivated to share their opinions, eWoM would not exist. Moreover, it is the initiators of conversations online who determine to a large extent what is being shared, where it is being shared and with whom.

Altruism is a motivation with the ultimate goal of increasing the welfare of one or more individuals other than oneself (Batson and Shaw 1991). Altruistic consumers share information and opinions online without any expectation of reward (Cheung and Lee 2012). Individual differences in altruism may also account for differences in consumers' likelihood to engage in eWoM, as well as the nature of their online communication activities. The purpose of this work is to explore altruism and altruistic personality in the context of eWoM, in order to further the understanding of consumers' motivation to share information and opinions online.

WoM Goes Digital

Traditional word of mouth (tWoM) involves the passing on of information concerning a brand, product or service between a non-commercial communicator who receives no reward and a receiver (Dichter 1966). However, since the advent of the Internet and social media, word-of-mouth is often mediated through electronic means (Kietzmann and Canhoto 2013). Since eWoM is an expanded version of tWoM, it has been generally assumed that they share the same core motivations. Notwithstanding their shared history, there are some important differences between them that may impact motivations. For example, because eWoM provides greater anonymity compared to traditional face-to-face communications, there may be an increased temptation and opportunity for individuals to post fake or untruthful messages online. Additionally because eWoM tends to involve asynchronous rather than two-way communication, (Hennig-Thurau et al. 2004; Cheung and Thadani 2010) consumers who might not ordinarily feel confident to voice strong opinions or complain to service providers directly, might be more inclined to do so in an anonymous eWoM setting where they feel less self-conscious and can vent negative emotions without fear of repercussions.

Anonymity and the asynchronous nature of eWoM raise another important question in relation to motivations. EWom is a behaviour that evolved organically without input from marketers (Kozinets et al. 2010) but rather as a consequence of technological developments facilitating knowledge and opinion sharing between consumers on the internet (Chan and Ngai 2011). Surprisingly, much of this activity appears to involve non-reciprocal sharing, raising the question why would an individual share information or offer advice online with those they are unlikely to encounter again. Individuals who are contributing online have no guarantee of receiving anything in return for their efforts. In the absence of reciprocation what drives these individuals to share consistently? From an economic perspective this is clearly irrational.

Communicators' Motivations for Engaging in eWoM

While early contributions to WOM research originate with Dichter (1966), Hennig-Thurau et al. (2004), were the first to research consumers' motivations to engage in eWoM specifically. Building on the earlier work of Dichter (1966), Balasubramanian and Mahajan (2001) and Sundaram et al. (1998), this seminal study on eWoM identified four key motivations for senders of eWoM; desire for social interaction, concern for other consumers, self-enhancement and economic gain. It is generally held that these have provided the foundation for most research into communicators' motivations in eWoM. They also noted that consumers could be differentiated and categorised according to their various motivations. These included self-interested helpers, consumer advocates, multiple motive consumers and true altruists. Self-interested helpers formed the largest cluster, 34 % of respondents, while true altruists formed the second largest cluster, 27 % respondents. Interestingly self-interested helpers appear to be driven by both a concern for other consumers as well as economic incentives. This could suggest that they may be more rational when deciding to engage in eWoM. Being motivated by economic incentives and a concern for others might lead this group to weigh costs and benefits before contributing online. This might also lead to greater possibility of bias, particularly if compensation is offered for making recommendations.

True altruists, on the other hand, appear to be motivated by both a concern for other consumers and a desire to help companies. Economic incentives appear to have little impact on this group (Hennig-Thurau et al. 2004), which is interesting given that consumers rely on eWoM largely because they believe the information to be generated by an individual who has no self-interest in promoting a particular product/service (Dichter 1966; Silverman 2001). Therefore consumers seeking advice and opinions online are quite likely to judge source credibility at least to some degree on whether they believe the contributor was incentivised. In the meantime, while some studies argue that monetary incentivisation should be encouraged for online contributions (Van der Lans 2010), others indicate that providing compensation for contributions could erode the value of recommendations if it became public knowledge (Phelps et al. 2004). However, as research into the effect of monetary incentives in eWoM is scant, further investigation is necessary before any conclusions can be drawn.

Nevertheless, it appears that altruists may be an important segment for providing reliable, honest and unbiased feedback that is not only beneficial for consumers trying to make better consumption decisions but also marketers wishing to understand their customers better. More recently, Cheung and Lee (2012) categorised motivations into egoist, (reputation and reciprocity) collectivist (sense of belonging), altruistic (enjoyment of helping) and principalistic (moral obligation and knowledge self–efficacy) motives. They found that collectivism (sense of belonging) and altruism (enjoyment of helping others) were the most significant motives for consumers' willingness to share online. Clearly, a need to help others and contribute towards society and community drives much of eWoM activity.

The Role of Personality in eWoM Motivations

More recently researchers have begun to turn their attention to the impact of personality, focusing on individual differences such as self-enhancement, (Hennig-Thurau et al. 2004), vengeance (Cheema and Kaikati 2010) and need for uniqueness (Cheema and Kakaiti 2010). To this end Wien and Olsen (2014) adopted an interesting perspective by exploring the effect of individualism on the need for self-enhancement and motivation to initiate eWoM. They posited that high-individualism consumers should be more likely than low-individualism consumers to initiate eWoM after a satisfactory consumption experience compared to an unsatisfactory one, when eWoM is unsolicited versus solicited and when perceived social risk is higher versus lower (Wien and Olsen 2014).

Through sharing satisfactory consumption experiences, consumers can appear competent, signaling their expertise (Wojnicki and Godes 2011) and providing an opportunity for self-enhancement. Similarly, because unsolicited WoM is proactive whereas solicited WoM is reactive, high individualism consumers can self-enhance by being proactive and initiating WoM. Finally, when social risk is high, it provides the opportunity for self-enhancement for those consumers who are willing to challenge social norms and express opinions. It is argued that high-individualism consumers are more likely to use these situations as a means of displaying their traits (Wien and Olsen 2014).

Moreover, individuals tend to consider their possessions as extensions of themselves (Belk 2013), therefore they may be less likely to recommend brands they feel reflect their personality because others may then adopt the product diminishing its uniqueness, thus having a negative impact on their own identity (Cheema and Kaikati 2010). In an online setting, communication is asynchronous, recommendations are typically anonymous and individuals are often geographically dispersed (Cheung and Thadani 2010), therefore it could be speculated that consumers with a high need for uniqueness may be able to avoid the cost (decreased uniqueness) associated with recommending products that enhance their uniqueness, because even if others adopt those products they are unlikely to ever meet each other in public or engage with them socially.

Along a similar vein but quite distinct from high-individualism or the need for uniqueness is 'consumption focused self-expression' (Saenger et al. 2013, p. 959) which has been defined as "the motivation to engage in WoM about consumption activities in order to gain attention and express one's self-concept" (p. 960). Social media and eWoM offer a multitude of ways in which consumers can express themselves and display self-concept. Consumers motivated by consumption-focused self-expression are likely to share eWoM about brands that reflect and communicate their self-concept.

eWoM—Altruism or Egoism?

A conundrum that remains within eWOM research is whether the motivations for generating word of mouth are ultimately altruistic or egoistic? Altruism according to Rushton is "social behaviour carried out to achieve positive outcomes for another rather than for self" (Rushton 1980 p. 8), however this does not necessarily preclude there being some form of self-benefit (such as positive affect from having helped another). On the contrary Staub (1978) states that altruism is also "likely to be associated with intrinsic rewards and the expectation of such rewards", such as "empathetic reinforcing experiences" (Staub 1978 p. 10). In contrast, egoism is defined as "the excessive concern with one's own pleasure or advantage at the expense of others and the standards of conduct endorsed by the wider community" (Weigel et al. 1999, p. 370), and is positively related to cynicism (low trust) and negatively correlated with agreeableness (trust, compliance and altruism) (Weigel et al. 1999).

Much online activity may be self-oriented, even narcissist in some cases, while some individuals do appear to act more altruistically by offering advice, knowledge and expertise with the primary intention of helping others. However, some researchers reject altruism on the basis that positive emotional rewards such as praise, honor and pride are ultimately driven by egoist motivations, that is, individuals' reason for helping is ultimately driven by an egoist motivation to acquire these emotional rewards. This implies that even seemingly altruistic motivations to communicate eWoM are be driven by the desire to feel good about one-self, rather than to help another. For example, a desire for increased status is often associated with greater selfishness, implying egoism. The idea of sharing and co-operation would appear antithetical to notions of status that is so often characterised by competition for success, yet recent theories on altruism appear to prove otherwise. For example, Griskevicius et al. (2007) argue that public acts of philanthropy signals that the individual has resources and is willing to share them, traits that are desirable in a potential mate, which in turn leads to increased status. In a separate study, it was also shown that conspicuous displays of altruism (e.g. buying green products), might also serve as a costly fitness signal associated with status (Griskevicius et al. 2010). Consequently, examining eWoM motivations through the lens of altruism may alter the cognitive landscape of eWoM by challenging some of the current assumptions, e.g. that consumers are primarily driven by selfish and egoist motives. It also offers an opportunity for a much deeper and richer understanding of communicators' motivations and eWoM in general.

A re-examination of altruism in consumer motivations for the generation of eWOM is increasingly being recognised. Munzel and Kunz (2013) drew attention to altruism specifically, arguing that it may be a key motive for creators of eWoM. Highlighting its importance in the communication of eWoM, they requested further research investigating reciprocation and exchange in the development of social capital (Munzel and Kunz 2013). Requests for greater research into 'writers motivations' (Chan and Ngai 2011) have called for studies that might help companies encourage consumers to provide more balanced, informative, honest feedback, "not just rants and raves" that would benefit all stakeholders (King et al. 2014, p. 172). Readers of online opinions tend to make decisions based on the causal inferences regarding the communicator's motivation for contributing (Sen and Lerman 2007). Readers are likely to judge credibility and honesty of online reviews and opinions to some degree at least, on whether the communicator is perceived to have their own interests or others' interests at heart. Consumers may be more cynical about advice provided by those who are perceived to be more self-centered than altruistic. Accordingly, because credibility enhances persuasiveness (Berger 2014), altruists' opinions should also have a greater influence on readers' attitudes and behaviours.

Similarly, what appears to be emerging in other research is that altruism may play a far greater role in pro-social motivations than was previously thought. Insights from the biological, social and evolutionary sciences seem to suggest that altruism may have played a key role in the success of our ancestors (Klein 2014). Neurological studies using fMRI indicate that altruism is socially rewarding at a neurological level (Garcia and Saad 2008), implying that human co-operation and altruistic behaviour may have evolved as a means of survival. Buss (2004) explains that altruism towards non-relatives may be contagious whereby the benefactor of an altruistic act wishes to then pay it forward by doing something for another individual in the future (Buss 2004). If this is the case then it has important implications for online sharing and eWoM in particular, in so far as altruists may be instrumental in the contagious spread of helping behaviour that is characteristic of eWoM. Moreover, developing a deeper understanding of altruism and altruists' role in eWoM would not only help marketers and platform operators design strategies that encourage this influential segment to share eWoM about their brands and services, but would also benefit consumers seeking to obtain reliable information relevant to their needs.

Towards a Reconceptualisation of Altruism

Despite increasing academic attention, very little effort has been made to conceptualise altruism specifically within an eWoM domain, or indeed consumer research. Early research into motivations for eWoM by Hennig-Thurau et al. (2004) did not provide any formal definition of altruism. Consequently, those researchers who have acknowledged it tend to define it very loosely as concern for other consumers, implying an element of altruism although without stating specifically what they mean when using the term. Others have adopted various definitions borrowed from different theoretical models. For example, Cheung and Lee (2012) linked it with empathetic emotion, defining it as "serving the public good to benefit one or more others" (Cheung and Lee 2012, p. 2), whereas Price et al. (1995) argued that empathy may not play as important a role in everyday marketplace helping behaviour, therefore their definition states that altruism is an intention to help others that reflects intrinsic values, regardless of social or motivational reinforcement (Price et al. 1995, p. 257). This would appear to be a significant oversight given the fact that altruism is such a contentious issue. Before any claim can be made for or against altruism, it is necessary to define and explain it in the context of the research in which it is being applied. Some researchers consider helping others to be a separate motive to helping companies even though they both signify altruism (Sundaram et al. 1998), others differentiate between pure and impure altruism (Dellarocas and Narayan 2006), whilst others again claim that altruism is ultimately driven by self-motives (Alexandrov 2013). Altruism according to Rushton is "social behaviour carried out to achieve positive outcomes for another rather than for self" (Rushton 1980 p. 8), however this does not necessarily preclude there being some form of self-benefit (such as positive affect from having helped another).

Batson and Shaw (1991) claim is that while altruism and egoism both refer to goal-directed motivation as well as the ultimate goal of increasing someone's welfare, determining whether the individual is driven by egoism or altruism depends on whose welfare is the ultimate goal, another person's, or one's own. This single determining factor is crucial to the explanation, definition and understanding of altruism. While they acknowledge that altruists may engage in a 'hedonic calculus' by weighing up costs and benefits to helping, as long as the cost of helping does not exceed the relative benefit of helping, the individual will be motivated to act (Bateson and Shaw 1991, p. 112). They systematically ruled out egoist explanations for various helping motives such as empathy-induced altruism, empathy-specific punishment, socially-administered empathy specific punishment and self-administered empathy specific punishments. Furthermore they argued that altruism need not necessarily incur a cost to oneself, nor need it involve distress or require reciprocation, but rather it arises from empathetic emotion, defined as "a set of congruent other focused feelings of compassion, tenderness, sympathy and the like" (Batson and Shaw 1991, p. 113). Finally, their research demonstrates empirically that although altruism may result in self-benefits, the motivation can still be altruistic "as long as obtaining the self-benefit is an unintended consequence of benefiting the other and not the ultimate goal" (Batson and Shaw 1991, p. 109).

An important contribution dovetailing Batson and Shaw's (1981, 1991) research highlights that it is the signal value of emotion on altruism that is paramount when making judgments about the ultimate motives for altruism (Barasch et al. 2014). Barasch et al. (2014) suggest that pro-social actors who are motivated by the expectation of emotional rewards should be judged more favourably than pro-social actors who are motivated by other benefits, such as reputational or material rewards. This implies that not only are emotions used in order to deduce the true intentions behind altruists' behaviour but also emotions can signify whether their true intention is more egoistic or altruistic. Unlike other personal benefits such as monetary reward or enhanced reputation, which are regarded more skeptically as being selfishly motivated, emotional benefits signal authentic concern for others and strengthen the view that the actor behaved altruistically (Barasch et al. 2014). Accordingly, contributors of eWoM who receive emotional benefits are likely to be perceived to be more genuine and altruistic than contributors who receive material or reputational rewards for contributing online. Feeling good from helping others is seen to be evidence of an authentic concern for others (Barasch et al. 2014).

In conclusion, whether or not altruism is ultimately motivated by egoism may depend upon the definition of altruism adopted. If the definition adopted for altruism excludes intrinsic "self-rewards" such as a positive "self-image as a good, responsible concerned person" then it appears to point more towards egoism (Batson et al. 1986, p. 219). If, on the other hand, the definition of altruism does not preclude self-rewards such as good feeling for helping others then the case for altruism still holds. Individual tend to act in ways that are consistent with their self-concept (e.g. Saenger et al. 2013), therefore it is how the individual sees themselves and how others perceive them that will be predictive of their behaviour.

Hence, from the research discussed above, it can be predicted that individuals who are high in altruism, including those who are motivated by emotional rewards, should still be judged more credible and honest than those who appear to be more self-serving. For this reason, it is important for companies and marketers to be able to identify altruists as well as understand what motivates them so that they can encourage them to share eWoM, influencing their target consumer market. Ultimately however, for the purposes of eWoM it may not be necessary to prove empirically the existence of altruism, rather it is important to understand what it is meant by altruism and how it is perceived from both the communicator's and receiver's perspective.

eWoM Through the Lens of Altruism

The critical question therefore is how might including altruism in the discussion of motivations contribute to the research on eWoM? The ensuing discussion points to some predictions relating to how altruism might alter, shape and deepen current understanding of eWoM and lead to a more balanced and comprehensive perspective on communicators' motivation to engage in eWoM.

Communication Channels and Platform Choice

Altruism is characterised by a desire towards helping others (Rushton et al. 1981), therefore it is likely that this will evidenced in their activities online. Additionally, because altruism is an important driver of pro-social behaviour individuals who are high in altruism are likely to be sociable with a large network of social contacts both offline and online. This should impact not only on the volume of eWoM they share but also the scope. It is also likely that they will generate and share eWoM that is dispersed across a broad range of platforms, both company and consumer-led, as well as other social channels such consumer review websites, social networking sites, blogs and even email, passing along content where they can benefit others seeking help in making consumption decisions. Altruists may also be more likely to pass along content they have no interest in themselves, merely because they wish to help others and believe it may be relevant or interesting to them. Consequently, environmental and incidental triggers such as watching an interesting documentary or seeing a video advertisement when browsing YouTube might have a greater impact on altruist's motivation to share.

Furthermore altruists heightened sensitivity to other individuals' needs means they might also be better at predicting what other individuals' preferences might be. Consequently, they are likely to provide more useful advice and information for those they communicate with online. Some studies indicate that consumers trust opinions from individuals who are perceived to be similar to themselves because they are likely to have analogous preferences even if they don't share close social ties with them (Steffes and Burgee 2009). When providing advice online or sharing opinions, altruists may not in fact be similar to the receiver but due to their greater ability to adopt the perspective of others (Batson et al. 1997), other consumers may perceive greater homophily and consequently place greater trust and value in their opinions. By the same token, they may also be important as consumer advocates, helping companies disseminate information, promoting their brands and services to consumers as well as providing valuable feedback both positive and negative, so that they marketers can align their efforts with consumer needs and desires.

Valence

Interestingly, altruism is the only motive that has been found to account for both positive and negative WoM. Negative WoM appears to be more diagnostic and influential in consumption decisions (Lee et al. 2008). However, because of impression management concerns, some consumers may be less likely to post negative feedback that might reflect negatively on them as individuals (Berger 2014). For example, De Angelis et al. (2012) revealed that consumers who wish to self-enhance tend to engage in more positive WOM about their own experiences but share negative WoM about other people's experiences, in order to make themselves look good (De Angelis et al. 2012). This suggests that consumers who are more concerned about their self-image will be likely to share eWoM strategically in order to manage impressions. Altruists, however, may be less concerned about image impression management and more concerned with helping others, therefore they will be more likely to post negative eWoM after a poor consumption experience. Even if they are concerned to some degree how others might perceive them, they are still more likely to act in accordance with their self-concept, by warning other consumers and by complaining or offering advice to companies in order to help them improve their service.

Brands

Brand characteristics appear to play an important role in what types of products and experiences are talked about most in online conversations (Lovett and Schachar 2013). Experience goods, luxury goods that signal status and less complex goods appear to get more mentions online (Lovett and Schachar 2013). Motivations to talk about particular brands online may also be shaped by the brand's characteristics. Furthermore, identifying who are the people talking about particular brands and what ultimately motivates them would help provide a more comprehensive picture of brand sharing in online networks. For example, consumers with a need for status, show off by acquiring expensive brands and luxury goods and then displaying them to others (Griskevicius and Kendrick 2013). It is also very likely that consumers use eWoM as a means of 'broadcasting' their status by talking about luxury and status brands (Lovett and Schachar 2013, p. 438). In consumption contexts where the focus is on providing benefits to others, this can lead to an increase in consumption of ethical goods (Ross 2011). However, status motives also appear to have a positive effect on consumption of 'green' products because these signal altruism (Griskevicius et al. 2010).

Sex differences in altruism may also reveal disparities in what is talked about online. Griskevicius et al. (2010) propose further studies to investigate how sex differences, status and altruism affect consumption. If altruism signals fitness, then men and women may use it in different ways to signal traits that are favoured by the opposite sex. For example, men might be likely to show off by generating eWoM signalling dominance and leadership, whereas women may be inclined to pass along more eWoM demonstrating co-operation and agreeableness. Differences may also translate into the types of brands and experiences men and women talk about, for example men might show off by talking about status brands that indicate intelligence and resourcefulness, or brands that are consumed when one is alone to exhibit leadership. Women, on the other hand, might tend to talk more about brands that are used socially or brands that signal caring.

Altruism may also lead to the development of other hypotheses in relation to social-tie strength. For example, while high openness is positively correlated with altruism towards strangers, high agreeableness appears to have a greater effect on sharing amongst friends and acquaintances (Oda et al. 2014). High openness is associated with greater novelty seeking whereas high agreeableness indicates greater co-operation. This suggests that, depending on their audience, altruists might be selective about what brands and experiences they discuss. For example, they may be more likely to talk about novel and unusual brands where recommendations are anonymous, whereas they may be more inclined to talk about brands their friends talk about when posting in social networks such as Facebook. The suggestions offered above provide just a small sample of potential avenues awaiting further investigation.

Conclusion

On account of the evidence provided throughout this paper as well as numerous calls from other researchers, it appears timely to adopt a new perspective on eWom motivations by incorporating ultimate explanations into the understanding of altruism. There is clearly much yet to be explored about altruism and altruists' role in communicating eWoM. Examining eWoM motivations through this lens provides an opportunity to view opinion sharing online from a different viewpoint, providing a more complete picture of communicators' motivations. Not only would this improve the understanding of eWoM, but would also build on current research to develop deeper insight into what ultimately drives consumers to share online.

References

Alexander RD (1987) The biology of moral systems. De Gruyter, New York
Alexandrov AL (2013) The effects of social and self motives on the intentions to share positive and negative word of mouth. J Acad Mark Sci 41:531–546
Balasubramanian S, Mahajan VT (2001) The economic leverage of the virtual community. Int J Electron Comm 5:103–138
Barasch A, Levine JE, Berman JZ, Small DA (2014) Selfish or selfless? On the signal value of emotion in altruistic behavior. J Pers Soc Psychol 107(3):393–413
Batson CD, Shaw LL (1991) Evidence for altruism: towards a pluralism of prosocial motives. Psychol Enquiry 2(2):107–122
Batson CD, Duncan BD, Ackerman P, Bucldey T, Birch KJ (1981) Is empathic emotion a source of altruistic motivation? J Pers Soc Psychol 40:290–302
Batson CD, Bolen MH, Cross JA, Neuringer-Benefiel HE (1986) Where is the altruism in altruistic personality? J Pers Soc Psychol 50(1):212–220
Batson CD, Early E, Salvarani G (1997) Perspective taking: imagining how another feels versus imaging how you would feel. Pers Soc Psychol Bull 23:751–758
Belk R (2013) Extended self in a digital world. J Consum Res 40:477–500
Berger J (2014) Word-of-mouth and interpersonal communication: an organizing framework and directions for future research. J Consum Psychol 24(4):586–607
Breazeale M (2009) Word of mouse. Int J Mark Res 51(3):297–318
Buss DM (2004) Evolutionary psychology, 2nd edn. Pearson Education, Boston
Chan YYY, Ngai EWT (2011) Conceptualising word-of-mouth. Mark Intell Plann 29(5):488–516
Cheema A, Kaikati AM (2010) The effect of need for uniqueness on word of mouth. J Mark Res 47:553–563
Cheung CMK, Lee MKO (2012) What drives consumers to spread electronic word-of-mouth in online consumer-opinion platforms. Decis Support Syst 53:212–225

Cheung CMK, Thadani DR (2010) The effectiveness of electronic word-of-mouth communication: a literature analysis. In: Proceedings of the 23rd Bled eConference eTrust: implications for the individual, enterprises and society, pp 329–345
De Angelis M, Bonessi A, Peluso AM, Rucker DD, Constabile M (2012) On braggarts and gossips: a self-enhancement account of word-of-mouth generation and transmission. J Mark Res 49:551–563
Dellarocas C, Narayan R (2006) What motivates consumers to review a product online? A study of the product-specific antecedents of online movie reviews. In: Proceedings of the international conference on web information systems engineering
Dichter E (1966) How word-of-mouth advertising works. Harvard Bus Rev 44(6):147–166 (Nov–Dec)
Garcia JR, Saad G (2008) Evolutionary neuromarketing: darwinizing the neuroimaging paradigm for consumer behaviour. J Consum Behav 7:397–414
Griskevicius V, Kendrick DT (2013) Fundamental motives: how evolutionary needs influence consumer behavior. J Consum Psychol 23(3):372–386
Griskevicius V, Tybur JM, Sundie JM, Cialdini RB, Miller GF, Kenrick DT (2007) Blatant benevolence and conspicuous consumption: when romantic motives elicit strategic costly signals. J Per Soc Psychol 93(1):85–102
Griskevicius V, Tyber JM, van der Bergh B (2010) Going green to be seen: status, reputation, and conspicuous conservation. J Pers Soc Psychol 98(3):392–404
Hamilton WD (1963) The evolution of altruistic behavior. Am Nat 97:354–356
Hennig-Thurau T, Gwinner KP, Walsh G, Gremler DD (2004) Electronic word-of-mouth via consumer-opinion platforms: what motivates consumers to articulate themselves on the internet? J Interact Mark 18(1):38–52
Kietzmann J, Canhoto A (2013) Bittersweet! understanding and managing electronic word-of-mouth. J Public Aff 13(2):146–159
King RA, Racherla P, Bush VD (2014) What we know and what we don't know about online word-of-mouth: a review and synthesis of the literature. J Interact Mark 28:167–183
Klein S (2014) Survival of the nicest. What made us human and why it pays to get along. Experiment Books, New York
Kozinets R, de Valck K, Wojnicki A, Wilner S (2010) Networked narratives: understanding word-of-mouth marketing in online communities. J Mark 74(2):71–89
Lee J, Park DH, Han I (2008) The effect of negative online consumer reviews on product attitude: an information processing view. Electron Commer Res Appl 7:341–352
Lovett MJ, Schachar R (2013) On brands and word of mouth. J Mark Res 50:427–444
Munzel A, Kunz WH (2013) Creators, multipliers and lurkers: who contribute and who benefits at online review sites. J Serv Manage 25(1):49–74
Nowak M (2006) Five rules for the evolution of cooperation. Science 314:1560–1563
Nowak MA, Sigmund K (1998) Evolution of indirect reciprocity by image scoring. Nature 393:573–577
Oda R, Machii W, Takagi S, Kato Y, Takeda M, Kiyonari T, Fukakawa Y, Hiraishi K (2014) Personality and altruism in everyday life. Personality Individ Differ 56:206–209
Phelps JE, Lewis R, Mobilio L, Perry D, Raman N (2004) Viral marketing or electronic word-of-mouth advertising: examining consumer responses and motivations to pass along email. J Advertising Res 44:333–348
Price LL, Feick LF, Guskey A (1995) Everyday market helping behaviour. J Public Policy Mark 14(2):255–266
Ross S (2011) Egoism and the everyday consumer: developing a new theory on prosocial behaviours in consumption contexts. Am Mark Assoc Summer 165–172
Rushton JP (1980) Altruism, socialization, and society. Prentice Hall, New Jersey
Rushton JP, Chrisjohn RD, Fekken GC (1981) The altruistic personality and self-report altruism scale. Personality Indiv Differ 2:293–302
Saenger C, Thomas VL, Johnson JW (2013) Consumption-focused self-expression word of mouth: a new scale and its role in consumer research. Psychol Mark 30(11):959–970

Sen S, Lerman D (2007) Why are you telling me this? An examination into negative consumer reviews on the web. J Interact Mark 21(4):76–79
Silverman G (2001) Secrets of word-of-mouth marketing. AMACOM Books, New York
Staub E (1978) Positive social behavior and morality: social and personal influences, vol 1. Academic Press, New York
Steffes and Burgee (2009) Social ties and online word-of-mouth. Internet Res 19(1):42
Sundaram DS, Mitra K, Webster C (1998) Word-of-mouth communications: a motivational analysis. Adv Consum Res 25:527–531
Van der Lans RV (2010) A viral branching model for predicting the spread of electronic word of mouth. Mark Sci 29(2):348–365
Weigel RH, Hessing DJ, Elffers H (1999) Egoism: concept, measurement and implications for deviance. Psychol Crime Law 5(4):349–378
Wien AH, Olsen SO (2014) Understanding the relationship between individualism and word of mouth: a self-enhancement explanation. Psychol Mark 31(6):416–425
Wojnicki AC, Godes DB (2011) Signaling success: strategically positive word of mouth. working paper, Rotman School of Management, University of Toronto

Customer Experience of Value in the Service Encounter

Shu-Ching Chen

Abstract Customer value is regarded as the fundamental basis for all marketing activity. It is also described as a source of competitive advantage for any organisation. In the critical service encounter, customer experience of value can improve business performance via customer satisfaction and/or customer loyalty. Customer satisfaction and customer loyalty are two imperative non-financial indices for measuring business success in a service-dominated organisation. Past studies suggest customer satisfaction can lead to customer loyalty. However, a satisfied customer may not be a loyal customer. Moreover, a review of literature on customer value, customer satisfaction and customer loyalty suggests the importance of exploring the role of customer value in understanding the relationship between customer satisfaction and customer loyalty for an organisation. How can the customer's experience of value impact the transformation of customer satisfaction into customer loyalty? Furthermore, what type of customer value experience in the service encounter is effective in strengthening the relationship between customer satisfaction and customer loyalty? In other words, what type of customer value will keep satisfied customers loyal? This article aims to explore the possible answers for those questions and provide mangers and service employees with insights into making a difference to the satisfied customer's loyalty through customer experience of value.

Keywords Customer experience · Customer value · Customer loyalty · Customer satisfaction · Service encounter

Introduction

> People will forget what you said. People will forget what you did. But people will never forget how you made them feel. ~ Maya Angelou

---

S.-C. Chen (✉)
Ritsumeikan Asia Pacific University, Beppu, Japan
e-mail: schen@apu.ac.jp

© Springer Science+Business Media Singapore 2016

C. Plewa and J. Conduit (eds.), *Making a Difference Through Marketing*,
DOI 10.1007/978-981-10-0464-3_11

A service is a source of experience from the consumer's perspective (Ostrom et al. 2010). Consumers perceive and evaluate value from their consumption experience in the service encounter (e.g. Anderson et al. 2006; Helkkula et al. 2012). Following the perspective of Helkkula et al. (2012) about "value in the experience" (p. 60), in this article the terms "customer experience of value" and "customer value experience" are defined as customers' perceived value in the experience of services. Customers' experience of value can improve business performance via customer satisfaction and/or customer loyalty (Reichheld and Teal 2001). Creating a positive service experience for consumers from a value perspective is thus imperative to an organisation's performance. In addition, scholars and practitioners have regularly called for further research on consumer consumption experiences and practices (e.g. Solomon et al. 1985; Helkkula et al. 2012; MSI 2014; Chen 2015). One challenge for managers of service outlets is the efficacy of value delivery during the service encounter to current satisfied customers, in order to drive their loyalty for business profitability.

Customer satisfaction and customer loyalty are two imperative non-financial indices for measuring the business success of an organisation. A review of past studies suggests a causal relationship between customer satisfaction and customer loyalty. Satisfying customer needs and wants is key to attaining customer loyalty (Oliver 1997). However, two contradicting premises have also been made: that customer satisfaction can lead to customer loyalty (Tsiotsou 2006), but a satisfied customer may not always be a loyal customer (Oliver 1999). This leads to the question of what factors are influential in transforming a satisfied customer into a loyal one. This question motivates subsequent research to identify possibly factors that influence the relationship between customer satisfaction and customer loyalty from different perspectives. In the field of marketing, customer value is identified as one prominent factor.

Customer value is regarded as being "…the fundamental basis for all marketing activity" (Holbrook 1994, p. 22). Customer value is also described as one source of competitive advantage for an organisation (Woodruff 1997). The identification of customer value as a key influential factor to transform satisfied customers into loyal customers raises an interesting managerial issue on customer relationships: the role of customer value in this transformation. In other words, how can customer experience of value impact the transformation of customer satisfaction into customer loyalty? Moreover, what type of customer value can keep satisfied customers loyal? Those questions motivate the current article's exploration of the role of the customer value experience with respect to the relationship between customer satisfaction and customer loyalty, as well as the effective type of customer value experience to strengthen the relationship.

In light of the research foci, this article reviews past studies of the associations among customer value, customer satisfaction and customer loyalty. The review of literature is included in the following sections, including the role of customer experience of value, the imperative viewpoints of consumers, the critical role of service employees, and the effective type of customer value experience. It provides suggestions to address issues regarding (1) the impact of customer experience of value on the transformation of customer satisfaction into customer loyalty; and (2) the approach to customer loyalty through customer value experience in the service encounter. The article consequently draws conclusions about influencing satisfied customers' loyalty through customer experience of value.

The Impact of Customer Experience of Value

The Role of Customer Experience of Value

Past studies identify varied relationships among customer value, customer satisfaction and customer loyalty, and suggest the variable of customer value is an antecedent of customer satisfaction and customer loyalty (e.g. Hume and Mort 2008). A literature review of relevant studies also suggests the moderating effect of customer value on the relationship between customer satisfaction and customer loyalty (e.g. Agustin and Singh 2005). In comparison, no studies provide empirical evidence of customer value as a mediator of the relationship between customer satisfaction and customer loyalty (Voss et al. 2010).

Investigating the mediating role of customer experience of value can help to understand the mechanism through which this causal variable affects the outcome of the relationship between customer satisfaction and customer loyalty. For example, Chen (2012) empirically examined customer value as a mediator of the relationship between customer satisfaction and customer loyalty in the context of online auction services. The results obtained from a structural equation modelling analysis provide support for the influential mediator of customer value, which has a completely mediated effect on the relationship between customer satisfaction and loyalty. In other words, customer experience of value can affect the pre-existing relationship between customer satisfaction and customer loyalty. For managers and service employees, this indicates the necessity of changing the mind-set from focussing on the casual relationship between customer satisfaction and customer loyalty. Instead, managers and service employees need to focus on how well they understand customer experience of value from the consumer perspective and implement customer value accordingly within their interactions with customers.

Transformation of Satisfied Customers

Retaining the loyalty of existing satisfied customers is regarded as a strategy to maintain a competitive advantage (Grönroos 2009). This leads to the critical issue of how to transform a satisfied customer into a loyal customer. To the best understanding of the author, transformation from customer satisfaction to customer loyalty can include two steps. The first is the initial stage of making customers satisfied (Chen and Quester 2006). Related to this step is the question of what type of customer value experience will lead to customer satisfaction. With an understanding of the drivers of customer satisfaction, the next step is retaining satisfied customers (Chen and Quester 2006) and eventually making them loyal customers (Chen 2012).

Interestingly, past studies suggest that customer value is essential in the two-step transformation of satisfied customers into loyal customers (e.g. Chen and Quester 2006; Chen 2012). Customer satisfaction can be achieved through overall customer satisfaction, customer expectations and the consumption experience by means of customer value (Chen 2012). The retention of satisfied customers paves the way to customer loyalty (Reichheld and Teal 2001; Chen and Quester 2006; Chen 2012). This can be achieved through implementing different types of customer value in services, which can trigger the satisfied customer's cognitive and/or emotional reactions in a positive way. This step of retaining satisfied customers highlights that managers of service outlets should understand the influence of different types of customer value experiences on the satisfied customer's formation of loyalty. Managers need to be able to identify effective types of customer experiences and take them into account in order to reinforce the strength of the linkage between customer satisfaction and customer loyalty. These tasks are challenging but the payoff of achieving customer loyalty by means of customer experience of value is worthwhile. Customers show their loyalty in different psychological and behavioural dimensions. For example, customers tend to have a preference for, and behave as frequent customers towards, an organisation or a specific store.

Going beyond understanding the role and the importance of customer experience of value in the formation of satisfied customers' loyalty, this study explores the effective type of customer value experience for keeping satisfied customers loyal. As such, it is necessary to understand the possible approaches to customer loyalty through customer experience of value in the service encounter. This paves the way for managers of service outlets to achieve desired customer loyalty.

Approach to Customer Loyalty

The Imperative Viewpoints of Consumers

Managerial recommendations from past studies suggest that in order to create and deliver effective types of customer value for customer loyalty, the customer value experience should be understood and created from the consumer perspective (e.g. Chen 2015). In a study of drivers of customer loyalty by means of customer value experience with matched dyads of service providers and consumers, it was found that the predictive validity of the loyalty model for consumers is significantly higher than for service employees (Chen 2015). This finding suggests that the factors driving satisfied customers' loyalty are better captured from the consumer perspective. Moreover, direct input from satisfied consumers about their experience of different types of value provides managers with better insights as to where to invest in generating customer value to match customers' needs and wants to achieve customer loyalty.

In addition, to understand customer experience of value from the consumer perspective, it is critical to pay attention to consumers' perceptions of competition in order to identify competing types of value. As stated in earlier sections, customer value is recognised as a means to generate and maintain the competitive advantage of an organisation (Woodruff 1997). Nevertheless, it is unclear what type of customer value can provide a competitive advantage in serving customers. The significant role of competition has been found in the formation of customer loyalty by means of customer experience of value. Chen (2015)'s dyadic study of service employees and consumers found that service employees perceive competition as a critical driving force for customer loyalty, but consumers do not. Rather, consumers take certain types of value delivery elements into consideration when choosing a service outlet from among competitive offers, for example, the experience of the social-psychological interaction with service employees. Furthermore, consumers use the available alternatives to assess certain types of value they experience from service employees. The type of value, for example, can be service quality, servicescape and service equity. This suggests to managers of service outlets while they try to identify what types of value can be effective, they should consider the consumers' view on competition from the perspective of both their individual absolute evaluation against needs and relative evaluation among competitors in terms of customer value. In order to identify effective types of customer value, managers should be aware that it may be ineffective to use service employees or other organisational personnel to answer questions on the drivers of customer loyalty by means of customer value, as their perceptions may not coincide with those of actual consumers.

The Critical Role of Service Employees

These days, co-creation of value with consumers is regarded as imperative for an organisation. Customer value can be co-created by both parties in the evolution of relationship (Grönroos 2009); it is therefore critical for management to understand the implications of customer perceived value from actual customers' service experience. Thus, service experience implies both efficiency and effectiveness of service delivery. This further highlights the important role of frontline employees in the customer's experience of value in the service encounter. Consequences of customer experience of value can highly depend on the service performance of frontline employees. The critical boundary-spanning role of frontline employees and the significant impact they have on business performance via customer loyalty are evident from past studies (e.g. Bove and Johnson 2009; Chen and Quester

2015). The relationship between customers and frontline employees exerts a direct influence on customer loyalty (e.g. Chen and Quester 2015) as well as an indirect link to firm loyalty (e.g. Yim et al. 2008).

In addition, co-creation of value between service providers and consumers raises an important issue on managing service employees during the service encounter. Recent studies suggest that managers of service outlets and frontline employees need to be aware of the role of competition on the impact of customer value experience in the service encounter. Competition is a significant global issue for businesses. Competition has been found to have a moderating effect on the formation of customer loyalty bas a result of satisfied customers' experience of different types of value from service employees (Chen 2015). Competition can lead to uncertainty in the consequence of achieving customer loyalty, as a consequence of service employees' effort to deliver certain types of value in the creation of customer experience, for example, customer experience of service quality, servicescape and service equity.

The Effective Type of Customer Value Experience

Two primary perspectives on customer value within the research domain of consumer behaviour are the rational perspective of value and the experiential perspective of value. According to Zeithaml (1988), the rational perspective of value is a kind of return for paying for a commodity, and such return involves an assessment of trade-off or a comparison of benefits and sacrifices in terms of the consumption experience. In contrast, the experiential perspective of value places an emphasis on personal and subjective perceptions such as emotion or preference (Holbrook and Hirschman 1982). Both perspectives are equally important to enhance the comprehension of value in consumption experiences (Holbrook and Hirschman 1982; Chen and Quester 2005).

Indeed, consumers can perceive and evaluate their experience of value in services in terms of both cognitive and emotional factors (Edvardson 2005; Han and Jeong 2013). Nevertheless, a cross-disciplinary examination of consumer experience of emotions and cognitions in the field of psychology suggests that consumers' emotional reactions are highly associated with their preference consistency, in comparison with cognitive reactions during choice decision making (Lee et al. 2009). Consumers who show stronger emotions towards an object tend to have higher preference consistency while making their choice decision. This implies an association between consumers' emotional experience and customer loyalty.

An ideal pre-condition for creating a positive customer experience is superior customer value, which is considered as the source of an organisation's competitive advantage and long-term business success (Woodruff 1997; Vargo and Lusch 2004). The following sub-sections explore some prominent and emerging types of customer value experiences from both cognitive and emotional aspects, which involve love, competition/service alternatives, service equity, service quality, servicescape, social-psychological interaction and trust. These types of value, derived from the consumer responses, have been evident empirically for their efficacy for customer loyalty in the service context. They should be helpful to address the issue on achieving customer loyalty through customer experience of value in the critical moments of truth, i.e., during the service encounter, and answer the question about what type of customer value experience can be effective in strengthening the loyalty of satisfied customers.

Love

Love is a concept relevant to the business context and is not limited to personal relationships. Chen and Quester (2015) provide empirical evidence of the applicability of the concept of love, which is originated from Sternberg's (1986) love theory, in the business context. It has been found that customer experience of love is a significant predictor of satisfied customers' loyalty. In order to translate the notion of love into service actions to achieve customer loyalty, frontline employees should display intimacy, passion and commitment towards their customers.

In particular, the factor of commitment deserves more attention, as it has been identified as the most critical factor among consumers who are with a specific frontline employee in an on-going business relationship lasting for years (Chen and Quester 2015). This finding provides managerial implications for recruiting frontline employees and customer relationship management. When managers recruit frontline employees, they should pay attention to applicants' personalities. People's attitudes towards love, which are derived from their individual personal experience of interpersonal interactions, influence their capacity to show love towards others. Recruitment of suitable employees for frontline services is therefore crucial. Managers of service outlets and service employees need to understand consumers' unspoken needs or wants for love in service encounters in order to perform better in their efforts to generate and maintain customer loyalty.

Competition

In this article, competition means the service alternatives offered by competitors as seen from the customer's perspective. Customers' understanding of competition may come directly from the consumption experience of competitors' offers, or indirectly from consulting their reference groups such as relatives and friends. From the customer's perspective, competition increases choice, raises expectations and provides opportunities. Competition is reflected in a consumer's perception of service alternatives regarding professionalism, public praise, flexibility in price adjustment, and competent quality service (Chen and Quester 2005).

Competition is significant in the service encounter (Bolton et al. 2014). The achievement of customer loyalty requires taking market competition into consideration. Competition has been identified as a moderator of the relationship between customers' perceived value and customer loyalty from the satisfied customer's perspective (Chen 2015). Competition influences consumer evaluations of certain types of customer value which impact on their loyalty attitudes and behaviours, for example, consumer experience of service quality, servicescape, and service equity (e.g. Chen 2015). In order to survive competition and maintain competitive advantage, an organisation needs to keep creating and delivering something unique and of value to customers (Bolton et al. 2014) as judged especially by the satisfied customers from their consumption experience.

Service Equity

Equity has been defined as "fairness, rightness, or deservingness in comparison to other entities, whether real or imaginary, individual or collective, person or non-person" (Oliver 1997, p. 196). Similarly, it has also been defined as "The customer's overall assessment of the standard of fairness and justice of the company's service transaction and its customer problem and complaint handling process" (Hellier et al. 2003, p. 1765). Equity may include financial and psychological judgements of service performance such as payment equity and sense of fairness in service. In the service encounter, equity can be measured by consumers from their experience of frontline employees' positive response to service failure; their experiences of fairness of an exchange of payment for service outcome, service contents, and time spent; their experience of promotional offerings regarding the customers' interests; their experience of noticing sales promotion by different media; and their experience of service employees' assurance of low risk for participating in promotion activities (Chen and Quester 2005).

Service equity is important for an organisation to stay competitive by keeping satisfied customers' loyalty in a fierce business environment. Customer experience of service equity has been found to have an indirect influence on customer repurchase intention (Hellier et al. 2003) and an indirect (Johnson et al. 2006) and a direct (Chen 2015) influence on customer loyalty. It has also been found to be a moderator in the relationship between customer satisfaction and repurchase decisions (Olsen and Johnson 2003). Moreover, when service equity considerations are perceived as satisfactory by consumers, the level of competition has no effect on customer loyalty (Chen 2015). In other words, whenever consumers make a positive judgement for service equity, it will not evolve into a concern for consumers when the competitive situation changes.

Service Quality

Consumers experience service quality from personnel interaction and its performance outcomes (Brady and Cronin 2001). Service quality can be perceived from frontline employees' performance in politeness, friendliness, courtesy, consideration for the interests of consumers, meticulous attitude in service details, and consistent service quality (Chen and Quester 2005).

The quality of service experience has been highlighted as a determinant of service interaction outcomes (Solomon et al. 1985; Zomerdijk and Voss 2010). Customer experience of service quality is often regarded as a driving force for customer loyalty (Gilbert and Veloutsou 2006) and is also suggested as a means to enhance customer loyalty (Cronin et al. 2000). Moreover, it is found that the relationship between service quality and customer loyalty is strongest when competition is high (Chen 2015). In order to achieve the desired level of satisfied customers' loyalty in a competitive business environment, it is imperative for managers of service outlets to invest in the improvement of the creation and delivery of quality services.

Servicescape

Servicescape is an organisation's physical facilities or physical environment that are "the manmade, physical surroundings as opposed to the natural or social environment" (Bitner 1992, p. 58). It includes both tangible and intangible features such as decorations, music and general ambience. The servicescape has been shown to influence the actual enactment of employee-customer interaction (Bitner 1992; Schneider et al. 2005). Servicescape can be evaluated by consumers based on their experience and the performance of frontline employees regarding the aspects of delight in the service process, ease in service procedure, a tidy consumption environment, and the space design for privacy in services (Chen and Quester 2005).

Studies of servicescape are centred on the impact of the physical places in which services are performed on service employees' performance (Parish et al. 2008), on customer satisfaction, or on customer intention (Harris and Ezeh 2008). However, the impact of the servicescape on customer loyalty as seen by the customers has received limited investigation. Recent work by Chen (2015) provides empirical evidence about the influence of servicescape on customer loyalty. Servicescape has a positive influence on customer loyalty. Moreover, the relationship between servicescape and customer loyalty can be moderated by the effect of competition. It shows that the higher the competition, the stronger the link between servicescape and customer loyalty. The findings suggest to managers about the value of servicescape to customer loyalty, and a possible way to survive competition and maintain competitive advantage.

Social-Psychological Interaction

Social-psychological interaction helps to develop a personal as well as commercial relationship. Personal interaction between frontline employees and consumers is the basis for the development. The social features and psychological phenomena in the service encounter can exert a major impact on service outcomes. Consumer experience of social and psychological benefits such as social identity and personal identification generates customer value (Walker and Olson 1991). Customer experience of the social-psychological interaction with service employees is an effective type of customer value for achieving customer loyalty (Paul et al. 2009; Chen and Quester 2006).

The interpersonal nature of service highlights the need for employees to understand consumer service motivations. Social–psychological interaction has been verified by consumers as an important driving force of loyalty in the service context (e.g. Chen and Quester 2006). Specifically, consumers experience of the service employee's practices consists of paying attention to customers, recognising and greeting customers whenever they visit, valuing the customer's needs of expressing their opinions and receiving feedback from the service employees, and retaining interactions with customers after the end of the service experience.

Trust

Consumers can experience trust from cognitive and emotional perspectives in the service encounter (Johnson and Grayson 2000). Specifically, frontline employees display credibility and benevolence in their interactions with customers by their thoughtfulness towards consumers, attentiveness to consumers' needs, and capacity to keep promises. On the other hand, consumers can evaluate trust from their feelings of dependability, competence, integrity, and responsiveness derived from their consumption experience.

Customer experience of trust is salient for the satisfied customers' decision making on staying loyal in a business relationship. It is proven to be a significant and positive factor for predicting customer loyalty (e.g. Doney and Canoon 1997; Chen and Quester 2015). Customers' experience of trust can significantly influence their loyal attitude and behaviour toward an organisation (Guenzi and Georges 2010). In addition, trust has been found to be a mediator between customer satisfaction and customer loyalty (e.g. Chen 2012). The findings suggest that there is not only a significant relationship between trust and customer loyalty, but also some direct relationship between customer satisfaction and customer loyalty. It is imperative for managers of service outlets and service employees to understand the influences of trust in order to develop customer loyalty and maintain the quality of relationship.

Conclusion

Customer experience of value can be varied. Past studies suggest that customer value consists of several varied types and each type of value can include several dimensions. Customer value has also been found in different roles in the formation of customer loyalty with other variables in varied research contexts. This article addresses the possible outcomes as to how customer experience of value in the service encounter can make a difference to the transformation of customer satisfaction to customer loyalty for an organisation. Suggestions for marketing practitioners in the service industry or employees in the service encounter are that customer satisfaction is an essential ingredient for customer loyalty, but that customer experience of different types of value can exist as a mediator and a moderator between customer satisfaction and customer loyalty. Moreover, it is evident that certain types of value can be effective to transform satisfied customers into loyal customers. This helps managers of service outlets reduce uncertainty about where to invest in generating customer value for the satisfied customer to achieve desired customer loyalty.

References

Agustin C, Singh J (2005) Curvilinear effects of consumer loyalty determinants in relational exchanges. J Mark Res 42:96–108

Anderson, JC, Narus, JA and van Rossum, W (2006) Customer value propositions in business markets. Harvard Bus Rev: 90–99

Bitner MJ (1992) Servicescapes: the impact of physical surroundings on customers and employees. J Marketing 56(2):57–71

Bolton RN, Gustafsson A, McColl-Kennedy J, Sirianni NJ, Tse DK (2014) Small details that make big differences: a radical approach to consumption experience as a firm's differentiating strategy. J Serv Manag 25(2):253–274

Bove LL, Johnson LW (2009) Does "true" personal or service loyalty last? A longitudinal study. J Serv Mark 23(3):187–194

Brady MK, Cronin JJ Jr (2001) Some new thoughts on conceptualizing perceived service quality: a hierarchical approach. J Mark 65(3):34–49

Chen SC (2012) The customer satisfaction-loyalty relation in an Interactive e-service setting: the mediators. J Retail Consum Serv 19(2):202–210

Chen SC (2015) Customer value and customer loyalty: is competition a missing link? J Retail Consum Serv 22:107–116

Chen SC, Quester P (2005) Developing a value-based measure of market orientation in an interactive service relationship. J Mark Manag 21(7–8):779–808

Chen SC, Quester P (2006) Modelling store loyalty: perceived value in market orientation practice. J Serv Mark 20(3):188–198

Chen SC, Quester P (2015) The relative contribution of love and trust toward customer loyalty. Australas Mark J 23(1):13–18

Cronin JJ, Brady MK, Hult GTM (2000) Assessing the effects of quality, value, and customer satisfaction on consumer behavioral intentions in service environments. J Retailing 76(2):193–218

Doney PM, Cannon JP (1997) An examination of the nature of trust in buyer-seller relationships. J Mark 61:35–51

Edvardsson B (2005) Service quality: beyond cognitive assessment. Managing Serv Qual 15 (2):127–131
Gilbert RG, Veloutsou C (2006) A cross-industry comparison of customer satisfaction. J Serv Mark 20(5):298–308
Guenzi P, Georges L (2010) Interpersonal trust in commercial relationships: antecedents and consequences of customer trust in the salesperson. Eur J Mark 44(1/2):114–138
Grönroos C (2009) Marketing as promise management: Regaining customer management. J Bus Ind Mark 24(5/6):351–359
Han H, Jeong C (2013) Multi-dimensions of patrons' emotional experiences in upscale restaurants and their role in loyalty formation: emotion scale improvement. Int J Hospitality Manag 32:59–70
Harris LC, Ezeh C (2008) Servicescape and loyalty intentions: an empirical investigation. Eur J Mark 42(3/4):390–422
Helkkula A, Kelleher C, Pihlström M (2012) Characterizing value as an experience: implications for service researchers and managers. J Serv Res 15(1):59–75
Hellier PK, Geursen GM, Carr RA, Rickard JA (2003) Customer repurchase intention: a general structural equation model. Eur J Mark 37(11–12):1762–1800
Holbrook MB (1994) The nature of customer value: an axiology of services in the consumption experience. Serv Qual: New Dir Theory Pract 21:21–71
Holbrook MB, Hirschman EC (1982) The experiential aspects of consumption: consumer fantasies, feelings, and fun. J Consum Res: 132–140
Hume M, Mort GS (2008) Satisfaction in performing arts: the role of value? Eur J Mark 42:311–326
Johnson DS, Grayson K (2000) Sources and dimensions of trust in service relationships. In: Swartz TA, Iacobucci D (eds) Handbook of services marketing and management. Sage, London, pp 357–370
Johnson MD, Herrmann A, Huber F (2006) The evolution of loyalty intentions. J Mark 70(2):122–132
Lee L, Amir O, Ariely D (2009) In search of homo economicus: cognitive noise and the role of emotion in preference consistency. J Consum Res 36(August):173–187
MSI (2014) 2014–2016 research priorities: a guide to MSI research programs and procedures. Marketing Science Institute, Cambridge
Oliver RL (1997) Satisfaction: a behavioral perspective on the consumer. McGraw-Hill International Editions
Oliver RL (1999) Whence consumer loyalty? J Mark 63:33–44
Olsen LL, Johnson MD (2003) Service equity, satisfaction, and loyalty: from transaction-specific to cumulative evaluations. J Serv Res 5(3):184–195
Ostrom AL, Bitner MJ, Brown SW, Burkhard KA, Goul M, Smith-Daniels V et al (2010) Moving forward and making a difference: research priorities for the science of service. J Serv Res 13 (1):4–36
Parish JT, Berry LL, Lam SY (2008) The effects of the servicescape on service workers. J Serv Res 10(3):220–238
Paul M, Hennig-Thurau T, Gremler DD, Gwinner KP, Wiertz C (2009) Toward a theory of repeat purchase drivers for consumer services. J Acad Mark Sci 37:215–237
Reichheld FF, Teal T (2001) The loyalty effect: the hidden force behind growth, profits, and lasting value. Harvard Business Press
Schneider B, Ehrhart MW, Mayer DM, Saltz J, Niles-Jolly KA (2005) Understanding organization-customer links in service settings. Acad Manag J 48(6):1017–1032
Solomon MR, Surprenant C, Czepiel JA, Gutman EG (1985) A role theory perspective on dyadic interactions: the service encounter. J Mark 49(1):99–111
Sternberg RJ (1986) A triangular theory of love. Psychol Rev 93(2):119
Tsiotsou R (2006) The role of perceived product quality and overall satisfaction on purchase intentions. Int J Consum Stud 30:207–217
Vargo SL, Lusch RF (2004) Evolving to a new dominant logic for marketing. J Mark 68:1–17
Voss GB, Godfrey A, Seiders K (2010) How complementarity and substitution alter the customer satisfaction–repurchase link. J Mark 74:111–127

Walker BA, Olson JC (1991) Means-end chains: connecting products with self. J Bus Res 22 (2):111–118

Woodruff RB (1997) Customer value: the next source for competitive advantage. J Acad Mark Sci 25(Spring):139–153

Yim CK, Tse DK, Chan KW (2008) Strengthening customer loyalty through intimacy and passion: roles of customer-firm affection and customer-staff relationships in services. J Mark Res 45 (6):741–756

Zeithaml VA (1988) Consumer perceptions of price, quality, and value: a means-end model and synthesis of evidence. J Mark: 2–22

Zomerdijk LG, Voss CA (2010) Service design for experience-centric services. J Serv Res 13 (1):67–82

Multiple Celebrity Endorsement

Sik Chuen (Max) Yu and Ravi Pappu

Abstract The use of multiple celebrity endorsers, to advertise a single brand, is becoming increasingly common. While the idea of using multiple endorsers is not entirely new, research on the topic is scant. This research contributes to the celebrity endorsement literature by introducing a previously unexplored dimension of source congruence: portfolio-brand fit. This research conceptualises fit as a multidimensional construct and offers empirical evidence for its impact on consumer brand evaluations. The conceptual model is based on information processing models. The conceptual model was tested in two different presentation formats for a fictitious brand in an experiment using a consumer sample. We measured the key variables using seven-point scales. Data were collected using online surveys. We tested the hypothesised model using SEM. The results provide support for the predicted effects. Results show that fit affects consumer attitudes toward multiple celebrity endorsement positively and attitudes toward the endorsed brand indirectly. Fit affects clarity of positioning of the endorsed brand differently in different presentation formats. The results suggest that managers should consider portfolio-brand fit in selecting the endorsers and should consider the potential impact on the brand's positioning when choosing multiple celebrity endorsement. Marketing practitioners should also consider the differential effects of fit in different types of multiple celebrity endorsement.

Keywords Congruence · Fit · Multiple-celebrity endorsement · Presentation format

---

S.C. (Max)Yu
The University of Sydney, Sydney, Australia
e-mail: Siyu7074@uni.sydney.edu.au

R. Pappu (✉)
University of Queensland, Brisbane, Australia
e-mail: r.pappu@business.uq.edu.au

© Springer Science+Business Media Singapore 2016

C. Plewa and J. Conduit (eds.), *Making a Difference Through Marketing*,
DOI 10.1007/978-981-10-0464-3_12

Introduction

The use of multiple celebrity endorsers, to advertise a single brand, is becoming increasingly common (Rice et al. 2012). Gillette has enlisted three athletes (Roger Federer, Thierry Henry, and Tiger Woods) for its *Champion* ad campaign to promote its Fusion men's razor.

Marketers have long known that fit (e.g. Till and Shimp 1998) or congruence (e.g. Kirmani and Shiv 1998) between endorser and brand is important in influencing consumer evaluations of the celebrity endorsements. The majority of the research on congruence in celebrity endorsement has focused on the evaluation of the brand in the context of a single endorser (e.g. Kamins 1990).

While the idea of using multiple endorsers is not entirely new, research on the topic is scant. Prior multiple celebrity endorsement studies (e.g. Rice et al. 2012) have continued to assume that fit operates on and influences consumer evaluations in the same fashion as it did in the context of 'single celebrity and brand' studies. How does fit operate in multiple celebrity endorsement?

When firms use multiple endorsers for promoting a brand, should the endorsers collectively be of good fit with the brand? Current literature does not provide satisfactory answers to this important question. Despite practitioners' increased use of multiple-celebrity endorsement, investigators have given relatively little attention to the effects of congruence in this strategy of endorsement.

Hence, the objectives of the present research are two-fold. First, we examine how *fit* affects consumer brand evaluations in multiple-celebrity endorsement. We introduce a new dimension of fit: portfolio-brand fit, which refers to the fit of the multiple elements in a campaign portfolio (e.g. celebrities/spokes people/cartoon characters) with the single brand. We use the term *celebrity portfolio* to refer to the endorsers collectively involved in an instance of multiple-celebrity endorsement. The advantage of the celebrity portfolio perspective is its consideration of the interdependencies among the brand and multiple celebrity endorsers with respect to consumer perceptions. Second, we also examine how portfolio-brand fit affects consumer brand evaluations in different formats of multiple celebrity endorsement currently used by practitioners.

We test the conceptual model for a fictitious brand in an experiment using a consumer sample. We find that portfolio-brand fit can favourably influence, consumer attitudes toward the endorsement and brand attitudes. The impact of portfolio-brand fit on clarity of positioning depends on the type of multiple celebrity endorsement. We find that portfolio-brand fit positively affects clarity of positioning when the endorsers are presented sequentially but not when both the endorsers are presented simultaneously. Consumers find it harder to process information presented sequentially hence they employ heuristic processing, where portfolio-brand fit serves as a peripheral cue, for inferring "hard to evaluate" concepts such as the brand's clarity of positioning. Peripheral cues are those that are not central to the true merits of the issue or message (Kirmani and Shiv 1998). We interpret the results of the experiment as support for the proposed multidimensional nature of fit in the context of multiple celebrity endorsement and for our prediction that consumers evaluate multiple-celebrity endorsements holistically rather than in a piecemeal fashion.

Conceptual Model

Fit

We adopt a consumer-based conceptualisation where fit with the endorsed brand depends on consumer perceptions of appropriateness of the connection or relationship between the celebrity portfolio and the endorsed brand. Specifically, we identify two types of fit consumers might perceive when evaluating a multiple-celebrity endorsement: *endorser–brand fit* and, celebrity *portfolio-brand fit*.

Endorser–brand fit refers to the fit between an endorser in the portfolio and the brand and this type of fit has been examined extensively in current celebrity endorsement research (e.g. Kamins and Gupta 1994). We define endorser-brand fit similar to Simmons and Becker-Olsen (2006). Fit between the endorser and the brand is high when the two are perceived as congruent (i.e. as going together), irrespective of from where that congruity is derived. Take from the opening example of Gillette. The fit between Roger Federer (Tiger Woods/Thierry Henry) and the endorsed brand would be referred to as endorser-brand fit. That is, researchers would be interested in three endorser-brand fits in this example: Roger Federer-brand fit, Tiger Woods-brand fit, and Thierry Henry-brand fit.

Portfolio-brand fit refers to how well the endorsers in the portfolio (i.e. Roger Federer, Thierry Henry, and Tiger Woods) *together* fit with the brand. We argue that, a consumer's perceptions of the fit between the celebrity portfolio and the brand can be different from the same consumer's perceptions of *endorser–brand fit*. That is, when a portfolio of three celebrities is used, we measure portfolio-brand fit once and endorser-brand fit three times: once for each of the three celebrities. For example, while a consumer may believe Roger Federer to be of high-fit with Gillette, the same consumer may not rate the celebrity portfolio which includes Roger Federer, Thierry Henry, and Tiger Woods, to be a similar high-fit with Gillette because of negative publicity received by the Golf supremo or lack of familiarity with the soccer champion.

Clarity of positioning refers to the absence of ambiguity in the information conveyed by the brand (Simmons and Becker-Olsen 2006). Brands signal attributes such as quality using their marketing mix. Clarity of positioning is a key determinant of how well a signal conveyed by the brand achieves its intended purpose and is often realised through marketing mix strategies (Erdem and Swait 1998). Brand alliances such as sponsorship, cobranding are known to affect clarity of positioning of the partner brands. For example, sponsorship researchers have observed positive impact of sponsorship relationship fit on clarity of positioning of the partner brands (Pappu and Cornwell 2014).

By definition, high portfolio-brand fit endorsements are those believed to be more appropriate and logical relationships for the brand and hence high portfolio-brand fit should be viewed as more consistent with the brand's marketing mix. Clarity of positioning is enhanced by consistency in the marketing mix (Erdem and Swait 1998). We argue that fit of the portfolio would enhance clarity of positioning because high portfolio-brand fit complies with consumers' expectations of the marketing mix and their perception of the brand's positioning.

Brand attitude formation or change, in response to marketing communications, occurs in a two-stage process and hence requires greater processing effort. Consumers first make a relatively effortless inference about the communication platform, such as a brand alliance (Simonin and Ruth 1998) or a celebrity endorsement (Pappu et al. 2011) or a sponsorship arrangement (Simmons and Becker-Olsen 2006). Then, on the basis of inferences about the communication platform, consumers form new brand attitudes or reinforce existing attitudes. For example, recent work in the areas of celebrity endorsement (Pappu et al. 2011) and sponsorship (Pappu and Cornwell 2014) shows that clarity of positioning and attitude toward the partnership are positively related to, and transmit the impact of relationship fit onto, consumer attitudes toward the brand. Consumers are cognitive misers (Fiske and Taylor 1984), hence they would base their inferences on heuristics (Garbarino and Edell 1997) such as portfolio-brand fit rather than evaluating endorser-brand fit of each individual endorser included in the portfolio. Thus, we propose that portfolio-brand fit affects attitudes toward the endorsement and clarity of positioning.

H1: Portfolio-brand fit positively affects attitude toward multiple celebrity endorsement.

Presentation Format

Prior research shows that people use different cognitive styles to process information presented simultaneously and sequentially. Sequential presentation discourages analytical processing, because one has to cognitively "recheck" materials presented previously (Krueger 1983). Moreover, materials presented sequentially are more vulnerable to memory decay (Allen et al. 2006) and are harder to recall, and hence could result in holistic processing. In contrast, simultaneous presentation allows more direct comparison of information (Reed 1973), and consequently aids analytical processing. Thus, the type of multiple-celebrity endorsement used (sequential vs. simultaneous presentation of the endorsers) could affect the way consumers process information and hence their evaluations. We argue that the processing routes and the type of processing consumers employ also vary by the type of judgments they are asked to make. Marketing actions such as clarity of positioning are relative harder to evaluate for consumers than expressing their attitudes toward a brand or an endorsement.

Specifically, the sequential presentation could result in heavier reliance on portfolio-brand fit, which serves as a peripheral cue for clarity of positioning evaluations, since information is more difficult to cognitively recheck. That is, it is much harder for participants in the sequential presentation format to assess the clarity of positioning of the brand in the ad and hence they rely more on portfolio-brand fit to make inferences. Evaluating the brand's marketing actions such as clarity of positioning should be more demanding for the participants than expressing their attitudes toward the endorsement. In contrast, it should be much easier to process the information presented together in the simultaneous format which should encourage information processing through the central route. Therefore, the relevance and importance of the information presented determines consumer evaluation of clarity of positioning in the simultaneous format. Participants are more likely to rely on the *arguments* presented in the ad. As previously discussed portfolio-brand fit serves as an argument in the simultaneous presentation. Therefore, we predict that portfolio-brand fit is more effective in the sequential presentation format than in the simultaneous presentation format in influencing consumer perceptions of hard to evaluate concepts such as clarity of positioning.

H2. Portfolio-brand fit affects clarity of positioning of the brand positively in multiple celebrity endorsement, such that consumer evaluations are more favorable in sequential presentation than in simultaneous presentation.

Attitude Toward the Brand

Alliances with other brands can serve as signals for a brand and hence can influence consumer attitudes toward the brand. As noted earlier, multiple-celebrity endorsement is a type of brand alliance between the celebrities as human brands and the brand they endorse. Enhanced clarity of positioning allows people to more easily learn and remember the information conveyed by the brand (Erdem and Swait 1998).

Previous research has shown that both clarity of positioning and attitude toward the partnership transmit the impact of sponsorship fit to attitude toward the sponsor (Simmons and Becker-Olsen 2006) and the impact of endorser-brand fit to nonprofit brand evaluations (Pappu et al. 2011). Thus, consumers make a relatively effortless inference of the endorsement which may in turn affect attitudes toward the brand. However, the current literature is unclear as to *how* the positive effect of portfolio-brand fit transfers to attitude toward the brand. We argue that portfolio-brand fit affects attitude toward the brand via attitude toward the endorsement.

H3: Attitude toward the endorsement mediates the impact of portfolio-brand fit on attitude toward the endorsed brand in multiple celebrity endorsement.

Higher clarity of positioning should elicit more favorable brand attitudes, all else being equal. In line with our earlier arguments in support of a two-step process of brand attitude formation, we expect clarity of positioning to mediate the positive effect of portfolio-brand fit on brand attitudes. Thus, clarity of positioning is expected to transmit the impact of portfolio-brand fit onto brand attitude. As previously mentioned, consumers are cognitive misers, hence we propose that portfolio-brand fit indirectly affects their attitudes toward the brand, via clarity of positioning.

Previous research has shown that multiple celebrity endorsement affects attitudes toward the brand positively when the endorsers appear sequentially (Rice et al. 2012). We argue that indirect effects of portfolio-brand fit on attitude toward the brand via clarity of positioning are more favorable in sequential presentation than in simultaneous presentation.

H4: Clarity of positioning mediates the positive impact of portfolio-brand fit on attitude toward the brand in multiple celebrity endorsement, such that consumer evaluations are more favorable in sequential presentation than in simultaneous presentation.

Experiment

Participants, Design, Stimuli and Procedure

We recruited 170 adult consumers (50 % females) through an online panel data provider. Participants (18–65 years old; mean age = 44 years) were randomly assigned to one of the two treatment conditions in a between-subjects design (Type of multiple celebrity endorsement: sequential presentation vs. simultaneous presentation). The order of presentation of the celebrities (John Travolta first vs. Russell Crowe first vs Hugh Jackman first) was counterbalanced. Portfolio-brand fit was a measured variable. We relied on the variation in the variable to estimate the latent variable interaction with presentation format.

Pretesting with a university student sample ($N = 93$, 54 % female, 18–29 year age group) helped in the selection of a fictitious brand ("Zertu"), ads used as stimuli and the celebrities used for endorsement. The pretest respondents expressed a favorable attitude toward the brand.

We designed portfolios that were more realistic and included endorsers, each of who individually offered a good fit with the selected brand. We selected three Hollywood actors (John Travolta [JT], Russell Crowe [RC], and Hugh Jackman [HJ]) as the endorsers on the basis of the results of the pretest. The selection of only male celebrities was to reduce extraneous variance due to gender effects of the celebrities. The pretest respondents considered each of the selected endorsers to be congruent with the watch brand. No major differences were observed among the endorsers in terms of source characteristics, such as attractiveness, expertise, familiarity, likeability, and trustworthiness.

We administrated the experimental tasks online using the fictitious watch brand, Zertu and fictitious ads professionally designed for the experiment. All the ads were identical in design and background except for the celebrities included. Participants completed the online questionnaire after viewing an ad showing two celebrities endorsing the watch brand either simultaneously or in a sequence.

Type of multiple celebrity endorsement varied at two levels (sequential presentation vs. simultaneous presentation). In the *sequential presentation* condition, the two celebrities were introduced sequentially through two separate ads, similar to the procedure used by Rice et al. (2012). For example, participants first saw an ad with John Travolta, then an ad with Russell Crowe. In the simultaneous condition, celebrities were presented together in a single ad. For example, participants in the *simultaneous presentation* condition saw an ad that included both John Travolta and Russell Crowe.

Measures

We measured the key variables using seven-point scales. We measured the independent variables (i.e. portfolio-brand fit and endorser-brand fit) in this experiment. We adapted Keller and Aaker's (1992, p. 42) scale from brand extension research to measure both *portfolio-brand fit* ($\alpha = 0.97$) and *endorser–brand fit* ($\alpha > 0.97$). We measured portfolio-brand fit once for each portfolio, and endorser-brand fit for each celebrity included in the portfolio.

Attitude toward the endorsement and clarity of positioning were the mediating variables, while attitude toward the brand was the dependent variable. We adapted scales from Simmons and Becker-Olsen (2006, p. 157) to measure *attitude toward the endorsement* ($\alpha = 0.96$), *clarity of positioning* ($\alpha = 0.94$) and *attitude toward the brand* ($\alpha = 0.97$).

We used source characteristics of the celebrities as covariates. We adapted scales from Ohanian (1990) to measure *attractiveness* ($\alpha = 0.97$), *expertise* ($\alpha > 0.97$) and *trustworthiness* ($\alpha > 0.97$) and scales from Simmons and Becker-Olsen (2006) to measure *likeability* ($\alpha > 0.98$) and *familiarity* ($\alpha > 0.96$) (2006). We also included consumer involvement with the product category ($\alpha = 0.98$) as a covariate in the analysis. We measured *involvement* using five semantic differential scales sourced from Zaichkowsky (1985).

Results

Preliminary analysis indicated that the design demonstrated variance in the key independent variables: Portfolio-brand fit ($M = 5.33$, $SD = 1.34$, range = 6) and endorser-brand fit (Celebrity 1: $M = 5.22$, $SD = 1.41$, range = 6; Celebrity 2: $M = 5.37$, $SD = 1.49$, range = 6).

We tested the hypothesised model using SEM. We conducted the analyses by including the source characteristics of individual celebrities and involvement as covariates, but the inclusion or exclusion of these variables as covariates did not change the overall pattern of structural relationships examined. Hence, we present the results of the parsimonious model without the covariates.

The results provide support for the direct and indirect effects of portfolio-brand fit and the predicted interaction effects. We tested nested models with (Model B) and without (Model A) the interaction terms. Model B, which included the interaction term, revealed significantly better fit to the data ($\Delta\chi_1^2 = 5.3$, $p = 0.021$).

Portfolio-brand fit affected consumer attitudes toward the endorsement significantly ($b = 0.66$, $p < 0.001$) indicating support for H1. As H2 predicted, the interaction between portfolio-brand fit and type of multiple celebrity endorsement had a statistically significant effect on clarity of positioning ($b = 0.22$, $p = 0.033$). Specifically, portfolio-brand fit affected clarity of positioning more favorably in the sequential presentation than in the simultaneous presentation. Portfolio-brand fit positively affected clarity of positioning in the sequential presentation ($b = 0.22$, $p = 0.046$) but not in the simultaneous presentation format ($b < 0.01$, $p = 0.886$). These results indicate support for H2.

The indirect effect of portfolio-brand fit on attitude toward the brand ($b = 0.33$, $p < 0.001$) was statistically significant, indicating support for H3. The joint indirect effect of portfolio-brand fit and type of endorsement on attitude toward the brand via clarity of positioning was not statistically significant ($b = 0.07$, $p = 0.078$). The indirect effect of portfolio-brand fit was not routed via clarity of positioning ($b < 0.01$, $p = 0.993$). These results do not indicate support for H4.

Discussion and Implications

The results indicate support for H1, H2 and H3. Portfolio-brand fit affected participants' attitude toward the endorsement significantly (H1). The interpretation of this result is that when people see an ad that features both John Travolta and Russell Crowe, people's attitudes toward the endorsement are likely to be shaped by the question "how well John Travolta and Russell Crowe together fit with the endorsed brand?" The results of the present study provide support for the multidimensional nature of source fit in the context of multiple-celebrity endorsement. Portfolio-brand fit affected consumer attitude toward the brand indirectly via attitude toward the endorsement (H3). Thus, this research makes an important theoretical contribution to the celebrity endorsement literature (e.g. Kamins and Gupta 1994; Kirmani and Shiv 1998) by introducing a previously unexplored dimension of source congruence: portfolio-brand fit. These results extend celebrity endorsement theory (e.g. Rice et al. 2012) by demonstrating that consumers evaluate multiple-celebrity endorsements holistically by integrating information about multiple endorsers and the brand.

Importantly, the results reveal that portfolio-brand fit affects clarity of positioning differently in different types of multiple celebrity endorsement. Specifically, portfolio-brand fit enhances clarity of positioning in the sequential presentation format but not in the simultaneous presentation format (H2). Thus, the results make an important contribution to the multiple celebrity endorsement literature (e.g. Rice et al. 2012) as the current literature does not explain how portfolio-brand fit affects consumer attitudes in different multiple celebrity endorsement formats. These results suggest that portfolio-brand fit serves as a peripheral cue for hard to evaluate concepts such as clarity of positioning when information is presented sequentially. In doing so, these results contribute to research on information processing models (e.g. Petty et al. 1983). The results do not support H4. The indirect effect of portfolio-brand fit on attitude toward the brand via the brand's clarity of positioning was not statistically significant.

The results of the present study suggest that portfolio-brand fit may have an important role in influencing consumer endorsement evaluations and imply that marketing practitioners should consider the multidimensional nature of fit in the context of multiple celebrity endorsement. Practitioners should consider how well different endorsers together fit when executing multiple celebrity endorsement. Marketing practitioners should also consider the differential effects of fit in different types of multiple celebrity endorsement.

References

Allen RJ, Baddeley AD, Hitch GJ (2006) Is the binding of visual features in working memory resource-demanding? J Exp Psychol Gen 135(2):298–313

Erdem T, Swait J (1998) Brand equity as a signaling phenomenon. J Consum Psychol 7(2):131–157

Fiske ST, Taylor SE (1984) Social cognition. Addison-Wesley, Reading

Garbarino EC, Edell JA (1997) Cognitive effort, affect, and choice. J Consum Res 24(2):147–158

Kamins MA (1990) An investigation into the 'match-up' hypothesis in celebrity advertising: when beauty may be only skin deep. J Advert 19(1):4–13

Kamins MA, Gupta K (1994) Congruence between spokesperson and product type: a matchup hypothesis perspective. Psychol Mark 11(6):569–586

Keller KL, Aaker DA (1992) The effects of sequential introduction of brand extensions. J Mark Res 29(1):35–50

Kirmani A, Shiv B (1998) Effects of source congruity on brand attitudes and beliefs: the moderating role of issue-relevant elaboration. J Consum Psychol 7(1):25–47

Krueger LE (1983) Probing proctor's priming principle: the effect of simultaneous and sequential presentation on same-different judgments. J Exp Psychol 9(3):511–523

Ohanian R (1990) Construction and validation of a scale to measure celebrity endorsers' perceived expertise, trustworthiness, and attractiveness. J Advert 19(3):39–52

Pappu R, Cornwell TB (2014) Corporate sponsorship as an image platform: understanding the roles of relationship fit and sponsor–sponsee similarity. J Acad Mark Sci. doi:10.1007/s11747-014-0373-x

Pappu R, Cornwell TB, Wallin A (2011) Endorsement: it's about how you identify with Kate and then how Kate fits with the brand. In: AMA summer educators conference 2011: delivering

value in turbulent times, AMA educators proceedings, American Marketing Association, vol 22, pp 40–41
Petty RE, Cacioppo JT, Schumann D (1983) Central and peripheral routes to advertising effectiveness: the moderating role of involvement. J Consum Res 10(2):135–146
Reed SK (1973) Pattern recognition and information processing. Academic Press, New York
Rice DH, Kelting K, Lutz RJ (2012) Multiple endorsers and multiple endorsements: the influence of message repetition, source congruence and involvement on brand attitudes. J Consum Psychol 22(2):249–259
Simmons C, Becker-Olsen KL (2006) Achieving marketing objectives through social sponsorships. J Mark 70(4):154–169
Simonin BL, Ruth JA (1998) Is a company known by the company it keeps? Assessing the spillover effects of brand alliances on consumer brand attitudes. J Mark Res 35(1):30–42
Till BD, Shimp TA (1998) Endorsers in advertising: the case of negative celebrity information. J Advert 27(1):67–82
Zaichkowsky JL (1985) Measuring the involvement construct. J Consum Res 12(3):341–352

Can Country of Origin Branding be a Competitive Advantage for Agri-Products from Emerging Countries?

Amal R. Karunaratna and Roberta Crouch

Abstract Country of origin research continues to generated interest and remain relevant in spite of the wide body of existing literature realised from studies generate around the world over many decades. The chapter presents a proposed conceptual framework of consumer decision pathways respective to agriculture based products, particularly those produced in emerging, underdeveloped economies. The proposed model illustrates the possible mediating effects of country of origin cues via low versus high involvement/motivations associated with low tech versus highly technical product endowment. The model further suggests that higher levels of technical product endowment will require more cognitively based assessments by consumers as compared to products based on lower levels of technology (like Agri-products) that will be assessed with a more affective approach. The chapter expands these concepts to present a possible matrix showing some suggested strategic approaches in the use of COO cue in country branding to leverage expected consumer responses and processing modes.

Keywords Country of origin · Emerging countries · Agri-products · Signalling · Country branding

Introduction

In the past, producers and manufacturers in emerging countries tended to be low cost providers of equipment for manufacturers in larger firms based in developed countries (Hussain and Jain 1999 in Magnusson Haas and Zhao 2008). Their only

A.R. Karunaratna (✉)
The University of Adelaide, Adelaide, Australia
e-mail: a.karunaratna@gmail.com

R. Crouch
School of Wine and Spirits, Groupe ESC Dijon Bourgogne, Dijon, France
e-mail: roberta.crouch@adelaide.edu.au

R. Crouch
School of Marketing &Management, The University of Adelaide, Adelaide, Australia

© Springer Science+Business Media Singapore 2016
C. Plewa and J. Conduit (eds.), *Making a Difference Through Marketing*,
DOI 10.1007/978-981-10-0464-3_13

source of competitive advantage being price based on low wage costs, leading to perceptions of lower quality and negative COO (Country of Origin) perceptions. Hence consumers in emerging and developed countries alike were less willing to pay high prices for products produced in these countries (Kotler and Gertner 2002; Srikatanyoo and Gnoth 2002). For the 43 countries where 20% or more of their total merchandise export is reliant on agriculture based commodities (FAO 2002) to bolster their hard-currency earnings, such negative perceptions, and lack of differentiation, traps these exporters into being price-takers rather than price makers. Thus they are condemned to being labour-intensive low-price suppliers to foreign firms that buy their products and add value. Hence, these already poor nations are further deprived of much needed export earnings. But, it is possible that sophisticated market development and innovation of capabilities, if realised, could enable exporters in these emerging economies to move further down the value chain, creating greater profits and a better quality of life for its citizens.

A few developing countries are, indeed, generating value and differentiating their products using inventive strategies that signal greater value by either building on a positive aspect of their COO image (where that is possible) or 'side-stepping' the issue by developing national brands of their own with credible value propositions. In this chapter, we use the COO literature and signaling theory to explore opportunities for developing countries to break out of the commodity trap via product differentiation, making them less susceptible to the winds of global supply-demand dynamics that contribute to continuing conditions of poverty. Here, we consider the concept of COO and its implications for agri-products, which are typically low-involvement products with a few notable exceptions such as 'fine wine'. This is followed by the application of signaling theory and nation branding and generally accepted COO based strategic implications that provide the basis for contrasting strategies for firms from developing versus emerging economies. Finally we consider the implications of these concepts to create products that eventually need to evolve from their COO based brands to strong brands in their own right rather than rely on their national origin based associations.

Country of Origin

Consumer purchasing decisions are based on their assessment of a variety of informational product cues that are moderated by their own their personal knowledge base or what they 'learn' during the 'search' and purchasing process (Han 1989, 1990; Mareswaran 1994). These cues can be related to the physical make up and objective performance of the product (intrinsic), for example the flavor of foods or drinks, colour, texture, actual ingredients etc., or cues that are extrinsic to the product but are related to it. Some extrinsic cues that consumers believe to be highly credible indicators of quality include price, brand name, retailer expertise and country of origin (COO). Given the difficulties consumers experience gaining and making objective evaluations of intrinsic cues (even in some cases post consumption), buyers often rely heavily on extrinsic information such as COO (Huber and McCann 1982) acts as "signals" for product quality (Steenkamp 1990) and, importantly, can be manipulated without changing the performance of the product itself (Verlegh and Steenkamp 1999).

COO theory provides historical illustrations of EMFs (Emerging Market Firms) branding their way out of the low-cost, low-quality cycle, for example coffee producers in Costa Rica and tea producers in Ceylon (Sri Lanka). In more recent times we see commodity producers from emerging economies such as China and Chile realising market success as wine producers without the stereotypical associations that have been relied upon for success in the past. These firms have built their own reputations, and in turn, enhanced that of their respective countries by establishing competencies linked to their locations not experienced before. This phenomenon has been seen in the past, where the expectations of quality and heightened perceptions of expertise has been built for countries such as Japan via the development and consumer support for brands like Sony and Honda (Lambert and Jaffe 1997) and Samsung and Hyundai in South Korea (Srikatanyoo and Gnoth 2002). Once it is accepted that quality products in a given category can be produced in a specific location, then it is possible (over time) to leverage those perceptions to other categories. For example, we may not readily associate Japan with the production of high quality fashion, but the more highly we think of Japan as a producer of quality products broadly, then the more highly we will regard their fashion products (Papadopoulos and Heslop 2002).

In addition to quality signaling, COO carries emotional and symbolic properties to consumers, particularly with food products. It is associated with product status, authenticity and exoticness (Batra et al. 2000), and makes connections between product-country imagery, with sensory, effective and ritual connotations (Askegaard and Ger 1998). It also connects consumers to products at an emotional level, relating to pride and autobiographical memories and transforms COO into an "expressive" or "image" attribute (Verlegh and Steenkamp 1999). Verlegh and Steenkamp classify COO influences into three groups: Cognitive, Affective and Normative.

Cognitive mechanisms are the form of signals inferring product quality attributes such as reliability and durability. Cognitive influences are based on stereotypical views about the nature of the country of origin and are formed as a result of direct or indirect product experiences. For example, German cars are associated with a perception of quality German engineering, while electronic products from Japan are associated with that country's established capabilities in manufacturing consumer electronics as a result of a high quality workforce and successful global manufacturing brands. The latter is testament to perceptions changing over time as this was not so for Japanese products when they first entered the market (Lambert and Jaffe 1997; Srikatanyoo and Gnoth 2002; Verlagh and Steenkamp 1999).

Affective processes include symbolic and emotional elements such as social status and national pride. Normative processes are those regarded as "the right way of conduct", that supports the local economy and consumers refraining from buying goods from countries with objectionable activities or regimes or when there is a feeling of animosity due to historical conflicts (Herche 1994; Klein 2002). Such views about countries may be also be formed during experiences with countries during holidays or encounters with foreigners through art, education and mass media (Han 1989, 1990). Consumers base affective associations to autobiographical memories, to national or ethnic identities, as well as impressions of status and pride associated with products from certain countries Hirschman (1985). Affective reactions to country associations can also be expected to influence consumer's consumer's self-image and their role within groups (Verlagh and Steenkamp 1999). An example of this is where "western" products have a positive association with brand attitudes (Batra et al. 2000), particularly where consumption and ownership are publicly visible.

Normative aspects are those that result in consumers making a conscious decision to purchase a product, or not, based on social or political views about the country of origin. Here we have examples of Jewish consumers boycotting German products because of the holocaust and Chinese consumers unwilling to purchase Japanese products because of the military rivalry between these countries. "Buy local" campaigns launched by governments, labour unions and industry groups to encourage purchase of domestic products appeal to consumers' tendencies towards ethnocentricism and motivates them to purchase domestic rather than foreign products (Balabanis and Diamantopoulos 2004; Klein 2002).

Verlag and Steenkamp (1999) note that while these influences are identified as separate components, they are not independent influencers and interact with each other. As consumers travel and migrate, they carry with them products with which they are culturally connected such food, wines, tea, coffee and so on. These are then exposed to their adopted countries through their cultural activities, art, education, mass media and everyday use and through retailing presence. Generally, each of the cognitive, affective and normative influences of COO appear to be associated with the level of economic development of a country (Papadopoulos and Heslop 2002). Specifically, the 'base' assumption by consumers is that across all product categories, in all markets (developed and emerging), products from 'first world' developed economies will be superior—as compared to those sourced from less developed locations.

However, often these assumptions related to expectations of lower quality don't result in a disadvantage for producers in emerging economies. Indeed, it can lead to higher sales and market advantaged because the expectations of lower quality are accepted by consumers in developed economies due to lower prices. Hence, these consumers will typically 'trade' off quality to save money especially where the difference is not seen to be significant and/or the products are low involvement. This 'tradeoff' is tempered, however, if there is a higher than acceptable perception of 'risk' in terms of bad product performance leading to unacceptable levels of dissatisfaction (Verlagh and Steenkamp 1999). As discussed, however, a country's image is not necessarily fixed and can be changed, but it is a slow process. In addition to leveraging the success of locally produced brands, special events such as the Olympics can accelerate the process and similar changes of attitudes to countries of origin have been apparent (Magnusson et al. 2008).

Signaling

As alluded to previously, while the concept of COO has been studied extensively, other cues such as pricing and branding have been shown to be stronger influences of product evaluations, particularly with high involvement products (Gurhan-Canli and Maheswaran 2000). Signaling theory is based on the assumption of information asymmetries in information based transactions. Therefore, firms in emerging economies have information to which consumers either have no access to, or are unwilling to get access, for a variety of reasons. Magnusson et al. (2008) have proposed that branding and COO ("made in") are two signals that are used in consumer decision making, but for a signal to influence attitudes, the information has to be accepted as true and result in a penalty to the sender if untrue (Rao et al. 1999). Hence, a firm can signal quality through warranties or loss of brand equity in the case of a brand name (Brouthers et al. 2005). Magnusson et al. (2008) propose COO is a weak 'signal' because its validity is based on a non existent bonding component and COO functions more as "noise" (distractions) to consumers, interfering with the firm's attempts to signal clearly to customers (Leclerc et al. 1994). Brands, on the other hand, function by reducing consumer search costs by focusing their attention on well-known names and symbols. The position is that consumers bond more readily with this approach than a COO cue. Further, perceptions of brands tend to be considered biased toward the hedonic (e.g. prestige) or utilitarian (e.g. convenience). Depending on the brand's country associations—real or implied (e.g. they have English or French spelling) Hence, COO based associations and perceptions of product quality can be generated by assumption and implicit rather that explicit signaling. Magnusson et al. (2008) have support their argument with the case of the $1.25 b acquisition of the IBM personal computer business by Lenovo (a Chinese company), including the brand name which was aimed specifically at changing negative associations with the notion of computers made in China. Such strategies are known as 'borrowing origins' (Papadopoulos and Heslop 1993). They suggest that, over time, Lenovo's reliance on the IBM brand has been increasingly marginalised as the Lenovo brand has been strengthened through its stable presence global markets. In time, other Chinese based brands may also work to enhance China's country image as has been achieved in Japan, Korea and elsewhere.

The previous examples relate to complex products. Li et al. (1993) also considered the signaling role of COO in product evaluations for complex products (watches) that included technical and style elements. They hypothesised that motivation played a key role in product evaluation. Motivation was defined as the effort exerted by consumers in information search about products under consideration. They argued that while COO was used as a signal to guess the product quality where an inference of belief was imputed to the product—where information was not available or difficult to comprehend. Their question was, if COO was used to infer belief about a product, then what are those beliefs based on?

Their research showed that COO was used when the information presented was limited, but consumers relied on COO much less when there was sufficient other information to make judgments about product quality. They also showed that consumers who were highly motivated, availed themselves of more information compared with less motivated individuals. Further, their research showed that consumer responses to COO indicated that they used this cue as more as a signal of style rather than the functional aspects of the product, indicating that subjective elements of a product are more susceptible to COO influences compared with more technical aspects. Information that has personal relevance results in high levels of information acquisition in the form of prior knowledge, or knowledge gathered during decision making (Dowling and Staelin 1994). It follows then, that consumers who have a high level of product category involvement will also conduct more extensive information searches (Zaichkowsky 1985). This suggests motivation and involvement have similar influences on information acquisition.

These findings indicate that COO may influence consumer evaluations via two possible decision pathways (see Fig. 1). Firstly, where products under consideration are technically complex and are, therefore, likely to require more information to be accurately assessed by consumers. Hence, higher levels of cognitive processes may take place during the evaluation process. Motivated and involved consumers are more likely to discount the COO cue, in favour of objective product information, unless extrinsic cues such as the COO of the product is deemed to be a credible cue to quality (e.g. French perfume, German cars) (Heimbach, Johansson et al. 1989; Rao and Olson 1990). Conversely, those consumers with lower levels of involvement are

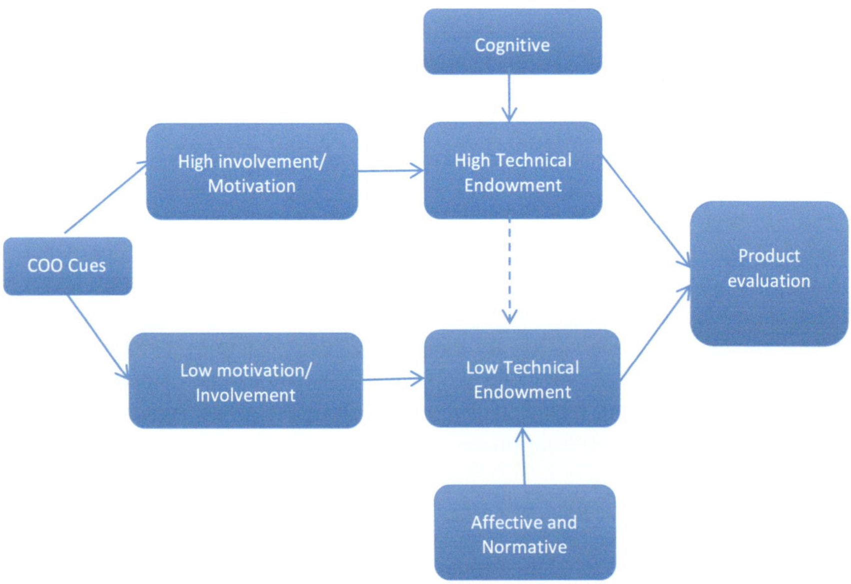

Fig. 1 Decision pathways under conditions of low/high involvement and products endowed with high versus low technical characteristics

likely to rely more heavily on the COO cue, even for complex products, because they lack the desire or ability to accurately evaluate objective, intrinsic cues. These consumers will be taking a decision path more likely to be based on the affective and normative product attributes. This is also likely to be the case where the products under consideration are less technically based and/or based on lower levels of category involvement. The product described in the study by Li et al. (1993) were watches which have elements of both technical complexity and styling whose intrinsic properties cannot be easily and accurately assessed by consumers, much like motor vehicles, computers, fine wines and complex services such as medical or legal advice. Conversely, less technical product examples include food and drink products, clothing and footwear, whose attributes are more easily determined.

The majority of agriculture based products are more likely to follow the lower pathway than the upper one. However, it could be conceivable that those who have the expertise and ability to make judgments about product quality in specialised agriculture based products such as wines, coffee and tea, may well follow the upper pathway. In this case, they may play an important role in influencing purchase decisions of those who would evaluate themselves with lower levels of expertise.

Country Branding

Country image profiles (country based beliefs and associations) are akin to a 'brand image' for respective countries (Kotler and Gertner 2002; Nebanzahl and Jaffe 1996; Papadopoulos and Heslop 2002; Srikatanyoo and Gnoth 2002)—it encompasses assumptions about values, competencies, strengths and weaknesses allowing consumers (like with product brands) to set a consistent expectation of quality. When a country is a co-component or a contributor to a product's branding characteristics such as with agri-products, the evoked image is subject to consumers using their past experiences with that country's products and other information that they may have. Hence, a country's brand (Country Brand) image associations on agri-food products send signals of particular quality characteristics about a country to consumers which have been created and re-enforced where consumers are cued to recall an image of the quality attributes associated with that country (Innes et al. 2007).

Governments promote country image building as brands and link them to industries for economic and political reasons. Canada, for instance, promotes the Canadian brand for Agriculture and Agri-food products in the Canadian market (Innes et al. 2007), the Australian government uses a program called "Australia Unlimited" as a brand Australia program for products that conform with the program (Australia Unlimited), and "Brand Korea" is a program run by the South Korean government as part of a cultural diplomacy campaign (Kim 2012).

These programs are subject to unexpected events and could have a positive influence on the country brand whereas in other cases, the reverse happens. In the case of South Korea, the South Korean Rapper's Gangnam Style music created an audience of 400 million and enhanced the government's program (Kim 2012) whereas criticism regarding Canada's policies over non-implementation of the Tokyo protocol which lead to increases in greenhouse gas emissions may have damaged Canada's image as a "trustworthy, reliable, competent, pristine and environmentally friendly" country brand (Innes et al. 2007). Hence a country brand is based on past experiences with the intrinsic attributes of the product carrying the country brand and the interactions between the individual's perception of the country, its marketing efforts, brand equity and expected quality create overall brand images of a country.

Because of the less differentiated nature typical of agri- products, building country brand attributes into these are more challenging. However, when certain conditions of production are controlled, it is possible to differentiate such products and command premium prices—for example organic or sustainably produced foods. Further, Innes et al. (2007) have shown that when agri-food products are country branded, enhancing consumers' perception of the product's quality, this differentiates the product from competing products, such as Hawaiian pineapples or Canadian Maple syrup. For such products, there is a potential for higher profits via price differentiation where there is sufficient country brand equity associated with them in a credible way, and the supply of products sold is limited. Further, fulfilling the purported value proposition is critical for the country brand to be a strong quality signal resulting in a sustained boost for the quality associated with the brand. They point out that ensuring the integrity of the production practices of firms using the country's brand is essential to maintaining the brand's credibility because it is via these processes that the uniqueness of the country associations is confirmed. Although this may not be directly observable to the consumer, positive country brand equity can only be sustained in the long-term if the claims and its image are consistent. A credibility gap between actual production practices and quality image is of concern because a profit-maximising firm will have little incentive to adhere to the quality standards unless they are required to do so. Hence, just like in a firm branding situation, sustaining a country brand image is highly contingent on maintaining consistent quality.

Strategies for Countries with a Weak Versus a Strong COO Brand Image

As new suppliers enter international markets with unknown brands, COO continues to play a role in determining consumer purchasing decisions. Where products enhance social relationships and possession of such products are suggestive of high social status, products from western developed countries are still at a significant advantage compared with developing nations. Whilst some countries have reversed this situation over time, surprisingly countries like China, despite investments in the Olympics Games, greater openness in the media, education of their population about western culture and tradition and customs have been far less successful in changing perceptions (Herstein et al. 2014). This may be due to their lack of quality global brands to underpin the enhancement of their country image brand. Moreover, despite the growth of manufactured exports from emerging countries, agriculture based exports to other developing countries (15.6 %) and to industrialised countries (48 %) in even as far back as 2001 was significant (Aksoy and Beghin 2005). Value adding opportunities through unique and desirable production and processing methods and working to enhance country branding are important means of improving profitability. As a negative country brand image represents a key source of negative consumer perceptions restricting the ability to achieve premium prices, overcoming this via branding is central to business development opportunities in high value markets and market segments.

Herstein et al. (2014) presented a typology to analyse the relationship between COO image and the level of economic development and its implications for branding strategies. They proposed a "Made-in" matrix to enable the positioning for companies originating from developing versus developed countries and their human capital status as a means of suggesting different mechanisms for overcoming the made-in problem. This model has two dimensions: the vertical axis (global political status) represents the external aspect of the economic development variable and the horizontal axis represents the internal aspect of economic development. The global political status represents the level of influence the home country has on designing political agendas all over the world or on certain geographic areas or regions. This dimension has a powerful influence on consumer evaluations of COO (Bilkey and Nes 1982) and since a country's political power positively influences its export capabilities, countries that influence other countries political agendas are evaluated to have greater brand equity compared to those who are on the receiving end of political influences who suffer from low brand image (Herstein et al. 2014).

The top 10 nations according to a survey by Gfk (2014) are Germany, USA, UK, France, Canada, Japan, Italy, Switzerland, Australia and Sweden. The positioning of these countries is based on their country brand image in terms of international diplomacy, exports, governance, culture, people, tourism immigration and investments. While the US has fallen in this ranking compared with Germany due to its role in world peace and security, Russia has been downgraded due to its negative role in international peace and security to be overtaken by Argentina, China and Singapore. Despite their size, BRIC (Brazil, Russia, India and China) are weaker in terms of their political influence on other countries political agendas as being limited (Herstein et al. 2014). In practical terms, empirical country brand rankings such as the Gfk survey or Brand Finance (2014) can be used to map countries onto this axis or political risk analysis such as the PRS (2015) which may correlate with the Gfk survey or a composite score of both.

The horizontal axis (Fig. 2) refers to a country's human capabilities, where workers in developed countries tend to have higher levels of education, greater exposure to local and global information and technology with greater levels of workforce skills compared with those from developing countries. As discussed earlier, consumers globally tend to evaluate brands from these countries more positively than those from developing countries (Bjorkman and Xiucheng 2002).

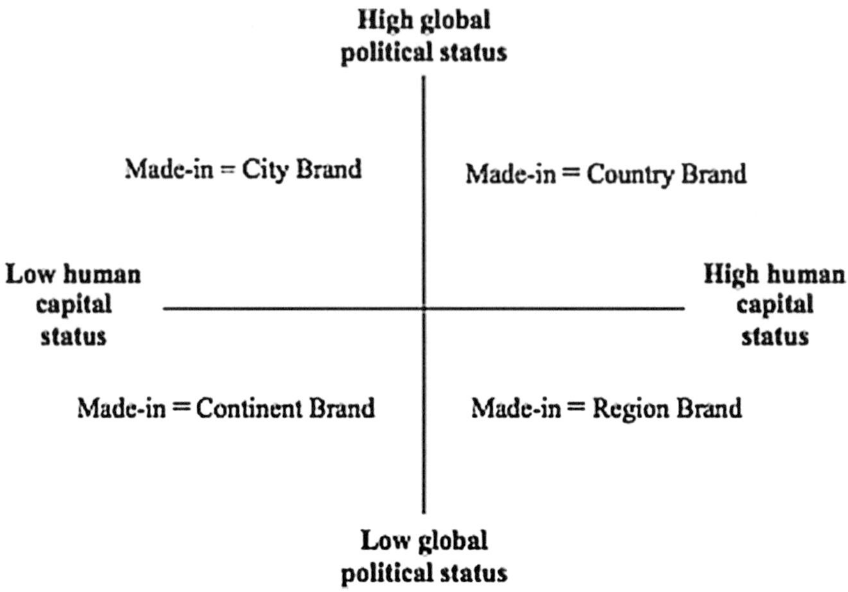

Fig. 2 Made-in matrix positioning model" (Herstein et al. 2014, p. 299)

The authors use this matrix develop generic strategies based on these two dimensions. The top right quadrant **high global political—high human** capital status applies to companies from developed nations where they have an advantage over most other countries. They have advantages that are strong in both dimensions, and while Herstein et al. (2014) state that organisations from the USA, Germany, Japan, France and the UK are likely to be high on this scale, The World Economic Forum (2013) ranks the US, Germany, Japan, France, and the UK as 16, 6, 21, 15, 8 respectively. Countries ranked in the top 10 are: Switzerland (1), Finland (2), Singapore (3), Netherlands (4), Sweden (5), Germany (6), Norway (7), UK (8), Denmark (9) and Canada (10). Companies from these countries are in a position to exploit their generally positive country brand image; emphasizing their heritage and history is likely to further enhance their country equity in this regard.

The second positioning, working clockwise from the first, **low global political—high human capital** refers to companies from powerful emerging markets strong only in human capital and China and India are presented as examples. However the World Economic Forum (2013) ranks China as 43, India at 78 and Sri Lanka as an example of a small country with a long standing agribusiness industry at 50. These countries have a relatively well educated workforce but histories of an unstable political environment or non-democratic governments with less influence on other nations representing lower global political status. India's status as a young democracy is still in a state of development. However, there is strong evidence that both India and China are increasingly influential in the region of south east Asia.

For companies from these countries, the authors recommend a regional branding strategy that highlights the unique features of specific regions. The authors suggest examples of regional branding such as Champagne from France, Toscana from Italy and for the Chinese region of Liaoning for wine and Shanghai for fashion. Other examples could include the Nilgiri Hills in India for tea, Kashmir for wool (particularly Pashminas) and the Uva region in Sri Lanka for top quality tea. Other examples will be considered later.

The third quadrant **low global political—low human capital** represents companies from countries that have no advantage or leverage. The authors list Thailand (44), Vietnam (70), Nigeria and South Africa that have no or little political influence over other countries and are recommended to implement a continent branding strategy. Their basis of creating a competitive advantage could be based on leveraging the continent in which they are located. Hence, Thai or Vietnamese products should emphasise an exotic status by their location in the Far East or the most exotic continent in the world—East Asia. Companies from countries such as Nigeria and South Africa could emphasise the "heart of Africa" as their location, emphasising the African continent. The aim here is to emphasise the continent instead of the lack of equity of the country and to leverage the perceptions of the continent and blur the association of a single developing country.

The fourth quadrant **high global political status—low human** capital status has one advantage. They have a strong political status but suffer from a low human capital status. Examples include Russia (51) with high political influence over countries within the Eastern European region, it's commonwealth states, such as Armenia (73), Azerbaijan (64), Kazakhstan (45), Kyrgyszstan (94), Moldova (83), Turkmenistan (ND), Tajikistan (ND) and Uzbekistan (ND). Another example is Egypt (111) with its apparent influence over regional nations such as Jordan, Morocco and Saudi Arabia which also has a low perceived human capital status and index. It is recommended that companies from these nations engage in a city branding strategy where they leverage positive affective reactions to the most famous cities in their country. In the case of Russia, they suggest St. Petersberg and Moscow, Cairo and Alexandria for Egypt and Istanbul and Ankara for Turkey. These famous cities present a highly positive image due to their history and heritage and these shine brighter than the rest of the country image to create a positive impression on the consumer. They provide the examples of leather manufacturers from Turkey emphasising Istabul or Ankara and Russian companies manufacturing food such as chocolate, caviar and beverages such as liquors and vodka and jewelry and marble should emphasise their origins in St. Petersberg for cachet, design and style.

While it can be seen that this typology and the examples provided are not perfect in terms of their potential fit with the types of data that could be used here, it is a highly efficient means of developing strategies and deconstructing the general COO concept into a more refined context. In the following section we consider the application of this typology to agribusinesses in emerging economies.

Agricultural Food Commodities and Differentiation

Of the many problems faced by emerging countries in developing their economies and enhancing their country brand images are the challenges they face in value adding to their major exports. UNIDO (2013) estimates that where high-income countries add over US$200 to value by processing one tonne of agricultural products, developing countries add less than US$50 and consumer perceptions of products are associated with income per capita of the country of origin. This apparent and real link between value adding and perceptions of emerging economies makes it difficult to use a price signal even where quality may be high, particularly with respect to consumer goods. Emerging economies, therefore, are trapped in a difficult position where branding and word of mouth dynamics are less accessible to them (Hudson and Jones 2003). One way to provide a price signal is to obtain a quality certification such as ISO 9000 which can be an expensive process. Depending on the extent of the requirements, the cost ranges from $5,000–50,000 plus the costs of a consultant if necessary (The 9000 Store) which can be prohibitive for small producers.

Hudson and Jones (2003) have shown that the availability of quality certification based signals such as ISO 9000 have poor take up, particularly by smaller exporters, due to compliance costs and a greater challenge in establishing brand reputations. This is seen as an information asymmetry (signaling) problem where there are significant barriers to communicate the product and brand attributes of products from producers from less financially well resourced countries with weak currencies. These authors found that rather than ISO certification, smaller exporters attempt to comply with the quality requirements of each of their markets. This suggests differential branding positions that are likely to create inefficiencies and inconsistencies that may create additional cost burdens. Hence, what other mechanisms have been used by emergent economies as a means of brand based competitive advantage?

Research done by Moreda-Piñeiro et al. (2003) on the physical attributes of tea from Sri Lanka, India, China, Malaysia China, Japan, Bangladesh, Malaysia and Papua New Guinea have shown that in terms of their physical properties of 17 elements including Aluminum, Barium, Cadmium and so on show that while tea from Sri Lanka is closely grouped and overlaps Indian teas, it is quite distinct from most of the others such as China whose properties are spread and different to Japan, Bangladesh and the others. This implies that tea from Sri Lanka appears to have distinct characteristics although they may overlap or be close to those of Indian teas. This means Sri Lankan teas have the potential to be physically unique—not just perceptually so, which is often the case with consumed products. This uniqueness is evident at auction pricing. It is reported that tea branded as Ceylon Tea (the former name of Sri Lanka during colonial times), fetches $US1 more than tea from other origins (Business Times 2010). This indicates potential for a price signaling effect based on quality.

Based on the Herstein et al. (2014) typology, this suggests a regional branding based strategy on locality effects linked to the brand to be most effective for this country. Although it is not totally clear if the association between Ceylon and Sri Lanka are well understood within key market segments, and it is likely that the older "Ceylon" represents a heritage brand evoking images of a colonial past with languid tea plantations, pith helmet clad planters and leisurely tea parties and tea pluckers on confluent green hillsides with friendly, smiling faces and more than a touch exotic compared with recent images of Sri Lanka which are more likely to be associated with terrorism and human rights issues. Recent informal research has suggested a somewhat positive set of images evoking suggesting diversity, authenticity, compactness and friendliness (Ericsson and Rudell 2013). Evoked words such as these indicate attitudes to brands. Reflecting a possible change of attitude to Sri Lanka, Brandfinance, an organisation that tracks the overall financial value of a national brand annually and published in its Nationbrands report showed that Sri Lanka's national brand improved from being ranked 73 in 2012 to 65 in 2013 with a value improvement of 48 %, which, while still not in the stellar regions of the USA (ranked 1st), China (2nd) and Germany (3rd) and India (9th), the improvement in positioning is a positive sign and Sri Lanka is ranked fourth in South Asia.

Region of origin effects are also apparent in the coffee industry. In a study on pricing opportunities in the coffee industry of single origin coffee and the relationship between price and quality, where price is obtained on internet auctions and the quality score is a ranking based on a taste score in Japanese, US and European markets, price is influenced by the sensory score and varies according to the country of origin (Teubner 2010). They also found that prices varied according to its region of origin. There is, therefore, an elasticity effect where an increase in quality of 1 % resulted in a price premium of 7.7 %. However, there was a negative association between quantity and price where a 1 % increase in availability of coffee resulted in a 0.39 % reduction in price. Product differentiation in agricultural products may take other forms, including geographic indicators such as country branding which may also include regional branding and product quality signaled by certification. For instance, the Dominican Republic has gained international leadership as a source of organic bananas with exports of $200 m in 2011 which was dramatic growth from the $70 m in 2010 based on fair-trade certification granted to 400 companies in June 2011. The Dominican Republic is gaining further sophistication in value-adding in the coffee industry by launching their first origin brand "Barahola Coffee" (Agritrade 2011). Such a move within the coffee industry may be a beneficial spillover from established COO connections from Dominican cigars which are regarded as some of the finest in the world. Dominican coffee, with its soft and mild flavour and a particular taste, originating from a region that is of granite origin matches the taste profile popular with the Japanese market which has a clear preference for Caribbean coffee products (Luxner 2004).

Considering the pricing coffee with a stipulated country of origin, with reference to a standard, Guatamala coffee fetched a price premium of 75 % compared to Honduran coffee and Bolivia obtained a price premium of 63 % whereas the

Ethiopian region of Yirgachefe commanded a price premium of 50 % over other regions. The author also commented that coffee professionals express a preference for traditional varieties of coffee over modern varieties. Further, coffee that is organic also resulted in a pricing premium of 27 % compared to non-organic coffee. Overall the study found that COO played a significant role in the price for coffee and the highest ranked coffee judged as excellent achieved a pricing premium of 143 % compared to coffees ranked fourth and lower. Interestingly, Columbia was known to have invested substantial funds on creating a positive image in the mass market for coffee, and it appears to have paid off. Using these strengths, for countries such as Guatamala, Honduras and Bolivia, branding opportunities based on continent branding and niche markets may present strong strategic opportunities for branding signaling based on South America and the region.

The limited search a consumer makes with food products may restrict the potential cognitive processing of the subtle differences in COO based branding effects discussed here. For food based agri-products, product differentiation may represent a serious perceptual challenge as differences may be more subjective and personal rather than for high involvement products such as electronic goods or fashion products. Further, if a customer is satisfied with a product, it may be difficult to provide sufficient reasoning to motivate them to look for other brands unless there is a compelling reason to do so where brand loyalty has been established and expert opinion may be one way of opening interest in consumers via cooking shows and print media.

Branding effects may represent the strongest opportunity for differentiating products from competition and the types of COO approaches described above. This has been done very successfully within the wine industry where research has shown that the distinction between higher and lower quality wines are not easily distinguished (Veale 2008; Veale and Quester 2009). As a result, wine drinkers resort to labels and pricing to make inferences about the quality of the wine, along with the taste, and geographic indicators or country and region of origin are major determinants of brand equity.

Conclusions

In this chapter we have examined the problems confronting developing or emerging countries and their opportunities for differentiating their products. Given the large number of emerging economies that are based on agri-foods, finding opportunities for them to add value and gain greater profit advantages enjoyed by developed nations represents an important enabler for social and quality of life improvements for many of these nations. While the COO effect decomposed using the typology by Herstein et al. (2014), provides a starting point for developing generic strategies, eventually, signaling theory suggests that COO has to be eventually transferred into the brand for products to be strongly cognitively established. Mechanisms for achieving this with the majority of products in agri-foods due to their low involvement and low complexity results in low levels of motivation to indulge in search activities to learn about these products.

Further, many of these products are subject to fads and fashions such as the recent international interest in coconut-based products, believed to be the health product of the moment. For producers who rely on a few agricultural products to sustain their lives, opportunities for building brands and generating ongoing streams of income is a life-giving process and innovations with brands provide the basis for this kind of income longevity. For producers of such products, diffusion and sustainability can be greatly assisted by the role of innovators and opinion leaders and market development processes such as the identification of niche markets to which such products are likely to appeal and developing products for these markets such as specific products, blends and characteristics that change with changing tastes. All this, coupled with COO and branding provides opportunities for producers to differentiate themselves and create new business opportunities.

References

Agritrade (2011) Growing Competition in Differentiated Product Markets. http://agritrade.cta.int/Agriculture/Commodities/Bananas/Growing-competition-in-differentiated-product-markets. Accessed 17/7/15

Aksoy MA, Beghin, JC (ed.) (2005) Global agricultural trade and developing countries. The International Bank for Reconstruction and Development/The World Bank, http://www-wds.worldbank.org/external/default/WDSContentServer/WDSP/IB/2005/11/22/000090341_20051122134826/Rendered/PDF/344290PAPER0Gl101official0use0only1.pdf. Accessed: 27/7/15

Askegaard S, Ger G (1998) Product-Country Images: Towards a Contextualized Approach. In: Basil G (ed) E - European Advances in Consumer Research, vol 3. Englis and Anna Olofsson, Provo, UT: Association for Consumer Research, pp 50–58

Australia Unlimited, http://www.australiaunlimited.com/brand-australia/brand-australia-engagement-program Accessed 24/7/15

Balabanis GR, Diamantopoulos A (2004) Domestic Country Bias, Country-of-Origin Effects and Consumer Ethnocentrism: A Multidimensional Unfolding Approach. Journal of the Academy of Marketing Science 32(1):80–96

Batra R, Ramaswamy V, Alden DL, Steenkamp JBE, Ramachander S (2000) Effects of Brand Local and Nonlocal on Consumer Attitudes in Developing Countries. Journal of Consumer Psychology 9(2):83–95

Bilkey WJ, Nes E (1982) Country-of-Origin Effects on Product Evaluations. J Int Bus Stud 13(1): 89–100

Brouthers LE, Story JW, Hadji-Marcou J (2005) Can developing country firms overcome negative country of origin stereotypes? Paper presented at the 2005 Academy of International Business Annual Meetings. Quebec, Canada

Brand Finance (2014) The annual report on nation brands December 2014, http://www.brandfinance.com/images/upload/brand_finance_nation_brands_report_2014_final_edition.pdf . Accessed 27 July 15

Business Times (2010) Protecting the Ceylon Tea Brand 23rd March http://sundaytimes.lk/100523/BusinessTimes/bt39.html Accessed 27 July 15

Bjorkman I, Xiucheng F (2002) Human resource management and the performance of western firms in China. Int J Human Resource Manage 13(6):853–864

Dowling GR, Staelin R (1994) A model of percieved risk and intended risk-handling activity. J Consum Res 21(June):119–134
Eriksson G, Rudell S (2013) Branding Sri Lanka http://www.diva-portal.org/smash/get/diva2:646392/FULLTEXT01.pdd. Accessed 3 May 15
FAO (2002) Dependence on single agricultural commodity exports in developing countries: magnitude and trends http://www.fao.org/docrep/005/y3733e/y3733e0d.htm. Accessed 17 July 15
Gfk (2014) Germany knocks USA off top spot for 'best nation' after 5 years http://www.gfk.com/documents/press-releases/2014/2014-11-12_anholt_gfk%20nation%20brand%20index%202014.pdf. Accessed 27 Nov 15
Gurhan-Canli Z, Maherswaran D (2000) Determinants of country-of-origin evaluations. J Consum Res 27:96–108
Han CM (1989) Country image: Halo or summary construct? J of Mark Res 26 (May):222–229
Han CM (1990) Testing the role of country image in consumer choice behaviour. Eur J Mark 24 (6):24–40
Heimbach AE, Johansson JK, MacLachlan DL (1989) Product familiarity, information processing and country-of-origin cues. Adv Consum Res 16:460–467
Herche J (1994) Ethnocentric tendencies. Mark Strategy Import Purchase Behav Int Mark Rev 11 (3):4–16
Herstein R, Berger R, Jaffe ED (2014) How companies from developing and emerging countries can leverage their brand equity in terms of place branding. Competitiveness Rev 24(4):293–305
Hirschman EC (1985) Primitive aspects of consumption in modern American society. J Consum Res 12:142–154
Huber J, McCann J (1982) The impact of interential beliefs on product evaluations. J Mark Res 19 (August):324–333
Hudson J, Jones P (2003) International trade in "Quality Goods': signalling problems for developing countries. J Int Dev 15:999–1013
Innes BG, Kerr WA, Hobbs JE (2007) Branding as a marketing strategy for agricultural products. CATPRN Commissioned Paper, CP 2007-05, http://www.catrade.org. Accessed 17 July 15
Kim H (2012) The importance of nation brand. http://www.culturaldiplomacy.org/pdf/case-studies/Hwajung_Kim_The_Importance_of_Nation_Brand.pdf. Accessed 24 July 15
Klein JG (2002) Us versus them, or us versus everyone? Delineating consumer aversion to foreign goods. J Int Bus Stud 33(2):345–363
Kotler P, Gertner D (2002) Country as brand, product and beyond: a place marketing and brand management. Brand Manage 9(4):249–261
Lampert SI, Jaffe ED (1997) A dynamic approach to country-of-origin effect. Eur J Mark 32:61–78
Leclerc F, Schmitt B, Dube L (1994) Foreign branding and its effects on product perceptions and attitudes. J Mark Res 31(2):263–270
Li W-K, Leung K, Wyer RS (1993) The roles of country of origin information on Buyers' product evaluations: signal or attribute. Adv Consum Res 20:684–689
Luxner L (2004) Dominican republic gets serious about coffee exports. Coffee International, 176 (9) (Sept–Oct) http://www.teaandcoffee.net/0904/coffee.htm. Accessed 17 July 15
Magnusson P, Haas SM, Zhao H (2008) A branding strategy for emerging market firms entering developed markets. J Int Consum Mark 20(3–4):95–107
Maheswaran D (1994) Country of origin as a stereotype: effects of consumer expertise and attribute strength on product evaluations. J Consum Mark 21:354–365
Moreda-Piñeiro A, Fisher A, Hill SJ (2003) The classification of tea according to regions of origin using pattern recognition techniques and trace metal data. J Food Compos Anal 16:195–211
Nebanzahl I, Jaffe ED (1996) Measuring the joint effect of brand and country image on consumer evaluation of global product. Int Mark Rev 13(4):5–22
Papadopoulos N, Heslop L (1993) Product country images—impact and role in international marketing. International Press

Papadopoulos N, Heslop L (2002) Country equity and country branding: problems and prospects. J Brand Manage 9(4–5):294–314
PRS (2015) Regional political risk index. https://www.prsgroup.com/category/risk-index. Accessed 27 July 15
Rao A, Qu L, Ruekert R (1999) Signaling unobservable product quality through a brand ally. J Mark Res 35(May):258–268
Rao AR, Olson EM (1990) Information examination as a function of information type and dimension of consumer expertise: some exploratory findings. Adv Consum Res 17:361–366
Srikatanyoo N, Gnoth J (2002) Nation branding—country image and international tertiary education. Brand Manage 10(2):139–146
Steenkamp J-BEM (1990) Conceptual model of the quality perception process. J Bus Res 21:309–333
Teuber R (2010) Geographical indications of origin as tool of product differentiation: the case of coffee. J Int Food Agribusiness Mark 22:277–298
The 9000 Store http://the9000store.com/ISO-9000-Tips-How-Much-Does-it-cost.aspx. Accessed 27 July 15
UNIDO (2013) http://www.unido.org/fileadmin/user_media_upgrade/What_we_do/Topics/Agribusiness_and_rural/UNIDO_Agribusiness_development.pdf. Accessed 26 July 15
Verlegh PWJ, Steenkamp J-BEM (1999) A review and meta-analysis of country-of-origin research. J Psychol 20:521–546
Veale R, Quester PG (2008) Tasting quality: the roles of intrinsic and extrinsic cues. Asia Pac J Mark Logistics 21(1):195–207
Veale R, Quester PG (2009) Do consumer expectations match experience? Predicting the influence of price and country of origin on perceptions of product quality. Int Bus Rev 18:134–144
World Economic Forum (2013) The human capital report. http://www3.weforum.org/docs/WEF_HumanCapitalReport_2013.pdf. Accessed 27 July 15
Zaichkowsky JL (1985) Measuring the involvement concept. J Consum Res 12(December):341–352

Decomposition of Country of Origin Effects in Education Services: A Conjoint Analysis Approach

Daniel Aruan and Roberta Crouch

Abstract Research in the area of international marketing has shown that consumers' assessments of product quality may change (positively/negatively) according to country of manufacture, country of design and/or country of parts of the products. While this notion has been established in the product context, no research has attempted to isolate similar effects of the country of origin construct in relation to service offerings. This research deconstructs the country of origin (COO) construct for international services along country of origin of the brand (COB), country of origin of where the service is delivered (COSD), and country of origin of the person providing the service (CPI). A total of 143 respondents participated in the online survey undertaken in Australia. The service to be evaluated in the experiment was education service. Results of conjoint analysis in education service confirmed the effects and the importance of the proposed COO dimensions on consumers' expectations of service quality. More specifically, the experiment revealed that CPI is more important than COB and COSD on consumers' expectation of service quality.

Keywords Country-of-origin · Education · Conjoint · Service delivery · Image

Introduction

Today's products may result from a series of design and production processes in more than one country (so-called hybrid products), hence, the COO of a product can be multiple. For example, a computer can be designed and manufactured in different

D. Aruan
The University of Adelaide, Adelaide, Australia
e-mail: Daniel.aruan@adelaide.edu.au

R. Crouch (✉)
School of Marketing and Management, The University of Adelaide, Adelaide, Australia
e-mail: roberta.crouch@adelaide.edu.au

R. Crouch
School of Wine and Spirits, Groupe ESC Dijon Bourgogne, Dijon, France

© Springer Science+Business Media Singapore 2016

C. Plewa and J. Conduit (eds.), *Making a Difference Through Marketing*,
DOI 10.1007/978-981-10-0464-3_14

countries so that the product has a different COO in terms of design and manufacturing. In that case, the term 'COO' is no longer the same as the country of manufacture. Instead, the product has multiple countries of origin. A number of scholars have examined COO elements such as country of design, country of manufacturing/assembly, country of parts and country of target (Chao 1998, 2001; Essoussi and Merunka 2007; Insch and McBride 1999, 2004). They found that consumers' perceptions of quality change when a product is manufactured or designed in a country different from its brand origin (Erickson et al. 1984; Han and Terpstra 1988). For example, when a product is manufactured in a country with less reputable image than its brand origin, that information can impact negatively on quality evaluations. On the other hand, when a product from a less reputable image country is designed in a more favourable image country, that information can serve as quality assurance and increase quality evaluation (Chao 2001; Chetty et al. 1999). For example, Ssangyong, a Korean car company, communicates to the market that the engineering technology of their products was designed by Mercedes Benz, a reputable car company from Germany (Morley 2000). A study by Chao (2001) found that consumers have positive attitudes towards and prefer to buy products which are assembled in the U.S. rather than in Mexico, if the parts are also from the U.S. rather than from Mexico. When the product is assembled in the U.S. with some of its parts from Mexico, consumers' attitudes and likelihood to buy are lower than when both the product's parts and assembly are U.S. based. A similar finding was also reported by Johansson et al. (1985), in relation to different types of products.

Few studies have sought to understand the theoretical foundation of the COO effects associated to hybrid product or services evaluation. The principle of congruity assumes that when congruent and incongruent information presents, the congruent information is preferred because incongruent information creates dissonance in the mind of consumers (Osgood and Tannenbaum 1955). Consumers will react more positively to congruent conditions than to incongruent conditions. Further, Osgood and Tannenbaum (1955) posit that when two paired objects of judgment are incongruent, they tend to shift in the direction of congruence with their evaluation of the other. This means that when a negatively valued object is paired with a positively valued object, the evaluation of the negatively valued object becomes less negative, and vice versa, the evaluation of the positively valued object becomes less positive. Jacoby and Mazursky (1984) reported that a combination of a strong brand and a weak store resulted in a dilution of the brand image and an improvement in the store image. An experiment by Chao (2001) found that perceived congruency positively moderates COO effects on consumers' product evaluation. Similarly, Jossiassen and Assaf (2010) reported that a greater perceived congruency between a product and country increases the relationship between COO image and product evaluation.

In the context of hybrid product evaluation, the perception of congruity can be understood as perceived fit (similarity) amongst the country images of a product's multiple COO. For example, a perception of fit between the country of manufacture and country of design influences perceptions of product and design quality respectively, because country of design can affect product quality through reflection of symbolic meanings, such as prestigious brands (Essoussi and Merunka 2007).

Furthermore, the magnitude of the effects of each COO dimension varies based on the aspects of quality. For example, it was found that the effect of country of design is greater on the functionality and brand image aspects (Chao 1993; Essoussi and Merunka 2007; Insch and McBride 2004), while country of manufacturing and country of parts have a stronger impact on product quality (Chao 2001; Essoussi and Merunka 2007). Whilst the effects of COO dimensions are also found to vary according to product category, the extent to which such effects vary according to product category is yet to be concluded. Some scholars found that on durable products such as TVs and radios, country of manufacture has stronger effects than country of brand (Chao 2001, 1993; Knight 1999). Others argue that country of brand has stronger effects than country of manufacturing, on the basis that through the brand name, consumers can infer quality more quickly, thus making country of manufacturing or country of parts irrelevant (Hui and Zhou 2003; Leclerc et al. 1994; Usunier and Cestre 2007). The above discussion demonstrates the multidimensionality of COO construct, where each dimension contributes differently according to product types and situational factors.

COO Effects in the Services Context

It appears that very few studies have examined the difference of COO influence between product and services (Elliott 2006; Michaelis et al. 2008). However, among those few empirical studies, scholars argue that COO effect varies according to product and services characteristics. A study by Michaelis et al. (2008) conducted a direct comparison of COO effects on consumers' trust between products and services evaluation. Their Polish findings revealed that the effects of COO on perceived trust is stronger in services than in products. Another direct comparison study conducted by Elliott (2006) also found that the COO effect for services is more important than for tangible goods. Further, in association with perceived risk, COO effects on service evaluation seem greater than those on product evaluation (Berentzen et al. 2008). Greater perceived risk associated with service provision is actually related to the nature of service characteristics, such as its intangibility and inseparability from consumption, thus making it difficult to evaluate their quality prior to purchase (Bebko 2000; Bitner et al. 2008; Grewal et al. 2007; Lovelock and Gummesson 2004). In addition, consumers have fewer choice alternatives in services (Brand and Cronin 1997) and higher exit barriers imposed by service providers (Mittal and Kamakura 2001) which leads to a greater perceived risk when compared to products. Therefore, in order to reduce risks, consumers seek additional external cue information such as reputation and COO (Keh and Xie 2009; Michaelis et al. 2008).

Gaps in the Existing Literature

In the product context, many COO studies have investigated the effect of COO on hybrid products evaluation (Chao 2001; Essoussi and Merunka 2007; Sharma et al. 2009). Those studies have proven demonstrated that consumers' perception of quality and purchase intentions are affected by the interplay of COO dimensions effects such as country of manufacturing (assembly), country of parts, country of design and country of brand. They also indicated that incongruent image information among the COO dimensions affects consumer attitudes towards the product. Yet, the extent to which this premise applies in the context of hybrid service is still not widely known. Prior research has put attempted to identify potential important dimensions of COO for services, such as country of service delivery image (Roggeveen et al. 2007; Walsh et al. 2011). They found that inconsistency of this country image can change consumer attitude towards service offered. Whilst Speec and Pinkaeo (2002) examined consumers' assessment on the quality of COO dimensions, such as quality of brand, quality of design and quality of the service provider in educational services, they did not examine which dimension is more important than another in forming overall image. This present study addresses this issue by investigating the possible dimensions of COO that might influence on consumers' expectations of service quality. Particularly, this present study examines the extent to which consumers' expectations of service quality varies according to country of origin of the brand (COB), country of origin of where the service is delivered (COSD), and country of origin of the person providing the service (CPI).

Country of Service Delivery (COSD)

Prior research has indicated the importance of the location of services delivery as one key attribute in consumer evaluations of services, particularly in the course of offshore services. Hence, the image of COSD can significantly change consumer expectations of quality as has been indicated in several types of services, such as education, cruise lines, and call centres services (Ahmed et al. 2002; Sharma 2012; Srikatanyoo and Gnoth 2002). A negative COSD image can reduce consumers' perceived quality of the services, experienced or expected (Acton 2007; Roggeveen et al. 2007; Srikatanyoo and Gnoth 2002), leading to an unwillingness to purchase the services. For example, a U.S. medical school offering offshore programs in Belize suffered from quality denigration because U.S. consumers perceived that this country was not able to provide adequate facilities and human resources service as well as its counterparts at home (Acton 2007). Similar findings are also reported that consumers of cruise line holidays considered the services provided by American providers to be better than those provided by Malaysians under the same brand name (Ahmed et al. 2002). In call centre services, consumers' perceptions of quality towards an offshore call centre (India) were found to be lower than an onshore call centre (the U.S.) due to the unfavourable image of India as a less developed country, which in turn reduced consumers' expectations of the service quality provided by Indian staff (Sharma 2012; Walsh et al. 2011).

Unlike products, the production/delivery of services must occur at the same time as they are used. Hence, in the context of hybrid services, where the country of service delivery is different from the country of brand, at least two countries are involved in the provision of that service, thus the images of those 'participating' countries would enter into consumers' minds. In addition, consumers' dependence on COO cues when evaluating expected quality is more critical in the service context than in the tangible product context. However, which COO dimension, COB or COSD, would exert the most influence on consumers' expectations remains unclear since the discrimination between them has never been tested before.

Country Person Image (CPI)

The literature has demonstrated that consumers possess stereotypical beliefs about people from various locations. For example, consumers in the U.S. perceived services provided by Indian or Mexican providers to be 'less serious' in providing good services than their American counterparts (Acton 2007; Ouellet 2007). Hence, consumers have low expectations of the quality of services provided by these people and, consequently avoid using their services. Therefore, consumers' stereotypical beliefs about a country are also likely to be transferred to people from that country. For example, less developed countries are believed to have lower capabilities in terms of technology and skill, so that service providers (people) from less developed countries are also perceived as having lower skill levels and less expertise in providing the same services relating to technology compared to those from developed countries.

Furthermore, the literature has shown the influence of CI on product evaluation (Roth and Diamantopoulos 2009). County image, which is conceptualised as the overall perception of a country, includes not only a country's economy, politics, and technology, but also includes a people factor. This people factor is known to be associated with the characteristics of individuals, such as friendliness, likeability, artistry, responsibility and technical skills. Prior studies have employed these characteristics as attributes of the people factor (or CPI) in evaluating the quality of foreign products (Parameswaran and Pisharodi 1994; Parameswaran and Yaprak 1987), thus indicating its importance.

Country of Brand (COB)

As products can increasingly be designed and manufactured in different countries, the COO of a product now consists of more than one country; thus country of origin of a brand (COB) may no longer be the same as the country of production. For example, Chevrolet, an American brand car, is manufactured in several countries such as Vietnam, India, Korea, and Brazil. Thus, the COB of Chevrolet is the U.S. and the country of manufacturing relates to countries where various stages of the production process take place. Prior research has indicated a change in consumer perceptions of the quality of a product when the country of manufacturing and/or country of design or brand are different, and COB has been found to be a strong predictor of quality (Bae 1999). Similar to tangible products, this research argues that COB also has important effects on the evaluation of hybrid services.

The focus of this research is to investigate the extent to which the service COO dimensions (COB, COSD and CPI) serve to drive in consumer expectations of service quality and purchase intentions. This research examines three dimensions of COO deemed important for hybrid service evaluations:

H1a: COB will significantly influence consumer expectations of service quality.
H1b: COSD will significantly influence consumer expectations of service quality.
H1c: CPI will significantly influence consumer expectations of service quality.

Research Methods

This research employs full-profile conjoint analysis to measure consumer preferences. The full-profile approach has the advantage that each profile is presented individually, allowing respondents to focus only on one profile at a time. Full-profile analysis was chosen because this approach can best accommodate the aims of this research, which is not only to identify which profile is considered the most desirable, but also to investigate the strength of each attribute (and level) affecting perception of service quality and subsequent intentions to purchase.

In designing a full profile conjoint analysis experiment, a researcher decides a set of related product or service attributes (real or hypothetical) in which each attribute has varying level of choices for evaluation. From every possible combination of these varying levels, a set of product bundles (so-called profiles) is generated and presented to respondents. Respondents then assess each profile by scoring them. By doing this, the researcher can identify respondent's preference structure on the basis of the relative importance of each attribute and the 'worth' (utility) of each level within an attribute that determines a respondent's overall preference. The total worth for a profile will be obtained from the accumulation of part-worth of each level (Hair et al. 1998).

The part-worth of a level represents the utility a respondent can gain from that level expressed in a common scale, where the total worth (utility) of levels in that attribute is zero. In other words, the utility of a level in an attribute is relative to other levels within that attribute (Dean 2004; Orme 2006). The difference (gap) between utility levels in an attribute indicates the importance of that attribute for the respondent in assessing the product or services. A higher gap between the maximum and minimum utility levels indicates a higher level of importance of that attribute for the respondent because changes from one level to another leads to significant impact on respondent's overall assessment in differentiating between profiles. Therefore, the relative importance of an attribute can be obtained by dividing the gap of that particular attribute with the total gaps of all attributes in that product or services (Jaeger et al. 2001; Kupiec and Revell 2001).

A combination of three dimensions of country of origin (COB, CPI, and COSD) was examined for—education services. The attributes for education were university name, campus location, and nationality of lecturers. Each attribute had three levels: Australia, Indonesia and Singapore. In this scenario, respondents were asked to imagine a situation where they, as a student, they are being supervised for a long period in order to get a university research degree. Respondents were then asked to rate the quality of service expected from each alternative university from low quality to high quality. This approach will support, or otherwise, the degree to which results may be generalised across service types and COO.

In selecting brands, the researcher sought to ensure that those chosen were available, and real. To achieve equality across services, the brands also needed to have a brand name that consumers in all locations could identify with the country of origin of that service. The brands used were Australian National University (Australia), University of Indonesia (Indonesia) and National University of Singapore (Singapore) were selected (Table 1).

There were 27 or (3^3) possible combinations that could be generated from the full-profile method. To reduce the number of combinations, a fractional factorial design was applied. A fractional factorial design calculates and estimates only the main effects of the attributes, assuming that the composition rule applied is the additive model (Table 2). By employing fractional factorial design, only nine profiles (plus two holdouts) were necessary to show respondents for their evaluations. A hold-out is a profile presented to respondents to be assessed but it is not included in the analysis in the calculation of part-worth scores. The purpose of a hold-out is to test the internal validity of the data. Part-worth statistics obtained from the hold-outs were compared to those in the fractional factorial design to check for the consistency of both sets of data.

Non-probability sampling was employed in this research, resulting in a convenience sample. The unit of analysis in this research was defined as individual

Table 1 Attributes and levels for each service

Attributes	Levels
University name	Australian National University University of Indonesia National University of Singapore
Campus location	Canberra (Australia) Jakarta (Indonesia) Singapore
Nationality of lecturers	Australians Indonesians Singaporeans

Table 2 Combination of profiles

Profile No	University name	Lecturers nationality	Campus location
1	University of Indonesia	Indonesian	Canberra
2	Australian National University	Singaporean	Jakarta
3	University of Indonesia	Australian	Jakarta
4	Australian National University	Indonesian	Singapore
5	National University of Singapore	Indonesian	Jakarta
6	University of Indonesia	Singaporean	Singapore
7	National University of Singapore	Singaporean	Canberra
8	National University of Singapore	Australian	Singapore
9	Australian National University	Australian	Canberra
10 (holdout)	Australian National University	Singaporean	Canberra
11 (holdout)	University of Indonesia	Singaporean	Canberra

Australian consumers, male or female, aged between 18 and 70 years old. Also, the individual needed to be a citizen of their country. A web based survey was used to collect the data.

Respondents were approached through electronic invitations (emails and social networking websites), and a variety of communications (telephone, and face-to-face). They were asked to go to the link and participate in the survey. They were also guaranteed confidentiality. They were further informed of the nature and purpose of the research and were invited to ask for further information, if they needed it. The survey used Qualtrics software, a web based professional survey panel that provides survey templates enabling the researcher to exclusively customise the questionnaire.

Results

In total 148 respondents completed the online survey (Table 3). The sample was determined based on gender and age. Around 65 percent of the respondents were female, distributed almost equally in five age groups. Compared to the general Australian population (ABS 2010), these variations are not expected to substantially limit results.

Conjoint Analysis Validity Testing

Pearson's R, Kendall tau and Kendall tau for holds-out correlations were used to test the internal validity of the model as shown in Table 4 The correlation coefficients signify the degree to which the correlations between predicted and observed ESQ.

Table 3 Demographic profile based on age and gender

Variables	Count	%	National stat. (%)
Age			
20–29	38	25.4	14.69
30–39	33	22.3	14.13
40–49	27	18.5	14.12
50–59	24	16.2	12.57
60 up	26	17.7	18.98
Gender			
Male	51	34.5	49.2
Female	97	65.5	50.8
N=	148		

Table 4 Conjoint analysis validity testing

	Corr.	Sig.
Pearson's R	0.966	0.000
Kendall-tau	0.944	0.000
Kendall-tau (hold-out)	1.000	

The table shows that the correlations were high and significant. Hence, internal validity was achieved. Internal validity signifies a causal-effect relationship between predictor and criterion variables. The table shows high coefficient correlations in all categories, confirming the internal validity. Thus, COO dimensions and ESQ conform to a significant causal-effect relationship.

Part-Worth Utilities and Attribute Relative Importance

Table 5 shows that the utility scores for Australia level were high and positive for all COO dimensions, indicating respondents' preference for Australian services in

Table 5 Summary of part-worth utilities and relative importance

	Level	Part-worth utilities	Relative importance
COB	Australia	0.539	30.86
	Singapore	−0.220	
	Indonesia	−0.320	
COSD	Australia	0.462	28.63
	Singapore	−0.179	
	Indonesia	−0.284	
CPI	Australia	0.880	40.50
	Singapore	−0.197	
	Indonesia	−0.684	

all dimensions (COB, COSD and CPI). Part-worth utilities of Indonesia were the lowest. Negative scores suggest that services provided by Indonesian service providers were viewed unfavourably. These low scores were consistent for all services, indicating that Australian respondents perceived services provided by Indonesian brands, Indonesian people and processed in Indonesia relatively inferior than those provided by Singaporean and Australian service providers. On the other hand, Australian services received the highest positive scores for their COB and CPI attributes. Such scores indicate that services provided by Australian providers were preferred by Australian respondents.

For relative importance, the table shows that respondents relied highly on CPI (40.50 %), followed by COB (30.86 %) and COSD (28.63 %) respectively. This research provides some clarity about the multidimensionality of COO in the context of hybrid services. Respondents placed CPI as the most important predictor of quality of service (around 40 %), while COB was considered more important than COSD. CPI was most important in this service because consumers tend to be more selective and more risk averse in order to minimise associated risks. Respondents were asked to imagine that they were research students with a supervisor seeking a degree from a university. In this scenario, respondents may have thought that the perceived risk associated with the supervisor (a person) would be greater than that associated with university name (a brand). For example, respondents might have thought that they would encounter communication problems. This finding was consistent with that of (Harrison-Walker 1995), who investigated consumers' preferences in choosing ophthalmologists and found that patients relied heavily on the nationality of service providers (CPI) rather than other cues (e.g. warranty, availability, facilities, etc.). Overall, based on these findings, it could be concluded that COB, COSD, and CPI serve as important dimensions of COO in predicting consumers' expectations of service quality with variations according to service category, thus confirming the hypotheses.

Theoretical Contributions

This research adds to the literature by providing evidence that COB, COSD, and CPI are important dimensions of COO effects for service quality evaluation. Although research established the significant influence of COO dimensions on consumers' evaluations of hybrid products, this research confirmed the dimensionality of COO in the context of hybrid service. Researchers have examined the effects of COO only as a single or separate dimension such as location (COSD) or personal stereotypes (CPI) on expected quality or purchase decisions (Ganguli and Roy 2010; Thelen et al. 2011; Walsh et al. 2011). Whereas the effect of a single COO dimension does not ignite conflict in consumers' minds, the effect of multiple COO dimensions can trigger conflict particularly when the country images of those dimensions are not congruent. This research, therefore, is the first study to examine the extent to which each COO dimension has a simultaneous effect on consumers' evaluation of hybrid services when varying country image combinations are presented to consumers Managerial Implications.

This research supported a recommendation related to service marketing and brand management, especially for firms launching offshore strategies. Service managers must understand that COO is not merely a single dimension (COB) as traditionally thought. COO is a multidimensional construct that consists of COB, COSD, and CPI. They must identify which dimensions are important to the perception of the quality of their services and then allocate resources and act accordingly.

Specifically, firms engaging in education sector should be aware of CPI and treat it with great care. For example, educational institutions such as universities can provide to the public information about their academic staff such as background, qualifications, research publications and interests, professional experience, awards, and so on. Consumers might weigh this information more heavily as an added value to reduce level of perceived risk (Ostrom and Iacobucci 1995). Service firms can also provide reviews and testimonies about their professional staff through neutral media or open free-session seminars to provide further physical and tangible cues to the public.

Future Research Directions

This research may provide an impetus for further research on this important topic. First, further research could expand on the development of the COO construct—for example by generating items for the COB, COSD, and CPI dimensions. Second, it might be useful for future studies to introduce other dimensions that might serve as important COO dimensions, such as country of training image and other extrinsic cues such as price and reputation, in order to achieve a more accurate measure of COO dimensions as determinants of hybrid services evaluation.

As this research focused on the assessment of consumers' expectation of service quality, future research might also compare the effects of COO on expected and perceived quality and on potential and real customers. Lastly, further research might also apply the model to a wider area of services—for example by examining COO effects according to level of contact between consumers and service providers.

References

Acton R (2007) Students gamble on offshore education. Tribune Review, Pittsburgh

Ahmed Z, Johnson J, Ling C, Fang T, Hui A (2002) Country-of-origin and brand effects on consumers' evaluations of cruise lines. Int Mark Rev 19(3):279–302

Bae SW (1999) Effects of partitioned country of origin information on buyer assessment of binational products. Adv Consum Res 26:344–351

Bebko CP (2000) Service intangibility and its impact on consumer expectations of service quality. J Serv Mark 14(1):9–26
Berentzen J, Backhaus C, Michaelis M, Blut M, Ahlert D (2008) Does "made in…" also apply to services? An empirical assessment of the country-of-origin effect in service settings. J Relat Mark 7(4):391–405
Bitner M, Gremler D, Zeithaml V (2008) Services marketing: integrating customer focus across the firm. McGraw-Hill, Irwin
Brand RR, Cronin JJ (1997) Consumer-specific determinants of the size of retail choice sets: an empirical comparison of physical good and service providers. J Serv Mark 11(1):19–38
Chao P (1993) Partitioning country of origin effects: consumer evaluations of a hybrid product. J Int Bus Stud 24(2):291–306
Chao P (1998) Impact of country-of-origin dimensions on product quality and design quality perceptions. J Bus Res 42(1):1–6
Chao P (2001) The moderating effects of country of assembly, country of parts, and country of design on hybrid product evaluations. J Advertising 30(4):67–81
Chetty S, Dzever S, Quester P (1999) Country of origin perception and industrial purchase decision-making in New Zealand. Eur J Purch Supply Manag 5(3–4):185–196
Dean DH (2004) Evaluating potential brand associations through conjoint analysis and market simulation. J Prod Brand Manag 13(7):506–513
Elliott G (2006) A less-developed country perspective of consumer ethnocentrism and "country of origin" effects: Indonesian evidence. Asia Pacific J Mark Logistics 18(2):79–92
Erickson G, Johansson J, Chao P (1984) Image variables in multi-attribute product evaluations: country-of-origin effects. J Consum Res 694–99
Essoussi LH, Merunka D (2007) Consumers' product evaluations in emerging markets: does country of design, country of manufacture, or brand image matter? Int Mark Rev 24(4):409–426
Ganguli S, Roy SK (2010) Service quality dimensions of hybrid services. Manag Serv Qual 20(5):404–424
Grewal D, Iyer G, Gotlieb J, Levy M (2007) Developing a deeper understanding of post-purchase perceived risk and behavioral intentions in a service setting. J Acad Mark Sci 35(2):250–258
Hair JF, Anderson RE, Tatham RL, Black WC (1998) Multivariate data analysis, 5th edn. Prentice Hall, New Jersey
Han CM, Terpstra V (1988) Country-of-origin effects for uni-national and bi-national products. J Int Bus Stud 19(2):235–255
Harrison-Walker LJ (1995) The relative effects of national stereotype and advertising information on the selection of a service provider: an empirical study. J Serv Mark 9(1):47–59
Hui MK, Zhou L (2003) Country-of-manufacture effects for known brands. Eur J Mark 37(1/2):133–153
Insch GS, McBride JB (1999) Decomposing the country-of-origin construct. J Int Consum Mark 10(4):69–91
Insch GS, McBride JB (2004) The impact of country-of-origin cues on consumer perceptions of product quality: a binational test of the decomposed country-of-origin construct. J Bus Res 57(3):256–265
Jacoby J, Mazursky D (1984) Linking brand and retailer images: do the potential risks outweigh the potential benefits? J Retail
Jaeger SR, Hedderley D, MacFie HJH (2001) Methodological issues in conjoint analysis: a case study. Eur J Mark 35(11/12):1217–1239
Johansson JK, Douglas SP, Nonaka I (1985) Assessing the impact of country of origin on product evaluations: a new methodological perspective. J Mark Res 22(4):388–396
Josiassen A, Assaf A (2010) Country-of-origin contingencies: their joint influence on consumer behaviour. Asia Pac J Mark Logistics 22(3):294–313
Keh HT, Xie Y (2009) Corporate reputation and customer behavioral intentions: the roles of trust, identification and commitment. Ind Mark Manage 38(7):732–742

Knight GA (1999) Consumer preferences for foreign and domestic products. J Consum Mark 16 (2):151–162
Kupiec B, Revell B (2001) Measuring consumer quality judgements. Br Food J 103(1):7–22
Leclerc F, Schmitt BH, Dube L (1994) Foreign branding and its effects on product perceptions and attitudes. J Mark Res 31(2):263–270
Lovelock C, Gummesson E (2004) Whither services marketing?: In search of a new paradigm and fresh perspectives. J Serv Res 7(1):20
Michaelis M, Woisetschlager DM, Backhaus C, Ahlert D (2008) The effects of country of origin and corporate reputation on initial trust: an experimental evaluation of the perception of Polish consumers. Int Mark Rev 25(4):404–422
Mittal V, Kamakura WA (2001) Satisfaction, repurchase intent, and repurchase behavior: investigating the moderating effect of customer characteristics. J Mark Res 131–142
Morley D (2000) Musso-Mercedes match was a rocky road: Fairfax Media
Orme, BK (2006) Getting started with conjoint analysis: strategies for product design and pricing research. Research Publishers, LLC
Osgood CE, Tannenbaum PH (1955) The principle of congruity in the prediction of attitude change. Psychol Rev 62(1):42–55
Ostrom A, Iacobucci D (1995) Consumer trade-offs and the evaluation of services. J Mark 59(1):17–28
Ouellet J-F (2007) Consumer racism and its effects on domestic cross-ethnic product purchase: an empirical test in the United States, Canada, and France. J Mark 71(1):113–128
Parameswaran R, Pisharodi RM (1994) Facets of country of origin image: an empirical assessment. J Advert 23(1):43–56
Parameswaran R, Yaprak A (1987) A Cross-national comparison of consumer research measures. J Int Bus Stud 18(1):35–49
Roggeveen AL, Bharadwaj N, Hoyer WD (2007) How call center location impacts expectations of service from reputable versus lesser known firms. J Retail 83(4):403–410
Roth KP, Diamantopoulos A (2009) Advancing the country image construct. J Bus Res 62(7):726–740
Sharma P (2012) Offshore outsourcing of customer services–boon or bane? J Serv Mark 26(5):352–364
Sharma P, Mathur R, Dhawan A (2009) Exploring customer reactions to offshore call centers: toward a comprehensive conceptual framework. J Serv Mark 23(5):289–300
Speece M, Pinkaeo K (2002) Service expectations and consumer ethnocentrism. Australas Mark J 10(3):59–75
Srikatanyoo N, Gnoth J (2002) Country image and international tertiary education. J Brand Manag 10(2):139–146
Thelen ST, Yoo B, Magnini VP (2011) An examination of consumer sentiment toward offshored services. J Acad Mark Sci 39(2):270–289
Usunier JC, Cestre G (2007) Product ethnicity: revisiting the match between products and countries. J Int Mark 15(3):32–72
Walsh G, Gouthier M, Gremler DD, Brach S (2011) What the eye does not see, the mind cannot reject: can call center location explain differences in customer evaluations? Int Bus Rev

Part IV
Making a Difference—University Education and Innovation

Knowing Me, Knowing You: Mentorship, Friendship, and Dancing Queens

Vinh N. Lu and Brett Scholz

Abstract The relationship between a supervisor and a research student can 'make or break' the student's success and pursuit of original contribution to knowledge development. Although the nature of the supervision relationship has evolved over time, studies about supervisor-student relationships have not fully examined the influence of the key factors associated with relational exchange. In this paper, we develop a conceptual model depicting the antecedents of supervisory relationship satisfaction. In developing the current paper, we draw from the extensive relationship marketing literature and are inspired by the relational model of focal sponsorship exchange by Farrelly and Quester (2005). Our arguments are also supported by a comprehensive reflection of the research supervision relationship between Professor Pascale Quester and the first author of this paper, as well as that between the second author and his supervisor. We argue that supervisor's trust and commitment in the relationship are two key drivers of student's and supervisor's satisfaction with the relationship. We also propose congruence moderates these key relationships such that the relationship is stronger with higher congruence.

Introduction

> Sit back, relax, and enjoy the process! (Pascale Quester)

Those were the wise words that Professor Pascale Quester frequently said to the first author of this paper when he was frustrated by various challenges along his PhD research candidature. Professor Quester, through her research prominence,

V.N. Lu (✉)
Research School of Management, College of Business and Economics,
The Australian National University, Canberra, Australia
e-mail: Vinh.lu@anu.edu.au

B. Scholz
Synergy Nursing and Midwifery Research Centre, Faculty of Health,
University of Canberra, Canberra, Australia
e-mail: Brett.scholz@canberra.edu.au

© Springer Science+Business Media Singapore 2016

C. Plewa and J. Conduit (eds.), *Making a Difference Through Marketing*,
DOI 10.1007/978-981-10-0464-3_15

sustained discipline leadership, and significant supervision experience, has inspired generations of PhD students who have gone on to accomplish major success both within and outside of academia in Australia and overseas. Professor Quester has had a profound impact on her students' research and career accomplishments through the art of supervision and through her command of what constitutes a mutually satisfying supervisor-student relationship.

Indeed, the supervision relationship is one of the key factors in facilitating the research students' learning outcomes (Heath 2002). A satisfying relationship is also pivotal to the timely completion of the research degree (Hemer 2012) and remains a major part of the higher degree by research experience. Evidence-based recommendations for research supervisors emphasise the importance of regular meetings during candidature, as well as the need for effective feedback to be provided to students (Heath 2002). While these are important considerations for supervisors, less attention has been provided to the nature of the supervision relationship and how to maximise the benefits of regular meetings and effective feedback.

Traditional models of research supervision can be likened to a master-apprentice relationship, where supervisors are more experienced and hierarchically superior to less experienced supervisees. Recent research suggests that traditional master-apprentice models of supervision may be problematic because (a) they position supervisors as the single resource available to students, (b) students need more well-rounded skill sets post-graduation than supervisors alone can provide, and (c) hierarchies of power might damage supervision relationships and put the candidature at risk (Harrison and Grant 2015). Thus models of supervision that move away from master-apprentice styles of relationship might provide more useful frameworks for supervision practice.

Contemporary models of supervisory relationships conceptualise supervision as more of a collaborative activity undertaken without strict hierarchies of power (Hemer 2012). Indeed, when supervision is not too didactic, students may be more likely to engage in candid conversations about their needs and future goals (Duxbury 2012). An important part of the supervisory relationship is the role of supervisors in instilling confidence in research candidates (Duxbury 2012). Sidhu et al. (2015) describe ideal research supervision as facilitative across relevant domains, with the goal to support the participation of the candidate in academic practice. Through more equal relationships, research students should be better endowed to engage in driving their own research processes, and to develop a better sense of trust in supervisors.

In order to understand the mechanics of the supervision relationship, it is useful to turn to Hockey's (1994) discussion, which elaborates on two dimensions of the relationship: an intellectual dimension, and a pastoral dimension. In discussing how to balance these dimensions of supervision, Hemer (2012) suggests that supervisors consider having some research meetings over coffee or in more informal locations. Although some supervisors report a sense of anxiety over how to maintain boundaries in establishing social relationships with students, some positive aspects of engaging with research students in neutral locations include the levelling of hierarchies, greater willingness of students to engage in more open communication with supervisors, and a strengthening of relationships. Indeed, in order to develop more collaborative partnerships between supervisors and supervisees, researchers have emphasised the importance of supervisors having a better understanding of students' needs (de Kleijn et al. 2015). As yet, there has been little research exploring how this might be done, and how to integrate adaptability into the supervisory relationship. In this conceptual paper, we propose a framework through which supervisors might consider how to develop particular aspects of the supervisory relationship.

This brief conceptual piece extends the relationships in sponsorship effectiveness to the research supervision relationships. To this end, our framework draws inspiration from the model of satisfaction in sponsor-sponsee relationships developed and empirically tested by Farrelly and Quester (2005). Their findings focus on sponsors' commitment and trust in the sponsorship relationship as antecedents of both noneconomic and economic relationship satisfaction in the sports industry. They also suggest that sponsors' non-economic satisfaction acts as an antecedent to their economic satisfaction in the relationship. In the current study, we argue that the elements of trust and commitment are important in supervisory relationships in similar ways to the propositions of Farrelly and Quester (2005) in regards to sponsorship relationships. Instead of focusing on economic and noneconomic satisfaction, our model of supervision relationships focuses on intellectual and pastoral dimensions of supervision proposed by Hockey (1994). Thus our model of supervision satisfaction proposes that supervisors' trust and commitment in a supervision relationship are antecedents of satisfaction with both the intellectual and the pastoral dimension of the relationship.

Take a Chance on Me (Andersson and Ulvaeus 1978)

Trust is one of the most common and historical variables in the literature (Seppänen et al. 2007) and is a critical construct in relational exchange (Dwyer and Oh 1987). Trust reflects the belief of an exchange party that its requirements will be fulfilled through future actions undertaken by the other party (Anderson and Weitz 1989; Barney and Hansen 1994). As a result, a trusting relationship is one in which the involved parties do not engage in opportunistic behaviour, thereby decreasing uncertainty in the relationships (Morgan and Hunt 1994). In the sponsorship model developed by Farrelly and Quester (2005), trust from the sponsors has a direct effect on their satisfaction with the relationship. Farrelly and Quester (2005, p. 216) highlight that "risk-laden activities, such as sponsorship leveraging, are more likely to be attractive if there is the knowledge that the sport entity will not take advantage of the vulnerability associated with the investment".

Similarly, trust, warmth and honest collaboration are the key relationship characteristics driving successful supervision of students (Blumberg 1977). Indeed, the supervisor's trust is critical to the student's focus and progress. From our own experience in working with our PhD supervisors, there are multiple ways for a supervisor's trust to be demonstrated. The supervisor can show their appreciation of the students' work ethics and self-initiatives. The supervisor can also instil the belief that the student will be honourable with the delivery of the research milestones or outputs, and that the student can work productively and independently with limited supervision. Further, the supervisor can actively encourage the student to voice his/her feedback and opinions.

From a student's point of view, the activities by the supervisor affirm the supervisor's faith and a sense of respect toward his or her own capabilities. Without trust on the part of the supervisor, the students will either give up or refrain themselves from going beyond the acceptable boundaries defined by the supervisors (Pearson and Brew 2002). In other words, the supervisor's trust will lead to a satisfying working relationship. More specifically, such satisfaction results from the fact that the students will make the most of their learning and intellectual development opportunity offered by the supervisor, and the supervisor is confident that their 'investment' in the supervisory relationship is worthwhile. As such, we propose that:

P1: Supervisors' trust in the relationship is positively related to both students' and supervisors' satisfaction with the relationship.

I Do, I Do, I Do, I Do, I Do (Andersson et al. 1975)

Commitment refers to "an enduring desire to maintain a valued relationship" (Moorman et al. 1992, p. 316), and is an essential element for a successful relationship (Gundlach et al. 1995) that leads to achieving valuable outcomes (Morgan and Hunt 1994). For instance, commitment can significantly influence customer loyalty and expectations of relationship continuity (Palmatier et al. 2006).

In their study of the focal sponsor-sponsee relationship, Farrelly and Quester (2005, p. 212) define commitment was "a willingness of the parties in the sponsorship relationship to make short term investments in an effort to realise long-term benefits from the relationship". They argue that the sponsor can signal their long-term commitment to the relationship in the form of additional investments and leveraging activities (e.g. allocation of additional resources over and above the initial agreement). In order to promote the relationship and realise its long term and strategic benefits, Farrelly and Quester (2005) further suggest the sponsor (i) develop a clear set of sponsorship objectives, (ii) integrate sponsorship agreements into their marketing or corporate plan, and (ii) foster a confident future outlook for the relationship. In our experience, these elements also lay a very robust foundation for the development of commitment in the context of supervisor-student relationship.

A reflection of our working relationship during and beyond the doctoral research candidature with our own supervisors indicates that they indeed undertook a wide range of activities to demonstrate their full commitment to us and to the relationship. From the beginning of the relationship, and even before students commence their candidatures, a supervisor can show a great deal of enthusiasm towards the student's potential research topic. Extending Farrelly and Quester's (2005) focus on the sole perspective of the sponsor, we argue that, in the research supervision context, the supervisor should enable the student to co-create a meaningful learning experience by working together on an agreed set of clear and achievable goals. Through an effective two-way interaction, the supervisor remains a strong source of aspiration and guidance for the student when he/she is confronted by various research and career uncertainties.

Additionally, the supervisor's commitment to the relationship is strengthened by their willingness to invest additional time and resources, such has having an open door policy for the student, maintaining a 24-h turnaround time for feedback on research papers or thesis chapters, and even providing extra funding for the student's research endeavour and conference attendance. Such commitment is further extended to the supervisor's efforts in introducing and integrating the student into their own network of professional connections and relationships, which is instrumental to the student's future career success. Further, we support Farrelly and Quester's (2005) argument that the supervisor's commitment to the supervisory relationship creates a rewarding relational atmosphere. Such atmosphere allows both supervisor and student to achieve their individual and mutual goals without opportunistic behaviours. It also fulfils the supervisor's desire to nurture an academic talent and foster a long-term collegial and professional relationship. As such, we propose that:

P2: Supervisors' commitment to the relationship is positively related to both students' and supervisors' satisfaction with the relationship.

I Have a Dream (Andersson and Ulvaeus 1979)

Congruence, in the context of sponsorship, has been conceptualised as the relevancy and expectancy of the relationship between sponsors and those sponsored (Fleck and Quester 2007). It has been claimed that congruence between perceptions of sponsors and sponsees has been one of the most commonly researched concepts within the literature about sponsorship (Spais and Johnston 2014). While the dominant trend in the field appears to support the argument that congruence between sponsors and sponsees would have a positive impact on the sponsor's brand, Fleck and Quester (2007) propose that the relationship may be somewhat more complex. They argue that some incongruence between the sponsor and the sponsored partner may be more cognitively stimulating, and therefore more successful than complete congruence (and certainly more than complete incongruence).

Critical readings of congruence have noted that perceptions of congruence might differ across contexts in at least two ways. First, perceptions of congruence might differ between individuals. For instance, Spais and Johnston (2014) suggest consumer perspectives about sponsor-sponsee congruence might be quite different from the perspectives of those in management positions. It is, thus, beneficial to examine this phenomenon across contexts, rather than assuming the similarity between different individuals' perspectives of congruence. Second, there might be multiple aspects in which two entities are congruent. For instance, Macdougall et al. (2014) expand on two different kinds of sponsor-sponsee congruence: mission congruence (where the two entities are congruent in terms of what they do) and value congruence (where the entities are congruent in terms of aspirations). It might be useful to be mindful of congruence between two entities as encompassing multidimensional aspects.

Surprisingly, congruence in research supervision relationships has received little research attention. There have, however, been some useful insights into how congruence between supervisors and supervisees is currently being theorised in studies of higher education.

One way in which congruence can be theorised in terms of the supervision relationship, is in terms of supervision styles. Deuchar (2008) focuses on congruence in supervision styles in terms of the extent to which students valued autonomy or dependency, and how hands-on or hands-off a supervisor might be. He argued that these dimensions of the supervision relationship might change throughout the course of the research project, and, therefore, that congruence in the relationship could depend on flexibility of supervisors and supervisees to renegotiate needs over time.

A second way in which congruence in supervision has been researched is in terms of the cognitive congruence between supervisors and supervisees. Armstrong et al. (2004) categorise supervisors and students into either primarily analytic or primarily intuitive cognitive styles. They find that although similarity in cognitive styles within the supervision dyad did not appear to be related to the socioemotional aspects of the relationship, it did appear that a mismatch in cognitive styles might be beneficial. Thus, consistent with Fleck and Quester's (2007) proposal that congruence in sponsorship is unlikely to be unidimensional, congruence in supervision also appears likely to be more multidimensional and contextual.

We contend that there are other factors within the supervision dyad that have yet to be researched that might impact on the relationship between the supervisor and supervisee. For instance, congruence between students and supervisors on dimensions of epistemology, methodology, and goals are likely to influence interactions between them. It is also easy to imagine cases where supervisor's perspectives on congruence differ from those of students, as is the case for sponsors, sponsees, and consumers. As with understandings of congruence in sponsorship, nuance of understandings of congruence in supervision is still developing.

In our experience, we chose our supervisors because we saw a shared vision and our relationship worked because of a mutual view on the collaborative nature of the relationships. This may be different from person to person—it may be a shared vision for social change, a shared way of understanding the world, or a shared way of completing projects. These shared attitudes, orientations, or processes strengthen the relationship between supervisor and student over time. We suggest that this is because greater congruence increases the strength of the relationships between trust and relationship satisfaction, and commitment and satisfaction, such that:

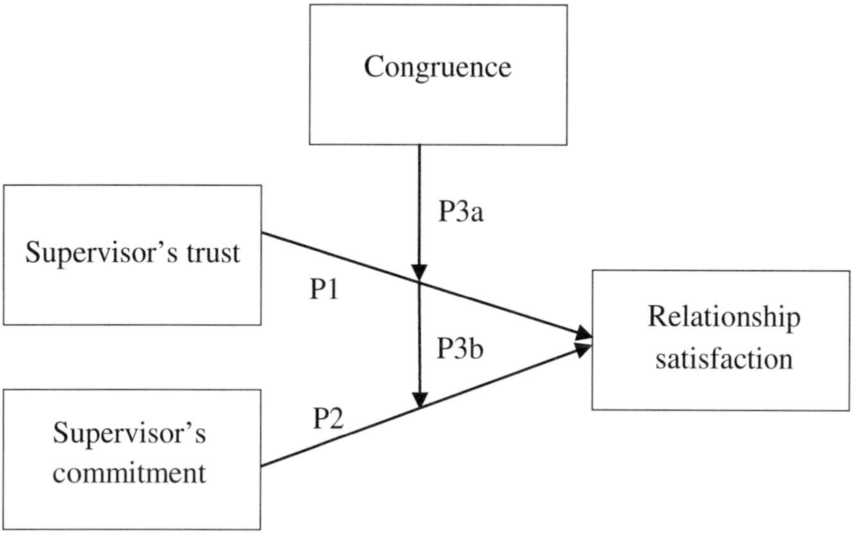

Fig. 1 Proposed conceptual framework

P3: C*ongruence moderates the relationship between (a) supervisor trust and supervisory relationship satisfaction and (b) supervisor commitment and supervisory relationship satisfaction, such that the relationship is stronger with higher congruence.*

Figure 1 depicts our conceptual framework for the positive influence of supervisor's trust, supervisor's commitment, and congruence on student's and supervisor's satisfaction with the relationship. In this framework, we only took into account the level of trust and commitment exhibited by the supervisor. Future research can empirically test our propositions and extend this relational framework by including the effects of trust and commitment demonstrated by the student in their working relationship with the supervisor.

When All Is Said and Done (Andersson and Ulvaeus 1981)

Ideal dyadic relationships in a supervision context should be driven by trust, openness, mutual understanding, communication, and collaboration (Carifio and Hess 1987; Johnson 2007). Nevertheless, such relationships can be challenged by uncertainty and confusion, creative tensions and even disjunction in expectations (Malfroy 2005). Importantly, the current system for higher degree research puts a significant emphasis on timely completions and financial implications, adding an additional layer of external pressure on supervisor-student relationships.

Inspired by the focal sponsorship exchange model by Farrelly and Quester (2005), we develop a conceptual model in which supervisor's trust, supervisor's commitment, and relational congruence drives satisfaction in the supervisory relationship. The foundation of a satisfactory relationship can be established at the candidate selection and supervisor-student matching phase. It is then that the supervisor can judge the student's level of enthusiasm, confidence, and commitment to the potential research topic (or other factors that might be important to individual supervisors). Students might approach individual researchers because of particular congruence they perceive between themselves and these potential supervisors, and thus it might be useful to listen to their perspectives about their specific preferences and ideas.

In the early stages of the relationship, it is essential that the supervisor and the student identify working styles and supervisory styles that they are both comfortable with. For instance, this can be partially done via a completion of the questionnaire on supervisor-doctoral student interaction (Mainhard et al. 2009). The mutual agreement on expectations and shared vision from both sides of the relationship can act as a form of psychological contract that drives the quality of and the degree of trust in the relationship. Given that trust and commitment accumulate over time, these initial steps will provide supervisors and supervisees with better understandings of how they will work together as the project progresses.

During the research candidature, the supervisor can create initiatives to shape a collegial environment (Malfroy 2005) through research retreats and encouragement of knowledge-sharing amongst research students. Open and quality communication can also offer an important venue to foster congruence (whichever form of congruence there may be between any given supervisor and supervisee). Supervision meetings over a coffee (Hemer 2012), or in other more informal settings can create a more welcoming atmosphere for a student to discuss their concerns and seek feedback from the supervisor. The authors also fondly remember dancing at conferences with their supervisors just because sometimes "you're in the mood for a dance" (Andersson et al. 1976). These informal aspects of the relationship might increase overall supervision satisfaction.

Finally, we believe that the relational model in research supervision can, and should, continue beyond the student's candidature. As today's students will be tomorrow's supervisors, sustained working relationships between the supervisor and their (former student) colleague might also benefit the progress and success of the future generation's PhD students.

Acknowledgements The first author would like to thank Professor Pascale Quester for excelling in both intellectual and pastoral dimensions of supervision. Both authors would like to thank her for her trust on and commitment to good research practice, and for being the ultimate dancing queen when she gets the chance. The first author was, has been, and will be forever grateful to Professor Quester for being his career and supervisory role model. The second author would also like to thank Dr Shona Crabb—whom he sought as a supervisor because of a congruence in world views that has enriched his approach to subsequent post-doctoral research. We also thank ABBA for putting music to our thinking of the proposed model of supervision.

References

Anderson E, Weitz B (1989) Determinants of continuity in conventional industrial channel dyads. Mark Sci 8(4):310–323

Andersson B, Ulvaeus B (1978) Take a chance on me [Recorded by ABBA]. On ABBA: The album. Polar Music, Stockholm

Andersson B, Ulvaeus B (1979) I have a dream [Recorded by ABBA]. On Voulez-Vous. Polar Music, Stockholm

Andersson B, Ulvaeus B (1981) When all is said and done [Recorded by ABBA]. On the visitors. Polar Music, Stockholm

Andersson B, Ulvaeus B, Anderson S (1975) I do, I do, I do, I do, I do [Recorded by ABBA]. On ABBA. Polar Music, Stockholm

Andersson B, Ulvaeus B, Anderson S (1976) Dancing queen [Recorded by ABBA]. On arrival. Polar Music, Stockholm

Armstrong SJ, Allinson CW, Hayes J (2004) The effects of cognitive style on research supervision: a study of student-supervisor dyads in management education. Acad Manag Learn Educ 3 (1):41–53

Barney JB, Hansen MH (1994) Trustworthiness as a source of competitive advantage. Strateg Manag J 15:175–190

Blumberg A (1977) Supervision and interpersonal intervention. J Classroom Interact 13(1):23–32

Carifio MS, Hess AK (1987) Who is the ideal supervisor? Prof Psychol Res Pract 18(3):244–250

De Kleijn RAM, Meijer PC, Brekelmans M, Pilot A (2015) Adaptive research supervision: exploring expert thesis supervisors' practical knowledge. High Educ Res Dev 34(1):117–130

Deuchar R (2008) Facilitator, director or critical friend? Contradiction and congruence in doctoral supervision styles. Teach High Educ 13(4):489–500

Duxbury L (2012) Opening the door: portals to good supervision of creative practice-led research. In: Allpress B, Barnacle R, Duxbury L, Grierson E (eds) Supervising practices for postgraduate research in art, architecture and design. Sense Publishers, Rotterdam, pp 15–24

Dwyer FR, Oh S (1987) Output sector munificence effects on the internal political economy of marketing channels. J Mark Res 24(4):347–358

Farrelly FJ, Quester PG (2005) Examining the importing relationship quality constructs of the focal sponsorship exchange. Ind Mark Manage 34(3):211–219

Fleck ND, Quester P (2007) Birds of a feather flock together… definition, role and measure of congruence: an application to sponsorship. Psychol Mark 24(11):975–1000

Gundlach GT, Achrol RS, Mentzer JT (1995) The structure of commitment in exchange. J Mark 59(1):78–92

Harrison S, Grant C (2015) Exploring of new models of research pedagogy: time to let go of master-apprentice style supervision? Teach High Educ 20(5):556–566

Heath T (2002) A quantitative analysis of PhD students' views of supervision. High Educ Res Dev 21(1):41–53

Hemer SR (2012) Informality, power and relationships in postgraduate supervision: supervising PhD candidates over coffee. High Educ Res Dev 31(6):827–839

Hockey J (1994) Establishing boundaries: problems and solutions in managing PhD supervisors' role. Cambridge J Educ 24(2):293–305

Johnson WB (2007) Transformational supervision: when supervisors mentor. Prof Psychol Res Pract 38(3):259–267

Macdougall HK, Nguyen SN, Karg AJ (2014) 'Game, set, match': an exploration of congruence in Australian disability sport sponsorship. Sport Manag Rev 17(1):78–89

Mainhard T, van der Rijst R, van Tartwijk J, Wubbels T (2009) A model for the supervisor-doctoral student relationship. High Educ 58:359–373

Malfroy J (2005) Doctoral supervision, workplace research and changing pedagogic practices. High Educ Res Dev 24(2):165–178

Moorman C, Zaltman G, Deshpandé R (1992) Relationships between providers and users of market research: the dynamic of trust within and between organizations. J Mark Res 29(3):314–328

Morgan RM, Hunt SD (1994) The commitment-trust theory of relationship marketing. J Mark 58 (3):20–38

Palmatier RW, Dant RP, Grewal D, Evans KR (2006) Factors influencing the effectiveness of relationship marketing: a meta-analysis. J Mark 70:136–153

Pearson M, Brew A (2002) Research training and supervision development. Stud High Educ 27(2):135–150

Seppänen R, Blomqvist K, Sundqvist S (2007) Measuring inter-organizational trust: a critical review of the empirical research in 1990–2003. Ind Mark Manage 36(2):249–265

Sidhu GK, Kaur S, Chan YF, Lee LF (2015) Establishing a holistic approach for postgraduate supervision. In: Tang SF, Logonnathan L (eds) Taylor's 7th teaching and learning conference 2014 proceedings. Springer, Singapore, pp. 529-545

Spais GS, Johnston MA (2014) The evolution of scholarly research on sponsorship. J Promot Manag 20:267–290

Beyond the Obvious: Facets of Diversity in Marketing Student Groups

Claire Eloise Sherman and Carolin Plewa

Abstract Student cohorts at higher education institutions worldwide are more diverse than ever due to international student mobility and a greater inclusion of previously underrepresented groups within the higher education system. Despite the potential effects of diversity on student academic performance and wellbeing, related studies have commonly been limited by a focus on cultural diversity. To better understand the importance of cultural diversity, we expand the literature by exploring various types of diversity simultaneously. A two-step research process, including a series of in-depth interviews and a survey, was used to examine the extent to which different dimensions of diversity, including characteristics brought to the group (language skills, academic goals and extroversion) and those that emerge during the group process (external commitments, commitment to task and adherence to rules), can influence the students' satisfaction with the process and satisfaction with the outcome. Furthermore, bi-directionality of communication and information-sharing emerge as processes that mediate the influence of diversity, in particular influencing the effect of differences in academic goals and differences in language skills, on group satisfaction with the process and outcome respectively. Implications for marketers are provided.

Keywords Diversity · Group work · Satisfaction · Group process · Mixed method

---

C.E. Sherman (✉)
Zayed University, Abu Dhabi, United Arab Emirates
e-mail: Claire.sherman@zu.ac.ae

C. Plewa
The University of Adelaide, Adelaide, Australia
e-mail: Carolin.plewa@adelaide.edu.au

© Springer Science+Business Media Singapore 2016

C. Plewa and J. Conduit (eds.), *Making a Difference Through Marketing*,
DOI 10.1007/978-981-10-0464-3_16

Introduction

Research on student group work within marketing courses has often purported various benefits of diversity for student learning, such as the development of teamwork skills (McCorkle et al. 1999), a multicultural experience (Williams et al. 1991) and a higher level of motivation (McCorkle et al. 1999). Group work is also often favoured as it is thought to closely replicate the style in which marketers work within practice. And it is perhaps for these benefits that Professor Pascale Quester initially designed her Introduction to Marketing assignment as a group experience; a format that has stood the test of time via many successive instructors. Despite these accolades, studies have found varied results regarding the functioning and outcomes of group work. For instance, a study by Sweeney and Weaven (2005) suggests that group work promotes deep learning, a greater appreciation of the contributions of different cultural backgrounds, and leads to changes in students' feelings and behaviours from a more egoistic to a more collectivist style. Yet, Kates (2002) found various barriers to deep learning due to an avoidance of confrontation, lack of dealing with free loaders and issues with control/dominance. In direct contrast to Sweeney and Weaven (2005), students were often found to disregard others' efforts, misleading them and reworking contributions to obtain a 'higher grade'. This study, thus, aims to shed some light on these incongruous results by exploring multiple dimensions of group diversity and their effect on outcomes, as mediated by group processes.

Our current study is warranted now more than ever, as universities across the globe have experienced a substantial change in the diversity of the student body, as evidenced by the doubling of the number of students studying abroad globally since 2000 (UNESCO Institute for Statistics 2014). Importantly, researchers have so far focused strongly on student group composition with particular reference to international student status. However, it may be important to broaden our focus on diversity to understand the relative importance of such status. Hence, the following discussion starts with a review of research surrounding various types of diversity within groups. Students' reflections on their group experience are then explored via interviews with an aim to better understand all relevant dimensions of diversity and their potential influence on group processes and outcomes (phase 1). Our refined framework is then tested in a preliminary survey (phase 2). The paper concludes with an outline of implications for marketing educators, limitations and directions for future research.

Diversity Within Groups

Diversity is a broad term for a multitude of differences between group members. Indeed, diversity can be categorised as either readily detectable attributes such as age, gender or nationality, most commonly studied (Paulus et al. 2005), or underlying attributes such as skill levels or values (Jackson et al. 1995). In general, differences in observable traits tend to negatively influence the affective outcomes for the group, such as satisfaction and identification with the group; yet can have a positive effect on cognitive outcomes such as the number of alternatives considered and the quality of ideas (Milliken and Martins 1996). Students who have found similar underlying attributes, such as their values, will enjoy working together due to positive reinforcement. However, similarity of values and attitudes may also hinder the creativity and critical argument that arises from differing opinions (Milliken and Martins 1996).

Nationality Diversity

Despite the identification of a large number of factors that may characterise group diversity, the majority of previous studies have focused on nationality or cultural diversity. For example, students working in groups encompassing domestic and international students are more likely to learn to look at issues from different perspectives (Williams et al. 1991), in turn inducing greater performance measured by mean grades (Bacon et al. 1998). Other studies also confirmed better grades for more ethnically diverse groups (Watson et al. 2002). In contrast, using a number of national clusters, Thomas (1999) found that homogeneous groups performed higher than heterogeneous groups with respect to grades.

While grades certainly provide one form of evaluation for group performance, a more comprehensive measurement might help in understanding the seemingly disparate results of the aforementioned studies. For example, Kates (2002) suggested that students may not be dealing with problems of skill diversity and may be submitting work without the full input of the members they perceive as less able. While the group may gain a higher grade, all students, including those with greater workloads and those who have their work disregarded, have a negative experience (Kates 2002). Van Der Zee et al. (2004) also found that diversity, measured as perceived difference in backgrounds, negatively affects satisfaction with undergraduate student groups. This refocus on the perception of diversity is an interesting development as it deals with the student's own measure of difference.

More recently, Kimmel and Volet (2010) introduced a bi-dimensional measure of cultural diversity where non-local schooling and multilingual skills denoted an 'other' culture student. Consequently they found particular manifestations of cultural differences, such as language proficiency, to negatively affect attitudes towards intercultural group work. In light of these distinctions, this study addresses the call for further refinement by exploring different ways in which diversity may arise in student groups and what effect various dimensions of diversity may have on the groups' performance. To allow a more comprehensive investigation of nationality diversity, three factors will be further explored, including international student status (enrolment as a domestic or international), ethnic background (Van Der Zee et al. 2004) and language skills (Paulus et al. 2005). In addition, further dimensions of diversity relevant to group work will be examined to explore their relative importance.

Prior (Pre-existing) Characteristics

The propensity of a particular personality trait to affect group processes and outcomes may be greater when the trait affects our ability to interact. For instance, in exploring multiculturalism, several personality traits have been found to influence the success of culturally diverse groups, such as cultural empathy, open mindedness, social initiative, emotional stability and flexibility, whilst several other traits relating to task orientation, outgoingness (Van Der Zee and Van Oudenhoven 2000) and Type A personalities (Watson et al. 2005) did not. In addition to their personality, students are also likely to differ in their academic goals. This could include differences in more surface oriented goals, such as their expectations for the grade they want to achieve, or deep-oriented goals, such as the skills and knowledge needed for their future career or existing job (Volet 1997). A student with high academic goals is likely to be a self-directed learner, who is proactive and motivated to learn (Zimmerman et al. 1992).

Diversity Surfacing During Group Work

The level of a student's external commitment has seldom been studied as a factor influencing student group work. The Australasian Survey of Student Engagement (AUSSE 2009) reports that 68 % of students surveyed were working for pay while studying. Such a high level of external commitment is likely to not only influence the time a student is able to commit to studying but also limit their interaction with others. Indeed, individuals value group work less and have significantly lower appraisal of the group experience when more than half its members work more than two days a week (D'Alessandro and Volet 2012).

Alternately, students may simply differ in relation to their commitment to the task at hand. The concept of task commitment is manifested in the actual completion of tasks and the amount of effort expended on those tasks. In an individual context, a student's effort is mediated by their general ability to maintain and enact their goals as well as their cognitive and emotional motivation towards the task (Volet 1997). For instance, if many group members are committed to the task, this may enhance overall members' interest and emotional states, thus increasing performance. However, if there is significantly lower commitment from only some members, this may have two opposing effects. That is, it either instigates even more attention or commitment from those students concerned about the achievement of their goals, or incites less commitment from previously committed members due to a decrease in motivation, both cognitively and emotionally.

A Framework of Diversity and Its Effects

Drawing from our review of the existing literature on diversity and students' group work, we have developed a broad framework depicting the impact of multiple dimensions of diversity (namely, international student status, ethnic background, language skills, academic goals and personality (prior to group work), as well as external commitments and commitment to task (during group work)) on group outcomes. Several group processes were also included within the framework so that a deeper exploration could be undertaken, where these processes may mediate any effects of diversity on group outcomes. For instance, external commitments may be managed differently depending on the level to which the group still engages in dialogue, which in turn may affect the satisfaction of each member in the group.

This exploratory study uses a mixed methods approach, enabling us to make use of the advantages of both qualitative and preliminary quantitative research. The qualitative phase (one) will be discussed first, leading to the discussion and results of the quantitative phase (two).

Phase 1—In-Depth Interviews

Method

A qualitative approach was employed in phase one of this study, as it enables the capture of rich data and the understanding of complex concepts and interrelations (Ticehurst and Veal 1999). More specifically, in-depth interviews were preferred as they may elicit more honest, less constrained responses reflecting a wide range of experiences. Using judgment sampling, nine students from a mid-sized Australian University were chosen from a third year marketing class. This late stage in the degree was selected to allow for a greater number of group experiences to be discussed. The students were chosen to represent various types of diversity, including age, gender (five males, four females), educational background, academic performance, extra or introversion and ethnic background (five local students, one each from China, Singapore, Malaysia and the United Arab Emirates).

An interview protocol was used, offering a systematic approach to a series of interviews without limiting the opportunity to uncover and explore new issues. While this qualitative research phase aimed at identifying the most relevant processes for students, the following concepts were included in the interview guideline based on available literature: communication (Kates 2002), leadership (Sy et al. 2005), role allocation (Batra et al. 1997), and group atmosphere (Jehn and Mannix 2001). Several group outcomes were also included so that a well-rounded exploration of the impact of diversity on the student group experience could be made.

The interviews lasted for approximately 40 min each. Interviewing continued until responses began to converge. All interviews were voice recorded and transcribed, as advantages of recording are believed to outweigh its limitations (Carson et al. 2001). Both researchers conducted a thematic analysis of the data, followed by a comparison and discussion of results.

Discussion of Results

The successive framework based on our preliminary findings is provided in Fig. 1, with a detailed discussion of results following.

Prior Characteristics

Consistent with our findings in the literature review, the more easily identifiable factors such as age, gender and educational background did not emerge as relevant factors affecting group performance. Interestingly, international student status and the ethnic background of students were also not perceived as factors significantly influencing group functioning and outcomes. This finding is in contrast with previous studies conducted within the US context (Bacon et al. 1998) and might be explained by the characteristics of the Australian student cohort. With more than half of the students enrolled in Australian business degrees classified as international, a group task bringing these groups of students together is a common experience.

However, three types of diversity emerged as relevant, including differences in relation to language skills, academic goals and personality. One type of nationality diversity, language skills, emerged as a significant inhibitor. The interviewees described language skills as a primary reason for a perceived inequality of work and an alleged lower mark. For example: "*One guy didn't contribute at all. He was an*

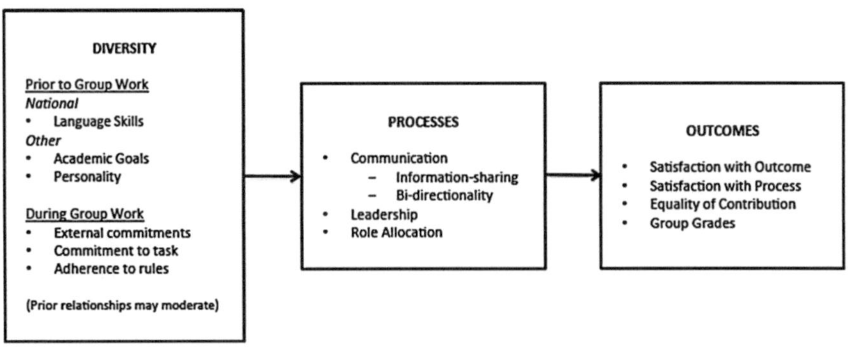

Fig. 1 Framework of group diversity, processes and outcomes

international student and couldn't speak a lot of English... we just said 'mate, it's OK. We'll do this". Students who did not speak English well were often excluded from deeper discussions and contributed in only a very structured way. Although initial attempts at inclusion were often made, groups tired of this effort as it slowed the process of creativity. Interestingly, international students whose English was not their native language but who spoke it relatively well also held this view; thus language skill rather than nationality or student status appears relevant.

Diversity in academic goals appeared to have an even greater influence on students' frustration and satisfaction with group work. Depending on what individuals aim to achieve in regards to their studies, or a specific task, they choose varied timings for milestones and quality levels for their work. Diversity in academic goals clearly limited not only the students' satisfaction with the group but also the quality of work produced:

> There can be issues. Especially when there are different people … trying to attain different goals in the end; and that could be from international students through to Australian students. If you have got an assignment where you have got someone who is doing university because it is a stop gap measure and all they are interested in is getting a piece of paper in the end; and so what they do normally is they are usually quite happy to do their assignment on the last day. That doesn't work if you want to produce high quality work. And then you can have problems.

Overall, group work seems to be easier if people in the group are generally similar: "*I found that people that are like me, it is easier to work with*". In the given context, students primarily identified one personality facet as influencing group work; namely extroversion (or introversion). A consensus within the interviews regarding the benefit of outgoing personalities was apparent. These people were seen as good at managing groups and generating ideas, allowing for a thorough discussion and in turn deep learning. Shy and passive individuals, on the other hand, were described as neither opening up to ideas nor contributing to discussions: "*… when you've got people that are submissive it can become very difficult because you can't tell whether you are on the right track*".

Another characteristic that influenced group functioning is the prior relationships amongst individuals on entering the group. While some described working with a friend as highly satisfactory, due to mutual support, motivation and established modes of communication, others perceived existing friendship as a disadvantage due to a lack of focus. Moreover, students outside of these friendship groups often felt awkward and excluded, in turn limiting their mutual learning: "*I wasn't expecting to do something on the weekend with them but I did feel left out. Maybe they did talk about the assignment. I didn't know about it*". Although this prior characteristic of the group is not diversity per se, it may moderate the effects of diversity, due to established communication and group norms or a greater distance between those who were and were not already within the relationship.

Diversity During Group Work

Interviewees also identified differences in group members' attributes and behaviours throughout the group work. Three major differences appeared to influence group functioning and success, namely the extent of external commitments, the level of commitment to the task and adherence to rules. Interviewees identified external commitments, particularly work commitments, as hindering group work functioning and success:

> Are they studying full-time or not full-time, are they studying and working at the same time? Or do they think that studies are just for the fun of it, just to get a degree regardless of the mark? … This plays a very important part.

Students felt that work commitments often meant that group work was not as efficient, partially because students could not spend large amounts of time working together.

Task commitment was manifested in the students' dedication to the work. One student mentioned that groups with only one or two committed individuals are most likely to struggle and achieve less than favourable learning outcomes. While the committed individuals may complete the group task, free riding puts extra pressure on them and excludes loafers from the deep learning process. Interviewees indicated that an individual's commitment to the task correlates with the academic goals the individual wants to achieve.

Perhaps related to task commitment are differences in the students' tendency to adhere to group rules. Adherence to rules relates to issues of being punctual or attending meetings and providing the work agreed upon at the appropriate time. In particular, when someone places a high importance on sticking to these rules or relies on this to organise their study schedule whilst others do not, this can cause angst and is more likely to lead to unequal workloads and a lack of deeper learning for those who break the rules, due to their exclusion from the process. While the management literature has discussed group norms, and thus informal rules aimed at conforming group behaviour (Van Engelen et al. 2001), the effect of diversity in adherence to these rules has received little attention to date.

Group Processes

Interviewees highlighted three primary processes that mediated their experience of success, namely communication, leadership and role allocation. Communication, in particular information-sharing and bi-directionality, is critical for group functioning and success. The difference between these two processes lies in the different nature of communication. Information-sharing relates to the expectations of openly sharing information and has been conceptualised previously with items measuring the belief that information sharing is important and that all relevant information is exchanged between parties (Fisher et al. 1997). Bi-directional communication, on the other hand, relates to the dialogue between parties, the feedback that is provided and the level of two-way communication between parties (Fisher et al. 1997).

While some interviewees described a true collaborative approach within some groups, where no leader was necessary, the importance of a good group leader emerged from the majority of interviews: "*I think a group leader is very important; but even more important than that is to have a 'good' group leader*". Students defined good leadership as taking the responsibility for directing the group while ensuring a collaborative approach. Dominance, which interviewees related to a student's personality, language skills and the 'type of group' they are in, reflected bad leadership. One student described a negative experience in which the work produced by one very dominant individual was not good, however, he did not feel it was appropriate for him to tell the individual or change the work. This resulted in a bad mark and also limited learning, as most group members did not engage with the task or each other.

Lastly, students highlighted the importance of role allocation, which relates to how the roles are divided between students. Role allocation by task (research, writing, editing) or sections (i.e. external analysis, promotion section, conclusion) allows for the use of individual students' strengths, provides for a relatively equal contribution to the group, and is a method for dealing with diversity. In particular, it was used by groups to deal with differences in language skills. For example, "*We had two students that had English as a second language so we said 'OK, they won't be doing any of the final writing up*". Despite their 'good' intentions, this approach can mean that students do not learn relevant skills, affecting variety and depth of learning (Kates 2002), particularly if groups did not discuss individual contributions.

Phase 2—Exploratory Quantitative Survey

Method

Phase two of the research project involved the distribution of a self-administered questionnaire to students attending the lecture of a third-year marketing course, where groups were asked to develop an integrated marketing communications campaign. With 70 students attending the lecture and 48 usable questionnaires, a response rate of 68.6 % was achieved. While the relatively small sample size should be noted as a limitation of this paper, it was deemed sufficient for a preliminary assessment of the interrelationships proposed (although categorical variables such as role allocation could not be included). Fifty-five point six % were domestic and 44.4 % international students while 27.1 % worked 5 h or less a week, 33 % of students worked 15–20 h, with another 31.3 % of students working 25 h or more.

Appropriate measurement items for the constructs were identified in the available literature and adapted to the current context of the study. Measurement items and respective sources are outlined in the Appendix. The most significant adaptations of items occurred in relation to the dimensions of difference. While academic goals, personality, external commitments and others have been individually measured for a respondent, a direct measurement of difference has to the authors' knowledge not been reported in the literature. Hence, individual items had to be re-worded to reflect the level of perceived difference within the group.

Results—The Impact of Diversity

A series of multiple regression analyses was conducted to identify which dimensions of diversity significantly influence group outcomes and processes. First, multiple regressions were conducted testing diversity dimensions 'prior to group work' on satisfaction with group outcomes. As shown in Table 1, language skills have a moderately significant ($\alpha \leq 10$) negative effect on satisfaction with the outcome. This result is in line with our qualitative findings, which indicated that differences in language skills lowered satisfaction with the outcome due to a shift of workload to native speakers. Students with a poor grasp of English language were often excluded from deeper discussion and appeared to have limited contribution to the outcome. This situation is also likely to cause dissatisfaction with the outcome for the educator. When testing diversity dimensions (during group work), none of the regression coefficients were significant. Hence, diversity appears to have very limited direct influence on satisfaction with the outcome.

A second multiple regression analysis was then conducted employing satisfaction with the process as the dependent variable (Table 2). The model examining

Table 1 Regression results of diversity on group outcomes

	Satisfaction with outcome	Satisfaction with process
Prior group work		
Diff. in language skills	$\beta = -0.284^a$	$\beta = 0.087$
Diff. in academic goals	$\beta = -0.090$	$\beta = -0.294^b$
Diff. in extroversion	$\beta = -0.035$	$\beta = -0.307^b$
Presence of prior relationships (control)	$\beta = 0.201$	$\beta = 0.125$
Total for all prior diversity	$R^2 = 0.15$	$R^2 = 0.25$
During group work		
Diff. in external commitments	$\beta = -0.048$	$\beta = -0.284^b$
Diff. in commitment to task	$\beta = -0.206$	$\beta = -0.246$
Diff. in adherence to rules	$\beta = -0.010$	$\beta = -0.131$
Total for all during diversity	$R^2 = 0.05$	$R^2 = 0.23$

Standardised regression weights reports
[a]Significant at $\alpha = 0.10$
[b]Significant at $\alpha = 0.05$

Table 2 Regression results of diversity on group processes

	Information-sharing	Bi-directionality	Leadership
Prior group work			
Diff. in language skills	β = −0.215	β = −0.228[a]	β = 0.208
Diff. in academic goals	β = −0.082	β = −0.287[b]	β = 0.035
Diff. in extroversion/introversion	β = 0.397[b]	β = −0.153	β = 0.274[a]
Presence of prior relationships (control)	β = 0.074	β = 0.264[b]	β = 0.190
Total for all prior diversity	R^2 = 0.13	R^2 = 0.33	R^2 = 0.20
During group work			
Diff. in external commitments	β = 0.113	β = −0.160	β = −0.099
Diff. in commitment to task	β = −0.019	β = −0.282[a]	β = 0.416[b]
Diff. in adherence to rules	β = 0.056	β = −0.144	β = −0.145
Total for all during diversity	R^2 = 0.01	R^2 = 0.22	R^2 = 0.12

[a]Significant at $\alpha = 0.10$
[b]Significant at $\alpha = 0.05$

diversity ‘prior to group work’ shows an R-squared of 0.25, with differences in both extroversion and academic goals showing significant negative effects. In addition, diversity of external commitments emerged as negatively affecting satisfaction with the process. These results further confirm our earlier discussion, highlighting the relevance of common academic goals, which was identified as the most critical dimension of diversity in the qualitative phase. In addition, similar personalities and similar levels of external commitments within groups may ease interaction and significantly contribute to higher levels of satisfaction with the process.

In a second step, multiple regressions were employed to test the effect of diversity on group processes, namely information-sharing, bi-directionality and leadership. Interestingly, while all dimensions of diversity ‘prior to group work’ significantly affected group processes, the results showed both positive and negative effects. As expected, differences in language skills and academic goals negatively influenced bi-directionality, and thus the dialogue within the group. Alternately, differences in extroversion positively influenced leadership and, unexpectedly, information sharing. With the inclusion of prior relationships, the significant positive influence it had on bi-directionality was controlled for.

These results suggest that students implement specific processes to overcome challenges brought on by diversity within the group. For example, if only one or two extroverted students are part of the group, these students are likely to see no option but to take on a leadership role (Barry and Stewart 1997). One example of this situation emerged in the qualitative phase of this research: “*I take charge of groups (but) I don’t necessarily want to take charge of groups*”. Results from a study by Barry and Stewart (1997) may provide guidance in understanding the positive relationship between extroversion diversity and information sharing. The proportion of extroverts within a group had a negative curvilinear effect on task focus, thus, the greater the weight of intro- or extroverted students within a group, the less focus on the task.

When considering diversity 'during group work', only differences in task commitment emerged as significantly influencing group processes, in particular bi-directionality. This finding is in line with the qualitative phase: If some group members are not committed to the task while others work hard, a meaningful dialogue within the group is unlikely to be established. However, such a situation is likely to require the committed students to take on a leadership role to at least gain some contribution from the less committed students. In line with this argument, differences in task commitment emerge as significantly and positively affecting leadership.

Results—The Mediating Role of Group Processes

To examine the potential mediating role of group processes, two additional tests were undertaken. Multiple regressions were conducted to assess the effect of group processes firstly on group outcomes and then on group processes (Table 3). The results show a significant positive effect of both communication variables, information-sharing and bi-directionality, on satisfaction with the outcome, as well as a significant effect of bi-directionality on satisfaction with the process. The relatively large R-squared, particularly for the model explaining satisfaction to outcome ($R^2 = 0.56$), shows the importance of communication for satisfaction with group work.

The results of the exploratory regressions indicated two potential mediating effects, namely bi-directionality mediating (1) the effect of goal differences on satisfaction with the process, and (2) the effect of language skills on satisfaction with the outcome. Only these paths meet the prerequisites of mediation (Baron and Kenny 1986). Further analysis was thus undertaken in relation to the two potential mediating effects, which were found to be significant (see Fig. 2).

Specifically, the effect of differences in academic goals on satisfaction with the group process and the effect of diversity in language skills on satisfaction with the group outcome were shown as fully mediated, such that the direct effects become non-significant once bi-directionality within the group process is introduced.

Table 3 Regression results of group processes on group outcomes

Independent variables	Dependent variables	
	Satisfaction with outcome	Satisfaction with process
Group processes		
Diff. in information-sharing	$\beta = 0.352^a$	$\beta = -0.047$
Diff. in bi-directionality	$\beta = 0.605^a$	$\beta = 0.588^a$
Diff. in leadership	$\beta = -0.009$	$\beta = 0.194$
Total for all group processes	$R^2 = 0.56$	$R^2 = 0.30$

[a]significant at $\alpha = 0.05$

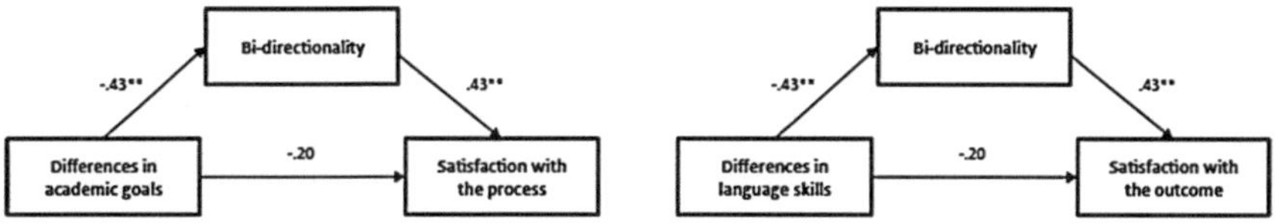

Fig. 2 Mediating effects of bi-directionality

Although these results are only exploratory in nature, they provide preliminary insight into the dynamics of diversity effects on student satisfaction with their group experience. In particular the important role of bi-directionality is highlighted, providing a potential focus for instructors in dealing with diversity.

Implications for Marketing Educators

Our study has drawn together several important dimensions of diversity, such as academic goals, language skills, extroversion and task commitment. With many of these dimensions not readily observable, it is suggested that educators should undertake more than a basic analysis of individuals prior to establishing groups. In particular, working habits, personality and their goals need to be understood. In dealing with diversity, group projects may be split into a number of components, allowing students to understand their group members' language skills, academic goals, commitment to the task, as well as the personalities involved before a final hand-up is required. Perhaps students may be allowed to change group members after each component, as proposed by Aggarwal and O'Brien (2008), or provided with guidance on how to overcome specific group challenges. For example, if difference in language skills is the primary challenge for a group, online discussion forms may be considered as a complement face-to-face discussions, providing students with lesser language skills an opportunity to find the right words in their time and thus actively contribute to the discussion.

Educators also need to provide assistance to students on how to deal with diversity. Tools may include a template for their first meeting, facilitating discussion regarding their working habits (e.g. completing tasks early on versus at the last minute), commitments (work, sport, other) and personalities (e.g. need for structure and planning). In particular, the academic goals of each student should be discussed, with reference to grades but also the skills and experience students wish to gain from the group work. A greater alignment of goals may be achieved by asking students to reflect on how they might achieve each other's unique goals together or by providing added motivation for those students who have 'lesser' goals, by outlining how the group work supports their original motivations for undertaking marketing studies.

Understanding what mediates group performance allows marketing educators to target these processes. For instance, with bi-directional communication shown as a strong predictor of satisfaction with the process and the outcome, dialogue and open discussions should be fostered. For example, educators may be part of group discussions at the beginning, providing some examples of how to moderate discussion. Groups can then be asked to assign a moderating role to one individual or to assign the role on a rotating basis. In addition, information sharing can be encouraged in a number of different ways; more formally, by asking individuals to present their contributions to the group at certain intervals, and assigning some class time for this. Informally by asking students about their knowledge of other group member's assigned areas, prompting them to share each other's work.

From the outset, instructors should provide guidance for students in relation to suitable levels of external commitments. Asking students to devise group meeting times and outlining the reasonable time commitment that is necessary for face to face contact within groups will serve to reinforce the commitment of students. In addition, the instructor might want to establish allocated mentoring sessions during which they provide additional face-to-face or online guidance to individual groups, focusing on the group's diversity and functioning.

Conclusions, Limitations and Directions for Future Research

This study has confirmed the need to go beyond nationality and cultural diversity. In particular, exploring the factors that students themselves believe to manifest diversity, as well as how they may be dealing with diversity, is important as this may have unintended consequences for the learning experience of all types of students. Our study serves as an exploratory platform for further research in this area and should be interpreted in view of its limitations. First, the scope of findings reported here is limited to a small sample and perhaps consequently, sometimes a low variance is explained (R^2). While it served the purpose of identifying and discussing a range of factors relating to diversity and processes in teamwork, further empirical research is required to confirm these results across various student groups, projects, classrooms, universities and countries.

Our results suggest that students struggle with diversity on many levels and that various types of diversity can significantly affect both tangible and intangible outcomes of group work. Depending on the reasons for using group work this struggle may or may not be perceived as warranted. By understanding the effects of various types of diversity at a broader level we, as providers of education, can hope to control and direct the student experience so that greater satisfaction and deeper learning can be achieved through group work. It is important to note that responsibilities for the success of group work do not lie solely with the instructor. Not only should students be reminded of their responsibilities, university support staff and senior management should help to ensure the best possible learning environment is established for all students. Lastly, these results may help us to understand students and thus become better teachers. Teachers that are more than just content providers and teachers that can make a difference through facilitating positive experiences between students, helping to gain more than a good grade but to learn how to be members of a well-functioning and productive team.

Appendix: Measurement

Prior group work
Diff. in language skills (New) (Cronbach alpha = 0.915)
• Our level of written English language skills differed • Our level of verbal (spoken) English language skills differed
Diff. in academic goals (Marsh et al. 2003)—different goal orientations bracketed (Cronbach alpha = 0.91)
• Group members differed in what we wanted to achieve • We differed in the extent to which we aimed to get the best mark we possibly could (approach success) • We differed in the extent to which we aimed to work to the best of our ability (mastery) • We differed in the extent to which we aimed to do better than other students (competition)
Diff. in extro-/introversion (John and Srivastava 2001) (Cronbach alpha = 0.88)
• Are talkative • Are reserved (r) • Are full of energy • Generate a lot of enthusiasm • Tend to be quiet (r) • Have an assertive personality • Are sometimes shy, inhibited (r) • Are outgoing, sociable
Diff. in commitment to task (Marsh et al. 2006) (Cronbach alpha = 0.94)
• We differed in the extent to which we worked as hard as possible • We differed in the extent to which we kept working even when the assignment was difficult • We differed in the extent to which we tried our best to acquire the skills and knowledge pertaining to the assignment • We differed in the extent to which we put forth our best effort
Diff. in external commitments (new)
• We differed in the amount of external commitments we had
Group processes
Information-sharing (Fisher et al. 1997; Mohr and Sohi 1995) (Cronbach alpha = 0.84)
• We shared any information with others in the group • We provided the others in the group with any information that might help the them • We kept each other informed about events or changes that may affect the other • We believe that sharing information in the assignment group is important
Bi-directionality (Fisher et al. 1997) (Cronbach alpha = 0.89)
• We discussed things a lot • We had great dialogues in the group • We provided a lot of feedback to each other • There was a lot of two-way communication between me and others in the group

(continued)

(continued)

Leadership emergence (Barry and Stewart 1997) (Cronbach alpha = 0.84)
• A leader emerged in the group • The group had one member who assumed the leader role • Our group did not have a specific leader (r)
Outcomes
Satisfaction with outcome (not at all—to a great extent) (Reinig 2003) (Cronbach alpha = 0.87)
• How satisfied are you with the quality of your group's solution? • To what extent does the final solution reflect your inputs? • To what extent do you feel committed to the group solution • To what extent are you confident that the group solution is correct?
Satisfaction with process (Reinig 2003; Cronbach alpha = 0.91)
• Efficient–inefficient • Coordinated–uncoordinated • Fair–unfair • Understandable–confusing • Satisfying–dissatisfying

References

Aggarwal P, O'Brien CL (2008) Social loafing on group projects: structural antecedents and effect on student satisfaction. J Mark Educ 30(3):255–264

Australasian Survey of Student Engagement (AUSSE) (2009) Student Report Australasian University. http://www.acer.edu.au/files/ausse_2009_australasian_uni_student_report.pdf. Accessed 30 June 2015

Bacon DR, Stewart KA, Stewart-Belle S (1998) Exploring predictors of student team project performance. J Mark Educ 20(1):63–71

Baron RM, Kenny DA (1986) The moderator-mediator variable distinction in social psychological research: conceptual, strategic, and statistical considerations. J Pers Soc Psychol 51(6):1173–1182

Barry B, Stewart GL (1997) Composition, process, and performance in self-managed groups: the role of personality. J Appl Psychol 82(1):62–78

Batra MM, Walvoord BE, Krishnan KS (1997) Effective pedagogy for student-team projects. J Mark Educ 19(2):26–42

Carson D, Gilmore A, Perry C, Gronhaug K (2001) Qualitative marketing research. Sage Publications, London

D'Alessandro S, Volet S (2012) Balancing work with study: impact on marketing students' experience of group work. J Mark Educ 34(1):96–107

Fisher RJ, Maltz E, Jaworski BJ (1997) Enhancing communication between marketing and engineering: the moderating role of relative functional integration. J Mark 61(3):54–70

Jackson SE, May KE, Whitney K (1995) Understanding the dynamics of diversity in decision-making teams. In: Guzzo RA, Salas E, Associates (eds) Team effectiveness and decision making in organisations. Jossey-Bass, San Francisco, pp 204–2610

Jehn KA, Mannix EA (2001) The dynamic nature of conflict: a longitudinal study of intragroup conflict and group performance. Acad Manag J 44(2):238–251

John OP, Srivastava S (2001) The big-five trait taxonomy: history, measurement, and theoretical perspectives. In: John OP, Pervin L (eds) Handbook of personality: theory and research, 2nd edn. Guilford, New York

Kates SM (2002) Barriers to deep learning in student marketing teams. Australas Mark J 10(2):14–25

Kimmel K, Volet S (2010) University students' perceptions of and attitudes towards culturally diverse group work: Does context matter? J Stud Int Educ 16(2):157–181

Marsh HW, Craven RG, Hinkley JW, Debus RL (2003) Evaluation of the big-two-factor theory of academic motivation orientations: an evaluation of jingle-jangle fallacies. Multivar Behav Res 38(2):189–224

Marsh HW, Hau K-T, Artelt C (2006) OECD's brief self-report measure of educational psychology's most useful affective constructs: cross-cultural, psychometric comparisons across 25 countries. Int J Testing 6(4):311–360

McCorkle DE, Reardon J, Alexander JF, Kling ND, Harris RC, Iyer RV (1999) Undergraduate marketing students, group projects and teamwork: the good, the bad, and the ugly? J Mark Educ 21(2):106–117

Milliken FJ, Martins LL (1996) Searching for common threads: understanding the multiple effects of diversity in organizational groups. Acad Manag Rev 21(2):402–433

Mohr J, Sohl Rs (1995) Communication flows in distribution channels: impact on assessments of communication quality and satisfaction. J Retail 71(4):393–416

Paulus TM, Bichelmeyer B, Malopinsky L, Pereira M, Rastogi P (2005) Power distance and group dynamics of an international project team: a case study. Teach High Educ 10(1):43–55

Reinig BA (2003) Toward an understanding of satisfaction with the process and outcomes of teamwork. J Manag Inf Syst 19(4):65–83

Sweeney ADP, Weaven S (2005) Group learning in marketing: an exploratory qualitative study of its usefulness. In: Proceedings of the Australian and New Zealand marketing academy conference, Perth. School of Business, University of Western Australia, pp 195–202

Sy T, Côté S, Saavedra R (2005) The contagious leader: impact of the leader's mood on the mood of group members, group affective tone, and group processes. J Appl Psychol 90(2):295–305

Thomas DC (1999) Cultural diversity and work group effectiveness. J Cross Cult Psychol 30 (2):242–263

Ticehurst GW, Veal AJ (1999) Business research methods: a managerial approach. Longman, Frenchs Forest, NSW

UNESCO Institute for Statistics (2014) Global flow of tertiary-level Students, released 5 May 2014. http://www.uis.unesco.org/Education/Pages/international-student-flow-viz.aspx. Accessed 26 June 2015

Van Der Zee K, Van Oudenhoven JP (2000) The multicultural personality questionnaire: a multidimensional instrument of multicultural effectiveness. Eur J Pers 14:291–309

Van Der Zee K, Atsma N, Brodbeck F (2004) The influence on social identity and personality on outcomes of cultural diversity in teams. J Cross Cult Psychol 35(3):283–303

Van Engelen JML, Kiewiet DJ, Terlouw P (2001) Improving performance of product development teams through managing polarity. Int Stud Manag Organ 31(1):46–64

Volet S (1997) Cognitive and affective variables in the academic learning: the significance of direction and effort in students' goals. Learn Instr 7(3):235–254

Watson WE, Johnson L, Zgourides GD (2002) The influence of ethnic diversity on leadership, group process, and performance: an examination of learning teams. Int J Intercultural Relat 26 (1):1–16

Watson WE, BarNir A, Pavur R (2005) Cultural diversity and learning teams: the impact on desired academic team processes. Int J Intercultural Relat 29(4):449–467

Williams DL, Beard JD, Rymer J (1991) Team projects: achieving their full potential. J Mark Educ 13(2):45–53

Zimmerman BJ, Bandura A, Martinez-Pons M (1992) Self-motivation for academic attainment: the role of self-efficacy beliefs and personal goal setting. Am Educ Res J 29(3):663–676

Student Engagement: A Multiple Layer Phenomenon

Jodie Conduit, Ingo O. Karpen and Francis Farrelly

Abstract Universities are seeking to actively and strategically manage student engagement through providing opportunities for students to interact and engage with the institution on a range of levels and in different ways. However, this increasingly complex and multi-layered nature of student engagement within a tertiary education environment is not well understood. Through qualitative focus groups and a series of interviews with undergraduate and postgraduate students, this study explores and articulates the cognitive, emotional, behavioural and social dimensions of engagement that depict the nature of student engagement. This is one of the first studies that considers social engagement as a dimension of the broader engagement construct and provides an illustration of social engagement at different levels within a tertiary education setting. Further, we demonstrate that engagement occurs with three key focal objects (or levels) embedded within the university structure; the lecturer, course and the institution itself. Hence, this paper contributes to the literature by providing a multi-layered consideration of student engagement and demonstrating the nested nature of engagement across the broad service system (the university), the narrow service system (the course), and the individual dyadic level of engagement (the student-lecturer interaction). These findings could be further considered and empirically tested in other engagement contexts (e.g. employee engagement, customer engagement).

Keywords Student engagement · Social engagement · Tertiary education · Service system · Students

---

J. Conduit (✉)
The University of Adelaide, Adelaide, Australia
e-mail: Jodie.conduit@adelaide.edu.au

I.O. Karpen · F. Farrelly
RMIT University, Melbourne, Australia
e-mail: Ingo.karpen@rmit.edu.au

F. Farrelly
e-mail: Francis.farrelly@rmit.edu.au

© Springer Science+Business Media Singapore 2016

C. Plewa and J. Conduit (eds.), *Making a Difference Through Marketing*,
DOI 10.1007/978-981-10-0464-3_17

Introduction

With Professor Pascale Quester as Deputy Vice Chancellor (Academic), the University of Adelaide developed and implemented a $41.8 million student learning hub that brought together informal learning and social spaces, university facilities, and retail services spaces for student use on campus. This flexible space was designed and co-created with students, in response to trends that were seeing students retreat off campus as soon as formal classes had finished (Quester et al. 2014). Given the demand-driven nature of the education sector in Australia and the University's strategic focus on becoming more student-centric (Quester et al. 2014), there was a recognised need to improve student engagement both among the student body and between students and the university. This large-scale investment demonstrated a serious commitment to making a difference in student engagement at the University of Adelaide.

Student engagement has become an increasingly important notion for educators because of its demonstrated impact on student's educational outcomes (Bravo et al. 2014) as well as retention and completion rates at tertiary institutions (Hennig-Thurau et al. 2001; Quaye and Harper 2014). Current educational thinking recognises that students are not passive recipients of their education, but rather are co-creators of their learning experience (Taylor et al. 2011). However, in today's environment, large class sizes, time poor students (Stafford 2011), access to technology, and the role that technology plays in people's lives (Northey et al. 2015) have changed the way both students and institutions seek to engage with each other. Universities are implementing initiatives such as flipped classroom, online courses, and enhanced facilities such as those described in the opening scenario, but the impact on student engagement is not fully understood (Taylor et al. 2011). A greater understanding of how student's engage with tertiary institutions is required to enable universities to deploy resources, organise curriculum, and provide support services to effectively facilitate student engagement (Kuh et al. 2011).

Within contemporary student engagement literature there is general consensus that engagement manifests as cognitive, affective and behavioural dimensions (Bryson and Hand 2007). There is also limited recognition that engagement occurs at the personal, situational and institutional level (London et al. 2009). However, extant studies typically consider engagement at one of these levels and there are few studies that consider engagement with multiple touch-points or at multiple embedded levels within the institution. While it is recognised that students interact with lecturers, course materials, other students, and university staff and facilities to co-create learning outcomes (Harrison 2013), there is a lack of understanding of how engagement with each of these focal objects combine within an institutional paradigm. This research will investigate the multiple focal objects with which students engage within a tertiary institutional environment and hence will further explicate the holistic perspective of student engagement in this setting.

The purpose of this chapter is to examine the complex and multi-layered nature of student engagement within a tertiary education environment. Firstly, through qualitative focus groups and a series of interviews with undergraduate and post-graduate students, we identify the presence of social engagement as a dimension of student engagement rarely discussed in educational literature. Further, we demonstrate that engagement occurs with three key focal objects that are embedded within each other (i.e. the lecturer, course and institution). Hence, this paper contributes to the literature by providing a multi-layered consideration of student engagement. It demonstrates nested engagement with the broad service system (the university), the narrow service system (the course), and the individual dyadic level of engagement (the lecturer), which can be considered for other engagement settings (e.g. customer engagement). Further, we provide examples of the cognitive, emotional, behavioural and social engagement that occurs at each of these levels of engagement. Given these findings, we argue for the need for future research to adopt and further investigate this multi-layered approach to engagement.

The remainder of this chapter is organised as follows. The next section provides a brief discussion of the dimensions and levels of student engagement in higher education. An explanation of the research method follows, which leads to a discussion of the results. The paper concludes with theoretical and educational implications as well as an outline of future research directions.

Student Engagement

While the terms 'student engagement' and 'institutional engagement' have been previously coined in the literature (e.g. London et al. 2007), there is a lack of consensus regarding the concepts' definition and scope with confusion surrounding the focal engagement subject and object of interest. While some authors propose the student as the focal engagement subject, and a particular task, course of study, or lecturer as the focal engagement object (London et al. 2009), others cite the institution as the focal engagement subject and the broader community as the focal engagement object (e.g. Keener 1999). In our study, consistent with London et al. (2009), the student is viewed as the focal engagement subject and this study seeks to further understand details regarding the focal object with which students engage through their learning experiences.

In general, student engagement requires an intrinsic motivation from students to invest effort into interactions related to their studies and/or the educational institution (Kuh 2003). It reflects the students' effort and absorption in initiating and sustaining learning activities (Furrer and Skinner 2003). It is argued that the effects of student engagement are enduring, and the broader psychological connection and sense of belonging toward their institution may endure for a period of time after their completion of their university courses and degrees (London et al. 2009). For the purposes of this study, we define student engagement as:

> A student's willingness to invest their own cognitive, emotional and behavioural effort to interact with resources related to their education experience.

Recent scholarly discussion has seen student engagement manifest as three dimensions; cognitive engagement, affective engagement and behavioural engagement (Lam et al. 2014). *Cognitive engagement* reflects a student's level of concentration and mental focus given to their education experience (Northey et al. 2015; Scott and Craig-Lees 2010). Indicators of cognitive engagement could include activities that reflect the students' cognitive strategies and approaches to learning, such as self-regulated learning (Lam et al. 2014). *Affective engagement* reveals the level of positive emotion toward a focal engagement object (Northey et al. 2015) and hence how students feel about their education experience. The notion of affective engagement often is strongly associated with aspects such as a sense of belonging, identification with the institution, and commitment (London et al. 2007; Lam et al. 2014). It reflects the students' attitudes toward learning (Skinner and Belmont 1993) and the institution they attend (Voelkl 1997). *Behavioural engagement* focuses more on interactions for task achievement and has historically included measures of class participation, attendance, participation in extra-curricular activities, and task completion (Finn et al. 1995; London et al. 2007; Lam et al. 2014). For the purpose of this study, behavioural engagement is considered a student's willingness to spend energy and time on their educational experience.

While many studies recognise the multi-dimensional nature of student engagement, very few recognise that students may engage with multiple touch-points within a tertiary institution. Most studies will focus on only one of these focal levels of engagement. As an exception, London et al. (2009) recognise that there are layers of engagement, at the personal, situational and institutional level. Several studies recognise the importance of the student-teacher interactions for facilitating student engagement (e.g. Skinner and Belmont 1993; Klem and Connell 2004). Recently, Pianta et al. (2012) posit that these personal interactions are so critical to student engagement that teachers need better knowledge and training of how to facilitate engagement and should receive personalised feedback about their interactive behaviours. Taylor et al. (2011) concentrated on engagement at the course-level and examined the motivations behind course-level engagement. While it is argued that few research studies have examined course-level engagement (Taylor et al. 2011), there are several studies which examine the effects of educational approaches (e.g. team-based learning; Chad 2012) and technological tools (e.g. asynchronous learning through Facebook; Northey et al. 2015) on student engagement, which are set in course-based situational settings. It is reasonable to assert that overall student engagement with the total educational experience is at least a partial function of student engagement at the component level (e.g. individual classes) (Taylor et al. 2011).

Baron and Corbin (2012) argue that the student experience as a whole is the key to engagement and, thus, a 'whole-of-university' approach is necessary to re-engage students. A focussed approach that aligns the university mission and engagement initiatives and reflects the campus environment and student cohort is required (Harper and Quaye 2009; Baron and Corbin 2012). To achieve this, a greater understanding of the overall learning experience from the perspective of the student is necessary. This will facilitate a better fit between the resources of the student and the resources of the University and enable a clear understanding of the meaning of engagement in the higher education sector to emerge.

In line with the theoretical grounding of service-dominant logic (Vargo and Lusch 2008), engaged students are interactive and co-create their learning experiences within the university (Brodie et al. 2011). As a co-creator of the learning experience, students integrate resources though interactions with other students, lecturers, course materials and university services for the purpose of obtaining a valued outcome (Díaz-Méndez and Gummesson 2012). Without the students' interaction in the experience, no value is derived from the resources of the lecturer, course-related resources, or other resources deployed by the university (Diaz-Méndez and Gummesson 2012; Vargo and Lusch 2008). Hence, an understanding of where and how students engage with the resources of the university is important for not only facilitating engagement, but also for driving value outcomes for students and the university. This perspective does not relinquish authority or control to students (e.g. McCulloch 2009), but rather identifies students as active contributors (rather than passive consumers) that significantly shape their education experiences and value perceptions associated with the usage of university resources. However, given the increasingly limited resources available to universities, being able to utilise them effectively is critically important. Indeed, universities can benefit from embracing a co-creation perspective by becoming the preferred education institution through better student-centered and meaningful education experiences. Hence, further research is required to understand how students engage with the university, and at what level is the focal object of engagement (i.e. lecturer, course, or university).

Research Method

This study was conducted in a large Australian University and respondents were drawn from all year levels of undergraduate and postgraduate students, across a cross-section of predominantly business departments, including accounting, design, entrepreneurship, marketing, and logistics. As the main objective of this study was to investigate the nature and interrelationship of student engagement, an exploratory, qualitative approach was adopted to enable rich insights and begin to understand the complexities and nuances of this domain. Thereby semi-structured interviews and focus groups were pursued (Smith 1995), enabling data triangulation (Coffey and Atkinson 1999). Specifically, we undertook four focus groups (between 6 and 10 participants each) and eleven subsequent in-depth interviews with students. We selected students who were involved in university-related activities beyond the classroom (e.g. student club memberships and associations) and/or who had parallel work-placement activities. These students could draw on a greater variety of university-related interactions and thus offer thick descriptions of their experiences. The sample size for this research was data-driven and data collection discontinued when saturation was reached; that is, where few new insights were gleaned from additional data (Lincoln and Guba 1985). Each interview ranged from 60–90 min in duration. The data were audio-recorded (Morgan and Spanish 1984) and transcribed by the researcher (Boland 1995), generating a total of over 361 pages of single spaced text. NVIVO 9 was utilised to support the data coding and analysis. Based on the Gioia et al. (2013) approach, we began with identifying and noting first-order incidents, which in this case represent different manifestations of engagement. These incidents were then clustered and aggregated to create second-order themes. The themes included for example different dimensions of engagement and engagement reference objects. In a final step we then investigated the links between these themes to better understand the potential interdependent nature of different levels of student engagement.

Results

The following results will provide overall insights into students' reference points with regards to their university-related engagement. That is, the qualitative study shows that engagement manifests in different forms (e.g. cognitive, emotional and behavioural) and across different levels of touchpoints and experiences (e.g. that are associated with a lecturer or course). These individual engagement levels likely contribute to overall engagement perceptions. While we show illustrative quotes in text with de-identified and hypothetical student names to support the emerging theorising, we further present additional quotes to enrich the empirical data upon which our findings rest.

An overarching theme to emerge from the student interviews was a general consensus that throughout their encounters at the university, students engaged with the university, the university community, and their learning experience. Students widely acknowledged their own personal involvement and interaction within the service system and the learning process and didn't consider themselves as passive recipients of a service delivery process.

> We get more of an opportunity to share our experiences with other students or maybe inform them about things that they aren't aware of and vice versa. We can become informed about things that we might not necessarily be aware of and just kind of knowledge share. I'd really love an approach to learning that is similar to like the experience of working at Google, or something like that, where there's like really open environment, discussion is encouraged because it's kind of built into the physical structure of the Google premise, like there's areas for people to congregate and meet. (Greg, male)

Students make use of a variety of resources that have the potential to become important engagement objects. Thereby the nature of engagement was routinely seen to be interactive and required an ongoing, active involvement from both parties. Without this reciprocated interaction, the level of engagement would drop off or would cease all together.

> If you make an effort but you don't get that same response back, you just don't care, you just don't bother (Lea, female)

Social Engagement Dimension

The thematic coding of our data to understand the concept of engagement in an educational context illustrated a dimension of engagement not often depicted or characterised in literature on student engagement. We found strong evidence of the students' willingness to interact with lecturers and other students on a personal level and through social exchanges for a stronger sense of engagement with the university at different levels. Consequently, we depict the notion of social engagement, which complements the dimensions of cognitive, emotional and behavioural engagement in the broader concept of student engagement. We define this social engagement dimension as:

> A student's willingness to invest effort in social interactions and personal exchanges with the resources of other actors (e.g. lecturers, peers) in relation to their education experience.

Although the notion of social engagement is not prevalent in the student engagement literature, the importance of social networks and teamwork is well recognised (Chad 2012). However, this literature focuses predominantly on the teamwork processes required to enhance learning performance (e.g. Bravo et al. 2014), and does not consider the social nature of the peer-to-peer (or peer-to-lecturer) engagement and its existence across different levels of engagement. While marketing literature has cursorily considered social engagement (e.g. Calder et al. 2009; Vivek et al. 2012), there has not yet been any substantive recognition of the need to engage students on a social level.

Many respondents articulated that having a personal connection and social interaction with the lecturer, not only ensured they felt more engaged at an individual level, but it also enhanced their learning experience.

> I think it's about connecting with somebody on a social basis as opposed to a professional basis, you know like anybody can really go in there and talk about accounting and it's all very professional… It's just that, you don't get the same connection from just talking about course work, it is a very kind of teacher-student relationship when it's just course work, whereas if you bring social aspects in you can still have the professional teacher/student relationship but there's something extra that just comes into it. (Helga, female)

In addition, the sense of engagement that arises from social interactions among student peers builds a community and network of support throughout the learning experience.

> If you have that similar experience that other people are going through, you can kind of help them through it or they can help you through it, you know, there's an understanding of where you currently are and where you're going to. And I suppose it's good if your peers are all experiencing the same thing and it's all something that you're equally passionate about, then you're going to get more out of the experience. (Greg, male)

This type of social comfort and support may arise naturally or spontaneously through social interaction and bonding, but it might also be professionally facilitated by the university. For example, students might be part of mentoring or advisory networks and thereby combine social support with educational support.

> This semester I think was definitely a highlight. Just starting SLAMS [student learning advisory mentors] and working with other students, mentoring in the subject that I did well in and that I actually really enjoyed; it's rewarding to know that you're helping students get through a time where they're struggling and because I've been there I know exactly what they're going through. (Lisa, female)

Given that the cognitive, emotional and behavioural dimensions are well identified and discussed in the literature, they will not be specifically explicated again here. The focus in the next sections will focus on the three focal institutional sub-objects that were uncovered through the interviews and subsequent analysis. That is, it was identified that students discriminate between and engage primarily with the lecturer, the course and the aggregate level of the institution (university). The initial engagement with the lecturer is a personal, dyadic relationship, whereas engagement at the course and university level represents engagement with a service system and is more multi-faceted. The nature of engagement with each focal object (lecturer, course and university) will be discussed in turn, followed by a discussion of the interaction between the levels of engagement. The cognitive, emotional, behavioural and social dimensions that manifest at each of those levels are further illustrated in Table 1.

Table 1 Illustrative quotes—student engagement levels and dimensions

	Cognitive engagement	Affective engagement	Behavioural engagement	Social engagement
Individual dyadic (lecturer)	"The teachers and the lecturers are there as resources but students have to do their own work and they have to apply themselves and motivate themselves." (Helga, female)	"I know I can't expect every teacher to take the time to meet with the student, but it made me feel really comfortable to be in their class knowing that they actually know who I am and that I'm not just you know someone who's just paying to listen to them, so that's also something that made me feel quite good." (Lisa, female)	"He'll (the lecturer) ask us a few questions and the whole lecture theatre is silent. The whole tutorial is silent. He goes 'OK well I'm not moving on until you answer my question. He sits there for five minutes and that is fair enough because nobody is answering the question." (Student, focus group 1)	"I can feel that the lecturer/tutor is actually trying to teach us something. And because they are telling us a little bit about their personal selves, basically then that relationship goes from a teacher/student perspective, to more acquaintances, so you sort of get like a more personal type level. And that … then from that you can then be free to open up, to generate discussions, ask questions" (Harry, male)

(continued)

Table 1 (continued)

	Cognitive engagement	Affective engagement	Behavioural engagement	Social engagement
Narrow service system (course)	"I think you have to be interested about it, the subject and if you're not interested in it, you make it interesting somehow. […] like you're actually looking forward to coming home and working on this project. It's in your head constantly, you're constantly thinking about '*How can I do this*', '*How can I change it*', it become an obsession almost." (Thomas, male)	"I will go to a lecture that engages me, like even though I might not know the answer but I still want to participate, I love to have the feeling. And if University A can have that, I think it's good enough." (Lars, male)	"The best subject that I've got the most out of has been this Work Integrated Learning subject, where this company came to us and said, here's my problem, help me out. Solve it. For me that's the subject that I've done the best in because it's like this is my project, this is about me, and me showing my skills" (Student, focus group 1)	"…those friendship circles. I couldn't see myself being where I am today having done it on my own. As I said University A has given that… in the first trimester you are forced to work in groups, so you're having an interaction with five people at one time and you can say okay I get along with this person, this person not so much…. subsequently when you have to work on your own and have to build your own team, that's where it really comes into play. (Ralf, male)
Larger service system (University)	"It would be the applied learning and personal growth, I think is what University A stands for. I think, again the independent kind of growing as a professional growing as an individual and being ready for whatever career you set out to do, I think that's what	"I am very happy to be a University A student. I'm very proud to call myself that because of the positive experiences I've had through the mentoring programs that I've had, through being employed by University A, through my interactions with my teachers. So I	"I don't actually feel like I've really taken advantage of what the university offers you until this last semester of university when I became a mentor […] that wakened me up to kind of the opportunities within the university." (Lisa, female)	"I've recognised that interacting with people at the university is really important too and I've had a lot of fun in that, like doing side projects for the university or just having lunch with some people on campus instead of just studying alone". (Helga, female)

(continued)

Table 1 (continued)

	Cognitive engagement	Affective engagement	Behavioural engagement	Social engagement
	University A represents." (Helga, female)	think, you know, overall I'm very proud to be a University A student." (Harry, male)		

Individual Engagement (Lecturer)

A common focal object of engagement identified by students was the personal engagement they had with the lecturer. Students recognised the interaction between themselves and the lecturer both in relation to the course content and their learning experience, as well as on a personal level. Students often spoke of how their confidence to interact and engage with both the learning materials and other students emerged from the trust and confidence built through engaging with the lecturer.

> And so with the teachers, if they can sort of explain the question to you with personal examples, then you can see how it applies, I can see how it relates to me. Then you can see, okay, I really want to work it out because now I understand this actually and want to find out the solution. So … that's how you basically engage and interact with the students. (Harry, male)

The lecturer was seen as a pivotal engagement point. When engagement between the student and the lecturer is minimal or non-existent, it often has an impact on the broader engagement. Our findings suggest that the interaction with the lecturer has the potential to shape the holistic education experience and thereby engagement levels with the university overall. Although specific resources can act as reference points (or objects) of engagement, it is likely that these different resources and engagement levels mutually influence each other. The following quote highlights how one specific resource or experience element can significantly affect other experience elements, even to their perceived detriment.

> And I just felt kind of … ripped off by the teaching staff and the way that the course was done, because you know, if the teacher gets things wrong, then what sort of hope do we have? (Harry, male)

It should be noted that the above illustration depicts a low degree of engagement, or even negative engagement with the lecturer. Engagement has been recognised to vary in degrees of intensity in consumer contexts (Vivek et al. 2012; Bryson and Hand 2007), and also in its positive or negative valence (Hollebeek and Chen 2014). However, an understanding of the impact of the degree of intensity and valence in engagement has rarely been discussed in an educational context. Although this is beyond the scope of discussion in this study, our findings reflect this variation in engagement.

Engagement with the Narrow Service System (Course)

The classroom environment is often considered the primary vehicle for student engagement from an educational perspective (e.g. Taylor et al. 2011). We define this classroom and course experience as the narrow service system with a specific educational purpose (i.e. reflective of the content of the class). All enrolled students, lecturers and educational materials and activities designed for the class reflect this narrow service system. Consistent with this, students recognised the interaction and engagement at the course level was an essential part of their engagement in the learning experience. Within the narrow service system of the course undertaken by the student, engagement occurs as evidenced in the following quotes:

> I love the class. Maybe, I was really lucky, because I heard quite a number of horror stories about [the course]. … I was lucky in the sense that it wasn't just my group mates that were really awesome, it was everyone in the class, and everyone was participative … Best tutorial class in my opinion, because it really gets the students to engage and couple of games, and it was fun (Lars, male)

This quote also highlights again the participatory and contributory role that students play in shaping their own education experiences and outcomes. Consistent with a service-dominant logic perspective (Vargo and Lusch 2008), classroom interaction as manifestations of co-created value directly shape engagement levels. In this case, all four elements of cognitive engagement (the game challenge), emotional engagement (the fun part), social engagement (the personal exchanges), and behavioural engagement (everyone participated) surfaced. Although students that were engaged with a course routinely reported higher levels of motivation and participation, regular participation itself was not akin to being engaged per se in the course. This supports the notion in the literature that engagement is beyond a behavioural concept and requires an accompanying psychological connection to the focal object, as is highlighted in the following example with low engagement intensity.

> Well with the subject you just want to get something done, you know, like you do the research, you reference, you start writing, but there's not always a real passion for what you're completing, you know. Like sometimes it's like okay, it's part of the coursework, it's a requirement, but it's not necessarily something that I would do on my own accord. (Greg, male)

Engagement with the Broad Service System (University)

Engagement at the institutional level is not only an aggregate of engagement with the multiple touch-points within it, but manifests as a direct engagement between the student and the institution itself. Akin to the notion of engagement, students spoke about their participation in activities at an institutional level and the emotional bond with the institution that arose from that interaction.

> You don't want to just feel like a number, you want to feel like you really are part of the University and … I haven't felt like that until my last semester, where I've actually started to get involved with the University and to receive some recognition for that. (Lisa, female)

Students also expected that the institution, at an aggregate level, would seek to engage with them as an individual reflective of the interactive aspect of engagement.

> They again see students as individuals who are achieving things as opposed to just a number to attend class. It kind of … it seemed like University A had a real pride in their students and was really motivated to get them noticed by you know if not industry then other contacts, I think, so the recognition I think was really important for me. (Helga, female)

A key theme identified at all levels of engagement, but most prevalent at the institutional level, was the recognition of the resources that were provided with which the student could interact to achieve their learning outcomes. Students often spoke about the institutional facilities and support services which assisted their endeavours to engage.

> I think University A has to know that, has to know that some students don't have the initiative to start off with… and through university, you know, student skills and initiatives should slowly be built up […] I think initiative stems from being comfortable in your own environment, and if you can … make it more comfortable for students, having those resources, having say, you know, counselling services where students can go … and classrooms where students feel comfortable in, then they'll start to engage (Harry, male)I think the thing that changed for me was at the Village it was very easy to do work because there were so many silent zones and all this kind of stuff,… I don't know, I still don't use the computer labs, but I don't know it's just … it feels like a bit more of a … like a learning supporting environment. And nothing changed except my attitude I suppose towards Uni. (Nerea, female)

Consistent with the resource-centeredness of service-dominant logic, students clearly leveraged resources to create better university experiences. The resources provided by the university create opportunities for learning experiences and value perceptions to emerge. Through these resources and subsequent experiences, engagement levels are both enacted and impacted.

Interdependence of the Engagement Layers

Preliminary evidence suggests that the layers of engagement are interdependent, with engagement at the personal level and within the narrow service system (the course) building to a greater sense of institutional level engagement. Thereby some resources or reference objects can be more important than others, but ultimately all have the potential to contribute to overall engagement. Indeed, due to the embedded nature of the focal objects (i.e. the lecturer is employed by and part of the institution), engagement at one level will partially build engagement at the broader level. This can be achieved without direct referral to the broader engagement level, as described below.

> I think when you had a good tutor or a good lecturer that really made a connection… When you got a personal relationship with one of those, either the tutor or the lecturer, by extension you felt a bit more a part of University A. (Helga, female)

Similarly, students speak of emotional engaging with the course, and as a consequence slowly building this into a greater sense of engagement across the institution.

> University's not just for the teaching, it's also for fun and enjoyment …., slowly that translates then into the classroom, into your learning experiences and then you slowly get a lot more out of Uni because you want to be there as well. (Harry, male)

In the following example, the student speaks to how increased engagement with the lecturer led to enhanced engagement with the broader institution. However, in this instance the connection between the engagement layers was more explicit, with the lecturer directing the student as to how he could engage at the broader service system level.

> I could actually speak to my lecturers and tutors outside of class that I didn't realise that you could do in the first year, so I think the fact that I could get more out of them kind of made me feel a little bit more comfortable at university because I was getting a bit more than these three or four years … those three or four hours a week that you would normally get. And then, they pointed me in the direction to this function and then to that… I didn't know these things were an option. (Helga, female)

These quotes are indicative of the interdependent nature of the engagement layers identified in our thematic analysis. The embedded nature of the lecturer and course within the institutional service system gives rise to the interdependence of the engagement objects. However, there was also evidence of clear referral and transference between and among the layers of engagement. The interplay between the engagement foci in this setting requires further exploration.

Table 1 provides further illustrative respondent quotes reflecting the levels of engagement within the institution identified from our analysis. This table also considers the cognitive, emotional and behavioural dimensions reflected within each levels of engagement, consistent with the multi-dimensional nature of engagement in the marketing and educational literature.

Theoretical and Educational Implications

Theoretical Implications

Our findings build on and advance conceptual engagement understandings recognised in extant literature. The student respondents identified several focal objects within an educational context with which they engage including the lecturer, aspects of the course, and the broader institutional, or university, level. We thus shed significant insights on engagement as a multi-level phenomenon that varies in depth and breadth across focal objects. Our data demonstrates that single-level considerations might provide theoretical frameworks that are too simplistic in terms of their potential to account for the complexities underlying the engagement phenomenon.

We also find initial support that these levels of focal engagement objects are interrelated with lecturers nested within courses, and courses nested within the university service system. This contributes to the literature on student engagement as previous studies have focussed on only one level of engagement and have not explored the interrelated effects of engagement of different, nested, focal objects. A multi-layered consideration of student engagement provides a richer theoretical model and points towards challenges that need to be considered by both academic coordinators and University administrators when allocating resources for student engagement at all levels.

Consistent with recent literature in educational, organisational and marketing literature, which has conceptualised engagement as a multidimensional concept, we identified cognitive, affective and behavioural dimensions of engagement within the institutional environment. However, our data clearly identifies a fourth dimension: social engagement. The identification of social engagement extends the engagement construct to capture the students' willingness to engage in personal interactions and social exchanges with their peers and their lecturer. Hence, we propose an updated definition of student engagement with captures this important and distinct dimension:

> A student's willingness to invest their own cognitive, emotional, social and behavioural effort to interact with resources related to their education experience.

Importantly, our findings demonstrate a four-dimensional conceptualisation of student engagement is consistently identified at each level of engagement within the institution, providing further support for its relevance and applicability within the student engagement literature.

Educational Implications

Universities need to be cognisant of engaging students through all touch-points in the learning experience. Academic staff should be knowledgeable about how to facilitate effective student interactions and engagement and receive feedback on this aspect of their performance. Particularly the awareness and understanding of the need to facilitate cognitive, emotional, behavioural and social engagement components as an individual and also within their service system (i.e. the course and its content) seems crucial. Course designs may adopt more active learning pedagogies and/or the use of technologies to foster increased personalisation and interaction; however, this should be dependent on the student cohort and educational content. In addition, given the prevalence of social engagement identified in this data, educators should further consider the role this plays in determining value in the students' learning experience.

At an institutional level, consideration needs to be given to the facilities (much like was introduced by Professor Quester at the University of Adelaide), supporting services, and extra-curricular activities of the university. Indeed, all touch-points across the university seemingly contribute to a student's engagement with the institution and their learning experience and hence strategies to enhance student engagement need to be holistic and implemented at a senior level within universities. For universities it is important to design engagement environments that facilitate meaningful experiences across resources and service system contexts. Ideally, the different engagement reference objects positively reinforce each other in terms shaping and triggering individual and overall engagement levels.

Future Research Directions

While this study provides important conceptual and qualitative insights, practice (i.e. lecturers, university managers etc.) and theory would be benefit from further quantitative analysis. For example, researchers could study whether the engagement dimensions (cognitive, affective, behavioural and social) discriminate within a university context and whether students are able to discriminate in quantitative research between different engagement levels. This in turn would require further operationalisation of some of the engagement constructs at each of the identified levels.

Further exploration of the interconnected nature of the levels of engagement is also warranted. The influence and combined effect of engagement at each level and their interconnectedness deserves empirical investigation. Does the magnitude and intensity of engagement differ through each focal object and how does the level of engagement at each level influence engagement across other levels and in aggregate? Longitudinal effects of individual and narrow service system engagement should be explored and the impact on the broader service system depicted.

In addition, consideration should be given to the nomological network of student engagement; with mutual and independent antecedents and consequences of engagement at each level considered and the interdependence and mutual development among the engagement levels considered. Attention should also be given to the nature of student dis-engagement, its causes, and the pathway to establish re-engagement.

In contexts where there is an established national or institutional mandate for student engagement assessment, the effect of these programs on engagement policies, engagement strategies and their related outcomes should be examined at an institutional and aggregate level.

These findings provide educators and university administrators with a greater understanding of the notion of student engagement, which will hopefully make a difference to the students' educational experience.

Acknowledgement The authors would like to acknowledge that this research was funded by a RMIT University Learning and Teaching Investment Fund (LTIF) Grant. We also acknowledge the anonymous reviewers and their suggestions for improvement of this paper.

References

Baron P, Corbin L (2012) Student engagement: rhetoric and reality. High Educ Res Dev 31(6):759–772

Boland BD (1995) Transcription quality as an aspect of rigor in qualitative research. Qual Inq 1:290–310

Bravo R, Lucia-Palacios L, Martin MJ (2014) Processes and outcomes in student teamwork. An empirical study in a marketing subject. Stud High Educ (ahead-of-print) 1–19

Brodie RJ, Hollebeek LD, Juric B, Ilic A (2011) Customer engagement: conceptual domain, fundamental propositions, and implications for research. J Serv Res 14(3):252–271

Bryson C, Hand L (2007) The role of engagement in inspiring teaching and learning. Innov Educ Teach Int 44(4):349–362

Calder BJ, Malthouse EC, Schaedel U (2009) An experimental study of the relationship between online engagement and advertising effectiveness. J Interact Mark 23(4):321–331

Chad P (2012) The use of team based learning as an approach to increase engagement and learning for marketing students. J Mark Educ 34(2):128–139

Coffey A, Atkinson P (1999) Making sense of qualitative data: complementary research strategies. Sage Publications, Thousand Oaks

Díaz-Méndez M, Gummesson E (2012) Value co-creation and university teaching quality: consequences for the European Higher Education Area (EHEA). J Serv Manage 23(4):571–592

Finn JD, Pannozzo GM, Voelkl KE (1995) Disruptive and inattentive-withdrawn behavior and achievement among fourth graders. Elementary Sch J 421–434

Furrer C, Skinner E (2003) Sense of relatedness as a factor in children's academic engagement and performance. J Educ Psychol 95(1):148–162

Gioia DA, Corley KG, Hamilton AL (2013) Seeking qualitative rigor in inductive research: notes on the Gioia methodology. Organ Res Methods 16(1):15–31

Harper SR, Quaye SJ (2009) Beyond sameness with engagement and outcomes for all: an introduction. In: Harper S, Quaye S (eds) Student engagement in higher education. Routledge, New York, pp 1–15

Harrison T (2013) Conceptualising student engagement: a co-creation perspective. In: Derricott D, Kekäläinen H, Kelo M, Kristensen RS, Loukkola T, Michalk B, Palomares FG, Ryan N, Stensaker B (eds) Working together to take quality forward. European University Association, Brussels, pp 51–60

Hennig-Thurau T, Langer MF, Hansen U (2001) Modeling and managing student loyalty. An approach based on the concept of relationship quality. J Serv Res 3(4):331–344

Hollebeek LD, Chen T (2014) Exploring positively-versus negatively-valenced brand engagement: a conceptual model. J Prod Brand Manage 23(1):62–74

Keener M (1999) Strengthening institutional engagement: addressing faculty issues to facilitate change. J Public Serv Outreach 4(1):29–38

Klem AM, Connell JP (2004) Relationships matter: linking teacher support to student engagement and achievement. J Sch Health 74(7):262–273

Kuh GD (2003) What we're learning about student engagement from NSSE: benchmarks for effective educational practices. Change: The Mag High Learn 35(2):24–32
Kuh GD, Kinzie J, Buckley JA, Bridges BK, Hayek JC (2011) Piecing together the student success puzzle: research, propositions, and recommendations: ASHE higher education report, vol 116. Wiley, Hoboken
Lam S-F et al (2014) Understanding and measuring student engagement in school: the results of an international study from 12 countries. Sch Psychol Q 29(2):213–232
Lincoln YS, Guba EG (1985) Naturalistic inquiry. Sage Publications, Beverly Hills
London B, Downey G, Mace S (2007) Psychological theories of educational engagement: a multi-method approach to studying individual engagement and institutional change. Vanderbilt Law Rev 60:455–482
London B, Anderson V, Downey G (2009) Studying institutional engagement: utilizing social psychology research methodologies to study law student engagement. Harvard J Law Gend 30:389–407
McCulloch A (2009) The student as co-producer: learning from public administration about the student–university relationship. Stud High Educ 34(2):171–183
Morgan DL, Spanish MT (1984) Focus groups: a new tool for qualitative research. Qual Sociol 7:253–270
Northey G, Bucic T, Chylinski M, Govind R (2015) Increasing student engagement using asynchronous learning. J Mark Educ. doi:10.1177/0273475315589814
Pianta RC, Hamre BK, Allen JP (2012) Teacher-student relationships and engagement: conceptualizing, measuring, and improving the capacity of classroom interactions. Handb Res Student Engagem. Springer, US, pp 365–386
Quester P, Backstrom K, Kovacevic S (2014) The University of Adelaide student learning hub: a case study of education co-creation. Universities in transition: foregrounding social contexts of knowledge in the first year experience, pp 187–204
Quaye SJ, Harper SR (eds) (2014) Student engagement in higher education: theoretical perspectives and practical approaches for diverse populations. Routledge, London
Scott J, Craig-Lees M (2010) Audience engagement and its effects on product placement recognition. J Promot Manage 16(1/2):39–58
Skinner EA, Belmont MJ (1993) Motivation in the classroom: Reciprocal effects of teacher behavior and student engagement across the school year. J Educ Psychol 85(4):571–581.
Smith JA (1995) Semi-structured interviewing and qualitative analysis. In: Smith JA, Harré R, Van Langenhove L (eds) Rethinking methods in psychology, Chapter 2. Sage, London, pp 9–26
Stafford L (2011) Measuring relationship maintenance behaviors: critique and development of the revised relationship maintenance behavior scale. J Soc Pers Relat 28(2):278–303
Taylor SA, Hunter GL, Melton H, Goodwin SA (2011) Student engagement and marketing classes. J Mark Educ 33(1):73–92
Vargo SL, Lusch RF (2008) Service-dominant logic: continuing the evolution. J Acad Mark Sci 36 (1):1–10
Vivek SD, Beatty SE, Morgan RM (2012) Customer engagement: exploring customer relationships beyond purchase. J Mark Theor Pract 20(2):122–146
Voelkl KE (1997) Identification with school. Am J Educ 294–318

Marketing—Making a Difference for Entrepreneurial Universities

Thomas Baaken, Todd Davey and Sue Rossano

Abstract In the knowledge economy, Higher Education Institutions (HEIs) are facing increasingly competitive environments. On the one side knowledge is now produced in a variety of organisations, so therefore universities are no longer the only producers or sources of knowledge. Universities are also competing with other education providers due to the growing offers of commercial education providers with a strong vocational dimension, and the emergence of new technologies in the higher education market offering virtual programs (Ferreira et al. 2007). Against this background HEIs are now operating in markets where it is imperative for them to make usage of marketing instruments if they want to succeed and remain sustainable. In this vein, the two core activities of HEIs, research and education, are addressing different markets and target groups. Consequently HEIs need to apply marketing, its toolbox and instruments to be successful in those markets, and they need to be entrepreneurial to access them. In this paper the markets for research in HEIs are examined more closely. The paper describes the particularities of a Marketing approach for science and recommends a comprehensive "Science-to-Business Marketing" approach, exhibiting and combining knowledge from different Marketing disciplines.

Keywords Higher education institutions · University-business cooperation · Science-to-business marketing · Knowledge transfer · Entrepreneurial university · Research marketing

T. Baaken (✉) · T. Davey · S. Rossano
Science-to-Business Marketing Research Centre, Münster University of Applied Sciences, Münster, Germany
e-mail: Baaken@fh-muenster.de

T. Davey
e-mail: Davey@fh-muenster.de

S. Rossano
e-mail: Rossano@fh-muenster.de

© Springer Science+Business Media Singapore 2016

C. Plewa and J. Conduit (eds.), *Making a Difference Through Marketing*,
DOI 10.1007/978-981-10-0464-3_18

Introduction

Higher Education Institutions (HEIs) are seen as a crucial element of a functioning regional innovation system (Freeman 1987). Modern regional economic development places the university in a more prominent role (Gunasekara 2006) in both innovation and human resource value chains of industry (Wilson 2012). The HEI has become an integral component of an entirely entrepreneurially oriented innovation process for the benefit of society (European Commission 2005; UNESCO 2002–04) and is playing an increasingly important role in the innovation chain.

The notion of the university as an entrepreneurial organisation has gained a great deal of attention within the international collegiate landscape in recent years through the concept of the entrepreneurial university (Etzkowitz 1983; Davey 2015). The entrepreneurial university paradigm incorporates the central role that universities have assumed in regional development (Woollard et al. 2007), and has been subsequently used by policy makers, academics and practitioners to describe those universities succeeding in their 'third mission' (Lambert 2003), this being the capitalisation of knowledge.

Encapsulating the understanding of the entrepreneurial university taken in this paper, Shane (2005) positions the entrepreneurial university, with its research mission, as a quadrant within the innovation matrix (Bouette 2004) and consequently as part of a market-oriented process (Laine et al. 2008). Universities are assigned a significant role in the innovation process and regard their influence on the other three quadrants (industrial R&D, industry cluster, and technology) as extremely strong and indispensable. This view that universities are an essential part of the innovation process has been adopted by a growing number of authors (Pavitt 2001; Etzkowitz and Leydesdorff 2000; Etzkowitz 1998; Franco and Haase 2010).

Given that value chain integration involves a market-orientation, an active market-driven commercialisation of research is necessitated. The fact that business thought and action are growing factors in the organisation of higher education is evidence of this. For example, the application of business tools such as controlling the balanced scorecard, or the value chain, to HEIs requires a reconsideration and analysis of the factors that determine the use of these tools or even makes their application possible in the first place (Plewa et al. 2006; Baaken and Kesting 2009).

Engagement with HEIs' entrepreneurial orientation and the attendant acceptance of markets within the collegiate environment make marketing a task of the university's business orientation (Bok 2003). Representing the growing market-orientation of HEIs, this article will focus on the role of marketing in universities that behave entrepreneurially and show that this role is an important one for modern and entrepreneurial universities which want to succeed in their markets (Baaken et al. 2008).

Entrepreneurial Universities Are Market-Focussed

A core characteristic of the entrepreneurial university is research cooperation and commercialisation, a concept generally referred to as knowledge and technology transfer (Liyanage et al. 2009). The term 'knowledge and technology transfer' itself implies that knowledge and technology are transferred from a provider to a recipient (Corsten 1987; Audretsch 2002; Walter 2003). In other words, scientific research is transferred from a supplier to a customer.

The expression 'knowledge and technology transfer' therefore actually implies the existence of a market, as an exchange in the sense of a service and reward (financial or payment in kind) ensues. This can be described as a market for research services (research market). In scientific or academic literature, it is not uncommon to find terms such as 'producer' or 'provider' for originators of knowledge and technologies, or 'user' or 'taker' for the recipients of knowledge and technologies (e.g. Astor 2003; Walter 2003).

However, a transfer from a university to real-world practice can only occur if the object of the transfer meets a need, and if the customer recognises a benefit in adopting it. Therefore, the starting point for a successful transfer should be to take into consideration the needs and interests of potential users (Kesting 2012). This ensures that the research transfer is orientated towards the interests of both parties.

In the terminology of Gibbons et al. (1994), there is a noticeable change in the generation of knowledge at universities and higher education colleges from 'Mode 1' (theoretical knowledge) to 'Mode 2' (application-orientated knowledge). In their opinion, scholarship is currently undergoing a transitionary period, which will result in a new understanding of what is meant by the word. In order to make this epochal change more easily understood, the authors differentiate between traditional scholarship and post-traditional scholarship. In the former dominant model of reference, research is predominantly carried out within a self-referential academic framework, whereas in the latter, research is carried out in collaboration with clients or users in order to work out problems and co-develop solutions (Knie et al. 2002; Gouthier et al. 2006).

Etzkowitz and Leydesdorff (2000) also see a change in the academic system, and depict it in their 'triple helix' model as being a new kind of triple interaction relationship between science, industry and politics, shown in Fig. 1.

According to the authors, this represents the key to innovation in a knowledge-based society (Etzkowitz and Leydesdorff 1997; Leydesdorff 2000; Leydesdorff and Etzkowitz 2001; Etzkowitz 2004). The stronger relevance of knowledge in the innovation process across broader society leads Martin and Etzkowitz (2000) to the theory that knowledge arising in the universities as part of the information society will become the motor of the economy and of society as a whole. The triple helix concept aligns closely with the concept of the entrepreneurial university described earlier (Davey 2015).

Correspondingly, Slaughter and Leslie (1997) state that there is a transnational trend in respect to HEIs towards 'academic capitalism'. In their study of the US,

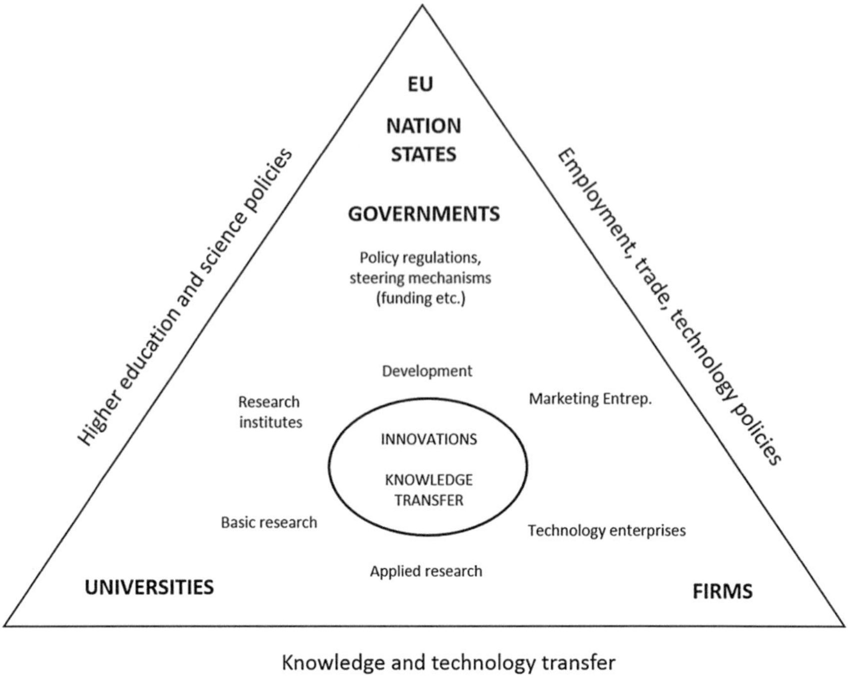

Fig. 1 Triple helix model (Etzkowitz and Leydesdorff 1995, p. 31)

Canadian, British and Australian higher education systems, they show that the shortage of public resources will lead to the more business-orientated establishments and marketing strategies increasingly gaining in importance.

On top of this Shane (2005) and Audretsch and Keilbach (2004) assign the entrepreneurial university a considerable role in the innovation process, and see their influence on industry, clusters and technologies as being extremely high and effective. In recent years, this thematising of the university as an entrepreneurial organisation, coupled with an actively market-driven commercialisation of research, has found increasing resonance in the international higher education sector (e.g. Berger 2008; Baaken and Plewa 2004; Kesting 2012).

The rise of this "entrepreneurial university" approach establishes novel perspectives within organisations, which entitles the consideration of marketing and management issues in the thinking and actions of academics (Kesting et al. 2014, p. 8). For example, universities now focus on creating more sustainable relations between organisations, an objective pursued under a relationship marketing perspective, and depicted by the stairway model to strategic partnerships (refer to Fig. 2). The stairway model is a research-based tool developed by the Science-to-Business Marketing Research Center (STBMRC) (Dottore et al. 2010; Kliewe et al. 2012) to guide universities' co-operators from their initial contact up

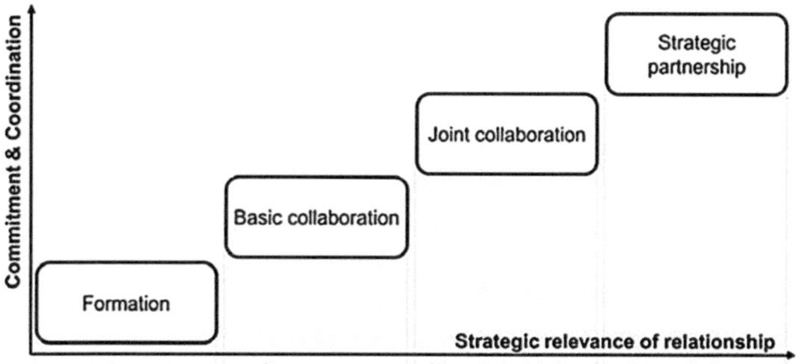

Number / Regularity of collaboration	Initial contact	One or several projects / irregular	One or several joint activities / regular	One or several joint activities / regular
Scope of collaboration	Initial contact	Low / medium	Medium / high	High
Time orientation of collaboration	Initiation of short-term activities	Short- / medium-term	Medium- / long-term	Long-term
Relevance of relation	Analytical / informational	Operational	Tactical	Strategic
Number of people involved	Few	Few	Multiple	Multiple
Management level	Individual (Professor) / TA*	Individual (Professor)	Faculty (Dean)	Organisational (University Mgmt.)
Focus of relationship management	Business Development Mgmt.	Customer Relationship Mgmt.	Partner Relationship Mgmt.	Key Account Mgmt.

*Transfer agency

Fig. 2 Stairway model to strategic partnership (Science-to-Business Marketing Research Centre 2010, p. 100)

to the formation of a strategic partnership. This strategic partnership level entails a deeper relationship between partners (Kesting et al. 2014).

In this vein, the concrete application of marketing strategies and instruments in higher education management becomes also part of the debate on higher education establishments' entrepreneurial orientation, which leads to the introduction of marketing as an essential component of the entrepreneurial university.

A market-oriented entrepreneurial university applies also to traditional missions of the university, such as its "education mission". Following this approach, universities are required to accomplish their duty and, as well, meet stakeholder's expectations.

On the one hand, universities need to meet students' expectations by preparing them for the economy in which they will operate, (Galloway et al. 2005). On the other hand, industry is increasingly demanding universities provide the right professionally trained graduates. This means the development of closer and more efficient cooperation with industry and the wider economic world to match the supply and demand for the skills needed in the knowledge economy (Wagner 2012; Davey 2015).

Science-to-Business Marketing Crucial for Entrepreneurial Universities

Science-to-business marketing is the term used to describe the advent of market-orientated entrepreneurial modes of thought and behaviour in universities and other research institutes (Baaken 2013). It is characterised by academic and scientific stakeholders actively seeking customers (users, applicants, clients) for their research results and services, and conveying them in return for suitable reward. Especially when the research undertaken is already orientated towards the needs of the market and the potential benefits for later users, the entrepreneurial universities' offerings satisfy businesses' market expectations, meaning that transfer is smooth and successful (Baaken 2007).

The term 'science-to-business marketing' therefore covers all those activities which (Baaken 2013):

- give knowledge and technology transfer a new conceptual basis due to the orientation towards the market and customers, and
- serve to build up, develop and manage relationships between research institutes and business undertakings (in the broadest sense of the term[1]), in the sense of forging stronger partnerships in future.

To achieve this, science-to-business marketing borrows from three different marketing disciplines: university marketing (in the sense of being the marketing agent), knowledge marketing (the object being marketed) and business-to-business marketing (the marketing's target group), shown in Table 1.

The following three sections clarify these borrowings, which go to make up science-to-business marketing: transfer attempts from university marketing, a discipline that is still at an early stage of its development, from the novel area of knowledge marketing, and finally from the well-established arena of business-to-business marketing (Baaken et al. 2005).

How Science-to-Business Marketing Borrows from University Marketing

The divergence of university marketing[2] from traditional marketing is a result of the fact that universities are not typical 'businesses'. Their academic members and staff

[1]'Business undertaking' in its broadest sense also encompasses non-profit organisations and public bodies. However, we will here make a distinction between public bodies as 'recipients (clients, customers, applicants), as opposed to them as institutions for funding research.

[2]In literature, university marketing is often understood to mean acquisition marketing (of highly qualified staff, or more specifically, university graduates) by businesses, as part of their staff recruitment processes (e.g. Wefers 2008 and many others). However, this interpretation is not used

Table 1 Marketing disciplines as suppliers of competencies for science-to-business marketing

Science-to-business marketing composition			
Discipline	University marketing	Knowledge marketing	Business-to-business marketing
Focus	The marketing agent	The object being marketed	The marketing target group
Process	Who is doing the marketing?	What is being marketed?	Who is the recipient of the marketing?
Agents	Universities, research institutes	Knowledge, technologies, results of research, findings	Businesses, organisations in a broader sense

have a wide-ranging freedom when it comes to shaping their openly defined fields of activity. Such levels of freedom would be unthinkable in business organisations. They form a relevant target group and can be embedded into market-orientated processes.

In universities, the focus today, with a certain level of implicitness, is increasingly on the importance of brand development, of strengthening their profile, on the university's 'customers' and of the importance of the deployment of university marketing (Pappu and Quester 2013). These developments do not always sit so easily with the university tradition, whose origins are in the 'Humboldtian' ideal, the freedom of research and teaching and the freedom of scholarship that is enshrined in institutional constitutions. This requirement for higher education establishments to orientate themselves towards the market and the customer goes against the grain of the longstanding understanding that research and teaching are traditionally explicitly decoupled from market considerations.

At present, the frameworks that higher education establishments have to work within, and the range of tasks that they carry out, are being considerably changed by the world of politics, in respect of:

- Expansion of universities' autonomy, accompanied by an expectation of an expanded spectrum of tasks,
- Benchmark-based allocation of funds, at the same time accompanied by reductions in public funding,
- Evaluation of the universities and their performance parameters.

In the same vein national and international competition for students, qualified lecturers, cooperation partners and third party funding is also increasing.

Universities are reacting to this and making their management and marketing more professional. This process of professionalisation is making deep inroads into the universities' structures and processes. For example, the universities' finance systems are being changed from public-budget management to cost-performance

(Footnote 2 continued)

in this paper. In this case, the application of marketing used by universities for the purposes to market academic services such as courses and research results.

accounting systems. HR departments and personnel development systems are gaining ground. Marketing specialists are recommending that universities apply a marketing philosophy (Bok 2003; Marcure 2004), and are even demanding that they demonstrate a consistent orientation towards the needs of the market (Meffert 2007; Baaken 2013).

Furthermore, Meffert (2007) defines the characteristics of unified university marketing at the most widely differing levels of university management:

- Philosophical aspect: conscious orientation towards needs
- Segmentation aspect: target-specific market cultivation
- Strategic aspect: determination of a long-term action plan
- Organisational aspect: organisational enshrinement of the concept
- Action aspect: application of marketing instruments in a way that is appropriate to the objectives

Meffert (2007) hereby addresses the needs of target groups. His view implies that universities' range of services be orientated towards these needs, and that they should go beyond the purely communicative activities to which universities' marketing publications have hitherto been dedicated.

In other countries, this approach is something that has been discussed for a long time, and has indeed partly crept in. American universities are at the pinnacle of these developments towards innovative university marketing. Indeed, the implementation of a marketing approach is already well established across a spectrum Anglo-American universities (Balmer 2001; Binsardi and Ekwulugo 2003).

A university's services and markets can be divided into core services (research, teaching and transfer of knowledge and technology) and the services that go beyond these. These include further training, promoting students' social interests, international cooperation with other universities, as well as the pastoral and supportive services (student advice bodies, social offerings, cultural offerings…). Therefore, from a marketing perspective, the university provides its customers with a core benefit and an additional value. According to Müller-Böling (2007), higher education establishments are comparable to multi-product firms. They provide different services to different groups of customers.

Whether the term customer can be used for all of a university's target groups and interest groups is however open to discussion. This is because their diversity is considerable and they display unique differences. What is recognisable from this statement is that there are external and internal target groups. The external core target group of science-to-business marketing comprises organisations (in the broadest sense) that acquire research services or results. Those are usually businesses, but can also be non-commercial organisations, including public institutions, public authorities or public service organisations.

Virtually all publications on university marketing concentrate on the communi-cation side of the marketing process. They are therefore not dedicated to the plane of strategic marketing, but focus instead on a rather operative branch of marketing. In terms of content, this literature stream essentially tackles the objectives of market presence, visibility, recognition and awareness, along with attaining these objectives using communication instruments and channels (Brüser 2006; Voss 2009; Siebenhaar 2008). Other publications embrace research marketing or knowledge marketing (University Dortmund 2003; Mager et al. 2003; Merten 2009), or Obermaier's publication on research to business. The latter stakes the claim that it contributes new theories (or theoretical components) to research or university marketing. However, this work too stalls at the action level of communication (Obermaier 2009).

It is remarkable that these publications firstly deal with (just) communication and secondly are targeted to the general public, forming part of a communication policy, as if they were a greater part of the instruments required for university marketing. Notwithstanding the importance of communication, the public only has an indirect function as the universities' target group. It is not the primary recipient of science-to-business marketing, since its representatives do not directly pay for research. But in the sense of public relations work, this group can definitely be the recipient, in order to achieve political results. Nevertheless, the public cannot be regarded as universities' customers, as they do not obtain any direct services. The primary target group is potential students, and in the sense of science-to-business marketing—as explained above—particular industries.

How Science-to-Business Marketing Borrows from Knowledge Marketing

The term 'knowledge marketing' covers the marketing of knowledge and its transfer to third parties in exchange for financial payment or payment in kind. In developed industrial countries it forms the economic basis for the country's future. Not without reason is the future knowledge-based economy regularly referred to as the vision and orientation of a sustainable economic system.

Knowledge is also important on the micro-economic level, because knowledge is one of the most important resources that a company has. Its creation and development are therefore a central role of management (Schmitz and Zucker 2003; Sjide v.d. and Ridder 1999). From an economic view, knowledge can be described as all "...investment-related, explicative, intrinsic, cognitive mental constructions..." (Rode 2001, p. 11). It therefore demonstrates an explanatory function; it is verifiable and consists of insights, know-what, know-why, know-how and know-who (Rode 2001).

Surprisingly, there is hardly any literature dealing with the marketing of knowledge. However in contrast, there is an abundance of literature that covers the term 'knowledge management'. This limited to businesses' internal dissemination of knowledge, and does not tackle the passing on of knowledge to external recipients in exchange for remuneration. Even Kuhn's work on "Marketing auf konzerninternen Wissensmärkten" (How to market knowledge internally on corporate organisations' markets) deals entirely with businesses' internal markets (Kuhn 2003).

According to Rode, knowledge marketing should be understood as a commodity-specific sub-discipline (Rode 2001). Knowledge commodities can be defined as "…all products and services whose main aim is that a recipient of the knowledge (who need not be the direct client) communicates with a knowledge bearer for the purposes of transferring knowledge." (Rode 2001, p. 13).

According to this, the separation of knowledge from other commodities is a result of its purpose and not the results obtained. Furthermore, Rode also names three peculiarities of knowledge commodities that serve to differentiate them further from economic commodities: a knowledge commodity is dependent on the recipient, as the recipient himself influences how it is used. Additionally, the transfer of knowledge is by its nature very time-consuming. The third characteristic property is that the knowledge bearer and his knowledge can only be protected against unauthorised disclosure, reproduction or use with great difficulty (Rode 2001).

Figure 3 provides an overview of the structure of a knowledge market, its commodities and stakeholders. In a knowledge market, providers can be businesses or institutions. Stakeholders in the area of pure research, whose objective is knowledge that does not yet exist, comprise researchers in universities, public research institutes and large companies, for example. Application research and development research are however based on existing knowledge. The aim of these types of research is to develop it further, for example by developers and engineers. On the other hand, the area of practical knowledge is based on knowledge that has already been applied, and on the provider's side, is represented by experienced consultants or staff in businesses and public authorities.

Therefore, knowledge marketing, as applied to the object being marketed, has a shaping influence on science-to-business marketing.

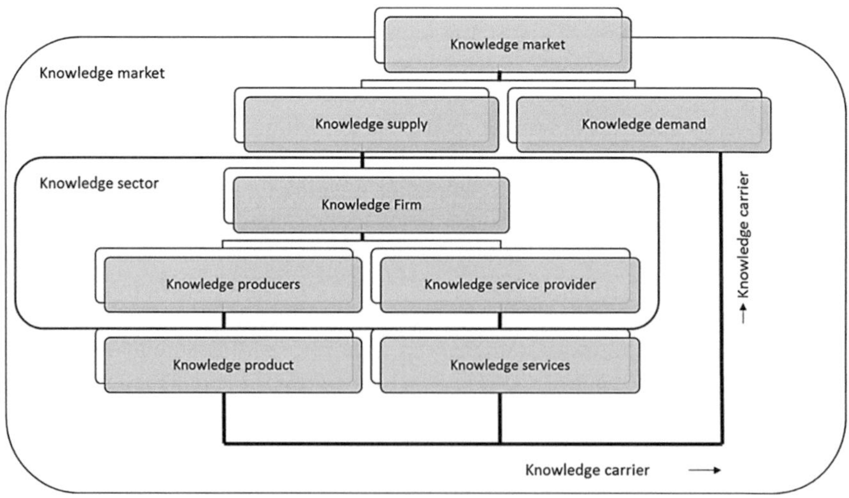

Fig. 3 Structure of a knowledge market (Baaken 2004b, p. 7)

How Science-to-Business Marketing Borrows from Business-to-Business Marketing

The term 'business-to-business marketing' primarily describes a market in respect of its stakeholders and the relationships that exist between them.

Demand generated by the end-customer or consumer triggers a resulting chain of demands that has a considerable influence on the business-to-business market. There are both decisive similarities as well as decisive differences that must be taken into account when looking at both markets as a unified whole. Even though an important difference is that, in business-to-business marketing, businesses act in the role of purchasers, the decisions themselves are made by human beings (Kotler and Pfoertsch 2006). These individuals take risks in their decisions that are of both a professional and personal nature.

However, the procurement process in business-to-business markets is clearly more rational and structured than in consumer goods markets (Baumgarth 2012). Individuals responsible for purchasing decisions in business-to-business markets follow the needs of their own business, and must be able to justify their decisions to co-workers in the company (Pförtsch and Schmid 2005; Brennan et al. 2014).

Because of the comparably high personal risks, for example due to technological innovations, purchasers have to rely above all on their own experience. Furthermore, their decisions are based on the trust that they have in a provider. Business-to-business marketing deals mostly not with the acquisition of individual products, but of comprehensive solutions to problems that have been specially tailored to individual customer requirements (Pförtsch and Schmid 2005; Backhaus and Muehlfeld 2005).

To adapt business-to-business marketing mechanisms into a theory that can then be transferred to HEIs, it makes sense to categorise the interaction processes between buyers and sellers in business-to-business markets (Pförtsch and Schmid 2005; Medlin 2004). Literature contains a great number of supply-orientated or demand-orientated categorisation approaches and typologies, which are researched in the context of their various classification criteria. These include, for example, product characteristics, processing levels and the perceived complexity of products. With many of these typologies, the transaction is in the foreground (transaction approach). The typology of business-to-business transactions of Kleinaltenkamp and Plinke (2002) devotes itself to two dimensions of observation: (i) the frequency of repeated procurement processes between the market parties, and (ii) the 'inter-activity' or intensity of the cooperation between the partners.

The above-mentioned transactions in business-to-business markets are generally characterised by uncertainties on both sides when it comes to the decision-making process. The high complexity of the products and services, along with the associated reciprocal integration of the business partners into the value-adding process, make a reliable, comprehensive assessment much more difficult, on the part of the supplier as well as the entity making the demand (Medlin 2004). This has the effect that, to compensate for any uncertainties that may arise, there is greater resort to experience and trust considerations. The latter is also characterised by image, brand and the existing business relationships (relationship approach) (Pappu and Quester 2013).

Both the transaction approach and the relationship marketing literature have an effect on science-to-business marketing. Individual transactions between business partners can also be found in technology transfer. In this environment, trust is established as a primary concept. Several authors have presented in the literature dealing with the private sector, the positive effect of trust on performance in general and on the utilisation of research in particular (e.g. Farrelly and Quester 2003). Trust becomes even more relevant in the context of transfer from university to industry, given the uncertainty involved in collaborating with a party from a different sector (Plewa et al. 2005).

The transaction approach is then used to provide theoretical support for a 'knowledge and technology transfer'. Alongside this, science-to-business marketing represents a second pillar to the relationship-marketing concept, since it increasingly signifies a long-term connection between the partners at a strategic level.

Dealing with Internal Target Groups in Science-to-Business Marketing

From the relational and services marketing perspective, authors have also reported on the importance of individuals (champions) engaging in relationship development with industry partners, where the time spent in building and cultivating the relationship is important for commitment (e.g. Howell et al. 2005; Plewa and Quester 2008).

However, building and cultivating relationships is not a natural role for academics, so this issue represents one of the peculiarities of science-to-business marketing. From this perspective, science-to-business marketing is a "2-sided-marketing" endeavour. This means that the external (potential) clients are only one target group to consider. S2B Marketing has to deal also with internal target groups, which are key players in this process. Academics, researchers and administrative staff are not prepared for working together with external parties since this is not part of their career criteria for promotion.

As opposed to commercial enterprises, in which staff are primarily behind the business's marketing objectives, the academic system is not market-driven, but knowledge-driven. Researchers do not pursue their careers so as to be able to establish relationships with business and work together with them. Instead, they are driven by the academic pursuit of knowledge, and not uncommonly, have visions of a technological or academic breakthrough. Their job satisfaction therefore comes predominantly from tasks whose content is largely self-defined. The conveyance of knowledge to students is a part of this.

However, an intrinsic motivation to collaborate with external organisations cannot be discounted per se. In the context of science-to-business marketing, however, the readiness and willingness to cooperate with the business sector often needs some initial encouragement (e.g. Baaken 2007; Sijde v.d.; Cuyvers 2003). This can take the form of argumentative persuasion, agreement about objectives, but also from incentives offered by university heads or management teams (Frey and Neckermann 2008).

As a result of universities engaging in activities beyond to what they traditionally do, managing a balance between general academic duties and activities of collaboration with industry is a challenging task (Jones-Evans 1997). In this respect, "time" is also a valuable resource for academics and should be considered as part of an incentives system. This assignment of time as a resource can be in the form of a reduction in teaching workload, allocation of human resources, such as student assistant hours, or space, among others.

In any case only a target-orientated incentives system, along with clearly worked out benefits for university members, can provide the basis for a successful university-business cooperation (Osterloh and Frey 2008; Davey et al 2011; Baaken 2013).

Discussion and Conclusion

Science-to-Business Marketing Driving Knowledge and Technology Transfer in the Entrepreneurial University

Over the last thirty years especially, knowledge and technology transfer has been the subject of much discussion and academic discourse, with the literature focusing more on obstacles and difficulties (e.g. Atzorn and Clemens-Ziegler 2010) than in drivers for University-Business-Cooperation (Davey et al. 2011). Only very few publications focus on drivers (Fernand and Cohendet 2001; Plewa 2010) for University-Business-Cooperation. Clearing away obstacles and barriers will not result in a smooth, trouble-free transfer. However if drivers are strong enough they will easily overcome all barriers. This paper has set up an enlightened focus on drivers, the adoption of marketing principles and instruments being some of them.

Just as is the case with businesses, if a modern university is to contribute in a more meaningful way to society, the university's market-orientated strategy must be based on information about the market. Market research and market analysis self-evidently belong to the range of marketing tasks, and therefore also to university marketing. Nevertheless, universities do not generally have a market-orientated culture, and the level of experience in dealing with market research and market analysis is low. Very often, strategies are simply formed on the basis of assumptions, and not on verified, 'defined' circumstances. So far, needs assessments, market potential analyses, studies on the universitys' awareness levels and image, customer satisfaction measurements and customer loyalty analyses have not made any headway in higher education establishments (Baaken 2004a).

From the viewpoint of a research institution in future, they will need to develop an understanding of the market that recognises processes and addresses these expectations and the various interests involved. This understanding of the market should include, on the one hand, the services (products and services) of the research institute itself, and on the other, it should also include a customer-orientated transfer of the services. Early recognition and acceptance of the various interests and needs, as well as taking them into consideration even during the knowledge creation and development process, forms the starting point for a market orientation in science-to-business marketing.

This understanding of the market entails a focus not only on processes, but also on outcomes and impacts, as well as the benefits experienced by individuals or institutions involved in this transfer (Franco and Haase 2010). These improved outcomes, can include a range of tangible and intangible benefits such as improved teaching, or increased income from research (Davey et al. 2014).

Early involvement of the customer in the development process goes hand in hand with a change in the traditional transfer process. Whereas academic or scientific achievement was once mostly isolated from potential user markets, the new, collaborative model connects academia and business right from the moment that the decision is made to begin a research project (Kesting 2012). At this point, both parties determine which research content will be worked on and how it will be methodically targeted. The involvement of the market in the knowledge creation process and new technologies factors in specific applications and potential right from the very beginning, and therefore creates a prerequisite for successful introduction to the market later.

An important finding in science-to-business marketing in relation to the transfer is that this does not represent a one-sided transfer of scientific knowledge from the university to the business. It is much more the case that there is a reciprocal exchange, that is to say, an interaction between both stakeholders, and for which on the research side, the practical consideration remains very much in the foreground. Businesses therefore provide the researchers with all the information that they need in order to be able to match the service that they provide to the requirements of the organisation making the request. In other words, the process secures the market relevance of scientific findings even before the research process or the research itself has begun (Holtkamp et al. 2005; Kröcher 2005).

The transfer of knowledge and technology also includes the tacit conveyance of experience, knowledge of the (potential) interactions between different technologies, and application know-how from operational practice in the institution undertaking the research. This is how (strategic) partnerships in business/science relationships come into being (Baaken 2010).

A Summary of Theses

The summary of this paper is made through four theses:

Thesis 1 Science-to-business marketing creates its own individuality based on special features taken from three areas: the entity carrying out the marketing (university or research institute), the object of the marketing (research) and the nature of the market (business as customer), together with high levels of uncertainty when it comes to decision making, which is due to the asymmetry of knowledge.

Thesis 2 Science-to-business marketing therefore diverges from the topic area of university marketing. This applies especially to the traits of the entity undertaking the marketing (the peculiarity of the university as active agent), from knowledge marketing, the object being marketed (the peculiarity of the object being marketed), and from business-to-business marketing, the target group of business, with its complex decision making processes (peculiarity of the market).

Thesis 3 The business-to-business marketing′s transactional approach focuses on individual business transactions and their special market mechanisms. From this perspective, the transfer of knowledge and technology will be aligned to market demands. In this respect, the business-to-business marketing concept and relationship marketing offer potential for science-to-business marketing.

Thesis 4 One of the primary peculiarities of science-to-business marketing is that an organisation that was traditionally never orientated towards markets must now at least in part orientate itself to them, as in future it will need to compete. This reorientation must take place within a framework of change management, both on an organisational level (processes and structures) as well as at the individual level of the university members. This change can occur as a result of changes in attitude and behaviour (for example, through an incentive system) induced either internally or by third parties. 'Internal marketing' therefore plays a decisive role.

References

Fernand A, Cohendet P (2001) Technology transfer revisited from the perspective of the knowledge-based economy. Res Policy 30(9):1459–1478

Astor M (2003) Kriterien der Evaluierung von Technologietransfereinrichtungen. In: Pleschak F (ed) Technologietransfer – Anforderungen und Entwicklungs-tendenzen. Dokumentation einer Tagung des Fraunhofer ISI, Stuttgart, pp 27–38

Audretsch DB, Keilbach M (2004) Entrepreneurship and regional growth: an evolutionary interpretation. J Evol Econ 14(5):605–616

Audretsch DB (2002) The dynamic role of small firms: evidence from the US. Springer, New York

Atzorn, H-H, Clemens-Ziegler B (2010) Ermittlung von Hemmnisfaktoren beim Aufbau von Kooperationen von KMU mit Institutionen der Wissenschaft, insbesondere den Fachhochschulen, Berlin

Baaken T (2004a) Satisfaction ratings by industry clients. In Marcure J (ed) Marketing scientific results & services—a toolkit, Sydney, Kyoto, Washington, DC, pp 40–50

Baaken T (2004b) Wissens-Marketing – ein Ansatz zur Vermarktung von Wissen in der künftigen Wissensgesellschaft in NRW. Gutachten für das Ministerium für Innovation, Wissenschaft, Forschung und Technologie des Landes Nordrhein-Westfalen, Düsseldorf, 09.06.2004

Baaken T (2007) Science Marketing—erfolgreiche Forschungsvermarktung. In: Meffert H, Backhaus K, Becker J (eds) Hochschulmarketing – Herausforde-rungen und Erfolgsfaktoren im Wettbewerb, Münster, pp 50–59

Baaken T (2010) Science-to-Business Marketing als Impulsgeber und Treiber für marktgerechte Innovationen. In: Baaken T. Höft U. Kesting T (eds) Marketing für Innovationen, Lichtenberg (Odw.), pp 3–12
Baaken T (2013) Science-to-Business Marketing. In: Hofbauer G. Pattloch A, Stumpf M (eds) Marketing in Forschung und Praxis, Berlin, pp 869–894
Baaken T, Kesting T (2009) Wertkettenkonzepte im Science-to-Business Marketing. In: Voss R (ed) Hochschulmarketing, 2nd edn, Lohmar/Köln, pp 181–200
Baaken T, Plewa C (2004) Key Success Factors in Research Commercialization. In: Hosni YA, Smith R, Khalil T (eds) Management of technology, new directions in technology transfer, Washington DC, Amsterdam et al., pp. 75–89
Baaken T, Plewa C, Quester P (2005) Science marketing: best practice, research agenda and a conceptual framework. In: 12th Biennial world marketing congress, marketing in an inter-connected world: opportunities and challenges, Münster, Germany, 6–9 July 2005
Baaken T, Davey T, Kliewe T, Francis A (2008) A model for the assessment and extraction of entrepreneurial value from university research. In: Ingle S, Neuvonen-Rauhala M-L (eds) Promoting entrepreneurship by universities, proceedings of the 2nd international FINPIN Conference, Hämeenlinna, Finnland, pp 204–212, 20–22 Apr 2008
Backhaus K, Muehlfeld K (2005) Strategy dynamics in industrial marketing: a business types perspective. Manag Decis 43(1):38–55
Balmer JMT (2001) Corporate identity, corporate branding and corporate marketing—seeing through the fog. Eur J Mark 35(3/4):248–291
Baumgarth C (2012) Markenorientierung als Nucleus einer erfolgreichen B-to-B Markenkommunikation. In: Baaken T, Kesting, T, Kliewe T, Pörner R (eds) Business-to-Business-Kommunikation. 2. überarbeitete u. erweiterte Aufl., Berlin, pp 129–150
Berger A (2008) Unternehmen Universität – Universität Unternehmen. In: Siebenhaar K (ed) Unternehmen Universität, Wiesbaden, pp 37–46
Binsardi A, Ekwulugo F (2003) International marketing of British education: research on the students' perception and the UK market penetration. Mark Intel Plann 21(5):318–327
Bok D (2003) Universities in the marketplace. The commercialisation of Higher Education, Princeton, Oxford
Bouette RD (2004) Creative Coupling Programme, Report prepared for the Government of Victoria, Melbourne
Brennan R, Canning L, McDowell R (2014) Business-to-business marketing. 3rd edn. Sage, Los Angeles, London, New Delhi, Singapore, Washington, DC
Brüser R (2006) Perspektiven des Hochschulmarketing: Eine theoretische und empirische Bestandsaufnahme, Saarbrücken
Clark B (2001) The entrepreneurial university: new foundations for collegiality, autonomy, and achievement. High Educ Manage 13(2)
Corsten H (1987) Technology transfer from universities to small and medium-sized enterprises—an empirical survey. Technovation 6(1):57–68
Davey T, Baaken T, Galán-Muros V, Meerman A (2011) Study on the cooperation between Higher Education Institutions and Public and Private Organisations in Europe. European Commission, DG Education and Culture, Brussels
Davey T, Plewa C, Galan-Muros V (2014) University-business cooperation outcomes and impacts —A european perspective. In: Kliewe T, Kesting T (eds) Modern Concepts of Organisational Marketing, Festschrift Thomas Baaken 60th birthday. Springer Gabler, Wiesbaden, pp 161–176
Davey T (2015) Entrepreneurship at Universities—exploring the factors influencing the development of entrepreneurship at universities. University-Industry Innovation Network Publishing, Amsterdam
Dottore A, Baaken T, Corkindale D (2010) A partnering business model for technology transfer. Int J Entrepreneurship Innovation Manage (IJEIM) 2(2):190–216
Etzkowitz H (1983) Entrepreneurial scientists and entrepreneurial Universities in American Academic Science. Minerva 21(2–3):1573–1871

Etzkowitz H (1998) The norms of entrepreneurial science: cognitive effects of the new university–industry linkages. Res policy 27(8):823–833

Etzkowitz H (2004) The evolution of the entrepreneurial university. Int J Technol Globalisation 1 (1):64–77

Etzkowitz H, Leydesdorff L (2000) The dynamics of innovation: from National Systems and "Mode 2" to a Triple Helix of university-industry-government relations. Res Policy 29(2):109–123

Etzkowitz H, Leydesdorff L (1997) Universities and the global knowledge economy. A Triple Helix of University-Industry-Government Relations, London, New York

Etzkowitz H, Leydesdorff L (1995) The Triple Helix: University—industry—government relations. A laboratory for knowledge based economic development, EASST Review. Eur Soc Study Sci Technology 14(1):18–36

European Commission (2010) Europa 2020 – eine Strategie für intelligentes, nachhaltiges und integratives Wachstum, Brussels

European Commission (2005) European Universities: Enhancing Europe's Research Base, reported by the forum on University-based Research, Brussels

European Commission (2006) Report on the implementation of the Entrepreneurship Action Plan. Brussels, SEC (2006): 1132

European Commission (2001) Benchmarking industry-science relations—the role of framework conditions. Report by DG Enterprise and the Ministry of Economy, Austria

Farrelly F, Quester PG (2003) What drives renewal of sponsorship principal/agent relationships. J Advertising Res 43(4):353–360

Ferreira JM, Leitao J, Raposo M (2007) The role of entrepreneurial universities in competitive advantage: the case of Beira Interior Region, MPRA Paper, No. 486, Madrid

Franco M, Haase H (2010) Do Universities impact regional employment? A cross-regional comparison. Actual Probl Econ 7(109):301–312

Freeman C (1987) Technology and economic performance: lessons from Japan. Pinter, London

Frey B, Neckermann S (2008) Academics appreciate awards—a new aspect of incentives in research. Universität Zürich, Institut für Empirische Wirtschaftsforschung

Galloway L, Anderson M, Brown W, Wilson L (2005) Enterprise skills for the economy. Educ Training 47(1):7–17

Gibbons M, Limoges C, Nowotny H, Schwartzman S, Scott P, Trow M (1994) The new production of knowledge. The dynamics of science and research in contemporary societies. London et al.

Gouthier M, Kleppel C, Schulze Wehninck R, Luhn A, Kremer A (2006) Service-related science-to-business collaborations: case studies from Germany. Int J Technol Intel Plann 2 (2):142–159 (Baaken T, Sugasawa Y (eds))

Gunasekara C (2006) The generative and developmental roles of universities in regional innovation systems. Sci Public Policy 33(2):137–151

Holtkamp G, Schüning T, Seeber J (2005) Einleitung. In: o.H. (Hrsg.): Wissens- und Technologietransfer – Analysen, Konzepte, Instrumente, Osnabrück, pp 5–8

Howell JM, Shamir B (2005) The role of followers in the charismatic leadership process: Relationships and their consequences. Acad Manag Rev 30(1):96–112

Jones-Evans D (1997) Universities, Technology transfer and spin-off activities: academic entrepreneurship in different European regions. Targeted Socio-Economic Research Project. University of Glamorgan

Kesting T (2012) Wissens- und Technologietransfer durch Hochschulen aus einer marktorientierten Perspektive. Wiesbaden

Kesting T, Kliewe T, Korff N, Serbin D (2014) Organisational marketing—making use of linkages and transfer potential between marketing disciplines. In: Kliewe T, Kesting T (eds) Modern concepts of organisational marketing, Festschrift Thomas Baaken 60th birthday, Springer Gabler, Wiesbaden, pp 3–21

Kleinaltenkamp M, Plinke W (2002) Strategisches Business-to-Business Marketing, Berlin

Kliewe T, Baaken T, Kesting T (2012) Introducing a science-to-business marketing unit to university knowledge and technology transfer structures: activities, benefits, success factors. In: Szopa A, Karwowski W, Ordóñez de Pablos P (eds) Academic entrepreneurship and technological innovation: a business perspective, Hershey, pp 53–74

Knie A, Simon D, Truffer B, von Grote C (2002) Wissenschaft als Cross-over-Projekt: Die Wandlung der Forschungseinrichtungen von Teilelieferanten zu Komplettanbietern. Eine Studie auf Initiative des Bundesministeriums für Bildung und Forschung, Berlin

Kotler P, Pfoertsch W (2006) B2B Brand Management, Berlin

Kröcher U (2005) Wissens- und Technologietransfer an Hochschulen – Konzepte und Entwicklungstendenzen. In: o.H. (Hrsg.): Wissens- und Technologietransfer – Analysen, Konzepte, Instrumente, Osnabrück, pp 9–50

Kuhn M (2003) Marketing auf konzerninternen Wissensmärkten. Bedarfsflexible Umsetzung von Wissensmanagement, Wiesbaden

Laine K, Sijde van der P, Lähdeniemi M, Tarkkanen J (Hrsg.) (2008) Higher education institutions and innovation in the knowledge society, Helsinki

Lambert R (2003) Lambert review of business-university collaboration. HMSO, Norwich, UK

Leydesdorff L (2000) The triple helix: an evolutionary model of innovations. Res Policy 29 (2):243–255

Leydesdorff L, Etzkowitz H (2001) A triple helix of university-industry-government relations: »Mode 2« and the globalization of »National« systems of innovation. In: The Danish Institute for studies in research and research policy (ed.): Science under pressure, Copenhagen, pp 7–34

Liyanage C, Ballal T, Elhag T, Li Q (2009) Knowledge communication and translation—a knowledge transfer model. J Knowl Manage 13(3):118–131

Mager B, Hamacher H (2003) Marketing und Kommunikation von Forschung, Köln

Marcure J (2004) Marketing scientific results & services: a toolkit, Washington DC et al

Martin BR, Etzkowitz H (2000) The origin and evolution of the university species. J Sci Technol Stud (Tidskrift för Vetenskaps- och Teknikstudier, VEST) 13(3/4):9–34

Medlin CJ (2004) Interaction in business relationships: a time perspective. Ind Mark Manage 33 (3):185–193

Meffert H (2007) Einführung in die Themenstellung. In: Meffert H, Backhaus K, Becker J (Hrsg.): Hochschulmarketing – Herausforderungen und Erfolgsfaktoren im Wettbewerb, Leipzig, pp 7–21

Merten W (Hrsg.) (2009) Wissenschaftsmarketing – Dialoge gestalten, Bonn

Müller-Böling D (2007) 10 Jahre Hochschulmarketing. In: Meffert H, Backhaus K, Becker J (Hrsg) Hochschulmarketing – Herausforderung und Erfolgsfaktoren im Wettbewerb, Leipzig, pp 7–21

Obermaier G (2009) Research-to-business Beziehungen. Technologietransfer durch Kommunikation von Werten (Barrieren, Erfolgsfaktoren und Strategien), Karlsruhe

Osterloh M, Frey B (2008) Anreize im Wissenschaftssystem, Zürich

Pavitt KLR (2001) Public policies to support basic research: What can the rest of the world learn from US theory and practice? (and what they should learn). Ind Corp Change 10(3):761–779

Pförtsch W, Schmid M (2005) B-to-B-Markenmanagement, München

Pappu R, Quester P (2013) Brand innovativeness effects on quality, satisfaction and loyalty. In: The 16th Biennial World Marketing Congress, Melbourne, Australia, Proceedings, pp 768–786

Plewa C (2010) Key drivers of university-industry relationships and the impact of organisational culture difference, Saarbrücken

Plewa C, Quester P (2008) A dyadic study of "champions" in university-industry relationships. Asia Pacific J Mark Logistics 20(2):211–226

Plewa C, Quester P, Baaken T (2006) Organisational culture differences and market orientation: an exploratory study of barriers to university-industry relationships. Int J Technol Transf Commercialisation 5(4):373–389

Plewa C, Rampersad G, Johnson CR, Baaken T, MacPherson G, Korff N (2013) The evolution of university-industry linkages – a framework. J Eng Tech Manage 30(1):21–44

Plewa C, Quester P, Baaken T (2005) Relationship marketing and university-industry linkages: a conceptual framework. Mark Theory 5(4):433–456
Rode N (2001) Wissensmarketing. Strategische Entscheidungen für Anbieter von Wissen, Wiesbaden
Schmitz C, Zucker B (2003) Wissensmanagement: Schnelleres Lernen im Unternehmen, Berlin
Science-to-Business Marketing Research Centre (ed) (2010) White paper on Science-Marketing, Münster
Shane S (2005) Economic development through entrepreneurship—government, university and business linkages. J Bus Ventur 9(5):397–421
Siebenhaar K (Hrsg) (2008) Unternehmen Universität: Wissenschaft und Wirtschaft im Dialog, Berlin
Sijde van der PC, Cuyvers R (2003) Training researchers to commercialize research results. Ind High Educ 17(1):29–35
Sjide van der PC, Ridder A (eds) (1999) Commercialising Knowledge, Enschede
Slaughter S, Leslie LL (1997) Academic capitalism. Politics, policies and the entrepreneurial university, Baltimore, London
Universität Dortmund (Hrsg) (2003) Forschung erfolgreich vermarkten, Heidelberg
Voss R (ed) (2009) Hochschulmarketing. Lohmar, Köln
Wagner T (2012) Creating innovators. The Making of Young People Who Will Change the World, New York
Walter A (2003) Technologietransfer zwischen Wissenschaft und Wirtschaft – Voraussetzungen für den Erfolg, Wiesbaden
Wefers U (2008) Hochschulmarketing in Deutschland: Chancen und Herausfor-derungen, Saarbrücken
Wilson T (2012) A review of business-university collaboration. https://www.gov.uk/government/uploads/system/uploads/attachment_data/file/32383/12-610-wilson-review-business-university-collaboration.pdf. Accessed on 23 July 2015
Woollard D, Zhang M, Jones O (2007) Creating entrepreneurial universities: insights from a new university business school. In: 30th institute for small business and entrepreneurship conference proceedings, Glasgow, Scotland, pp 1–13

Improving Innovation Process Performance and Service Quality in Innovation Networks

Carolin Plewa, Giselle Rampersad, Indrit Troshani and Tobias Kesting

Abstract The prevalence of innovation networks is ever increasing, with the role of universities in national innovation systems increasingly being emphasised. This chapter investigates the use of an innovation management application (IMA) by the technology transfer office of a university-focused innovation network that focuses on commercialisation of technologies developed by university researchers. Innovation process performance emerged as an important mediator between characteristics of the innovation management application (compatibility of the technology, perceived ease of use and perceived usefulness) on attitude towards the technology, and toward the intermediary's innovation orientation and service quality. Our research addresses marketing issues in the innovation context by relying on IMA as a means for fostering the underlying processes. Furthermore, the results extend the emerging literature on innovation process performance by not only establishing its relevance for an innovation network context but also by demonstrating its role as a mediator between IMA characteristics and attitude towards technology. The chapter concludes with an outline of managerial implications and future research directions.

Keywords Innovation networks · Innovation management application · Innovation process performance · Service quality · Technology transfer offices

---

C. Plewa (✉) · I. Troshani
The University of Adelaide, Adelaide, Australia
e-mail: Carolin.plewa@adelaide.edu.au

I. Troshani
e-mail: Indrit.troshani@adelaide.edu.au

G. Rampersad
Flinders University, Adelaide, Australia
e-mail: Giselle.rampersad@flinders.edu.au

T. Kesting
Münster University of Applied Sciences, Münster, Germany
e-mail: Kesting@fh-muenster.de

© Springer Science+Business Media Singapore 2016
C. Plewa and J. Conduit (eds.), *Making a Difference Through Marketing*,
DOI 10.1007/978-981-10-0464-3_19

Introduction

Innovation is increasingly moving beyond organisational boundaries and occurring within inter-organisational networks, given scarce research and development (R&D) funding and shorter product life cycles (Bunn et al. 2002). These innovation networks comprise groups of organisations including government, business, research institutes and universities (Möller and Svahn 2009; Rampersad et al. 2009). Marketing and innovation literatures emphasise the need for firms to collaborate with other organisations in achieving strategic innovation outcomes including the development of new products and services (Möller and Svahn 2009; Rampersad et al. 2009). To ensure the effectiveness of innovation networks, authors points out the necessity of more research on the factors driving innovation process performance, including those pertaining to service innovation within networks (Salunke et al. 2011; Soosay and Chapman 2006).

A stream of research has emerged noting the role of intermediaries in innovation networks in bridging research and business throughout the innovation process (Yusuf 2008). Such intermediaries may engage in a broad range of activities throughout the innovation process and contribute to reaching the planned outcomes. With numerous literature contributions dealing with the different roles of intermediaries such as technology transfer offices (Gassmann et al. 2011) and mechanisms through which intermediation occurs (Yusuf 2008), our current understanding of these actors within an innovation network remains limited, leading to growing calls for further research in this area (Gassmann et al. 2011).

In a higher education context, university technology transfer offices (TTOs) are commonly expected to take over the role as intermediaries coordinating and supporting research commercialisation (Wood 2011; Perkmann et al. 2013). As service providers, they support researchers, students and doctoral candidates in making use of the university's innovation network potential (Kesting and Wurth 2015). As part of their service offering, TTOs have started to engage technology, such as innovation management applications (IMA), for innovation processes. Existing literature has not been based on strategic innovation process oriented technologies like IMAs but have focused on tactical technologies used in operations such as radio frequency identification systems (RFID); global positioning systems (GPS); point of sales (POS); electronic data interchange (EDI) (Bendoly et al. 2007). However, there are calls for more attention to be placed on strategic technologies like IMAs in supporting the link between research and development (R&D) and marketing in commercialising new technologies (Chapman et al. 2003).

This study is therefore pertinent as it focuses on such IMAs which serve to support these processes. They are important with respect to fostering relational advantages for organisations both internally and externally (Lengrand and Chartrie 1999), thereby enabling a holistic approach to commercialisation. Yet, their ability to improve innovation process performance and contribute to perceptions of the TTO remains unknown. Universities are increasingly identifying the need to innovate to contribute to economic and regional development, particularly given the decreasing levels of public R&D funding, requiring the need to build relationships with other organisations (Patel et al. 2012). While they may focus on commercialising technologies that lead to either product or process innovations in industry, the process of innovation by which they commercialise these technologies are of increasing interest.

In particular, researchers are yet to examine what drives network actors' perceptions of such organisations in an innovation network context. In this respect, perceptions of innovation orientation and service quality are deemed critical. Innovation orientation can be defined as the openness of an organisation to new ideas and its capacity to change through the adoption of new technologies, skills, resources, and systems (Chen et al. 2009a; Siguaw et al. 2006). Given its implications for sustained customer demand, perceptions of value, loyalty and competiveness, service quality has been attracting considerable attention from both researchers and practitioners. Benefits arising from high levels of perceived service quality include service loyalty (Bitner 1990), word of mouth intentions (Parasuraman et al. 1991), service acceptance (Olorunniwo et al. 2006) and willingness to pay a price premium (Zeithaml et al. 1996).

An important outcome of innovation processes surrounding service innovation is the perceived service quality and whether perceived service quality with a focal innovation is higher than before. TTOs service both inter- and intra-organisational groups, by not only focusing on external clients in the business and government communities but also by servicing researchers, students and other actors within the university. Such a complex approach requires an integrative view of marketing perspectives, previously described as organisational marketing (Kesting et al. 2014). Despite the prolific research on service quality and its benefits on an organisational level, scholars in a technology context have tended to examine the service quality of the technology-based service rather than of the organisation (i.e. Carlson and O'Cass 2010). In particular, technology represents a strong facilitator of effective and efficient service delivery as it provides customers and employees with tools to optimise the service experience (Bitner et al. 2010). However, service quality is yet to be conceptualised and tested in an innovation network domain where IMAs are employed.

Hence, our chapter addresses the following research question: How does an IMA implemented by a TTO impact on innovation process performance and service quality perceptions within innovation networks? With hypotheses developed next, our empirical study examining the users' perception of an IMA implemented by an Australian TTO is discussed. We finalise our chapter by outlining conclusions, implications and future research directions.

Hypotheses Development

Compatibility has been shown to be an important driver of technology adoption in a business-to-consumer context (Liang et al. 2007). It is defined as the "degree to which the innovation is seen as consistent with potential users' existing values, previous experiences, and needs" (Wu and Wang 2005, p. 721). The greater the fit between the individual's work style and a technology, the more likely acceptance will be (Saaksjarvi 2003). In our research, this means that if the IMA is perceived to be well-suited to the individuals' current way of working, they are more likely to regard it as useful and, consequently, become motivated to integrate it into their current work routines (Meuter et al. 2005). Increased compatibility reduces the efforts required for technology adoption, suggesting that individuals might view the technology as easier to use than one that is not compatible with their respective working habits (Chau and Hu 2002).

Perceived ease of use is the "degree to which a person believes that using a particular system would be free of effort" (Davis 1989, p. 82). While the impact of perceived ease of use on technology adoption has been well documented, its role in the technology acceptance research remains controversial, as the nature of a technology, task or related service may influence its perceived ease of use (Fang et al. 2005). Perceived usefulness is "the degree to which a person believes that using a particular system would enhance his or her job performance" (Davis 1989, p. 320). A technology is expected to be highly useful when a potential adopter believes that there is a direct relationship between use and productivity, performance, effectiveness or satisfaction (Lu et al. 2003). Another relevant aspect is a user's attitude towards technology, defined as an evaluative summary judgment or predisposition to respond either favourably or unfavourably to a computer system and software, staff, or procedures related to it (Hong et al. 2008; Melone 1990). In work settings where innovation network partners from different organisations collaborate in technology usage, IMA use is likely to be voluntary. Under such conditions, technology acceptance and usage is only likely to ensue when users hold favourable attitudes towards it (Liker and Sindi 1997), suggesting the need for including attitude as a relevant construct in this research. Therefore:

Hypothesis 1: Compatibility is positively related to IMA's perceived ease of use (H1a) and perceived usefulness (H1b).

Research has conceptualised and confirmed the direct effects of ease of use and perceived usefulness on attitude towards a technology in multiple contexts (Davis 1989). While demonstrating general applicability, it should be noted that both antecedents, ease of use and perceived usefulness, are very broad in their conceptualisation and have primarily been tested in individual user contexts without considering the manner in which they operate in networks. With multiple actors engaging in innovation, it is likely that an actor's attitude towards a technology supporting collaborative innovation processes depends on individual perceptions concerning innovation outcomes rather than merely on the perceived IMA characteristics, even if these are perceived to support individual efforts. That is, drawing on social cognitive theory (Compeau and Higgins 1995), the ease with which an IMA can be used and its usefulness for individual work effectiveness may positively impact on innovation development by driving individual actions. However, the individual's attitude towards the technology is likely to depend on the actual outcome of using the technology within the innovation network; for example, whether suitable industry partners have been engaged and if the outcome of commercialisation in actually leading to a successful product or service.

This outcome can be measured by using innovation process performance, which refers to whether the commercialisation pace of new products or services is accelerated; and whether new products or services are developed, are profitable and enhance market value (Chen et al. 2009b; Rampersad et al. 2012a). Despite growing calls for research on better performance measures to assess innovation processes within networks (Soosay and Chapman 2006), the construct of innovation process performance is yet to be tested empirically within the context of innovation networks (Rampersad et al. 2012b). Based on these considerations, we thus hypothesise that:

Hypothesis 2: Perceived ease of use is positively related to innovation process performance.
Hypothesis 3: Perceived usefulness is positively related to innovation process performance.
Hypothesis 4: Innovation process performance is positively related to attitude towards the IMA.
Hypothesis 5: Innovation process performance mediates the associations between IMA characteristics (ease of use [H6a] and perceived usefulness [H6b]) and attitude towards the IMA.

In further conceptualising innovation process performance in a network, we note that research has yet to examine its association with the perceptions of intermediaries in the innovation processes. For example, while previous research has investigated the adoption of innovation orientation (Simpson et al. 2006), it has omitted the role such orientation can play for intermediaries within a network context. We expect the success in innovation development to positively influence the perception of the TTO. The greater such success, the more likely the involved actors will perceive the TTO as innovation-oriented. Therefore, we hypothesise that:

Hypothesis 6: Innovation process performance is positively related to the perceived innovation orientation of the TTO.

Whilst considerable research is devoted to improve our current understanding of service quality (Brady and Robertson 2001), there is a paucity of studies concerning its role in innovation domains. Specifically, research has yet to examine whether the provision of an IMA in innovation networks helps to improve the users' perceptions of the service quality offered by the intermediaries involved. While the services marketing literature converges in relation to the importance of perceived service quality, many conceptualisations and measurements of this construct exist. Brady and Cronin (2001) developed a framework aimed at integrating earlier divergent perspectives. It suggests that service quality entails three dimensions, namely interaction (functional), outcome (technical) and physical environment quality. Hence, if an intermediary utilises an IMA as an extension of its service provision, a positive attitude towards the IMA is likely to transfer to the intermediary. This is consistent with the work of Dabholkar (1996), who finds that attitude towards a technology is directly related to service quality when technology-based self-service options were used by customers in a fast-food domain. The argument also aligns with research on self-service technologies (Liljander et al. 2006). Hence, we hypothesise that:

Hypothesis 7: Attitude towards the IMA is positively related to perceived service quality of the TTO.

Despite Hurley and Hult (1998) pointing out the necessity to explore the impact of innovation orientation on perceived service quality more than 15 years ago, the relationship between a firm's innovation orientation and perceived service quality remain under-researched in innovation networks (Chen et al. 2009a). With innovation central to the network facilitated by the intermediary, a positive evaluation of the intermediary's emphasis and attention to innovation is likely to positively affect service provision evaluations. This reasoning is consistent with Simpson et al. (2006), who offered a comprehensive analysis of innovation orientation outcomes and propose a number of market advantages arising from innovation orientation, including a positive impact on company image and reputation (Simpson et al. 2006). Hence, we propose that:

Hypothesis 8: Innovation orientation is positively related to perceived service quality of the TTO.

Method

Research Context and Sampling

Our research focuses on a newly developed IMA, which had recently been implemented at a mid-sized Australian university, namely by its TTO. This TTO promotes exchange and partnership between university actors and external entities and aims at fostering engagement of relevant stakeholders throughout the innovation process and in general. The IMA in question constitutes a web-based platform that has been successfully commercialised and facilitates information exchanges amongst the members of an innovation network project as well as flexible planning and reporting mechanisms for innovation portfolios. The underlying environmental conditions reflect a typical scenario in which a TTO is embedded in the university and acts as an intra-organisational service provider. In addition, due to its emphasis on promoting interaction between members of the innovation network, the IMA implemented by this Australian TTO was deemed a suitable technology for investigating the factors impacting on innovation process performance and service quality perceptions within innovation networks.

The relevant population of IMA users comprises in total 100—students, university researchers and university's TTO staff members. A sample size of 100 is deemed suitable for the relevant structural equation modelling analysis technique that will be applied (Hair et al. 2006), as discussed in Sect. 4. Students represent the largest user group. 65 students extensively used the IMA over the period of one semester as they worked on the commercialisation of an idea as part of an innovation management course. In addition to students, 22 university researchers employed the IMA for managing their commercialisation projects and engaging with the TTO at the time of data collection. The third group included in the population comprises 13 TTO staff members that routinely engage with the IMA. Having sent out the questionnaire, we achieved a rather high response rate of 68 %. The final sample is composed of 57 students, nine TTO staff members and two researchers.

Construct Operationalisation

Existing and validated measurements for all constructs were adapted from extant literature to the current context. Specifically, the framework entails four constructs relating to technology and its connection with the user: compatibility, ease of use, perceived usefulness and the attitude towards the technology. The measurement of compatibility with the technology reflects the extent to which the technology is compatible with an individual's work practices and preferences (Meuter et al. 2005). Much of the extensive work examining perceived ease of use and perceived usefulness have adopted scales developed by Davis (1989), also employed here. Similarly, we conceptualise attitude towards the technology in line with research on technology adoption models (TAM), measured as seen in Taylor and Todd (1995).

Innovation process performance refers to the advancement of new products and services (Chong et al. 2011), considering the level of perceived development and profitability as well as the extent to which the innovation provides market value (Chen et al. 2009a, b; Rampersad et al. 2012a). The firm-related constructs are based on marketing and innovation literatures. Service quality of the TTO was captured by a global measure of quality based on Dagger and Sweeney (2007) and Brady and Cronin (2001). Hence, rather than focusing on individual aspects or separate episodes of service delivery, the measure takes a cumulative perspective, asking respondents about their general perceptions of the TTO's service. Regarding innovation orientation, we employ the measurement proposed by Chen et al. (2009a) (see Appendix for the complete list of construct items included in the framework).

Construct Reliability and Validity

Construct reliability was confirmed using Cronbach's alpha (α) (Cronbach 1951) and composite reliability scores (Diamantopoulos and Siguaw 2000), all of which

Table 1 Reliability, convergent and discriminant validity scores

Construct	No. items	α	p_η	AVE	Highest λ^2
Compatibility of technology	3	0.90	0.90	0.74	0.61
Perceived ease of use	3	0.90	0.90	0.74	0.24
Perceived usefulness	4	0.97	0.97	0.87	0.61
Attitude towards technology	3	0.91	0.92	0.79	0.50
Innovation process performance	3	0.94	0.93	0.83	0.50
Perceived service quality	3	0.94	0.94	0.85	0.65
Innovation orientation	4	0.95	0.94	0.80	0.65

α = Cronbach's alpha (Cronbach 1951)
p_η = Composite reliability (Diamantopoulos and Siguaw 2000)
AVE = Average variance extracted (Fornell and Larcker 1981)
Highest λ^2 = Highest shared variance (Fornell and Larcker 1981)

are 0.90 or higher (Table 1). Average Variance Extracted (AVE) was employed to test for convergent validity (Fornell and Larcker 1981), with all scores above the required 0.5. Finally, discriminant validity was substantiated as the highest shared variance emerged as higher than the AVE scores (Fornell and Larcker 1981). With proven construct reliability and validity, composite scores were created for further analysis (Farris et al. 1992). As detailed in Table 1, results demonstrated acceptable construct reliability and validity.

Discussion

Hypotheses were tested with Structural Equation Modelling (SEM) principles using AMOS 19. SEM is advantageous in this context as it enables the analysis of complete and complex models (Kline 2005). To allow its use despite a small sample size, we employed composites scores and utilised bootstrapping, a re-sampling procedure which derives confidence estimates based on numerous sub-samples of the original sample (Kline 2005). The results reported below were also confirmed by linear regression analysis using SPSS, confirming that the sample size did not affect the results. The analysis shows a model that fits the data well (χ^2: $p > 0.05$, χ^2/df = 1.20, RMSEA = 0.05, GFI = 0.94, TLI = 0.98, CFI = 0.99, NFI = 0.93). Overall, the model explains 65 % of the variance in the firm's perceived service quality.

As shown in Fig. 1 and Table 2, all hypotheses are supported. Compatibility of the technology has a strong positive impact on perceptions relating to the technology, including its perceived ease of use and usefulness. In particular, compatibility explains a strong 53 % of the perceived usefulness of the IMA. Hence, whether an IMA is seen as useful depends to a great extent on whether users perceive a close alignment between their current way of working on the one hand, and the IMA on the other. This finding contributes to the literature by substantiating

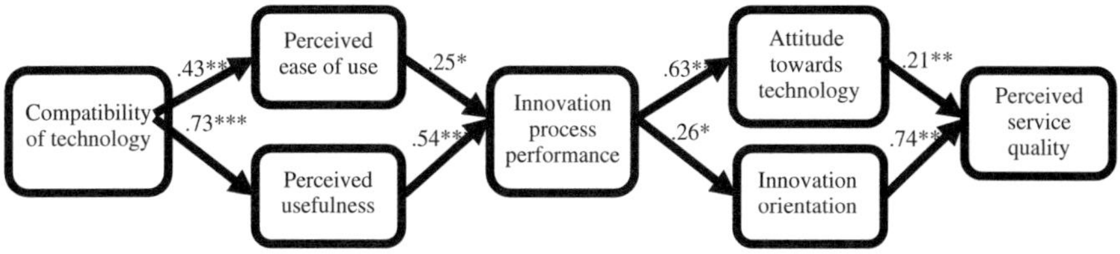

Fig. 1 Path Model

Table 2 Path model results

Hyp.	Independent variable	Dependent variable	Standardized Effects	Critical ratio
1a	Compatibility of technology	Perceived ease of use	0.43	3.88***
1b	Compatibility of technology	Perceived usefulness	0.73	8.69***
2	Perceived ease of use	Innovation process performance	0.26	2.49*
3	Perceived usefulness	Innovation process performance	0.54	5.28***
4	Innovation process performance	Attitude towards technology	0.63	6.84***
6	Innovation process performance	Innovation orientation	0.26	2.24*
7	Attitude towards technology	Perceived service quality	0.21	2.96**
8	Innovation orientation	Perceived service quality	0.74	10.21***

χ^2: $p > 0.05$, $\chi^2/df = 1.20$, RMSEA = 0.05, GFI = 0.94, AGFI = 0.87, TLI = 0.98, CFI = 0.99, NFI = 0.93

*$p < 0.05$; **$p < 0.01$; ***$p < 0.001$

Results are based on Bootstrap = 500; 95 % confidence level

the association between compatibility and perceived usefulness identified in a consumer context (Koenig-Lewis et al. 2010; Wu and Wang 2005) within an innovation management context. Furthermore, it illustrates the importance of considering the users' work routines and customs in the design of technology aimed at supporting intra-organisational innovation processes.

Researchers argue that the compatibility of a technology with an individual's working habits is particularly critical if repeated performance of a particular role has reinforced specific work customs and patterns of behaviour (Chau and Hu 2002). As our sample primarily comprises students, this reasoning does not explain our findings. These students represent early career innovation managers lacking long-established work behaviour patterns. Rather, our findings suggests compatibility as critical for IMA adoption independent of the length of practice, emphasising the importance of considering behavioural work patterns and working habits when arranging the use of technology in networked innovation management contexts.

Both ease of use and perceived usefulness impact innovation process performance, supporting H2 and H3, with IMA's perceived usefulness showing a stronger impact than ease of use. Hence, the more the IMA is seen to increase work effectiveness and productivity, the more positive the individuals' evaluations are relating to the innovation project. This means that ease of use and perceived usefulness drive innovation advancement by fostering actions that lead to an accelerated commercialisation pace and/or improved product development. In turn, innovation process performance positively impacts attitude towards the technology (H4), as shown by a strong path coefficient of 0.63. This finding may be explained by the context, which entails a strong emphasis on work performance. This means that the achievement of a positive outcome within the innovation network will determine whether the individual user develops a positive attitude towards the IMA. Moreover, considering the integration of multiple actors, these actors use the outcome relevant for the network (i.e. the innovation process performance) as a key driver for their attitude towards the IMA.

Given the integration of innovation process performance as a mediator into the commonly investigated associations between perceived ease of use and perceived usefulness on attitude towards the technology, further analysis of this mediating role was undertaken. Based on Barron and Kenny (1986), perceived ease of use, perceived usefulness and innovation process performance significantly impacted on attitude towards technology individually (0.42, $p < 0.000$; 0.52, $p < 0.000$; 0.64, $p < 0.000$, respectively). However, the direct paths between the independent variables and attitude towards technology became insignificant once innovation process performance was included into an overall framework. Hence, innovation process performance is shown here to fully mediate the central paths of the technology acceptance model, confirming H5.

Embedded in the network context of this study, the results support the proposed association between innovation process performance and the perceptions of an innovation orientation of the TTO in the innovation network (H6), providing insight into the drivers of such perceptions. Research has investigated the relevance of innovation orientation, an organisational resource commonly investigated at an organisational level, for innovation outcomes of the firm (Simpson et al. 2006). However, this study provides an initial examination that the level to which an innovation is seen as developed, profitable and valuable in the marketplace impacts on perceptions of the network actor responsible for innovation management. Hence, it broadens our understanding by going beyond the organisational unit of analysis: Outcomes of collaborative activities enhance perceptions relating to resources, which are embedded in the network (Baraldi et al. 2007), and thus may positively impact on other actors and joint activities.

Results further show that a positive attitude towards the technology fosters the perceived service quality of the TTO implementing the IMA (H7). These findings contribute to the literature by surpassing a common focus on technology usage intentions or actual usage (Chau and Hu 2002; Meuter et al. 2005) and endorsing an association between attitude towards technology usage and performance on an innovation project as well as on the perception of central actors within the network. This extension is critical as it validates the benefits of IMA adoption at both a project and organisational level in an innovation network.

Perceived service quality also emerged as dependent on the respondents' perceptions of the TTO's innovation orientation, supporting H8 with a path coefficient of 0.74. While earlier research has confirmed the relevance of innovation orientation as an organisational resource for achieving competitive advantage and firm performance (Chen et al. 2009a; Matzler et al. 2010), customer perceptions resulting from such resource have not been considered previously. This is despite attitudes such as perceived service quality being known to improve loyalty and word-of-mouth behaviour as well as service acceptance (Olorunniwo et al. 2006).

Conclusion

Scholars have been seeking to develop a comprehensive understanding of innovation networks and their success factors, taking into account some of the inherent challenges, such as the diversity of the actors' goals (Corsaro and Snehota 2011). We contribute to the discussion by examining the impact of an IMA on innovation process performance and service quality perceptions within a university-focused innovation network. The university TTO served as the intra-organisational service provider in this context.

This research improves our understanding of the importance of compatibility in the innovation context, confirming a particularly strong relevance for perceptions of usefulness, which in turn emerged as a strong predictor of innovation process performance. Furthermore, our contributions extend the emerging literature on innovation process performance by not only establishing its relevance for an innovation network context but also by demonstrating its role as a mediator between IMA characteristics and attitude towards technology. This mediating relationship reflects an important feedback loop as the adoption of a technology not only impacts on performance but this performance, in turn, subsequently impacts on attitude towards the technology and orientation and perceptions of service quality. Adopting IMA in organisational networks can instead maximise network externalities and innovation development efficiency (Troshani and Doolin 2007; Troshani et al. 2011). Importantly, this research directly addresses recent calls in the literature for research providing a better understanding of the role of and impact of boundary-spanning actors (Gassmann et al. 2011), as perceptions relating to the innovation orientation and perceived service quality of TTOs in an innovation network context have remained under-researched.

Managerial Implications

As shown in our research, when choosing an IMA and encouraging its adoption within a network context, emphasis should be placed on the extent to which the technology fits with the way actors work. That is, these actors should assess the extent to which an IMA fits with existing systems, processes, and practices (Troshani et al. 2011). Not only does compatibility directly impact on perceived usefulness, but it also indirectly impacts on innovation performance. This is likely to be challenging in innovation networks, as it brings together a multitude of actors (Rampersad et al. 2009), most of whom are likely to differ not only in their innovation goals but also in their ways of working (Plewa et al. 2005). Intermediaries should evaluate and foster identified drivers of service quality perceptions. Our results show that perceptions of innovation orientation are partly formed by innovation process performance. However, TTOs may also seek to further build and communicate their innovation orientation across networks.

Limitations and Future Research Directions

Despite its contributions, our research suffers from some limitations. First, the sample largely consists of student respondents. While student samples may affect the external validity of the study, they were deemed suitable as these students not only represent one important IMA user group in university contexts, but they also worked on real-life innovation projects with viable and realistic commercialisation outcomes. Nevertheless, a replication of the study across different IMAs, TTOs and across countries is recommended to test for generalisability. Second, based on these findings, additional qualitative surveys among the IMA users would allow researchers to establish in-depth insight regarding the implementation of IMAs in different contexts and the mediating role of innovation process performance on technology and firm-related outcome factors as discussed here.

To sum up, our research serves as an important first step for validating relevant measures as well as proposing and testing a conceptual model in examining the use of technology in fostering innovation process performance and in turn improved service quality in an intra-organisational context.

Appendix: Measurement Items

Variable and items used (all measured on 7-point Likert scales)
Compatibility of technology (α = 0.90)
Using [the technology] is compatible with my way of working
Using [the technology] is completely compatible with my needs

(continued)

(continued)

Variable and items used (all measured on 7-point Likert scales)
[The technology] fits well with the way I like to get things done
Perceived ease of use (α = 0.90)
I find it easy to get [the technology] to do what I want it to do
My interaction with [the technology] is clear and understandable
I find [the technology] easy to use
Perceived usefulness **(α = 0.97)**
Using [the technology] in my work enables me to accomplish tasks more quickly
Using [the technology] improves my work performance
Using [the technology] in my work increases my productivity
Using [the technology] enhances my effectiveness on the work
Attitude towards technology**(α = 0.91)**
Using [the technology] is a good idea
Using [the technology] is a wise idea
I like the idea of using [the technology]
Innovation process performance (project for which the technology has been or is being used) **(α = 0.94)**
The new products or services are developed
The new products or services are profitable
The new products or services enhance value to the market
Perceived service quality of the firm (α = 0.94)
The overall quality of the service provided by [the TTO] is excellent
The quality of the service provided by [the TTO] is impressive
The service provided by [the TTO] is of a high standard
Innovation orientation of the firm (α = 0.95)
[The TTO] pays close attention to innovation
[The TTO] emphasizes the need for innovation for development
[The TTO] embraces, accepts, and measures innovation
[The TTO] actively seeks innovative ideas

References

Baraldi E, Brennan R, Harrison D, Tunisini A, Zolkiewski J (2007) Strategic thinking and the IMP approach: a comparative analysis. Ind Mark Manage 36(7):879–894

Barron RM, Kenny DA (1986) The moderator-mediator variable distinction in social psychological research: conceptual, strategic, and statistical considerations. J Pers Soc Psychol 51 (6):1173–1182

Bendoly E, Citurs A, Konsynski B (2007) Internal infrastructural impacts on RFID perceptions and commitment: knowledge, operational procedures, and information-processing standards. Decis Sci 38(3):423–449

Bitner MJ (1990) Evaluating service encounters: the effects of physical surroundings and employee responses. J Mark 54(2):69–82

Bitner MJ, Zeithaml VZ, Gremler DD (2010) Technology's impact on the gaps model of service quality. In: Maglio PP, Kieliszewski CA, Spohrer JC (eds) Handbook of service science. Springer, New York, pp 197–218
Brady MK, Cronin JJ (2001) Some new thoughts on conceptualizing perceived service quality: a hierarchical approach. J Mark 65(3):34–49
Brady MK, Robertson CJ (2001) Searching for a consensus on the antecedent role of service quality and satisfaction: an exploratory cross-national study. J Bus Res 51(1):53–60
Bunn MD, Savage GT, Holloway BB (2002) Stakeholder analysis for multi-sector innovations. J Bus Ind Mark 17(2–3):181–203
Carlson J, O'Cass A (2010) Exploring the relationships between e-service quality, satisfaction, attitudes and behaviours in content-driven e-service web sites. J Serv Mark 24(2):112–127
Chapman RL, Soosay C, Kandampully J (2003) Innovation in logistic services and the new business model: a conceptual framework. Int J Phys Distrib Logistics Manag 33(7):630–650
Chau PYK, Hu PJ (2002) Examining a model of information technology acceptance by individual professionals: an exploratory study. J Manag Inf Syst 18(4):191–229
Chen J-S, Tsou HT, Huang AY-H (2009a) Service delivery innovation: antecedents and impact on firm performance. J Serv Res 12(1):36–55
Chen Y-S, Lin M-JJ, Chang C-H (2009b) The positive effects of relationship learning and absorptive capacity on innovation performance and competitive advantage in industrial markets. Ind Mark Manage 38(2):152–158
Chong AYL, Chan FTS, Ooi KB, Sim JJ (2011) Can Malaysian firms improve organizational/innovation performance via SCM? Ind Manag Data Syst 111(3):410–431
Compeau DR, Higgins CA (1995) Application of social cognitive theory to training for computer skills. Inf Syst Res 6(2):118–143
Corsaro D, Snehota I (2011) Alignment and misalignment in business relationships. Ind Mark Manage 40(6):1042–1054
Cronbach LJ (1951) Coefficient alpha and the internal structure of tests. Psychometrika 16(3):297–334
Dabholkar PA (1996) Consumer evaluations of new technology-based self-service options: an investigation of alternative models of service quality. Int J Res Mark 13(1):29–51
Dagger TS, Sweeney JC (2007) Service quality attribute weights: how do novice and longer-term customers construct service quality perceptions? J Serv Res 10(1):22–42
Davis FD (1989) Perceived usefulness, perceived ease of use, and user acceptance of information technology. MIS Q 13(3):319–340
Diamantopoulos A, Siguaw JA (2000) Introducing LISREL: a guide for the uninitiated. Sage Publications, London
Fang X, Chan S, Brzezinski J, Xu S (2005) Moderating effects of task type on wireless technology acceptance. J Manag Inf Syst 22(3):123–157
Farris PW, Parry ME, Ailawadi KL (1992) Structural analysis of models with composite dependent variables. Mark Sci 11(1):76–94
Fornell C, Larcker DF (1981) Structural equation models with unobservable variables and measurement error: algebra and statistics. J Mark Res 18(3):382–388
Gassmann O, Daiber M, Enkel E (2011) The role of intermediaries in cross-industry innovation processes. R&D Manag J 41(5):457–469
Hair JF, Anderson RE, Tatham RL, Black WC (2006) Multivariate data analysis. Prentice Hall, New Jersey
Hong S, Kim J, Lee H (2008) Antecedents of use-continuance in information systems: toward an integrative view. J Comput Inf Syst 48(3):61–73
Hurley RF, Hult GTM (1998) Innovation, market orientation, and organizational learning: an integration and empirical examination. J Mark 62(3):42–54
Kesting T, Wurth B (2015) Knowledge and technology transfer support potential of intermediate organizations: theory, empirical evidence and practice cases. In: Szopa A, Karwowski W, Barbe D (eds) Competitive strategies for academic entrepreneurship: commercialization of research-based products. Hershey, IGI Global, pp 144–171

Kesting T, Kliewe T, Korff N, Serbin D (2014) Organisational marketing—making use of linkages and transfer potential between marketing disciplines. In: Kliewe T, Kesting T (eds) Moderne Konzepte des organisationalen Marketing—Modern concepts of organisational marketing. Springer Gabler, Wiesbaden, pp 3–21

Kline RB (2005) Principles and practice of structural equation modelling, 2nd edn. The Guilford Press, New York

Koenig-Lewis N, Palmer A, Moll A (2010) Predicting young consumers' take up of mobile banking services. Int J Bank Mark 28(5):410–432

Lengrand L, Chartrie I (1999) Business networks and the knowledge-driven economy. European Commission, Brussels

Liang T-P, Huang C-W, Yeh Y-H, Lin B (2007) Adoption of mobile technology in business: a fit viability model. Ind Manag Data Syst 107(8):1154–1169

Liker JK, Sindi AA (1997) User acceptance of expert systems: a test of the theory of reasoned action". J Eng Tech Manage 14(2):147–173

Liljander V, Gillberg F, Gummerus J, van Riel A (2006) Technology readiness and the evaluation and adoption of self-service technologies. J Retail Consum Serv 13(3):177–191

Lu J, Yu C-S, Liu C, Yao JE (2003) Technology acceptance model for wireless internet. Internet Res 13(3):206–222

Matzler K, Bailom F, Anschober M, Richardson S (2010) Sustaining corporate success: what drives the top performers? J Bus Strategy 31(5):4–13

Melone NP (1990) Theoretical assessment of the user-satisfaction construct in information systems research. Manage Sci 36(1):76–91

Meuter ML, Bitner MJ, Ostrom AL, Brown SW (2005) Choosing among alternative service delivery modes: an investigation of customer trial of self-service technologies. J Mark 69 (2):61–83

Möller KK, Svahn S (2009) How to influence the birth of new business fields—network perspective. Ind Mark Manage 38(4):450–458

Olorunniwo F, Hsu MK, Udo GJ (2006) Service quality, customer satisfaction, and behavioural intentions in the service factory. J Serv Mark 20(1):59–72

Parasuraman A, Berry LL, Zeithaml VA (1991) Understanding customer expectation of service. Sloan Manag Rev 32(3):39–48

Patel F, Sooknanan P, Rampersad G, Mundkur A (2012) Information technology, development, and social change, vol 32. Routledge, New York

Perkmann M, Tartari V, McKelvey M, Autio E, Broström A, D'Este P, Fini R, Geuna A, Grimaldi R, Hughes A (2013) Academic engagement and commercialisation: a review of the literature on university—industry relations. Res Policy 42(2):423–442

Plewa C, Quester P, Baaken T (2005) Relationship marketing and university-industry linkages: a conceptual framework. Mark Theory 5(4):433–456

Rampersad GC, Quester PG, Troshani I (2009) Developing and evaluating scales to assess innovation networks. Int J Technol Intell Plan 5(4):402–420

Rampersad GC, Plewa C, Troshani I (2012a) Investigating the use of information technology in managing innovation: a case study from a university technology transfer office. J Eng Tech Manage 29(1):3–21

Rampersad GC, Plewa C, Troshani I (2012b) IOS adoption in innovation networks: a case study. Ind Manag Data Syst 112(9):1366–1382

Saaksjarvi M (2003) Consumer adoption of technological innovations. Eur J Innov Manag 6 (2):90–100

Salunke S, Weerawardena J, McColl-Kennedy JR (2011) Towards a model of dynamic capabilities in innovation-based competitive strategy: Insights from project-oriented service firms. Ind Mark Manage 40(8):1251–1263

Siguaw JA, Simpson PM, Enz CA (2006) Conceptualizing innovation orientation: a framework for study and integration of innovation research. J Prod Innov Manage 23(6):556–574

Simpson PM, Siguaw JA, Enz CA (2006) Innovation orientation outcomes: the good and the bad. J Bus Res 59(10–11):1133–1141

Soosay C, Chapman RL (2006) An empirical examination of performance measurement for managing continuous innovation in logistics. Knowl Process Manag 13(3):192–205

Taylor S, Todd, PA (1995) Understanding information technology usage: A test of competing models. Inform Syst Res 6(2):144–176

Troshani I, Doolin B (2007) Innovation diffusion: a stakeholder and social network view. European Journal of Innovation Management 10(2):176–200

Troshani I, Rampersad G, Plewa C (2011) Adopting innovation management software in university innovation commercialization. J Comput Inf Syst 52(2):83–92

Wood MS (2011) A process model of academic entrepreneurship. Bus Horiz 54(2):153–161

Wu J-H, Wang S-C (2005) What drives mobile commerce? An empirical evaluation of the revised technology acceptance model. Inf Manag 42(5):719–729

Yusuf S (2008) Intermediating knowledge exchange between universities and businesses. Res Policy 37(8):1167–1174

Zeithaml VA, Berry LL, Parasuraman A (1996) The behavioural consequences of service quality. J Mark 60(2):31–46

MIX
Papier aus verantwortungsvollen Quellen
Paper from responsible sources
FSC® C105338

If you have any concerns about our products,
you can contact us on
ProductSafety@springernature.com

In case Publisher is established outside the EU,
the EU authorized representative is:
Springer Nature Customer Service Center GmbH
Europaplatz 3, 69115 Heidelberg, Germany

Printed by Libri Plureos GmbH
in Hamburg, Germany